D0992007

Howling over Moab
Irony and Rhetoric in Isaiah 15–16

SOCIETY OF BIBLICAL LITERATURE

DISSERTATION SERIES

Number 157

HOWLING OVER MOAB
Irony and Rhetoric in Isaiah 15–16

by
Brian C. Jones

Brian C. Jones

Howling over Moab

Irony and Rhetoric in Isaiah 15–16

Scholars Press
Atlanta, Georgia

Howling over Moab

Irony and Rhetoric in Isaiah 15–16

by
Brian C. Jones

Library of Congress Cataloging in Publication Data
Jones, Brian C., 1957–
Howling over Moab : irony and rhetoric in Isaiah 15–16 / Brian C. Jones.
p. cm. — (Dissertation series / Society of Biblical Literature ; no. 157)
Includes bibliographical references.
ISBN 0-7885-0257-3 (alk. paper).
1. Bible. O.T. Isaiah XV–XVI—Criticism, interpretation, etc. 2. Bible. O.T. Isaiah XV–XVI—Language, style. 3. Rhetoric in the Bible. 4. Moab (Kingdom)—Biblical teaching. I. Title. II. Series: Dissertation series (Society of Biblical Literature) ; no. 157.
BS1515.2.J65 1996
224'.1066—dc20 96-28726
CIP

Printed in the United States of America
on acid-free paper

ACKNOWLEDGMENTS

I wish to express my gratitude to those whose advice and encouragement guided and sustained me during the writing of this book. I owe much to J. Maxwell Miller upon whose guidance, criticism and encouragement I depended throughout my research and writing. John Hayes and Carol Newsom read preliminary drafts of the book and offered advice and criticism that improved both my thinking and my writing. David Gunn generously allowed me to use his office and books during a crucial summer of writing. Members of my family offered practical support: my sister Kathy Johnstone and her family provided a place for my family to live while I wrote the final draft, and my brother Larry Jones photocopied and mailed to me numerous articles. Above all, I wish to express my profound gratitude to my wife and colleague, Judith Anne Jones. Her constant love and encouragement sustained my spirit, and her scholarly criticism, stimulating conversation, and expert editing improved this study on almost every page. To her I dedicate this book.

TABLE OF CONTENTS

ABBREVIATIONS

AB	Anchor Bible
ABD	*Anchor Bible Dictionary*
ASOR	American Schools of Oriental Research
BASOR	*Bulletin of the American Schools of Oriental Research*
BASP	*Bulletin of the American Society of Papyrologists*
B.C.E.	Before the Common Era
BDB	F. Brown, S. R. Driver, and C. A. Briggs, *Hebrew and English Lexicon of the Old Testament*
BEvT	*Beiträge zur evangelischen Theologie*
BHS	*Biblia hebraica stuttgartensia*
BKAT	Biblischer Kommentar: Altes Testament
BN	*Biblische Notizen*
BToday	*Bible Today*
CBQ	*Catholic Biblical Quarterly*
C.E.	Common Era
ConBOT	Coniectanea Biblica, Old Testament
D	Deuteronomist
E	Elohist Source
EI	*Eretz-Israel*
ET	*The Expository Times*
GKC	*Gesenius' Hebrew Grammar* (2d ed.) ed. E. Kautzsch, trans. A. E. Cowley
HAR	*Hebrew Annual Review*
HB	Hebrew Bible
HDR	Harvard Dissertations in Religion
HKAT	Handkommentar zum Alten Testament
HTR	*Harvard Theological Review*
HUCA	*Hebrew Union College Annual*
ICC	International Critical Commentary
IDB	*Interpreters Dictionary of the Bible*

IEJ	*Israel Exploration Journal*
J	Yahwist source
JAOS	*Journal of the American Oriental Society*
JBL	*Journal of Biblical Literature*
JQR	*The Jewish Quarterly Review*
JSNTS	Journal for the Study of the New Testament Supplements
JSOT	*Journal for the Study of the Old Testament*
JSOTS	Journal for the Study of the Old Testament Supplements
JSS	*Journal of Semitic Studies*
JThSt	*Journal of Theological Studies*
KAT	Kommentar zum Alten Testament
KAI	H. Donner and W. Röllig, *Kanaanäische und aramäische Inschriften*
KHAT	Kurzer Hand-Commentar zum Alten Testament
LXX	The Septuagint Version
LBH	Late Biblical Hebrew
MS(S)	manuscript(s)
NASB	*New American Standard Bible*
NCBC	New Century Bible Commentary
NEB	*New English Bible*
NedTTs	*Nederlands theologisch tijdschrift*
NICOT	New International Commentary on the Old Testament
NJPS	*New Jewish Publication Society of America Translation*
NRSV	*New Revised Standard Version*
OBO	Orbis biblicus et orientalis
OT	Old Testament
OTL	Old Testament Library
OTS	*Oudtestamentische Studiën*
P	Priestly source
PEQ	*Palestine Exploration Quarterly*
RB	*Revue Biblique*
RSV	*Revised Standard Version*
SANT	Studien zum Alten und Neuen Testament
SBL	Society of Biblical Literature
SBLDS	Society of Biblical Literature Dissertation Series
SJOT	*Scandinavian Journal of the Old Testament*

VT	*Vetus Testamentum*
WBC	Word Bible Commentary
WMANT	Wissenschaftliche Monographien zum Alten und Neuen Testament
ZAH	*Zeitschrift für Althebräistik*
ZAW	*Zeitschrift für die alttestamentliche Wissenschaft*
ZDPV	*Zeitschrift des Deutschen Palästina-Vereins*

CHAPTER 1

INTRODUCTION AND HISTORY OF THE INTERPRETATION OF ISAIAH 15 AND 16

I. Introduction

The subject of this study is Isaiah 15 and 16. These chapters contain a prophetic speech against Moab. In its present form, the speech consists of a description of the Moabites' lamentation following a nocturnal attack and of their subsequent flight southward (15:1–9); a description of a petition to Judah for assistance (16:1–6); a lament focusing on the destruction of Moab's crops (16:7–12); and an epilogue apparently updating the speech (16:13–14). This study offers a detailed examination of these chapters.

For several reasons Isaiah 15–16 deserve a new examination. The poem contains an unusual number of largely unresolved textual and translational problems, and it has become customary among recent interpreters to quote Otto Procksch's dictum that this text is a Schmerzenskind der Exegese. Most scholars discern signs of editorial activity, but there is little agreement about the redactional history of the chapters. Nor is there consensus about the historical situation behind either the final form of the text or its redactional units.

Also significant is the fact that serious genre issues remain unresolved. Two facets of the poem's genre require investigation. First, it is not clear whether the speech is to be taken as a frank lament or as a sarcastic taunt. Although this issue has been mentioned in passing by some commentators and even deliberated by a few, no thorough examination of the possibility of an ironic reading has yet been attempted. The question cannot be ignored, however, and, as the history of interpretation shows, it will not go away. One's answer to the question influences the analysis of the speech at a number of points. For example, many of the signs of redactional activity noted by commentators disappear if the poem is understood ironically. Inferring an ironic intention can result in an interpretation of the speech as a unified discourse with a coherent rhetorical purpose. Additionally, decisions about text-critical, geographical and historical issues are often affected by one's decision about the tone of the poem. Historical geography in particular plays an important role in the study of Isaiah 15–16 because of the unusual density of place names in the poem and the fact that the location of a number of the cities mentioned is uncertain.

The possibility of reading the speech as a unified discourse raises a second genre issue. The speech moves from lament by the speaker to petition by Moab, back to lament and finally to prophetic pronouncement. How is this mixing of genres to be understood? What comparative material exists? What is the over-arching genre? These questions are part of the larger discussion of the genre מַשָּׂא and of the nature and purpose of the oracles against the foreign nations (OAN). Ultimately, the question of form and function in Isaiah 15–16 is inextricably linked to the ongoing discussion of the nature of Israel's prophetic discourse and its relationship to the prophetic texts we now possess.

A final reason for the present study is simple topicality. Isaiah 15–16 is one of the primary sources of information about Moab in the Hebrew Bible, and Moab is the subject of much recent interest and research. A number of major studies have been published in the last decade: *Midian, Moab, and Edom* ed. by Sawyer and Clines (1983); *Moab zwischen den Mächten* by S. Timm (1989); *Studies in the Mesha Inscription and Moab* ed. by A. Dearman (1989); *Early Edom and Moab; the Beginning of the Iron Age in Southern Jordan* by P. Bienkowski (1992); and *Archaeological Survey of the Kerak Plateau* ed. by J. M. Miller (1993). Bienkowski comments in the preface to *Early Edom and Moab*, "In recent years there has been a huge increase in archaeological and historical work on the Iron Age kingdoms of Edom and Moab."[1] Moab has also figured prominently in a number of recent journal articles, principally by Miller, Worschech, Knauf, and Dearman (see bibliography). Finally, from the mid-1970s on, archaeologists have been active in Moab. Recent excavations and surveys in Moab include Heshbon and vicinity (Boraas, Horn and Geraty, 1973-76; Ibach, 1976-78); Baluʾ (Worschech, Rosenthal and Zayadine, 1983–86); and the Kerak plateau (Miller, 1978–79, 82; Worschech, 1983–85). Miller's study in particular has generated a great deal of interest in Moab; many of those who participated in his survey are now contributors to the ongoing discussion of Moab. Indeed, the present author became interested in Moab while working as Dr. Miller's assistant in the final preparation of the manuscript of the *Archaeological Survey of the Kerak Plateau*.

II. History of Interpretation

A. Overview and Orientation

Most of the post-Reformation discussion of Isaiah 15–16 has revolved around the issues of authorship, date, historical situation and redaction. Until the end of the eighteenth century, commentators analyzed the poem as a single composition, attributed it to Isaiah and interpreted the events it describes as an attack by an Assyrian ruler, usually Shalmaneser (Grotius, Usher, Vitringa) or Sennacherib (Jerome and most of the Rabbis[2]). Since the time of J. B. Koppe's German translation and annotation of Lowth's commentary (1780), however, many scholars have interpreted the poem as the work of an author or authors other than Isaiah. Suggestions regarding date have ranged from the time of Jeroboam II until the second century BCE. Similarly, the events described in the poem have been variously understood as the

[1]P. Bienkowski, ed., *Early Edom and Moab: the Beginning of the Iron Age in Southern Jordan* (Sheffield Archaeological Monographs 7; Sheffield: J. R. Collis/National Museums and Galleries on Merseyside, 1992) i.

[2]W. Gesenius, *Philologisch-kritischer und historischer Commentar über den Jesaia* (Leipzig: Vogel, 1821). Page-number citations refer to W. Tyler's translation of Gesenius's commentary on chapters 15 and 16: "Exegesis of Isaiah XV. XVI." *Biblical Repository and Quarterly Observer* 7 (1836) 122.

work of the transjordanian Israelite tribes, eighth-century Bedouin from the desert fringe, Edomites, and Nabatean Arabs. Complicating the authorship question is the fact that Jeremiah 48 duplicates much of the material in Isaiah 15–16. Most commentators agree that the writer of Jeremiah 48 has borrowed from and expanded the text in Isaiah, but a few voices have argued that the dependence runs the other way, or that the two used a common source. Perhaps in response to the uncertainties involved and the wide range of suggestions that have been offered, recent interpreters have become, with a few exceptions, increasingly agnostic on the issues of date and authorship.

The resolution of historical issues has been further complicated by the redactional analysis of the poem. Beginning with Ewald (1867), interpreters have divided the poem into increasingly smaller units which they date separately. In his landmark commentary (1978), Wildberger calls the poem a redactional *mosaikartigen Moabgemälde*, and notes that there is little agreement on the division and analysis of the pieces.[3] Indeed, agreement is widespread at only one point: most commentators since Ewald agree that the author of 15:1–16:12 is different from the author of 16:13–14. If one ignores the small details, it is safe to say that the majority of commentators since Ewald also agree on separating 15:1–8; 16:1, 3–6; and 16:7–11 as three distinct compositions, although some still argue that 15:1–8 and 16:7–11 were originally connected in some way. Additionally, most assign the earliest date to 15:1–8 (or 15:1–8 + 16:7–11) and designate 15:9, 16:2 and 16:12 as later additions.

The complicated redactional picture both derives from and influences genre and content analysis. Questions of genre and content have long been disputed. Some have interpreted the poem as a lament over an accomplished destruction, some as a prediction of coming events. In the latter case, the lament form is understood as a rhetorical device to add persuasive vividness to the prediction. Whether it be predictive or not, however, the poem is certainly no traditional lament. The petition at its very center

[3]H. Wildberger, *Jesaja*, vol. 2 (BKAT 10/2; Neukirchen-Vluyn: Neukirchener, 1978) 598–99.

invariably raises questions. As to the form and content of 16:1–6: Is it an exhortation or a petition? Is it Isaiah (or the Judeans) who exhorts the Moabites, or the Moabites who petition the Judeans? Is 16:6 an answer to the Moabites, or a disconnected reflection on Moabite hubris? Furthermore, what sense does it make to place this exhortation or petition between two sections that are primarily lament? Does the resulting text, the final form, communicate any coherent message, or is it a *mosaikartigen* with only superficial coherence, assembled by various hands over time? The latter option is favored by many modern interpreters, and the formal and thematic disruption caused by 16:1-6 is the single most important reason for this decision.

Bearing in mind this general summary of the issues, let us now review in detail the history of the interpretation of Isaiah 15–16. Although the following history is not comprehensive, neither is it merely representative. Effort has been made to include all the major commentaries and special studies, as well as several of the shorter treatments. Additionally, this study examines primarily those issues in the history of interpretation that have been raised by interpreters from the time of Lowth's commentary to the present. Although many fine treatments of Isaiah 15–16 were written prior to Lowth—one thinks particularly of the valuable grammatical notes in the commentary of Abraham Ibn Ezra (12th century) and the extensive commentary by C. Vitringa (1714)—a summary of these works has been omitted. References to these earlier commentaries do, however, appear in the chapters dealing with issues of text, grammar and historical geography. Two exceptions have been made to the exclusion of commentaries prior to Lowth: the commentaries of Luther and of Calvin, both of which offer interpretations that pertain directly to one of the major concerns of this study.

B. Luther and Calvin

The commentaries of Martin Luther and John Calvin on Isaiah are especially important in the history of interpretation of chapters

15–16.[4] Like their predecessors, Luther and Calvin understood the poem as a single, predicative prophecy and attributed it to Isaiah. They offered, however, a new interpretation of the tenor of the prophecy. Both held that the prophecy was antagonistic toward the Moabites and understood its expressions of grief (15:5; 16:9, 11) as ironic imitations of the Moabites. Credit for this line of interpretation must go to Luther, whose lectures on Isaiah were published in 1532, thirty-eight years before Calvin published his commentary. Given the number of similarities between the two treatments, it seems quite likely that Calvin was strongly influenced by Luther's commentary.[5]

Luther begins his treatment by noting that, "After the Philistines the most hostile enemies of the Jews were the Moabites, who were extraordinarily proud because of the fertility of their country" (146). This lays the foundation for his ironic interpretation. A sympathetic lament over the fate of one's greatest foe is, after all, suspicious. Luther sees an ironic intention in the very first section. The picture of a nocturnal attack (15:1) is designed to emphasize the ease with which the Moabites are defeated and to underline their "presumption" and "excessive pride" in the security of their defenses. The description of their lamentation (15:2) serves to ridicule "a foolish people in their pride." Arriving at the prophet's expression of grief over the fate of Moab in 15:5, Luther comments, "[My heart] cries thus: My heart grieves there because of Moab's wretchedness. Or this is prophetic irony, namely: How unjustly you are dealt with!" (146–47).

Luther understands all of 16:1–4 as "prophetic irony." Just as in 15:5, he offers both a straight reading and an ironic reading of 16:1,

---

[4]M. Luther, *Lectures on Isaiah: Chapters 1–39,* volume 16 of *Luther's Works,* ed. J. Pelikan, et al. (Saint Louis: Concordia, 1969) 146–53; J. Calvin, *Commentary on the Book of the Prophet Isaiah,* vol. 1 (Grand Rapids: Eerdmans, 1948) 468–96. Page number citations of works that are treated at length will be given in parentheses in the body text throughout the book.

[5]Cf., for example, their treatments of 15:1; 16:1, 6. Luther begins his comment on 16:6, "This is rhetorical anticipation" (150). In a similar manner Calvin begins, "The Prophet added this statement by way of anticipation" (488). I know of no common source from which both men might have drawn.

> [Isaiah] says: "You Moabites, who have withdrawn from the house of Israel and Judah and have stopped obeying it, I urge you: Return to your obedience. Give tribute to the king, and your affairs will prosper." Or, rather, it is prophetic irony, namely: "Send a lamb to Jerusalem now. Up until now you have despised us. Do you now crawl to the cross? Do you now wish to bring a sacrifice in Jerusalem? But it is too late. So you come at long last? (149)

He clearly favors the ironic reading, and in 16:2 he goes as far as to say, "These words prove that the preceding words were ironic." And 16:3, which he understands as an exhortation by the prophet to the Moabites, is "pure irony" (149).

He takes a slightly different approach to the expressions of grief in 16:9, 11. These he interprets as "an act" put on by the prophet in which Isaiah derisively repeats the words of the Moabites. Although he is less explicit than one would like here, it is plain that he thinks Isaiah quite incapable of any sympathy for the Moabites. In any case, his understanding of the general tone of this final section of the prophecy appears clearly in his comments on 16:9. He takes 16:9c to mean that the victory shout of the enemy (Assyria) has fallen upon Moab's harvest.[6] He comments, "[Isaiah] is taunting the Moabites by means of irony or sarcasm. That is to say, 'I truly think that the voice of people rejoicing has come into your harvest. Those who will be jubilant in your harvest will certainly come. Others will carry off what you have reaped, and they will be jubilant'" (151–52).

Luther's comments are brief and sometimes elliptical. His purpose throughout is homiletical rather than discursive, and this is only to be expected since the commentary was originally a set of lectures. Calvin offers a more detailed and closely reasoned treatment, but his overall interpretation runs along the same line. As does Luther, Calvin begins by reminding his readers that, although the Moabites were blood relatives and neighbors of the

---

[6]Luther's understanding of the verse is based on a translation of 16:9c ("Upon your fruit and your harvest [the shout of victory has fallen]" 151) that differs from that found in the NRSV ("for the shout over your fruit harvest and your grain harvest has ceased"). See textual and grammatical notes below.

Jews, they were forever harassing them most cruelly.[7] This gave "evidence of a savage and barbarous disposition." He returns to this theme of Moabite brutality again and again in his commentary (469, 474, 482, 489, 490). Their unjust and cruel treatment of the Jews is what justifies God's impending judgment and Isaiah's ironic tone. Calvin takes pains to explain that the prophecy is addressed not to the Moabites, but to "believers." Isaiah intended to comfort the Jews with the message that events were under divine control and that God would take "vengeance on [their] enemies by whom [they] had been barbarously treated" (470). Calvin speaks frequently as if Isaiah's taunts were addressed directly to the Moabites, but apparently he thinks of this merely as a rhetorical device employed for the sake of vividness.[8]

Like Luther, Calvin interprets the depiction of a nocturnal attack (15:1) as a criticism of the Moabites' confidence in their fortifications and consequent complacency. The description of their ascent to the temple in 15:2 (for so he understands בית) is intended as a condemnation of Moabite idolatry. This strong tone of condemnation in the prophecy is disrupted by the prophet's apparent cry of sympathy in 15:5. Calvin interprets these tears as playacting:

> At length he assumes the character of a mourner. But it may be thought to be strange and inconsistent in him to bewail the calamity of the Moabites; for he ought rather to have lamented the destruction of the Church, and to have rejoiced at the ruin of her enemies. It is customary with the prophets, however, to assume in this manner the character of those whose calamities they foretell, and thus to

---

[7]As is the case with other Christian commentators during this time, Calvin moves back and forth between "then" and "now," mixing terms as if there were no historical distance between Isaiah's time and his own. Thus, "the Jews" in the protasis of a sentence may become "the Church" or "believers" in the apodosis. I have attempted to be faithful to the historical setting of the commentators in my treatment of them so as to avoid introducing anachronisms. At times this means repeating their own anachronisms, as is the case with the term "the Jews."

[8]See especially 470–71, 482–84. Calvin may be thinking of the well-known device of satire by which one appears to address the person or group being satirized with no intention that that person or group should ever hear the satire. Satire does not seek to persuade its victim; it seeks to influence the public estimation of the victim.

> exhibit their condition, as it were, on a stage; by which means they produce a stronger impression than if they delivered their instruction in a direct form (473).

He deals with the apparent expressions of sympathy in 16:9, 11 in exactly the same manner. There, however, he feels obliged to counter the possible objection that even though the Moabites richly deserved punishment, Isaiah might still lament for them as fellow humans:

> It is undoubtedly true that believers always shudder at the judgments of God, and cannot lay aside the feelings of human nature.... Yet he does not describe his own feelings; but his intention is to give additional weight to his instruction.... He therefore represents in the person of a Moabite, as on a stage, the mourning and grief which shall be felt by all after that calamity (493).

Thus all the first person lament language in the prophecy is a rhetorical device and does not indicate that the prophet felt the least sympathy for the Moabites. Calvin differs from Luther only in that he does not suggest that these pretended expressions of sympathy are spoken sarcastically.

He does, however, sense great irony in 16:1–4a. Like Luther, he understands 16:1 as an ironic exhortation to the Moabites:

> Here the Prophet scoffs at the Moabites for not acknowledging God at the proper time, but recklessly waiting for the stroke of his hand, till they were completely destroyed.... Where the disease is incurable, an exhortation of this kind is appropriate; and this ought to be carefully observed, for both Jews and Christians misinterpret this passage.... We ought therefore, to view it as spoken ironically, (εἰρωνικῶς) *Send*; as if he had said that there is no hope of pardon, that they will *send* in vain (479–80).

The "mockery" continues in 16:2, Calvin suggests, with the prophet's description of the fleeing Moabites. The metaphor of birds suggests that the Moabites "flee even at the rustling of a leaf." The imperatives in 16:3 carry forward the ironic exhortation: "Isaiah ironically advises them to *assemble councils* and *execute judgments*, which they had formerly overturned through fraud and injustice" (481–82). In this way Isaiah underlines the poetic justice of the coming destruction of Moab.

The extent to which later commentators have ignored, or at least failed to mention, the ironic reading given the poem by Luther and Calvin is surprising. J. Alexander mentions (with disapproval) Calvin's treatment but says nothing of Luther's that lies behind it. Most commentators mention neither reformer. This is most surprising in the case of the few interpreters who do in fact suggest an ironic reading for at least a part of the poem; Luther and Calvin are not once mentioned by these commentators.

C. Eighteenth- and Nineteenth-Century Commentators

In the last quarter of the eighteenth century, scholars published a number of new ideas about Isaiah 15–16. R. Lowth's commentary on Isaiah (1778) presented, on the whole, a fairly conventional interpretation of the speech.[9] He understood it as a straightforward prophecy of a future event, probably delivered in the first year of Hezekiah and fulfilled in his fourth year when Shalmeneser invaded. His commentary primarily treats textual and grammatical issues, and in this area he made several original contributions to the study of the text. The chief importance of Lowth's treatment of Isaiah 15–16, however, lies not in his own ideas, but in the fact that his commentary was translated and copiously annotated and thus became the vehicle for the ideas of another scholar, ideas that radically broke with traditional interpretation.

This translator and annotator was J. B. Koppe. His translation of Lowth's commentary was published during the years 1779–1781, close on the heels of the English original.[10] In his notes,

---

[9]R. Lowth, *Isaiah: A New Translation with a Preliminary Dissertation and Notes* (Boston: William Hilliard; Cambridge: James Munroe and Company, 1834; originally published in 1778) 227–28. Of course, Lowth's commentary on the book as a whole was far from conventional; it was ground-breaking in its treatment of the prophets as poets and artists whose works should be interpreted according to the canons used for secular poetry. Also revolutionary was its free emendation of the Hebrew text. See chapter five below for this aspect of his work as it pertains to Isaiah 15–16.

[10]*D. Robert Lowth's Lord Bischofs zu London und der Londner und Göttingschen Societäten der Wissenschaften Mitglieds; Jesaias: neu ubersetzt nebst einer Einleitung und kritischen philologischen und erlauternden Anmerkungen; aus dem*

Koppe observed that the text of Isaiah 15–16 appeared to be a condensation of Jeremiah 48. This observation, coupled with his belief that certain figures and expressions in the poem sounded closer to the style of Jeremiah than to that of Isaiah, led him to the conclusion that Isaiah could not have written the poem (234–35). Koppe's attribution of the poem to Jeremiah has been rejected by all recent commentators, although several in his own time agreed with him.[11] His discussion of the stylistic peculiarities in Isaiah 15–16, however, raised questions of authorship that have persisted to the present.

Koppe's rejection of the Isaianic authorship of the poem was not accepted immediately by critical scholars. Writing in 1816, J. G. Eichhorn could still assume that most would agree that the poem had been written by Isaiah; he takes no pains to defend this assumption.[12] He does, however, suggest that someone other than Isaiah added the epilogue (16:13–14), probably a prophet in the time of Nebuchadnezzar. In his view, the prophecy was written by Isaiah in the midst of an Assyrian invasion of Moab. Isaiah's purpose in the speech was to warn Judah not to receive the Moabite fugitives lest, in so doing, Judah draw the wrath of Assyria on itself (245–46; 253–55).

Writing soon after Eichhorn, W. Gesenius agrees with Koppe that the style of the prophecy points to some prophet other than Isaiah.[13] He reverses Eichhorn's construction and assumes that the

---

Englischen; mit Zusatzen und Anmerkungen (Leipzig: Weidmanns Erben und Reich, 1780), vol. 2. In the case of Isaiah 15 and 16, the majority of Koppe's notes consist of additional information on the location of the cities mentioned in the poem.

[11]Gesenius (123) lists Augusti, Bauer, and Bertholdt, as among those who accepted Koppe's idea. The chief defense of the primacy of Jeremiah 48, however, is found in H. Bardtke, "Jeremia der Fremdvölkerprophet," *ZAW* 54 (1936) 240–62; see esp. 247–48. Thorough and trenchant critiques of this reversal of the dependency may be found in the commentaries of Gesenius, Auvray and Wildberger. Wildberger provides perhaps the most satisfying arguments in favor of the view that the author of Jeremiah 48 used at least some form of Isaiah 15–16.

[12] J. G. Eichhorn, *Die hebräischen Propheten* (Göttingen: Vandenhoef and Ruprecht, 1816).

[13]"Exegesis of Isaiah XV. XVI," 120–24.

epilogue was from Isaiah, but that the speech itself was by "an ancient prophet," either a contemporary of Isaiah's or some even earlier writer (121). The language, imagery and presence of a high degree of paronomasia convince Gesenius of this:

> In the prophecy itself...the language and imagery certainly differ rather remarkably from the usual language and imagery of Isaiah. The repetition and frequency of geographical names, the play upon these names, the roughness and harshness of expression, many favourite phrases in the passage, (particularly the עַל־כֵּן with כִּי repeated many times after it), are foreign to the genuine passages of Isaiah; but bespeak for the most part an ancient prophet (120–21).

In fact, the paronomasia in the poem goes beyond puns on place names; in his comments on 15:4; 16:10 and 12, Gesenius points out three instances of word play not related to place names. He gives little indication of what specifically he has in mind when he refers to "the roughness and harshness of expression." Judging from hints spread throughout his verse by verse commentary, however, it seems that he has in mind the elliptical quality of the poetry, its terseness and abrupt transitions. For example, he once notes that compared to Jeremiah 48, the style is "short, compressed, and rough, as the early prophets write (comp. Hosea)" (123), and in his treatment of 16:7, he refers to the "harshness" of the expression לכן ייליל מואב למואב. It is thus the style of the prophecy that persuades him to reject Isaianic authorship, and yet he is cautious: "That the prophecy itself was not written by Isaiah, can hardly be satisfactorily proved; yet it is very probable..." (122).

Gesenius rejects Eichhorn's understanding of the poem as a description of events already past. He interprets it as a "wish and expectation of destruction, which is expressed in the form of a prediction" (121). In it the prophet proleptically both describes and laments the fate of the Moabites (15:1–9). He calls on them in their extremity to renew their tribute payments to Israel (16:1) and describes their imagined petition (vv 3–4), their "inducement to hearken to [the] petition" (v 5), and Israel's rejection of the petition (v 6).[14] In response to this rejection, Moab again takes up its

---

[14]Gesenius is not careful to separate the identities of Israel and Judah in his treatment of this passage. He uses "Israel" several times to designate

lament, to which the prophet adds his own expressions of sorrow (16:7–12) (pp. 146–53).

Gesenius is aware that some might consider it odd for the prophet to express sympathy for a foreign nation in a predictive lament. In response, he notes that expressions of compassion are "often found in threatening prophecies; chap. 16:11. 21:3, 4. 22:4. Mic 1:8. Jer 23:9. 48:36" (137). He does not attempt to distance the prophet from the expressions of sympathy, as had Luther and Calvin, nor does he think the conflict serious enough to propose dividing the poem into originally separate parts, as will those who follow him.

Writing in 1831, F. Hitzig agreed with Gesenius's contention that the style pointed to an "ancient prophet," and that Isaiah was responsible only for the epilogue. He went beyond Gesenius, however, by arguing that the prophecy was the same as the one attributed in 2 Kings 14:25 to Jonah ben Amittai, and that the attacking army was the transjordanian Israelite tribes in the time of Jeroboam II.[15] While some after him agreed that this was possible, few thought it more than one possibility among many. Indeed, most dismissed it as improbable. Hitzig based his rejection of Isaianic authorship of the main body of the speech on its vocabulary, syntax and style. He noted that in 15:7 the author uses פקדה for "store," whereas in 10:13 Isaiah uses עתידה to communicate the same idea. In contrast to Gesenius, his analysis of the style led him to characterize it as repetitive, verbose and ponderous:

---

what, by the logic of the petition, can only be Judah. Apparently, he assumes that the identity of Judah could be subsumed in the name "Israel" when the poem was written. Something at least akin to this assumption is necessary for his observation that 16:1 alludes to the payment of tribute that the Moabites once made to Israel (2 Kgs 3:4). For the allusion to work, one must assume either a political identity between Israel and Judah (at least in the minds of the poem's intended audience) or a situation in which all political prerogatives once held by Israel are, in the wake of Assyria's conquest in 722, transferred to Judah.

[15]See F. Hitzig, *Des Propheten Jonas Orakel über Moab, kritisch vindicirt und durch Übersetzung nebst Anmerkungen erläutert* (Heidelberg: Mohr, 1831). Page-number citations refer to his commentary, *Der Prophet Jesaja* (Heidelberg: C. F. Winter, 1833).

> There is no trace of [Isaiah's] light and lively cadences, of his frequently bold linking of ideas! The flood of words here rolls on slowly and ponderously, even reversing its course as the author constantly misconstrues the relationship of reason and order so that כי and על־כן or לכן, repeated again and again, are nearly the only conjunctions he uses. The reason that the author moves so slowly forward is not only because once he moves forward, he then steps back again (cf. 15:6 with v. 8), but also because the flow of words is unbelievably verbose. 15:3–5 enumerates the only cities and villages where there is lament and outcry; the plea for refuge in 16:3–4 is expressed five times; the description of the grapes of Sibmah stretching outward (16:8) itself stretches through four verbs with modifiers; and in v. 10, where the end of celebration in the fields and vineyards is described, half the material could be deleted without harm. On the whole, while with Isaiah the words are hardly sufficient clearly to express the ideas, here they hang like a baggy robe, flapping about the body of the ideas which are thereby diluted in expression and through the *nimium* [excess] weakened. The author's ideas are as poor in proportion as they are lacking in any power or vigor. Here we do not hear that fiery orator, that mighty spirit; on the contrary, an elegiac fluidity runs through the text, a tender-hearted nature expresses itself (cf. 15:4; 16:9, 11). Such speech in general has no part in prophetic speech, but is nearer to written poetry to whose rules it adheres from the first verse on. (180, translation mine)

Hitzig goes on to argue that the style of the poem does not compare to that of any of the known biblical authors, and consequently it could not have been written by any of them. On the basis primarily of historical considerations he dates the poem in the time of Jeroboam II and suggests Jonah ben Amittai as the author (181–84).

A. W. Knobel (1843) was one of the few who accepted Hitzig's suggestion concerning date and authorship.[16] He contributed still further reasons why the vocabulary and style pointed away from

---

[16]*Der Prophet Jesaia* (KHAT 5; Leipzig: Weidmann'sche, 1843); A. Dillmann took over responsibility for updating this commentary for the 1890 edition (Leipzig: S. Hirzel); R. Kittel was responsible for the sixth edition (Leipzig: S. Hirzel, 1898). It is unclear to what extent Knobel was influenced by H. Ewald's work on the prophets which was published in 1840 (on which, see below). Several of Knobel's points about the style of the poem are very similar to Ewald's observations. Knobel does not, however, mention Ewald's source division of the poem.

Isaiah. He notes five characteristics of the poem that point away from Isaiah:

(1) the "tender-hearted sympathy" expressed for an otherwise hated foreign nation (15:5; 16:9, 11)

(2) peculiar thoughts and expressions which are without parallel in Isaianic material: the idea that one should raise a funeral lament in the streets, that wailing would encircle the borders, that Sibmah's vintage should stretch over the whole territory, that its tendrils should intoxicate, that the heart should cry out over Moab like the sound of a zither, that tears should dampen Heshbon and Elealah (15:3, 5, 8; 16:8, 9)

(3) unique phrases and expressions: מים, ערער זעקה, ירד בבכי הידד נפל, שית צל, עשה פלילה, הביא עצה, נחל הערבים, משמות (15:2, 3, 5, 6, 7; 16:3, 9)

(4) peculiar forms: עֹעֵר, נִלְאָה, רֹמֵס, מֵץ, נוֹסָפוֹת, הֵידָד, פְּקֻדָּה, מַעֲבָרָה, גֵּא (15:5, 7, 9; 16:2, 4, 9, 10, 12); as well as the use of כִּי and כֵּן עַל throughout the poem.

(5) the style of the speech as a whole: its awkward conception; its lack of a strong vitality and lively, engaging flow; its tedious listing of place names.

(105–06)

As does Hitzig, he believes that nothing else in the Old Testament could have come from this same author. It is a style and usage without parallel. Knobel's contention that the "tender-hearted sympathy" of the poem points to an author other than Isaiah implies either that Isaiah was incapable of expressing sympathy for Moab or that the mode of expression was uncharacteristic of Isaiah. The latter possibility seems the most likely since there is no reason to believe that Jonah ben Amittai would have had any greater cause for expressing sympathy for Moab than did Isaiah.

Not all were inclined to agree with Hitzig and Knobel that the style and usage pointed conclusively away from Isaiah. In his 1838 commentary, C. L. Hendewerk disagrees with Hitzig's assessment of the style. In a long passage, he counters Hitzig's disparaging of the style point by point.[17] He argues that the style was in fact lively and showed great imagination. Hitzig's rather loose and unguarded discourse on the non-Isaianic features of the speech is an easy target for Hendewerk. He shows again and again that the style can be understood as terse and powerful exactly where Hitzig had found it repetitive and verbose. He notes that the listing of numerous cities in the poem is comparable to that in 10:28–32 and that other repetitions are part of the power and beauty of the poetry. In the end, Hendewerk maintains that all but 16:13–14 come from the hand of Isaiah.

Conservative commentators in the middle and latter part of the eighteenth century such as J. A. Alexander and C. von Orelli did not deeply engage the discussion of authorship; for the most part, they simply assumed that Isaiah had written the speech. From about this time on, commentators can be grouped into two classes: those who believed that Isaiah had written most, if not all, of the book, and those who ascribed less and less of the book to the hand of Isaiah. The first group held to the traditional interpretation of the chapters with only slight and occasional deviations. Alexander understands the speech as a prediction written by Isaiah of the downfall of Moab. The prophet probably had no particular invasion or invader in mind, but intentionally left the exact nature of the coming disaster vague.[18] Orelli interprets the passage as a prediction uttered by Isaiah at the time of Tiglath-Pileser's deportation of the transjordanian Israelite tribes.[19] F. Delitzsch departs from the traditional interpretation only in his assertion that 16:1–6 contains an exhortation urging Moab to repent and send tribute to Israel and a depiction of its subsequent repentance and further pleas for protection. 16:6 is thus not a

---

[17]C. L. Hendewerk, *Des Propheten Jesaja Weissagungen* (Königsberg: Gebrüder Bornträger, 1838) 416–20.

[18]J. A. Alexander, *Commentary on the Prophecies of Isaiah,* 2 vols abridged in 1 (Grand Rapids: Zondervan, 1970; originally published 1846–47) 312.

[19]C. von Orelli, *The Prophecies of Isaiah* (Edinburgh: T & T Clark, 1889) 106.

rejection of the Moabite petition but an allusion, given for the sake of contrast, to Moab's attitude before their repentance.[20]

H. Ewald's comments on the poem, brief as they are, mark a new stage in interpretation. Ewald is the first to divide 15:1–16:12 into historically distinct units.[21] He distinguishes three stages of tradition. The original poem consisted of a single elegy which was subsequently divided into two parts (15:1–9 and 16:7–12). The division was made at the second stage by the later writer who added 16:1–6. At the third and final stage a supplement was appended (16:13–14).[22] Stage one Ewald attributes to a northern prophet writing some time before Amos; stage two he places in the time of Uzziah and attributes to an unknown author; stage three he attributes to Isaiah (137–41). His criteria for distinguishing the layers are style, form and content. The first stage is distinguished by its elegiac form, extensive use of paronomasia, and tender expressions of feelings. It describes an attack on Moab, probably by their "Arabian neighbors." Concerning the tone of the elegy Ewald writes: "Among the more ancient prophets there is no one else whose feelings are like those we find here; the prophet is carried away by his grief and pity; his tone is rather that of melting tenderness, of elegiac lamentation, than [of] prophetic sternness" (138). The addition made at the second stage has a completely different language and tone from the original elegy. Moreover, its content suggests a time when a "righteous and prosperous" king sat on the Judean throne, and this, Ewald reasons, must have been the early reign of Uzziah (140–41). The

---

[20]F. Delitzsch, *Biblical Commentary on the Prophecies of Isaiah* (Grand Rapids: Eerdmans, 1960; originally published 1873 by T & T Clark) 330–33.

[21]*Die Propheten des alten Bundes, Ausg. 2: Jesaja mit den übrigen älteren Propheten* (Göttingen: Vandenhoeck & Ruprecht, 1867; first edition, Stuttgart: Adolph Krabbe, 1840–41). Citations are from the English translation of the second edition: *Commentary on the Prophets of the Old Testament*, vol. 2, trans. J. F. Smith (London and Edinburgh: Williams and Norgate, 1876). It is probably safe to assume that Ewald's deep involvement in the development of the source-critical analysis of the Pentateuch influenced his decision to divide Isaiah 15–16 into three sources.

[22]In the first edition of the commentary, Ewald is more tentative in distinguishing 16:1–6 as a separate source, and he thinks it possible, given the similarity between 16:4 and Isa 29:20, that Isaiah added 16:1–6 to an older lament in order to make his own point (230–31, first ed.).

addition to the original elegy came at a time when Moab was again in trouble and applied to Judah for help. The addition advises against providing help: "Inasmuch as our prophet, therefore, advised that protection should not be given, he properly inserted his addition between the two strophes, as if the prophetic lamentation of the second strophe were the result of the refusal of protection which had then been made for a time" (140). The third stage is reached when Isaiah takes up the whole of 15:1–16:12, adds a brief supplement, and uses it to refer to an impending attack, probably by the Assyrians (141).

The influence of Ewald's ideas spread quickly. This was facilitated in the English-speaking world through the translation of his commentary in 1876. Even before the English translation, however, T. K. Cheyne (1870) responded to Ewald's analysis. Cheyne agreed with the established critical opinion that the language of 15:1–16:12 points away from Isaiah, but he was unconvinced by Ewald's introduction of a third author into the picture.[23] He comments,

> [It is] true, that vv. 1–6 appear at first sight to interrupt the elegy. Let it be weighed, on the other hand, (1) that the first gush of lamentation is already brought to a natural close in xv. 9, and that its renewal in xvi. 7 requires a fresh motive; (2) that there are three interruptions hardly less serious in the passage xvi. 1–6 itself, since vv. 1–4*a* do not cohere with vv. 4*b*, 5 (which are unintelligible as an utterance of the Moabites), and vv. 1–5 do not cohere with ver. 6, which is unintelligible as the answer of Zion to Moab, and is simply the prophet's own statement of the historical characteristics of the Moabitish nation. If therefore we are to argue from the mere fact of an interruption to a difference of authors, we must infer the existence not of a single fresh hand only, but of three (43).

Cheyne goes on to conclude on this basis that 15:1–16:12 is a unified composition. He reasons that the author's detailed knowledge of Moabite geography and his "deep and tender interest in Moab" point to a native of the northern kingdom (43). He interprets the speech as a predictive prophecy that both encourages the Moabites to offer their obedience to the Judean throne (for this

---

[23]T. K. Cheyne, *The Book of Isaiah, Chronologically Arranged* (London: MacMillan and Co., 1870).

northerner is "like...Hosea...an adherent of Davidic rights") and expresses doubt that such obedience will be forthcoming (43–44).

In his later commentary on Isaiah, Cheyne gives his reasons for rejecting Isaianic authorship:

> (1) The flow of sympathy, unparalleled in Isaiah, towards the objects of the predicted judgment; (2) The writer's minute acquaintance with Moabitish topography...and (3) The tediousness and archaic simplicity of the style (note the accumulation of assonances in the Hebrew, and of 'for' and 'therefore'), combined with certain words and phrases unknown to Isaiah.[24]

The note about the writer's acquaintance with Moabite topography, the critique of Ewald's division of the poem into sources, and the observation on the use of assonance appear to be Cheyne's unique contribution to the discussion.

By this time in the history of the interpretation of the chapters, a strong difference of opinion has emerged over the possibility that Isaiah expressed sympathy for the Moabites. All agree that the expressions of sympathy are unusual, both because of their mere presence and because of their intensity, but interpreters explain the oddity in one of several ways: (1) the expressions of sympathy are insincere; (2) such expressions are found in other threatening prophecies and are normal for the genre; (3) the high moral character and sensitivity of Isaiah leads him to sympathize with those upon whom he pronounces judgment; and (4) the expressions of sympathy point to some prophet from whom sympathy might more naturally be expected.

Cheyne's argument that the principles behind Ewald's source-redactional analysis of the poem should, by their own logic, lead to even further division proved to be prophetic. What was for him a reason against dividing the speech became for others the next logical step in its analysis. Commentators after Cheyne focused on further refinements of the source-critical analysis begun by Ewald.

While disagreeing with Ewald's division of the material, B. Duhm used similar source-critical tools to discover several later

---

[24] *The Prophecies of Isaiah*, vol. 1 (New York: Thomas Whittaker, fifth ed., 1892) 96.

additions to an original poem.[25] In his 1892 commentary, he argues that the original form of the poem was lament, and that this lament consisted of 15:1–9a; 16:1, 3–11. To this were later added the predictions in 15:9b; 16:2, 12–14, thus changing the lament into a threatening prophecy. Duhm regards as possible Ewald's suggestion that 16:1–6 was added after the original composition since its tone was cooler and harsher than the rest of the lament, but thinks it more probable that the difference in tone results from the change of content (98, 103). He also notes that the later addition of 16:2 to 16:1–6 not only disrupted the formal unity of the lament; it also created a geographical improbability. The depiction of Moab at the fords of the Arnon in 16:2 seems to indicate that the immediately following petition to Judah was made at the Arnon ford, an idea that makes little sense. To overcome this problem, he moves 16:2 to the end of the previous section, immediately after 15:9. This strategy has been followed by a number of later commentators.

Duhm is guided in his division of the material almost exclusively by considerations of form. He notes that the obvious addition in 16:13–14 is threatening prophecy, and he determines that other elements of threat must also be additions. What is left is a pure lament (98).

Although Duhm is the first to treat 15:9b; 16:2, 12 as later additions, his discussion is best remembered for its dating of the chapters. He argues that the epilogue makes sense in only one period of history, a time when the hopes of the Moabites had been fully crushed. This, he concludes, could only be the first century, in the time of Alexander Jannaeus. The word "formerly" in 16:13 he interprets to mean that the preceding lament must have been issued not long before, and thus he tentatively dates the main lament to the second century and connects it with the Nabatean conquest of Moab. The messianic references in 16:1, 3–6 refer to John Hyrcanus, though he thinks this section might have been added secondarily, and if such is the case, he would prefer to date the original lament somewhat earlier (99). No commentator has

---

[25] *Das Buch Jesaia* (HKAT; Göttingen: Vandenhoek and Ruprecht, 1902^{2}; first edition 1892).

adopted Duhm's dating of the poem, though his influence is easily traced in the literary treatments in commentaries of the next century.

D. 1900–1950

Writing at the turn of the century, K. Marti divides the poem into four distinct levels of tradition.[26] The original elegy he defines as 15:1b–9aα + 16:7–10 (11). This elegy was written on the occasion of an attack by Arab nomads in the fifth century. The attack must have originated in the southeast of the country since it was Moab's chief cities south of the Arnon which suffered; the cities north of the Arnon merely raised a lament. For this reason Marti rules out Hitzig's suggestion that the attack was made by the transjordanian Israelite tribes (or the Assyrians) who would logically have come from the north. Furthermore, the expressions of heartfelt sympathy rule out Hitzig's suggestion, for what sense do they make in the mouth of a prophet of the conquering nation? Such compassion for Moab was, however, possible in the fifth century, as the book of Ruth shows. To the original elegy were added 15:9aβ–16:4a, 6, 12, probably in the fourth century. The presence of the divine "I" in 15:9aβ is a clear indication of a break, since what had preceded was straight elegy. These additions served to change the elegy into a threatening prophecy. Still later 16:4b–5 was added as a messianic gloss and 16:13–14 was appended as an epilogue; both were probably added in the second century, about the time of John Hyrcanus (139–41). Marti also notes several other late glosses. He observes that 15:9aβ is grammatically troubled and resolves the problem by designating the phrase as a later gloss (135–36). He thinks that 16:11 is also a late gloss since 16:10 already provides a good conclusion to the original elegy and since 16:11 is very short and looks very much like a variant of 16:7 (139).

Marti's analysis essentially combines the observations of Ewald and Duhm. As does Ewald, he assigns the interruption presented by 16:1–6 to a later hand; as does Duhm, he removes all elements of threatening prophecy so that only a pure elegy

---

[26] *Das Buch Jesaja* (KHAT 10; Tübingen: J. C. B. Mohr, 1900)

remains. He adds significant new elements, however, in his treatment of 15:9aβ–16:6. This later addition is itself not a unity but originally lacked 16:4b–5. In its earliest form, it referred to further woes that would force Moab (and possibly Edom) to petition Judah for protection, a petition that Judah would refuse to grant. Later tradents misunderstood this section, the text having been somewhat corrupted, and took it as a petition for protection addressed by the Judeans to Moab. This understanding then led to the addition of the messianic gloss in 16:4b–5 (138). Marti's idea that 16:4b–5 is a late messianic gloss was accepted by many after him.

One notes in the commentaries of Duhm and Marti a keen attentiveness to the details of the text. Such attentiveness reached a zenith in the commentary of G. B. Gray.[27] One of Gray's most significant contributions to the discussion is his observation that "whereas almost the whole of 15:1–7a, 16:6–11 is quoted, or has left its trace, in Jer 48, no trace of the long intervening section is to be found there." Furthermore, 16:12 is also absent from Jeremiah 48 (271). These omissions had been noted long before (see Gesenius, for instance), but Gray was the first to connect them with the other signs of disunity at the center and end of the poem and use them as further evidence that this material had been added later. The lack of synoptic parallel for 15:7b–16:5 coupled with the observations of Ewald, Duhm and Marti led Gray to conclude that the original poem had consisted of 15:1–7a and 16:6–11. This original "elegy" he designates source "A." The remainder (15:7b–16:5, 12) he designates source "B," material in which "the prophetic element is conspicuous." He thinks that "A" may have included 15:7b–9a, since these verses fit better with the elegy than they do with the "prophetic section." The fact that they are lacking in Jeremiah 48 may be simply an accident. Likewise, he notes that 16:6 ill suits the elegy and is thus probably a somewhat later reflection on Moab's pride (272).

After reviewing the history of Moab, Gray concludes that the most likely time in which to set the original elegy is the fifth

[27] *A Critical and Exegetical Commentary on the Book of Isaiah*, vol. 1 (ICC; Edinburgh: T. & T. Clark, 1912).

century, the time of the probable conquest of Moab by the Nabateans (276). This is partially confirmed by the direction of the attack, which comes from the south or east. He is vague about when the "B" source was added, some time later to be sure.

By the time of Gray's commentary, there appeared to be an emerging critical agreement on the source analysis of the speech—at least in broad outline. This consensus, however, did not go unchallenged. In 1926, E. König argued that the source division of the poem destroyed its conceptual unity (*Gedankenzusammenhang*).[28] He understands the flow of thought as follows: (1) The Moabites are threatened by a sudden raid from enemy bands, to which is added a terrible drought, so that the whole population is put to flight. (2) In their extremity, the Moabites come to Judah bearing a gift of tribute and requesting protection. (3) On account of the arrogance of the Moabites, this request must be denied. For this reason the prophet is deeply pained but sees even more misfortunes coming (192). This understanding closely resembles the traditional line of interpretation from the early part of the previous century. König thinks this conceptual unity sufficiently explicit in the speech to overcome the source-critical evidence. He also finds evidence of unity in the parallel that exists between the use of the divine 'I' in 15:9aβ and in 16:10. He is critical of the reasons that had been adduced to divide the poem. For instance, he calls into question Gray's assertion that no trace of 16:1–5 is found in Jeremiah 48 by pointing out traces of these verses in Jer 48:28. Furthermore, since in four other places 15:1–7a and 16:6–11 have no parallel in Jeremiah, Gray's argument has no decisive strength (192–93). König does agree with the source-critical assessment of the poem on one point; as does Duhm, he thinks the description in 16:2 of the Moabites at the Arnon ford is misplaced and should be moved instead to the end of chapter 15 (202, n. 6).

König attributes the speech to a Judean prophet living in the latter part of the ninth century, certainly not an Israelite since the petition in 16:1 is directed to Judah and certainly not Isaiah on account of the "rough expression" and repetitive use of כי. The attack was probably made by Bedouin tribes, aptly described as

[28]*Das Buch Jesaja* (Gütersloh: C. Bertelsmann, 1926).

"lords of the nations" (193). On the whole, König's work represents a step back to pre-Ewald interpretation.

An even more remarkable step back toward traditional interpretation was made by O. Procksch in his 1930 commentary.[29] For the first time in a century of historical-critical scholarship, an interpreter argued that much of the main poem was from Isaiah. Specifically, Procksch determined that all of 15:1–16:5 is from Isaiah's hand and refers to an attack on Moab's southern territory in 715 B.C.E. (225–26). It begins with a lament by the Moabites over an attack on their land (15:1–9). This is followed by a petition by the Moabites for help (16:1–4a). In response, Isaiah gives a messianic prophecy of salvation to the refugees (16:4b–5). This prophecy of salvation is the main point of the original speech. Procksch's starting point is his contention that the postscript in 16:13–14 indicates that a former *promise* is being revoked. Thus, the original composition must have offered a promise to Moab, and this could only be the case if it ended at 16:5 (219–20).

The remainder of the poem, 16:6–12, was added by a later prophet, perhaps Jeremiah. This later addition is distinguished from the original composition in two ways. First, it envisions a different sort of disaster from 15:1–9 since it contains no reference to the flight south and since its focus is on the loss of viniculture rather than on a destruction of cities and subsequent flight. Secondly, it is impossible that a further lament should follow a promise of salvation (219–20). As does König, Procksch stresses the importance of the logical flow of ideas. Procksch, however, also sees a generic propriety in the original composition; this is clear in his outline of its structure: "1. Klage (c. 15). 2. Bitte (c. 16, 1–4a). 3. Verheißung (c. 16, 4b. 5)" (215).

---

[29]*Jesaia I* (KAT; Leipzig: A. Deichertsche, 1930). Much earlier in his career, Procksch had laid out the main arguments for the position he takes in his commentary. The arguments are essentially the same with the exception that he did not argue that the style had been skewed by Isaiah's attempt to imitate Moabite speech. Hidden away in a footnote (in his *Geschichtsbetrachtung und geschichtliche Überlieferung bei den vorexilischen Propheten* [Leipzig: J. C. Hinrichs, 1902], 51–52, n. 3), his interpretation was not taken into account by other scholars until the publication of his commentary in 1930.

Procksch's argument in favor of Isaianic authorship is as ingenious as it is simple. He answers the objection that the style and vocabulary are not Isaiah's by suggesting that the stylistic peculiarities result from the fact that Isaiah put 15:1–9 in the mouth of the Moabites and adjusted the style and vocabulary accordingly (209). Having removed the key objection to Isaianic authorship, he offers as positive evidence the similarity of content in 16:4b–5 and 9:1–6 (218). These arguments are, perhaps, too ingenious; other scholars have not accepted Procksch's particular way of defending Isaianic authorship.

By Procksch's time, a considerable amount of disagreement existed over the specific details of the attack on Moab: the identity of the enemy, the direction from which the attack had come, the territory involved, and the specific effects of the attack. The poem is somewhat vague and confusing regarding these details, and as a consequence, speculation ranged widely. In his journal article treating Isaiah 15–16, E. Power attempted to solve some of the problems.[30] The heart of his argument is a reinterpretation of 15:9bc. He contends that the "additions" that are to be made to Dimon (=Dibon) are in fact territorial additions, not additional troubles. The reference is intended ironically, however: "The irony would consist in regarding the neutral territory and the land of the invaders, where the surviving Dimonites now dwell, as additions made to the city of the slain" (436). He goes on to argue that the two ironic additions are indicated by the terms אריה and אדמה, which, by means of textual emendation, he takes as Ariel (=Jerusalem) and Edom. Thus, Edom is the attacker and Judah is the place of refuge (436–37). The tribute in 16:1 is directed by Edom to Judah. The Edomites seek to persuade Judah to turn away the Moabites, and they offer to divide the spoils of conquest with Judah (16:2; part of which, Power suggests, has been lost). In response, Isaiah urges the Judean king to shelter the Moabites (16:3–4b) and offers him a promise (16:4c–5) (pp. 440–42).

As further evidence for this unique interpretation, Power argues that the order of the place names mentioned in chapter 15

[30]"The Prophecy of Isaias against Moab (Is. 15, 1–16, 5)," *Biblica* 13 (1932) 435–51.

indicates that the flight there described was from the area south of the Arnon toward the north, ending finally in "the extreme south of the east Jordan valley" (443–47). He offers a number of new site identifications in defense of this reading; most of his proposals have been rejected by other scholars. It is clear by the end of his article, moreover, that his central purpose in dealing with Isaiah 15–16 is to further his argument placing the cities of "the Pentapolis" in the area at the northern end of the Dead Sea. This becomes especially clear when he defers any treatment of 16:6–12 and the epilogue since they "lie outside the scope of this article, which is concerned with the historical background and the sequence of thought in the descriptive and narrative parts of the prophecy" (451, n. 4). Although Power's interpretation won no adherents, it did serve to underline the insecurity of the geographical assumptions underlying most interpretations as well as the ambiguous nature of 16:1–6.

Power attempts to defend the Isaianic authorship of the entire poem. His arguments consist of a comparison of the irony he sees in 15:9 with that found in Isa 28:10–13, the uniquely Isaianic use of "Ariel" to denote Jerusalem, the Isaianic character of 16:3–5, and the similarity of the use of place names in Isa 10:27c–32 (pp. 447–48). These arguments have had little influence because, among other reasons, they depend too much on textual emendations and on Power's unique interpretation of 15:9. In fact, apart from those committed to defending the Isaianic authorship of most or all of chapters 1–39 (Kissane, Barnes, Young, Leupold, Watts, Oswalt, Hayes and Irvine, Brangenberg) there are no other scholars after this time who attempt to uphold the Isaianic authorship of the chapters.

E. 1950–1980

There were, however, two more critical scholars who attempted to defend the unity of the poem. The first was W. Rudolph who argues in his 1963 article on Isaiah 15–16 that except for a few late additions (15:9; 16:2, 12) the poem shows clear signs of having been an original unity.[31] These signs consist mainly of content links between the sections. For example, he argues that 16:1–6 presupposes 15:1–8, since 15:7 states that the Moabites flee into Edomite territory and 16:1 depicts them sending the embassy from Edom to Judah. Moreover, the petition in 16:3–5 is answered negatively in 16:6, thus linking the middle and final sections of the poem. As for the difference in the depiction of the catastrophe in 15:1–8 and in 16:7–11, it does not indicate two separate events; it reflects only different aspects of the same event (138). Rudolph rejects the designation "prophecy." What is being described is not in the future, but already past. This is obvious from the concrete facts that are mentioned: the trespass of the Moabites on Edomite territory, the sending of an embassy to Judah, the rejection of the petition (138).

Rudolph's general interpretation is similar to that of Eichhorn. The poem is a lament in response to an attack (from the north) on Moab. The petition in 16:3–5 is made by the Moabites to the Judeans. The reference to the tent of David in 16:5 is not messianic, but a promise by the Moabites of fealty to Judah (140). This petition is rejected in 16:6 with the prophet's reminder of Moab's overweening pride. In response, the lament resumes in 16:7–11. Rudolph's treatment differs from Eichhorn's mainly in that it designates 15:9, 16:2, 12 as later additions, primarily because their genre (oracle) differs from the rest of the lament. The original poem Rudolph dates to pre-exilic times due to the indication in 16:5 that the Davidic dynasty still exists. He considers it impossible that Assyria could have been the enemy because in that case Judah would hardly have been willing or able to give help (141). Considering that the attack came from the north, he approves the old suggestion that it was part of Jeroboam II's territorial expansion (141–42). The author was a Judean, possibly with some personal connection with Moab. Such a connection is his attempt to explain the expressions of sympathy, about which he remarks: "Bemerkenswert ist, daß kein Haß gegen Moab vorliegt, beim Propheten sogar Mitleid, das man nicht für scheinheilig und

---

[31]"Jesaja XV–XVI," *Hebrew and Semitic Studies Presented to Godfrey Rolles Driver*, ed. D. Thomas and W. McHardy (Oxford: Clarendon, 1963) 130–43.

ironisch halten darf" (142–43). The author of the epilogue may have been Isaiah, but this is uncertain (142). Rudolph does not venture a guess about how the final form of the poem came to be included in the book of Isaiah.

The second critic who argued during this period for the unity of the poem is W. Eichrodt.[32] In his commentary published in 1967, Eichrodt follows closely Rudolph's line of interpretation. The original poem consisted of 15:1–16:11, excluding 15:9 and 16:2. It was a lament by an ancient Judean prophet from the time of Jeroboam II and Uzziah over the results of an Israelite attack on Moab (45). The purpose of the Moabites' petition in 16:3–5 is to obtain Judah's mediation of the conflict (44). The petition is rejected because Moab had wrongly assumed that Judah would want to check Israel's territorial expansion, even at the risk of war, and because Moab's promise of fealty seemed insincere in view of their previous arrogance (46). The resumption of the lament in 16:7–11 is a natural response to this rejection. The addition of the prophetic threats in 15:9, 16:2, 12 changed the tone of the whole poem (47). Eichrodt rejects all attempts to date these additions; he also thinks it fruitless to speculate on the date or author of the epilogue (48). The unity of the original poem is proven by the coherence of its content and by its artistry: "Trotzdem ist die dichterische Formgebung von dieser prophetischen Klage unabtrennbar und spricht durch ihre meisterhafte Handhabung, die sich dem Inhalt gut anzuschmiegen weiß, für eine schon im älteren Prophetismus gern geübte Kunst der dichterischen Rede" (42). The similarity to Rudolph's position is clear throughout, and Eichrodt tacitly acknowledges that he is dependent on Rudolph's study by referring to Rudolph's contribution as "entscheidender" (42, n. 7).

Excluding Rudolph and Eichrodt, the history of the critical examination of Isaiah 15–16 after the year 1950 may be seen primarily as variations on the themes already established by Ewald, Duhm, Marti and Gray. Generally speaking, opinions on the source-redactional analysis of the poem divide into two

---

[32] *Der Herr der Geschichte. Jesaja 13–23 und 28–39* (BKAT; Stuttgart: Calwer, 1967).

groups: those who contend that the original lament consisted of 15:1–8 (9a) + 16:6–11, and those who believe that the original lament consisted only of 15:1–8 (9a).

H. Hertzberg is among the first group.[33] He is cautiously conservative in his assessment of the question of authorship; he does not argue for Isaianic authorship, but he states that he sees no serious reason why Isaiah might not have written at least part of the present poem. For support, he quotes Delitzsch (77). His source-redactional analysis, however, follows in the footsteps of Ewald. The original lament consists of 15:1–8 + 16:6–12. The word of promise (16:1–5) and appendix (16:13–14) are later additions, as are the threats in 15:9 and 16:2 (74–75). His division of the material is based primarily on style and content (76).

In his book *The Moabites*, A. van Zyl analyzes the redaction of the poem in much the same way as Hertzberg.[34] The original poem consisted of 15:1–9a + 16:6–11. Isaiah took up this poem and added to it 15:9b–16:5, 12 in order to "stress the point that Judah should not rely on Moab for help against the Assyrians." The addition does this by predicting that in the near future Moab will be overwhelmed and forced to seek refuge with Judah (15:9b–16:5) and by pointing out the futility of the Moabite cult (16:12). The epilogue was probably added in 585 B.C.E., "shortly after the Moabites had mocked the fugitives from Judah in 586 B. C." (21–23).

Although his analysis of the redaction of the poem follows a well trodden path, van Zyl's interpretation of the original poem takes a surprising turn. He argues that it was

> ...no elegy on Moab, for the typical אֵיךְ is replaced by כִּי, and we can observe a certain triumphant note throughout the poem. Therefore it seems more probable that this older source was originally a mocking song, sung by the enemies of the Moabites. The signs of sympathy with the Moabites are mere expressions of sarcasm. This is also indicated by the rhythm, which is not קִינָה (20–21).

He notes that in some places the rhythm corresponds to that found in Judges 5, which is in part a mocking song (21, n. 2). The

---

[33] *Der erste Jesaja* (Kassel: Oncken, 1952).

[34] A. van Zyl, *The Moabites* (Leiden: Brill, 1960).

linguistic peculiarities of the poem lead him to conclude not only that was the poem not Isaianic, but also that it was not even Hebrew in origin. He thinks that the mocking song originated among the Bedouin, perhaps during the last third of the eighth century (21, 37). Unfortunately, van Zyl's treatment of the poem is very brief; it is part of his introduction to the sources available for the study of Moab and is not intended as a commentary. In view of the originality of his proposal, however, one wishes that van Zyl had expanded and defended his reading more fully.

A somewhat expanded treatment of this ironic reading of the poem appears in the commentary of P. Auvray, who adopts both van Zyl's redactional analysis and his reading of the original poem as a mocking-song.[35] Auvray repeats the evidence of the poem's rhythm, which, he notes, is usually symmetrical (2+2) and only occasionally the meter of lament (3+2). He cites 15:2–3 and 16:12 as verses in which the ironic tone is evident but gives no more precise indication of what marks this tone. He notes that the reproaches in 16:6 suggest comparison with Isaiah 14, Ezekiel 27–28 and the book of Nahum (169). Apparently he is thinking of the theme of the humbling of a once proud nation found in each of the texts he mentions. Once again, the reader is left wishing for a more thorough defense of this intriguing reading. Oddly, neither van Zyl nor Auvray mentions the ironic interpretations posed by Luther and Calvin. One is left with the impression that neither scholar was aware that the ironic line of interpretation had been previously proposed.

Turning now to the second group, those who limit the original poem to 15:1–8 (9), we come first of all to the work of G. Fohrer.[36] Fohrer thinks the original poem consisted of 15:1–9a + 16:2 (the latter verse having been displaced when later material was added). He interprets it as lament over a recent attack on Moab rather than as prediction cast in the form of a lament. Since the lament shows deep human sympathy toward Moab, he dates it in the post-exilic era, when friendly feelings toward Moab were possible as indicated by the book of Ruth (190, 193). The remain-

[35]*Isaïe 1–39* (Paris: Gabalda, 1972).

[36]*Das Buch Jesaja; 1. Band Kapitel 1–23* (Zürich/Stuttgart: Zwingli, 1960).

ing parts of the poem all come from later, though how much later is unclear. 16:1, 3–4a is a *Kriegslied* that has been reinterpreted in the light of eschatological theology. Through the addition of 16:4b–5, Moab's troubles are placed among those woes that are to come at the end of time (191–92). Finally, 16:6–12 is a further lament that is marked by "einem tiefen menschlichen Mitgefühl...[und] eine klare Einsicht in die religiöse Ursache des Unheils." The poet's main purpose is to point out that Moab's woes are directly related to its arrogance (193). Nevertheless, he mourns and laments the disaster that overtakes Moab (195). The author of the epilogue interprets the composite poem as a prophetic threat against Moab and adds the epilogue to suggest that the threatened downfall of Moab needs only a little human help for its realization. This represents an "activist" theology that is entirely out of keeping with the theology of genuine Isaianic thought (195). Fohrer's treatment of Isaiah 15–16 is brief, and he provides little argument for his interpretation.

O. Kaiser's interpretation is very similar to Fohrer's but is argued in more detail.[37] As does Fohrer, Kaiser sees eschatological concerns in all the later additions to the poem. He even thinks it possible that the original poem (15:1–9aα) might have been eschatological (69, 74–75), though he thinks it more likely that it referred to an actual historical event. This event would probably have been an attack from the south on Moab's heartland, the area south of the Arnon. The text is vague and confusing. It seems, however, that the cities north of the Arnon are in a state of mourning, but for the moment unmolested, while those south of the Arnon, Ar (er Rabbah) and Kir (Kerak), lie in ruins. On the other hand, 16:8 seems to indicate that the attack also affected the northern territory, as does the southward flight described in 15:5–7. After discussing the various uncertainties and options, he states, "We can come to the provisional conclusion that the poet

---

[37]*Isaiah 13–39: A Commentary* (OTL; Philadelphia: Westminster, 1974; German original, 1973). Kaiser's comment is marked by a great deal of uncertainty. What he says in one place, he contradicts in another. I have tried to be fair in my summary of his interpretation to what I discerned to be his final conclusions, but it would be easy to fault my summary by citing individual passages from his commentary.

has in mind an attack upon the heartland of Moab south of the Arnon, but possibly also upon the north of the country at the same time" (65–68, 75). The genre of the original poem is "funeral lament." The apparent sympathy expressed in v 5 is, however, "a stylistic device to re-emphasize the severity of the blow...rather than an expression of genuine feeling" (68), an interpretation not unlike those of Luther and Calvin. Kaiser says little about the date of the original poem, the uncertainties of interpretation being great. He notes only that 16:1 *may* imply that 15:1–8 (9aα) was written before the exile (75).

The petition in 16:1–6 Kaiser considers a later addition to the poem with its own redactional history. Originally, it consisted of 16:1, 3–4a, 6. The marks of redactional activity are immediately apparent in the disruption caused by 16:2, which probably came originally after 15:9aα and represents an explanatory addition from a later hand. Also, 16:4b–5 are not a promise made by the Moabites to Judah, but rather an answer to the petition in 16:1, 3–4a. This answer is an eschatological promise, made for the sake of the Jewish audience rather than for the Moabites, that at some future time Judah will again have a king to whom the Moabites can turn for help. The original petition, which ended with 16:6, evoked no such promise, but gave instead a refusal (70–74).

The final large addition in 16:6–12 takes its cue from v 6, the displaced original answer to the petition. This negative answer becomes "the introduction to the taunt in the form of a lament which now concludes the poem.... Moab's pride ended in a fall. And the poet goes to great lengths to describe a mocking lament" (73). Kaiser seems unclear about the expressions of sympathy in 16:9–11, however, and comments,

> In this stanza the poet appears to be emphasizing his profound distress at what he has experienced, or rather observed. Verse 6 does not suggest that he played a very honourable part in it. Deeply moved, he wishes to mourn with Jazer for the vines of the neighbouring Sibmah, and even water Heshbon and Elealeh with his tears (73–74).

Apparently, Kaiser is torn between a straight reading and an ironic one. He never resolves this tension, but it seems safe to assume that he regards the first-person expressions of sympathy in 16:9, 11 as insincere. The final verse of this section, v 12, he regards as a later addition intended to deny explicitly that the lamentations of the Moabites in 15:2 have any effect.

The "apocalyptic addition" in 16:13–14 Kaiser dates in the second century B.C.E. or later, a time when a writer "believed that he possessed a more exact knowledge of God's plan for history" (74). He refers here, of course, to the phrase "within three years, like the years of a hireling." His argument for designating the final verses an "apocalyptic addition" depends almost entirely on this reference to "three years." In light of the notorious difficulty of this phrase, however, such an attribution can only be viewed as speculative.

One remarks great uncertainty in many places in Kaiser's interpretation, a fact that makes comparisons with other interpretations difficult. The similarity between his reading and those of Luther and Calvin is noteworthy, however. He disputes the sincerity of the expressions of sympathy in both the original and the later lament. He does not explain why this is so in the case of the first lament, but 16:6 seems to have provided the hermeneutical key to the later lament. He does not, however, give either lament a thoroughly ironic reading in the manner that Luther had. Indeed, he gives almost no indication of specific points at which the mocking tone is obvious in the second lament, the "mocking lament," even when the material invites it (see esp. bottom of p. 73). His inconsistency about the expressions of sympathy in 16:9, 11 may indicate that he is not entirely happy with the designation "mocking lament." Remarkable, too, is the fact that he does not allude to or discuss other ironic readings of the poem. He notes in his survey of the history of interpretation that van Zyl regarded the two laments as a Bedouin taunt song (61), but in his own comments on the "mocking lament," he makes no mention of van Zyl. References to Luther and Calvin are lacking entirely. Perhaps Kaiser's uncertainty over the many vexing questions involved in these chapters prevented him from pursuing any particular line of interpretation very far.

H. Wildberger offers a much more closely argued and decisive interpretation than had Kaiser.[38] Indeed, Wildberger's interpretation of Isaiah 15–16 is the most detailed and complete offered by any modern commentator —forty-five pages of careful argument and keen interpretation. His treatment deserves close and detailed attention.

Wildberger discerns more redactional activity in the poem than any commentator before him. The original poem he limits to 15:1–8. This poem is a two-part lament consisting of (1) a lament over the devastation of Ar and Kir Moab (15:1b–4) and (2) a lament using the "I" form pertaining to the fate of the fugitives (15:5–8). It was most probably composed during the waning years of the Judean kingdom and was designed to warn of the disaster that had already overtaken the territory south of the Arnon (602, 606–11, 614). To this lament a number of later additions were made:

16:1, 3–5: a call to turn to the "daughter of Zion" (16:1, 3–4a) and a promise of salvation (4b–5). This addition dates from the post-exilic era when eschatological-messianic (even apocalyptic) hope ran high. The situation anticipated in Isa 2:2–4, the influx of the nations to Zion, may have been in the author's mind (619–24).

16:6–7: either a reproach and threat directed at Moab or a reflection on Moab's destiny. Its date is uncertain (624–26).

16:8–11: a lament marked by its strong sympathy for Moab and the author's use of the first person. It is later than 16:6–7 since its reference to Kir Hareseth assumes that 16:7 is already in the text (626–29).

15:9; 16:2; 16:12: later additions consisting of "threats of judgment," by means of which the poem was transformed into a משׂא (603). 16:2 may at one time have been simply a marginal note later inserted inappropriately (624).

16:13–14: an announcement of a total and final judgment to befall Moab within three years (630–32).

This source-redaction analysis is similar to that of Kaiser and Fohrer, but at one point it differs markedly. Wildberger divides

[38]*Jesaja*, vol. 2.

16:6–11 into two separate sources, 16:6–7 and 16:8–11. This is a new suggestion in the history of interpretation. He gives several reasons for this division. The geographical scene is different in the two sections; vv 6–7 mention Moab's capital city south of the Arnon while vv 8–11 focus mainly on cities north of the Arnon. In v 6 "we" is used, whereas in vv 8–11 the reader encounters "I." The word used for "therefore" is different in the two sections, לכן in v 7 and על־כן in v 9. Most importantly, however, the attitude toward Moab is completely different in the two sections; whereas vv 6–7 state that Moab deserved its punishment, vv 8–11 reveal a deep sympathy with Moab in its extremity. All of this points to a separate origin for the two units, though Wildberger holds open the possibility that the same author wrote both since laying blame does not necessarily mean that one would not feel compassion (601–602).

Geographical scene provides the single criterion by which Wildberger separates 15:1–8 from 16:6–11. His analysis of 15:1–8 leads him to conclude that the disaster depicted there consisted of the destruction of only the southern cities Ar (er-Rabbah) and Kir (Kerak). The cities north of the Arnon are depicted as sites of lamentation, not destruction (599–600). In 16:6–11, on the other hand, the lamentation primarily concerns a devastation of the territory north of the Arnon (601–602). Thus two separate incidents lie behind the two laments.

The petition section, 16:1, 3–5, he separates from the remainder of the poem because no part of it appears in Jeremiah 48 and because its content, unlike 15:1–8 and 16:6–11, points to no definite historical situation. This is clear from the use of unusual and vague designations where one would expect proper names. The petition is sent from "a rock in the desert" by "the sovereign of the land" to "the mount of the daughter of Zion," not from a specific city by a specific Moabite king to a specific Judean king or official. The reference to the "mount of Zion" suggests that the eschatological journey of the nations to Zion envisioned in Isa 2:2–4 is in the author's mind.[39] All indicators point to an origin in the post-exilic period when eschatological hope led to visions of a future salvation and exaltation of Zion. The sense of the petition section is that at some future date, Zion will again have a ruling king and be able to offer assistance to its neighbors. At that time, Moab will find the help it seeks. Wildberger holds that the phrase "in the tent of David" (16:5a) is a late gloss that keeps open the question of whether or not this ruler will be a Davidide and that imports terminology from temple ideology (619–24).

The remainder of the additions to the poem (15:9, 16:2, 16:12, 16:13–14) contain threats of judgment. Wildberger differs from other commentators in assigning all of 15:9 to a later addition. He reasons that it forms a poor conclusion to 15:1–8 since it (1) contains "Dimon," a variant form of Dibon, (2) assumes that Moab had already been severely damaged in contradiction to the tenor of vv 1–8, (3) introduces the divine "I" for the first time, and (4) is introduced with a כי that is at odds with the כי of v 8. In the case of 16:2, he notes that moving this verse to just after 15:9, as many commentators have suggested, provides no solution to the problem. The transition from 15:9 to 16:2 would be rough, and 15:9 does not lead one to expect anything after it (600). It probably entered the text as a marginal comment (on what, he does not say), and was later worked into the text along with the other additions designed to change the lament into an oracle. In its present position, it serves to illustrate the distress of the Moabites (624). The final prophetic threat (16:12) is distinguished from the lament both by its genre and by its introductory formula, והיה (602).

In summary, Wildberger's analysis leads him to see the final poem as "Stücke verschiedener Art und Herkunft zu einem mosaikartigen Moabgemälde zusammengestellt" (598). The final product is thus full of tensions that cannot be resolved, tensions of geography, of genre, of attitude toward Moab, and of temporal perspective. Perhaps for this reason, Wildberger offers no sketch

---

[39] Against the prevailing view that Isa 2:2–4 is an exilic or post-exilic addition, Wildberger has argued that the verses are from Isaiah's hand. See his "Die Völkerwallfahrt zum Zion: Jes. II 1–5," *VT* 7 (1957) 62–81.

of a final, unified redactional understanding. No part of the poem may be attributed to Isaiah himself, nor even to his age. Its inclusion in the book is the work of the post-exilic redactor. Why it should have been included in this particular book, he does not say.

The final commentator to be grouped among those who limit the original poem to 15:1–8 (9) is R. Clements.[40] The brevity of Clements's commentary no doubt partly accounts for the fact that he adds very little new to the discussion of these two chapters. He follows Wildberger in defining the original lament as 15:1–8 and attributing all of 15:9, as well as 16:12, to later editors. These later additions serve to turn the lament over Moab into a threat (151, 156). He rejects Wildberger's idea that 16:2 is only a gloss, however, and suggests that it should be attached after 15:8 as a continuation of the lament (153). In the case of 16:1–5, he follows Kaiser's analysis by limiting the original petition to vv 1–4a, verses 4b–5 being a later addition. All of it he dates in the post-exilic period (153). Finally, he reads 16:6–11 as a prophetic threat against Moab. In distinction from Kaiser, however, Clements thinks that the passage involves no taunt and no irony. The expressions of sorrow in vv 9 and 11 are intended as "warning[s] of the judgment which still lies in the future" (151, 155–56). Regrettably, he does not explain or defend this assertion.

In the middle of this century, an important perspective on the traditio-historical background of Isaiah 15–16 emerged. Several Israeli scholars put forward the argument that the speeches against Moab in both Jeremiah and Isaiah were based, in part, on an archaic fragment found in Num 21:27–29.[41] Their insights were published in modern Hebrew and as a consequence are not mentioned in most commentaries. In the 1960s, however, N.

---

[40]*Isaiah 1–39* (NCBC; Grand Rapids: Eerdmans; London: Marshall, Morgan & Scott, 1980).

[41]Y. Kaufmann, *The Religion of Israel* (Chicago: University of Chicago, 1960; New York: Schocken Books, 1972); M. (Diman-)Haran, "An Archaic Remnant in the Prophetic Call to War," *Bulletin of the Israel Exploration Society* 13 (1946–47) 7–15; I. Seeligman, "On the History and Nature of Prophecy in Israel," *EI* 3 (1954) 125–32. Haran's study deals most extensively with Isaiah 15–16.

Gottwald and B. Margulis published in English works that drew on this traditio-historical analysis.[42] We may observe the effect of this analysis in Gottwald's interpretation of Isaiah 15–16. He holds that Isa 16:1–5 is from the prophet Isaiah, and that it is probably a prophecy from the time of Hezekiah urging that the Moabites be offered a warm reception (173–74). The subsequent addition of this originally positive prophecy to an ancient taunt song against Moab resulted in the subordination of the sympathetic tone to one of condemnation. The prototype for the taunt song was "a non-Israelite composition (or compositions) celebrating in fact an Amorite defeat of Moab (173–74)." Evidence for the non-Israelite origin of this taunt song includes (1) "the explicitly non-Israelite context given to the taunt against Heshbon in Numbers 21:21–30;" (2) the fact that "the profusion of place names in the oracle, many of which were no longer identifiable in the time of the monarchy, has been rather imperfectly preserved as an archaic survival;" and (3) the "discrepancy between the anti-Moabite and pro-Moabite sentiments" in the poem (173). Gottwald concludes his treatment with a note on 16:5:

> [Isaiah] does not present his case on the ground of an existing treaty by which Judah is legally bound to assist Moab. He argues rather from the concept of Hebrew kingship by throwing the standards of the enthronement hymns before Hezekiah's conscience and reminding him that it is precisely in such acts of mercy, in the offering of asylum to political refugees, that the Davidic dynasty will show its mettle and will thus outlast all oppressors. The messianic allusion, which has jarred many commentators, is in fact a quotation from an enthronement hymn (cf. 14:32).... Isaiah here evidences the broad compassion of Amos and goes beyond it, for *he urges that even a nation which has committed wrongs and is a traditional enemy must be shown consideration in its time of need* (174–75; emphasis his).

---

[42]N. Gottwald, *All the Kingdoms of the Earth* (New York: Harper, 1964) 173–75; B. Margulis, "Studies in the Oracles Against the Nations," Ph.D. Thesis, Brandeis, 1967. For a brief description of the development and transmission of this idea, see D. Christensen, *Transformations of the War Oracle in Old Testament Prophecy* (HDR 3; Missoula: Scholars, 1975) 5–6. For a summary and critique of Margulis, see D. Petersen, "The Oracles Against the Nations; A Form Critical Analysis," *Society of Biblical Literature Abstracts and Seminar Papers* (Missoula: Scholars, 1975) 1: 41–45.

This interpretation of 16:5 is unique in that it envisions Isaiah speaking the verse to the Judean king. As we have seen previously, many of the differences among interpretations of the poem result to a significant degree from differing decisions regarding the identities of speaker and addressee in 16:5. The ambiguity lies in the simple fact that although it is clear that shifts in speaker occur in 16:1–5, the speaking voices are not identified.

Gottwald's interpretation reflects a desire common among some commentators not only to place distance between the prophet and any possible irony or sarcasm, but even to argue that he was surprisingly compassionate in a situation where one would have expected unalloyed condemnation. In distinction from most, however, Gottwald thinks that this compassion is present only in 16:1–5. Apparently, he believes the expressions of compassion elsewhere in the poem are intended ironically.

F. Recent Studies

The approach taken by J. Watts in his 1985 commentary is remarkable for its originality.[43] The key to this originality lies in his initial decision about the genre of the book as a whole. He understands it as "vision literature," by which he means something quite particular:

> In vision literature, the person of the prophet falls into the background. Yahweh becomes the dominant speaker, and the dominant sub-form is that of the Yahweh speech. His speeches are supported and amplified by others, but the speakers are seldom identified. They are understood to be Yahweh's aides, whether these are taken as members of his heavenly court or as prophets.... The Vision, because it consists of successive speeches by different persons...is much more dramatic and less realistic in setting than other books (xlv).

Watts's understanding of the genre leads him to read the entire book of Isaiah as a series of dramatic scenes, "a sort of drama in which Yahweh and his aides (Heavens and Earth, 1:2) are the principal characters" (xlix). This heuristic device enables him to explain the sudden transitions and changes of speaker that are

[43] *Isaiah 1–33* (WBC 24; Waco: Word, 1985).

characteristic of many parts of the book. He notes that his approach is "reader-oriented," but he does not mean by this that it is synchronic or ahistorical (xliv). In fact, his interpretation is based on a very detailed and specific understanding of the historical situation behind the various parts of the book.

The hermeneutical effect of his assumptions takes him in a new direction in his interpretation of Isaiah 15 and 16. He sets the events described in the poem at the beginning of Hezekiah's reign, about 718 B.C.E.[44] The reference in Isa 14:28 to the death of Ahaz provides the key for dating the passage. He reads the text in its final form and does not discuss redactional issues. Its structure he outlines as follows (228):

A Announcement of Moab's desperate situation (15:1b–4)
  B Yahweh's sympathy, but determined judgment (15:5–9)
    C Moab's decision to flee to Judah (16:1–2)
KEYSTONE Moab's appeal for refugees and its meaning (16:3–5)
    C´ Judah's choral recognition of Moab's collapse (16:6–8)
  B´ Shebna's lament over Yahweh's judgment on Moab (16:9–12)
A´ A tiny, weakened remnant will survive (16:13–14)

Each of these sections contains multiple voices. In *A*, both a "Herald" and an unidentified "Messenger" to the Jerusalem court speak. *B* contains the voices of "Shebna," "Messenger" and "Yahweh." In *C*, "Moab's spokesman" addresses the Moabites and then in the first half of the "KEYSTONE" petitions the Jerusalemites. The second half of the "KEYSTONE" is spoken by the "Herald." A chorus of Judahites replies in *C´* with a reflection on the cause of Moab's calamity. "Shebna," interrupted once by "Yahweh" and once by "Heavens," issues a lament in *B´*, and the dramatic scene closes in *A´* with a transition supplied by the "Herald" and a final proclamation by "Yahweh" (223–25). According to Watts, the drama portrays the result of an attack on Moab and Moab's petition to Judah for help in its time of need. The heart of the poem lies in this request and Judah's answer. The answer, which comes in 16:4b–5, promises protection for Moab on

---

[44]Watts perceives a large historical framework for the whole book, and his decision about the date of Isaiah 15–16 is based on this framework. See the explanation in his introduction (l–li).

the condition that she accept her old role as a vassal to the Davidic throne. "Judah's authorities and people are sympathetic to the appeal. Even Yahweh is sympathetic....The implication is that Moab becomes Judah's vassal again" (231–32).

Although this reading is radical in its refusal to engage the prior critical discussion and in its dramatic reading strategy, it is not without similarities to previous interpretations. Watts's decision to read the poem as a unity, though it is grounded in modern literary theory and is a decision made prior to the reading, returns to the traditional interpretation of scholars prior to Ewald. His reading of the petition section seems unique at first glance, but it is in a sense only a historicizing of Kaiser's eschatological interpretation. Instead of offering a future-oriented promise, the answer offers immediate assistance under the auspices of the messianic king Hezekiah during the heyday of his program of expansion. Perhaps Watts's most significant contribution to the discussion is his dramatic voice analysis. The poem seems to invite this strategy with its abrupt changes of voice and scene. The official petition to Judah at its heart also lends credibility to the attempt to imagine an interplay of voices, for such petitions would certainly have provided occasion for the high drama of court politics with many voices engaged in policy making. The dramatic voice analysis has a validity based in the particularities of the text, a validity that is not necessarily dependent on Watts's understanding of the genre of the whole book. His analysis is, therefore, pertinent to the discussion of the redactional analysis of the poem since many source divisions have been made on the basis of voice and scene changes.

Another interpretation that analyzes only the final form of Isaiah 15–16 is found in the 1986 Claremont Ph.D. dissertation of R. Weis.[45] Weis divides the poem in a manner very different from

[45]"A Definition of the Genre Maśśāʾ in the Hebrew Bible," (Ph.D. diss., Claremont, 1986). See pages 113–29. Although Weis's treatment is only a minor section of his dissertation, I include it here because I describe and evaluate his larger study of the genre maśśāʾ at length below. His method for analyzing Isaiah 15–16 reflects the method he employs on all the texts with which he deals, and an evaluation of his results depends to some extent on whether one accepts this method and its specific application.

any we have yet encountered. Following an analysis first proposed by D. Petersen,[46] Weis separates the poem into three blocks: 15:1b–7, 15:8–16:2 and 16:3–12. He offers two reasons for this analysis. First, the usual division of the poem after 15:9 results in an unclear geographical picture in 15:1–9. The cities mentioned up through 15:7 are all south of the Arnon, but the cities in 15:8–9 lie both south and north of the Arnon (113–114). Second, the grammatical formulae and certain rhetorical structures indicate that the poem is to be so divided. He observes a number of symmetrical patterns in the poem that are chiefly marked by logical particles (primarily כי and על־כן). In 15:1b–4 he notes the pattern "report of reason (introduced by *kî*), report of lamentation, report of consequence (introduced by *ʿal kēn*)." He notes a similar pattern in 15:5–7 (pp. 115–16). This pattern suggests that the poem should be divided after 15:7, and since this division also removes the geographical inconsistency, its fitness is confirmed.

The next block, 15:8–16:2, has a structure similar to that of the two sections of the first block: "report of reason (15:8–9), command (16:1), report of consequence (16:2)." Here, a command replaces the report of lamentation, but the structural similarity is clear. The final block is constructed in a like manner: "commands and prohibition (16:3–4a), report of reason (16:4b–11), report of consequence (16:12)" (pp. 116–18). Weis's analysis of the poem elicits a pattern of similarly constructed units that he believes demonstrates the poem's unity and points the way to its proper interpretation.

Weis's interpretation of the poem is equally as original as his structural analysis. He understands 16:1 as an imperative addressed by the Moabite embassy to certain Judean leaders

---

[46]"The Oracles Against the Nations." Petersen offers a brief form-critical analysis of Isaiah 15–16 (51–55). He divides the poem into four blocks: **I.** 15:1aβ–4, lament; **II.** 15:5–7, flight; **III.** 15:8–16:4 (5), exhortation; **IV.** 16:6–11 (12), lament of lost fertility. His reason for dividing the poem after 15:7 is the different rhythm in sections **II** (=3:2) and **III** (=2:2). This change in rhythm is not certain, however. For a different analysis of the rhythm see J. Watts, *Isaiah*, 223–25 and J. Brangenburg, "A Reexamination of the Date, Authorship, Unity and Function of Isaiah 13–23" (Ph.D. diss., Golden Gate Baptist Seminary, 1989) 294–95—analyses that tend to agree with one another against Petersen.

(designated by *mōšēl*, a collective vocative) requesting them to "transmit" the lamb that Moab has sent, to the temple (*har bat ṣîyôn*), i. e., to Yahweh (120–21). 16:3–4a are addressed by the prophet to the Judean leaders urging them to grant asylum to the Moabites. 16:4b offers an argument in favor of granting this request: the foe has departed from the land and there is therefore no possibility of reprisals should Judah decide to harbor the fugitives (122–23). A further argument in 16:5 speaks of Yahweh's enthronement in the temple (*ʾōhel dāwīd*) (123; Weis does not explain how this verse functions as an argument). With this introduction of Yahweh enthroned in the temple, the way is prepared for the divine speech which follows in 16:6–11. The "we" of 16:6 is a courtly usage encompassing the heavenly council. It introduces a דבר יהוה for which the *maśśāʾ* as a whole serves as an exposition (124–26). This word of Yahweh is a pre-existing decree which is now quoted in order to bring to light the meaning of the events of the time.[47]

Weis does not engage the long discussion of Isaiah 15–16 to any significant degree. He notes that the poem is "a notorious problem text," but instead of wrestling with other attempts to solve the problems he chooses "to start more or less *de novo*" (113). This new start proceeds largely as a stylistic analysis focusing on rhetorical structures and grammatical markers. His method has many similarities to the rhetorical-critical studies produced by J. Muilenberg and his students. Whether or not one accepts this method of analysis as valid, Weis's application of it raises objections. His interpretation of the poem is idiosyncratic to such a degree that it seems unlikely that it will be approved by others.[48]

---

[47]Weis's reasons for this interpretation are based on the results of his study of maśśāʾ. See my summary of the study as a whole in the following chapter.

[48]For example, Brangenburg ("Reexamination," 295–96) is uncritical of most of Weis's conclusions, but he rejects Weis's structural analysis of Isaiah 15–16. And this is all the more remarkable since he adopts Weis's outline of the chapters as a template for his own analysis of the structure. He changes Weis's outline primarily in the section between 15:8 and 16:5, at the very point at which it diverges markedly from more traditional analyses.

The interpretation presented by J. Oswalt in his 1986 commentary proceeds along a traditional line.[49] Oswalt affirms a unity of intention and thought in the poem, while remaining tentative about the question of an original compositional unity. Although he is committed from the outset of the commentary to defending the Isaianic authorship of the whole book (chs. 40–66 included), he allows that in the speech against Moab Isaiah may have drawn on "a standard poetic treatment of Moab" and acted as a compiler of sources older than himself (336, 348). The poem as he understands it consists of a lament (15:1–9), a plea on behalf of the refugees (16:1–5), an "elegiac reflection on Moab's pride" and a postscript (16:13–14) (pp. 336, 345). As a whole it forms a prophecy of a coming attack on Moab and dates from around 715 B.C.E. Its main thrust is "to discourage any who would be tempted to join with proud Moab for purposes of mutual security" (336). The plea he understands as the words of the Moabite to the Judeans, including the passage loaded with messianic import in 4b–5: "the prophet here puts words in the Moabite messenger's mouth. He looks forward to the day when the oppression which has driven the Moabites into the Hebrews' arms will be brought to an end by that ideal ruler of the Davidic house." The final section of the poem, 16:6–12, provides not so much a response to the petition as a reflection on "the ephemeral nature of human pride and glory" (343). Thus neither 15:4b–5 nor 16:6 provides a solid answer to the petition, but this presents little difficulty since the events described lie in the future and no actual decision need be rendered. The epilogue indicates that the body of the speech is soon to be fulfilled; it may also point to a non-Isaianic origin for the poem or at least some of its parts (348).

Oswalt is both aware of and uneasy with the ironic reading of the poem. He notes that 16:6 is often taken as an answer to the petition and comments, "As such they would contain a not-so-subtle mockery of the suppliants who...now come creeping with piteous cries for mercy." He finds this interpretation unsatisfactory, however, and chooses to read 16:6–12 as a general reflection

[49]*The Book of Isaiah: Chapters 1–39* (NICOT; Grand Rapids, MI: Eerdmans, 1986).

on the folly of pride, rather than as a direct answer. This interpretation "take[s] some of the sting of mockery away that seems somewhat inconsistent with the apparently genuine grief expressed in v 9" (345; cf. 346, 336–37). The grounds for this decision, however, go beyond the perceived inconsistency. He notes that Jeremiah wept over the fate of those he denounced, that the destruction of cultivated lands is a cause for grief no matter whose lands they are, and that the prophets identified themselves with God and thus expressed God's compassion, even for the objects of divine punishment: "So the God who has stilled the shouts of joy (v 10) is also the God who weeps for and with those who now cry (Hos. 11:1–9)." In a footnote, Oswalt cites his own experience of grief at reading the Assyrian Annals: "The record of burning, looting, and killing became almost intolerable to read" (346). Clearly, there are a number of factors at work in his decision to reject the ironic interpretation.

The analysis of the poem by J. Hayes and S. Irvine, on the other hand, takes the ironic line of interpretation further than any previous study, even that of Luther.[50] Indeed, their reading of the whole of Isaiah 1–39 is quite set apart from all previous scholarship, and their treatment is unique in the history of commentary on the chapter. The book is not a commentary in the traditional sense of the word. It proceeds from a number of theses that are not generally accepted by scholars; it does not engage in the wider critical discussion of the book; it reads the book as a series of chronologically arranged speeches which, except for a few glosses, come from the prophet Isaiah; it reconstructs a highly detailed historical background against which to interpret all the speeches; and it allows for prophetic speeches that are much longer than is usually thought possible.

The idea that prophetic discourse included long speeches is central to Hayes and Irvine's interpretation. They view the prophets as orators who sought to persuade their audience to adopt a particular viewpoint or take a particular course of action. They use rhetorical-critical methodology, a relatively recent

---

[50]*Isaiah, the Eighth-Century Prophet: His Times and His Preaching* (Nashville: Abingdon Press, 1987).

arrival in contemporary biblical studies.[51] This method of analysis avoids the atomization brought about by form- and redaction-critical analysis. As Hayes and Irvine practice it, however, it is not, as it was for Watts, merely a final form reading strategy designed to bracket out the question of the literary pre-history of the text. It is, rather, a thoroughly historical attempt to explain the text on other grounds, to see an original compositional unity where source and redactional analysis have seen a literary and historical pastiche. Their study thus presents a historical-critical analysis that proceeds under very different historical and literary assumptions from past critical analysis. It seeks to convince the reader by the sheer force of the consistency of its own reading and analysis, both of the speeches in the book itself and of the relevant historical sources (50–66).

Hayes and Irvine date Isaiah 15–16 to the beginning of the reign of Shalmeneser V, in 727 B.C.E. or shortly thereafter. It probably refers to an attack from the north by a small contingent of the Assyrian army, Shalmeneser having divided his troops into groups in order to fight on several fronts. Proof that Assyria was active in the area at the time is supplied partly by Hos 10:14b–15a: "'as Shalman destroyed Beth-arbel [a city in northern Transjordan] on the day of battle; mothers were slashed in pieces with their children. Thus it shall be done to you, O Bethel'" (239). The purpose of the speech is to persuade Hezekiah to reject the petition of the Moabite embassy that had been sent to Jerusalem to request asylum in the wake of the attack (240). The first section of the poem, 15:1–9, is a description of the calamity and the subsequent flight of the Moabites. The expression of empathy in 15:5 is not genuine: "His expressions of sympathy, however, may have been only diplomatic language and expressions of 'politeness' or, even more likely, pure sarcasm since, in the last analysis, Isaiah recommends that Judah close the border to any migration of Moabites into the country" (242).

---

[51]The terminology is confusing at present. In Old Testament studies, Rhetorical Criticism is best known as that school of interpretation whose founder was James Muilenburg. There are significant differences between what Muilenburg advocated and what Hayes and Irvine do, however. For further discussion, see ch. 6.

In 16:1–2, Isaiah describes the Moabites' decision to send an embassy with a gift to Jerusalem. The function of 16:2 is unclear, and it may belong after 15:9, but it may also have functioned as the Moabites' preface to their petition. The petition proper consists of all of 16:3–5. The difficult passage in 4b–5 is spoken by the Moabite embassy as flattery to the Judean king; Hayes and Irvine translate, "Established in mercy is a throne,/ and one sits upon it in truthfulness,/ in the tent of David;/ one who seeks justice,/ and is swift to do the right thing." The logic of the flattery implies that a truly just king "would surely do the right, proper, and merciful thing and aid the homeless of Moab" (243–44). While Hayes and Irvine are not the first to interpret 4b–5 as motivational rhetoric, they are the first to suggest this particular logic of flattery.[52]

The final section of the poem begins with a harsh condemnation of the Moabites (16:6–7) and then changes tone drastically. This shift is, however, a movement into sarcasm rather than sympathy. Isaiah's statements in vv 9–11 are "rife with cutting sarcasm." As evidence Hayes and Irvine observe that many of the towns listed in 16:8–11 were formerly Israelite towns, towns that had passed back and forth between Moab and Israel a number of times through history. The mention of these towns would certainly have reminded the Judeans that Moab was anything but a good neighbor in need of a helping hand: "Thus when Isaiah refers to weeping over the fall of these towns, his audience, whether Moabite or Judean, would have caught the glitter of his verbal sword" (245).

In a surprising move, Hayes and Irvine contest one of the most agreed upon points in the interpretation of the poem, the notion that 16:13–14 is a later addition. In their view, there is no

---

[52]See, for example, Gesenius on v 5: "The suppliants add their benedictions, and present the blessings, which this [act of] humanity would bring upon the house of David, as an inducement to hearken to their petition" (153). See also the summary of Gottwald's position given above. Note how the rhetorical force of the verse changes depending on who one imagines as the speaker of these words: if the speaker is Isaiah, the verse is either a promise of help (Procksch) or an encouragement to provide help (Gottwald); if the speaker is a representative of Moab, the verse is cajolery and flattery.

break in the logical flow from v 12 on through v 14. Their understanding of v 12 is the foundation for this interpretation. They offer an "expansive translation" of the verse: "And should it happen [should Moabites be admitted temporally into Judah], when the Moabites wanted to worship, when they wearied themselves over the *bamah* [a place of worship], and when they came to his [Yahweh's] sanctuary to pray, they would not be allowed" (bracketed material is Hayes and Irvine's, 246). The refusal of entrance into Yahweh's sanctuary is "the thing spoken formerly" by Yahweh concerning Moab. Isaiah has in mind here the prohibition in Deut 23:3 that "No Ammonite or Moabite shall enter the assembly of Yahweh; even to the tenth generation..." (246). His addition to this former word of Yahweh is that in three years Moab will be very nearly wiped out, a prediction which may also be hinted at in 15:9 (242, 246).

Hayes and Irvine's contention that the poem is ironic in all its expressions of sympathy brings us back to a crucial issue, the interpretation posed first by Luther and Calvin. Most importantly, it offers new evidence to support this interpretation. The recognition that the cities mentioned are the very ones that changed hands many times in the years of conflict between Moab and Israel adds one more argument on the side of the ironic reading. Hayes and Irvine's interpretation of the names in 16:8–11 also brings to the fore an aspect of the poem that is often noted but seldom analyzed: the high concentration of place names. What is the purpose of listing so many Moabite cities? Do we miss something if we see them as only a catalogue of sites of lamentation or destruction? Is there some rhetorical purpose at work that goes beyond the merely pictorial one usually suggested (i. e., to emphasize the plight of Moab through particular examples)? We shall return to these questions in a later chapter.

The most recent commentary to appear on Isaiah is that of C. Seitz.[53] His treatment of chapters 15–16 is brief. This results in part from the fact that his entire commentary is devoted to a final form reading of the book and engages little of the critical discussion, though he assumes some of its less contested results. For example,

---

[53]*Isaiah 1–39* (Interpretation; Louisville: John Knox, 1993).

he interprets the poem as a collection of oracles, probably older than Isaiah's time, which are integrated into the overall purpose of chapters 13–27 by means of the postscript. He perceives a unity in the content of the three sections of the poem:

> Wailing begins as a consequence of a terrible defeat; a request for asylum is then made of Judah; the request is refused as the great pride of Moab is recounted; and so the lamenting continues where it had first begun. The unknown mourner of 15:5 resumes his cry, which continues up to 16:11. A final response is then made from the perspective of Judah [vv. 12–14], as was the case in 16:6–7 (139–40).

He does not comment on whether this unity arises from a single act of authorship or from a redactional process. He perceives "the interpretive key to the Moabite oracles" in the final verses (16:12–14), where it is emphasized that Moab will continue to have trouble that no amount of supplication at their high place will avert. The main theme of the chapter is "God's judgment over all forms of human pride, of which Moab has its share (16:6)" (140). In Seitz's view, the idea that "*God's sovereignty over human pride and arrogance reaches to every nation on earth*" dominates and unifies all the oracles in the OAN section (122, italics his; see 120–32).

Seitz's emphasis on the theme of God's judgment on all human pride gives a central place to 16:6. The declaration of Moab's great hubris is the turning point of the poem and a more significant interpretive key than 16:12–14, the verses Seitz emphasizes. This emphasis is the product of his final form reading strategy. Other commentators have noted the important role that 16:6 plays in the poem, even without Seitz's particular hermeneutic. Much depends on how interpreters understand the function of this verse. Who speaks in the verse? Why is the first person plural employed? Is it an answer to the petition? Or is it merely a reflection on Moab's pride with no connection to the previous section? Does it cast an ironic light on what follows? Or is it sensible to lament the fate even of an arrogant rival? Seitz does not acknowledge the conflict between the extreme expressions of grief for Moab and what he has identified as the poem's central theme, God's judgment of Moab's pride. Perhaps he sees no conflict.

If one ignores the very different presuppositions underlying the studies prior to Eichhorn and those of the last decade, it begins to appear that interpretation of the chapter is coming full circle. This is the effect of the new literary criticism and its reading strategies. Watts and Seitz abandon the quest to determine the literary antecedents of the text; instead they focus on the final form (for Seitz, the final redaction) of the book and seek a meaning at that level exclusively. Hayes and Irvine undertake to challenge all previous research into the literary prehistory of the book by positing a different understanding of prophetic speech and the process by which the book came to its present state. Oswalt follows the traditional line of interpretation but allows that Isaiah may have borrowed some of the material he uses in chapters 15–16. He alone belongs to a continuous line of interpretation since he represents conservative scholars who have all along published commentaries that assumed the Isaianic authorship and unity of the book in all its parts. The other three interpretations of the poem are a part of the broad movement among many critically trained scholars toward interpretation that focuses on unity of meaning and communicative purpose. No doubt many motives play a role in this move, but in our survey of the interpretation of Isaiah 15–16 it is not difficult to see that the increasing fragmentation of the text had resulted in increasing uncertainty and disagreement about the text's origin and, correspondingly, in a hermeneutical quandary as interpreters sifted the rising stack of small fragments of uncertain origin and meaning and pondered what significance they might have. In this situation it is not surprising that some have decided that the way back is the way forward.

III. The Contribution of the Present Study

Isaiah 15 and 16 present scholars with a number of challenging questions. As we have seen, many of these questions have not been resolved even after much careful study. In light of this it is valid to ask, What significant contribution can be made to this complex and wide-ranging discussion? The preceding history of interpretation points to several areas in which further study may prove fruitful. First and foremost, the possibility of an ironic intention behind the lament form needs to be investigated in a thorough manner. Van Zyl, Aubray and Hayes-Irvine offer a few arguments to defend their ironic readings, but a full discussion of the reasons for such a reading is beyond the scope of their commentaries. The present study will establish the grounds upon which an ironic reading of Isaiah 15–16 may be validated or invalidated, and render a verdict on which reading is more probable. Even if the conclusions of the study do not satisfy the reader, the method by which evidence may be weighed and conclusions made will be clarified, and the discussion of this important issue will be stimulated.

A second area in which further investigation is needed is the text-critical and grammatical analysis of the chapters. One frequently finds it remarked that the textual corruptions spread throughout the poem prohibit any firm conclusions on key interpretive questions. A number of the perceived textual corruptions are, however, pointed out not because of significant variants in the ancient versions but because of contextual disharmony, or because the text seems "rough" or opaque. In such cases, the perception of textual corruption is based on assumptions about the style, poetics, genre, history, geography, and rhetoric of the text. The interpretation of the poem as a whole and in all its parts has played an important role in text-critical decisions. Even when a significant variant is found among the versions, textual criticism often cannot free itself from the influence of grammatical analysis and interpretation. For example, in Isa 15:9 a city named Dimon (דימון) is mentioned. 1QIs^a and the Vulgate have instead of Dimon the well-known place name Dibon. Many factors enter into the decision to prefer one reading over the other, but among these factors is the possibility of a word play: "The waters of Dimon are full of blood (דם)." If one has decided that the author is in a satirical frame of mind, the suggestion that a pejorative word play is present will have weight, and one will be more likely to decide that the reading in the MT is to be preferred. Although the places at which interpretation affects a text-critical decision to this extent are not numerous, they are important. Consequently, we shall offer an extensive examination of textual and translational issues in which our conclusions about the genre and integrity of the chapters shall serve as a guide.

Finally, the results of our study of the genre and the possibility of ironic intention suggest the need for a new interpretation based on a method appropriate to the material. The method employed will be a close reading informed by newer literary critical methodology. In particular, the study will draw on several of the key insights and techniques of rhetorical criticism. Rather than strictly adhering to rhetorical-critical method, however, it will be methodologically eclectic to a certain degree. A fundamental assumption of the interpretation is that the poem is an artistic literary creation, and the main goal of the reading is to provide an interpretation that makes the best possible sense of the details of the text, given this assumption. Further discussion of the method behind the interpretation of the text will be offered in chapter six.

CHAPTER 2

CHARACTERISTICS OF OAN AND מַשָּׂא TEXTS

I. Introduction

The analysis of the genre of Isaiah 15–16 must begin with the recognition that the text is a member of two, partially overlapping groups of material. First, it appears in one of the collections of topically similar prophetic texts usually referred to as oracles against the nations. Secondly, it is headed by the designation "מַשָּׂא מואב," and thus belongs to a group whose members are defined by the fact that each is headed by a brief introductory phrase containing the designation מַשָּׂא. We will begin our investigation of Isaiah 15–16, therefore, by asking what significance its membership in these two groups may have for its interpretation. In particular we will be interested in the characteristics of texts in these two groups. Neither group constitutes a genre category *per se*, but both contain certain typical characteristics that may provide interpretive clues for understanding individual members of the group. The investigation of these characteristics constitutes, therefore, the necessary background for understanding the particular genre of Isaiah 15–16, a task we shall take up in a later chapter.

II. The Oracles Against the Nations

The designation oracles against the foreign nations, or OAN, refers to a body of prophetic texts distinguished by the fact that they have as their subject nations other than Israel or Judah. Such texts are found scattered throughout the prophetic books. They appear alone and in extended collections. All three of the major prophetic books contain a collection of speeches concerning the foreign nations. These are commonly referred to as OAN collections and are found in Isaiah 13–23; Jeremiah 46–51; Ezekiel 25–32. Isolated oracles against foreign nations are also found in the major prophets; these include Isa 7:3–9, 10–16; 8:1–4; 10:5–34; 34; 37:22–29; 47; Jer 25:15–38; 27:1–11; Ezek 35; 38–39. In the minor prophets we find only one collection of OAN: Amos 1:3–2:3, although the comparison of this collection to the three found in the major prophets is problematic.[1] Two of the minor prophetic books, Obadiah and Nahum, consist entirely of an oracle against a foreign nation. Isolated OAN texts are found in Joel 4:1–17; Jonah 3:1–5; Mic 4:11–13; 5:5–6; 7:12–13, 14–17; Habakkuk 2; Zeph 2:4–15; Hag 2:21–22; Zech 9:1–8; Mal 1:2–5. Among prophetic literature, it would seem that only Hosea lacks material that may be designated OAN.

Scholars in the past have generally treated this material as of secondary interest compared to the prophetic words addressed explicitly to Israel or Judah. The lack of interest in the OAN results in part from the contextual isolation and obscure theological/thematic function of the collections in the prophetic books, in part from their vitriolic tone and nationalistic spirit and in part from the fact that much of the material in the OAN collections is considered to be "inauthentic," the work of later authors. R. H. Pfeiffer's comments are typical: "Although such anathemas against the heathen were inaugurated by Amos...they reflect on the whole not the moral indignation of the great pre-exilic prophets, but rather the nationalism of the 'false prophets' and of

---

[1]The structure (of the individual oracles, of their arrangement as a group, and of their position in the book), length, and function of the Amos oracles differ remarkably from other OAN and OAN collections. Most remarkably, the Amos oracles display a formal homogeneity found nowhere else in the OAN collections, and the entire collection seems to have been composed primarily to portray the sin of Israel from a startling perspective. Note also that whereas hubris is the sin of the nations mentioned in the OAN, in Amos specific historical infractions are made explicit. The attempt to connect Amos's oracles to the other OAN collections by hypothesizing a common origin in the war oracle lacks sufficient grounds and methodological controls (see Petersen, "Oracles," 47). These facts suggests that categorizing the Amos oracles with the other OAN collections is problematic and potentially misleading.

the later Jews chafing for centuries under alien rule."[2] There are signs that this view has moderated recently and that interest is increasing. Several studies have been devoted to tracing the origins and development of this material (see below), and the theological/thematic function of the collections within the prophetic books is now receiving a much more positive assessment.[3]

The majority of recent study of the OAN has focused on the questions of the historical origin and intention of these texts. A variety of suggestions has been made, and it has become increasingly clear that the OAN display a diversity of form,[4] original intention and possible *Sitz im Leben* that frustrates attempts to find one model to explain the phenomenon.[5] Several studies have attempted to trace the origin and development of the OAN and to

---

[2]*Introduction to the Old Testament* (NY: Harper and Brothers, 1941) 443. For further comments on and examples of the prevalence of this view see Brangenberg, ("Reexamination" 1–2); J. Smith, "The Destruction of Foreign Nations in Hebrew Prophetic Literature" (Ph.D. diss., Hebrew Union College-Jewish Institute of Religion, 1969) 1–3.

[3]See especially Seitz (*Isaiah 1–39,* 115–127). In a session devoted to the OAN at the 1994 annual meeting of the Society of Biblical Literature, I noted a very positive response to Seitz's construal of the theological function of the OAN in Isaiah. Moreover, four out of the five papers presented explicitly or implicitly argued for a positive assessment of the OAN.

[4]The word *form* is used equivocally in many discussions, and it is necessary to address briefly its use in the present study. Insofar as we use *form* as a technical term, we shall reserve it to indicate "the structure or shape of an individual passage or unit, [insofar] as...this may be described without regard to the content of the passage" (J. Barton, "Form Criticism: Old Testament," *ABD* 2. 839). The terms *Gattung* and genre will be used to indicate definite literary types distinguished by similarity of form, language (terminology and metaphor), setting and intention. For a discussion of the problems involved in the variability of use of the terminology, see T. Conley, "The Linnaean Blues: Thoughts on the Genre Approach," *Form, Genre and the Study of Political Discourse,* ed. H. Simons and A. Aghazarian (Columbia: University of South Carolina, 1986) 68–71; D. Greenwood, "Rhetorical Criticism and Formgeschichte: Some Methodological Considerations," *JBL* 89 (1970) 420.

[5]For surveys and evaluations of the various proposals see J. Hayes, "The Usage of Oracles Against Foreign Nations in Ancient Israel," *JBL* 87 (1968) 81–92; R. Clements, *Prophecy and Tradition* (Atlanta: John Knox, 1975) 58–72; P. Beentjes, "Notitie; Oracles Against the Nations; A Central Issue in the 'Latter Prophets,'" *Tijdschrift voor Filosofie en Theologie* 50 (1989) 203–209.

understand their diversity as a product of their development.[6] These studies have come to somewhat different conclusions, and no clear picture has emerged. At most, there is agreement that somewhere in the ancestry of the OAN is the war oracle and the situation of warfare and, perhaps, the situation of communal lamentation. Even if clarity about this ancestry could be obtained, however, it would remain unclear how, if at all, the suggested original settings and intentions of the genre would relate to the OAN texts we now possess. These texts represent a stage of development distant from their hypothesized origins; whatever generic constraints and typical settings might have pertained at some early stage have been loosened and transformed in various ways. The interpretative value of a reconstructed original setting of the genre is thus questionable. In any case, the decision about original intention and setting has had minimal effect on the actual interpretation of individual OAN, and it offers little help in our effort to locate Isaiah 15–16 in a generic category.

This would not be the case if the OAN texts demonstrated patterns of generic similarity. It is generally agreed, however, that they do not. D. Petersen states this problem in a manner particularly appropriate to the present study: "A brief survey of the OAN texts concerning Moab reveals a plethora of *Gattungen*, most of which derive from settings other than the martial institution. The ability to reduce these texts to an essential form... appears problematic."[7] Furthermore, the traditional designation of these texts as "*oracles* against the nations" suggests a generic homogeneity that the evidence does not support. The word *oracle* means "information transmitted from the deity to human beings, usually either answers to important questions or revelations about future events."[8] Not all of the OAN material fits this definition. In the OAN collections we find laments, taunt songs and other genres

---

[6]The principal studies are Margulis, "Studies in the Oracles Against the Nations"; Christensen, *Transformations*. See Petersen ("Oracles," 39–61) for a summary and critique of the position taken by each of these scholars.

[7]Petersen, "Oracles," 51.

[8]"Oracle,"*ABD* 5. 28. G. Tucker defines "oracle" as "a direct word of God, originally the short utterance in response to an inquiry" (*Form Criticism of the Old Testament* [Philadelphia: Fortress, 1971] 60–61).

that do not purport to be transmitted words of the deity. In short, the formal diversity of the OAN makes it difficult to speak of the OAN *genre* except in a general and inexact way.[9]

Though the OAN lack generic uniformity, they do deal with the same subject matter. The texts treat the topic of the foreign nations and, generally speaking, seek to show how the nations fit into YHWH's plan. The attitude that they express toward the nations is not, however, unequivocally negative as the appellation Oracles *Against* the Nations might suggest; indeed, on occasion the tenor of the texts is positive (e.g., Isa 18:7; 19:19–25).[10] Furthermore, not all the OAN texts deal with the "Nations," as their traditional designation would imply: Isaiah 22 is found in an OAN collection, and its subject is Judah. This final objection rests on an isolated case, however, and may best be considered an exception of the kind that proves the rule. Indeed, the bond established by virtue of the fact that the OAN texts deal with foreign nations is the most obvious reason for treating them as a group.[11]

Despite this unity of subject, however, the purpose for which these texts were collected remains unclear. Similarity of subject

---

[9]See Hayes, "Usage," 92; Beentjes, 207.

[10]See Seitz, *Isaiah 1–39*, 9, 117. Seitz notes (in agreement with Clements) that Isaiah 13:1–16 is, in the first place, a commission to Babylon for a task of judgment, not a judgment on Babylon. 'Against' is also potentially confusing since superficially it implies that these texts had the nations as their intended audience. This was certainly not the case; the intended audience was Israel and Judah (Hayes, "Usage," 81; Clements, *Prophecy and Tradition*, 62–63). In part the confusion derives from the fact that the prophetic oracles *against* Judah or Israel are usually thought to be addressed to them, and it is easy to draw an improper analogy. Moreover, the rhetoric of the OAN often encourages the reader to think of the nations as the intended audience. One finds numerous examples of direct address to a foreign nation, imperatives, rhetorical questions and the like. Perhaps for these reasons, the idea that the OAN texts might have been addressed to the nations persists among some scholars. For instance, R. Rendtorff comments, "One basic difference [between the OAN and other prophetic oracles] is that the prophet cannot confront his audience directly. (Isaiah 18 might be seen as an exception; here perhaps we have a direct address to an Egyptian delegation.)" (*The Old Testament: An Introduction* [Philadelphia: Fortress, 1986] 122).

[11]Perhaps we need a completely new designation for these texts, such as 'Prophetic Speeches Concerning the Nations,' or something similar. The present study will continue to use OAN for ease of recognition; a new designation could only legitimately result from a full examination of the matter.

would be a sufficient reason were it not for the fact that we also find individual OAN texts scattered through the prophetic books. Why were some of the OAN texts compiled and not others? The fact that some texts were collected into groups and others were included alone suggests that some reason greater than coincidence of subject matter lies behind the OAN collections. If one accepts the idea that the texts were collected solely or even primarily because they treated the same subject, one must admit that the motive for their collation was superficial at best. Some scholars do indeed view the OAN collections as "grab bags," disorganized heaps of miscellaneous oracles collected over a long period of time and linked only by the slender thread of their topic.[12]

The topical similarity of the OAN collections is indeed only a slender thread, and recent work on them, especially on the collection found in Isaiah, has sought to understand the unity of the collections on other grounds.[13] Among the possibilities put forward has been the intention of the texts. The search for a single intention has run into serious difficulties, however.[14] The texts do not, as a whole, point to any single intention. Some texts seem to be intended as threats against other nations; some seem to have been intended as veiled assurances of salvation for Israel and/or Judah. Some texts seem to be aimed at providing guidance for political policy; some seem to function as theodicy. Often a text can be construed to have multiple intentions—threat, assurance, and political advice intermingled. The question of intention is further complicated by the various possible uses made of the OAN: the original use, the use as part of an independent OAN collection, the use of OAN collections within particular prophetic books.

In recent work on Isaiah, the unity of the OAN collections has been sought at the level of the final form of the book and in

---

[12]See Gray, li; Clements, *Isaiah*, 129–31.

[13]See, for instance, Seitz, *Isaiah*, 115–127; Brangenberg, 325–43.

[14]Clements, *Prophecy and Tradition*, 64.

theological content.[15] This promises to be a productive avenue of investigation in the present situation. Studies based on the final form of the prophetic books have the advantage of studying a text we actually possess rather than one that has been reconstructed hypothetically. If we can understand why the OAN texts were collected, selected and compiled in their present form, we may gain some insight also into earlier uses of the material. One such study appears in the recent commentary by C. Seitz. Seitz focuses on a theme in Isaiah that is designated by many scholars as a, or even *the,* central theme in the OAN: the hubris of the nations.[16] Seitz summarizes the theme of the OAN in Isaiah as follows: "The oracles against foreign nations are not primarily oracles of salvation for Israel; rather, they make clear that God's sovereignty over human pride and arrogance reaches to every nation on earth."[17] M. Sweeney plausibly suggests that the inclusion of Judah in the Isaianic OAN (Isaiah 22) can be understood best as resulting from the unifying influence of this theme. Chapter 22 is included to point out that Judah's hubris (displayed both in its preparations for and attitude following the Assyrian siege of Jerusalem) has made it just like the other nations who trust in their own military might.[18]

The centrality of the hubris theme offers a clue to at least one intention of the Isaianic OAN texts. Most of these texts depict or predict the downfall of nations great and small in order to emphasize the vulnerability and unreliability of the nations as sources of help and hope. Isaiah 19, for example, discourages

---

[15]See Seitz, *Isaiah 1–39,* 115–27; Beentjes, 207; M. Sweeney, *Isaiah 1–4 and the Post-Exilic Understanding of the Isaianic Tradition* (Berlin: Walter de Gruyter, 1988) 1 (and sources cited there), 44–51.

[16]So Gottwald, *All the Kingdoms,* 204–205; Smith, "Destruction of Foreign Nations," 134–74; Christensen, *Transformations,* 137; Clements, *Prophecy and Tradition,* 60, 64–65; G. Hamborg, "Reasons for Judgment in the Oracles Against the Nations of the Prophet Isaiah," *VT* 31 (1981) 145–59; J. Barton, "History and Rhetoric in the Prophets," *The Bible as Rhetoric,* ed. M. Warner (London: Routledge, 1990) 56–57, 62. Texts in which the hubris theme is prominent include Isa 14:4–21 (a classic example), Isa 2:11, 17; 5:15; 13:11; 23:1–18; Ezekiel 28; 32:2–8.

[17]Seitz, 122.

[18]Sweeney, 49–50, and 50 n. 86.

alignment with Egypt both by the revelation of Egypt's present fragility and by the promise of Egypt's eventual conversion and humility before YHWH.[19] The practical intention behind this emphasis was either to promote a policy of non-alignment in Judah's political life or to offer a theodicy based on the failure of Judah's past alignments. This intention fits well with that found in the first part of the book in which Isaiah frequently expressed opposition to foreign entanglements (e.g., 7:1–9:7; 28–33). It seems likely that Isaiah's speeches against the foreign nations served originally to promote non-alignment.

The political intention in all the OAN collections is indeed quite obvious, even if the precise nature of the intention is often unclear. D. Christensen comments: "The dominant intent of the OAN tradition in the hands of Isaiah, Nahum, Zephaniah and Jeremiah from *ca.* 720–609 appears to be political....the major thrust of the formal OAN tradition of this period is aimed at shaping foreign policy in Judah with respect to the nations concerned."[20] This political intention conforms well to the political role of the prophets. The nations provided a primary topic in prophetic speech for obvious reasons. Israel and Judah lived in the midst of political push and pull, and their rulers had to make difficult and perplexing decisions about whom to trust, whom to help and ask for help, whom to refuse all relations and whom to fight. The prophets were often deeply involved in these issues. Gunkel and Gressman believed that the OAN were the oldest form of prophetic oracle,[21] and it is possible that the prophets' earliest role in the society was connected in some way with politics.[22] Whatever may have been the role of the early prophets,

---

[19]See Clements, *Prophecy and Tradition*, 64. Cf. 20:5–6 which stress the disappointment of those who hoped Egypt would save them.

[20]Christensen, 282.

[21]See discussion in J. Hayes, "The History of the Form-Critical Study of Prophecy," *Society of Biblical Literature 1973 Seminar Papers* (Missoula: Scholars, 1973) 1. 64–65. Gottwald (*All the Kingdoms*, 47–49) defends a similar position chiefly on the grounds of the Balaam oracles and Num 21:26–30.

[22]The Deuteronomistic literature has doubtless over-emphasized the political role of the early prophetic figures (e.g., Samuel, Nathan. See J. Blenkinsopp, *A History of Prophecy in Israel* [Philadelphia: Westminster, 1983] 61–

it is clear that the later prophets advised those in charge of the political life of the Israel and Judah. They frequently spoke in order to affect political policy and action, and played a significant and complex role in political life.[23] The prominent place and extensive space given to the OAN collections in Isaiah, Jeremiah and Ezekiel, as well as the fact that two of the so-called minor prophets, Obadiah and Nahum, consist entirely of speeches against foreign nations, testify to the importance of the issue of international politics in the thought and role of the prophets.[24]

The observation that two OAN texts are long enough to constitute entire books (Obadiah and Nahum) directs our attention to an important aspect of this material. Very frequently individual OAN texts are quite long. Although this may at times be attributable to redactional activity, in a number of instances long texts display clear signs of literary integrity. To use only Isaiah as an example, we find long unities in 13:2–22; 14:4b–21; 19:1–15 and 23:1–14. In the case of Isaiah 15–16, many scholars

---

77). Our view of prophecy in early Israel is substantially blocked by the shaping of the narratives by Deuteronomistic theology and ideology.

[23]For a similar position see H. Barstad, "No Prophets? Recent Developments in Biblical Prophetic Research and Ancient Near Eastern Prophecy," *JSOT* 57 (1993) 54–57. The political role of the prophet is increasingly acknowledged; see Gottwald, *All the Kingdoms*, 204–208, 388–89; K. Baltzer, "Considerations Regarding the Office and Calling of the Prophet," *HTR* 61 (1968) 567–81; J. Holladay, "Assyrian Statecraft and the Prophets of Israel," *HTR* 63 (1970) 29–51 (reprinted in D. Petersen, ed., *Prophecy in Israel: Search for an Identity* [Philadelphia: Fortress, 1987] 122–43); W. Dietrich, *Jesaja und die Politik* (BEvT 74; Munich: Kaiser, 1976); B. Lang, *Kein Aufstand in Jerusalem: Die Politik des Propheten Ezekiel* (Stuttgart: Katholisches Bibelwerk, 1978). R. Wilson states in his summary of his study of the southern prophets, "...for the most part the Judeans [i.e., prophets from Judea] seem to have operated within the central social structure" (*Prophecy and Society in Ancient Israel* [Philadelphia: Fortress, 1980] 294; on Isaiah specifically see 215–218; 271). The political involvement of Isaiah is particularly clear (see 2 Kgs 19:1–7; 20:12–19; Isa 7:3; 8:2; 22:15–16). As a corollary to this recognition, one also finds growing emphasis on the rhetorical intention and practice of prophetic discourse; see M. Fox, "The Rhetoric of Ezekiel's Vision of the Valley of the Bones," *HUCA* 51 (1980) 4, 8–9; R. Carroll, "Poets Not Prophets; A Response to 'Prophets Through the Looking Glass,'" JSOT 27 (1983) 26–27; Hayes and Irvine, *Isaiah*, 59–69; Barton, "History and Rhetoric in the Prophets," 51–64.

[24]Clements, *Prophecy and Tradition*, 64–65.

identify the original composition as consisting of between thirteen and fifteen verses. Moreover, one observes a high degree of rhetorical complexity in these long OAN texts. Taking only the safest of our examples, Isa 14:4b–21, we find there a complex composition displaying numerous changes of speaker, addressee, and perspective. The rhetorical complexity of this text is often noted and its artistry praised.[25] Thus we are not always, or perhaps even typically, dealing with brief prophetic sayings in the OAN.[26] Rather, we are frequently confronted with compositional unities of a length and complexity that suggest a high degree of artistry and reflection in the act of authorship. If these long compositions were intended for oral delivery (which seems likely), we would do better to use a term such as "speech" rather than the traditional term "oracle."

Thus the interpretation of the OAN must take into account both the possibility of long, rhetorically and generically complex speeches and the political nature of the task in which the prophets were engaged. And perhaps these two things are interrelated. It is probable that the prophets composed OAN to influence policy, decision and opinion of the time, and their rhetorical goals may often have been better served by long speeches than by short oracular pronouncements.

III. The Texts Designated מַשָּׂא

Isaiah 15 and 16 is distinguished not only by the fact that it is found in an OAN collection, but also by the fact that it is found under the heading מַשָּׂא. This designation is attached to twelve other speeches in Isaiah (13:2–14:23; 14:29–32; 17:1b–11; 19:1b–25; 21:1b–10; 21:11b–12; 21:13b–17; 22:1b–14; 23:1b–18; 30:6b–7).[27] Outside of Isaiah it introduces seven prophetic speeches: 2 Kgs

---

[25]See for instance O. Eissfeldt, *The Old Testament: An Introduction* (New York: Harper & Row, 1965) 97, 320.

[26]Such a view is at odds with the emphasis on short speech units that has typified form-critical work; see G. Tucker, *Form Criticism*, 58. We will deal further with this issue below.

[27]The actual heading מַשָּׂא is found at 13:1; 14:28; 15:1; 17:1; 19:1; 21:1, 11, 13; 22:1; 23:1; 30:6. The delimitation of the מַשָּׂא texts is according to Weis, "Definition," 43–59.

9:26a; Ezek 12:11a–16; Nah 1:2–3:19; Hab 1:2–2:20; Zech 9:1aα–11:3; 12:1b–14:21; Mal 1:2–3:24. Jeremiah has no speeches designated מַשָּׂא, but the term is used in the book to refer to prophetic speech (see esp. Jer 23:16–40). The distribution suggests that the term is of particular importance in the book of Isaiah, especially in the Isaianic OAN collection.

The term "מַשָּׂא" is usually translated "burden" or "oracle." The texts to which it is attached contain a variety of styles, structures and component genres, just as is the case with the OAN. The relationship between the מַשָּׂא and OAN texts is complex. Many מַשָּׂא texts are also OAN, but some are not (2 Kgs 9:26a; Isa 30:6b–7; Ezek 12:11a–16).[28] All of the texts that are both OAN and מַשָּׂא with the single exception of Nah 1:2–3:19 are found in Isaiah. The מַשָּׂא in Isa 22:1b–14 is contained in the Isaianic OAN collection, but it deals with Judah and not a foreign nation as one would expect. Several מַשָּׂא texts contain both material concerning the nations and material concerning Judah (Hab 1:2–2:20; Zech 9:1aα–11:3; Mal 1:2–3:24). The significance of the overlapping of the two groups of material is unclear, but the fact that most מַשָּׂא texts are either contained within an OAN collection or treat the subject of the nations suggests that the connection between the two groups is more than coincidental or superficial. The topic of the nations appears to be an essential aspect of מַשָּׂא texts.

R. Weis has recently undertaken a detailed examination of the term מַשָּׂא and the texts in which it is found.[29] He offers a detailed history of how others have treated the term, and breaks considerable new ground with his own insights and suggestions. Several of his proposals have proved helpful in the present study. We will return to Weis's work in a moment, but first we must discuss briefly the earlier treatments.

Studies prior to Weis's had analyzed the term primarily etymologically.[30] The general opinion was that מַשָּׂא was derived

---

[28]Note well, however, that in both Isa 30:6b–7 and Ezek 12:11a–16 the foreign nations play a significant role.

[29]"A Definition of the Genre maśśāʾ in the Hebrew Bible."

[30]The chief modern studies are those of H. Gehman, "The 'Burden' of the Prophets," *JQR* 31 (1940–41) 107–21; P. de Boer, "An Inquiry into the Meaning of the Term משא," *OTS* 5 (1948) 197–214; R. Scott, "The Meaning of maśśāʾ

from the verb נשא and indicated "a lifting up" of either the voice or a prophetic word. Those who favored the sense of 'a lifting up of the voice' thought the term equivalent to a prophetic "word" (דבר) and usually translated it "oracle" (e.g., NRSV, NASB, NEB). Those who favored the sense of 'a lifting up of a prophetic word' thought that מַשָּׂא indicated the object-like quality of prophecy and favored the translation "burden." H. Gehman's study is typical of this second group.[31] He begins his article with observations about the role of the prophet:

> He is a 'forth-teller' rather than a fore-teller....The prophet does not speak for himself, but is the mouthpiece of God. The prophetic words which he utters have inherent power. The prophet is merely the channel through which they flow, and, as the occasion demands, the prophecy is directed against a particular nation or people. (107–108)

Thus, in his estimation, the prophetic word has an autonomous potency deriving from its true source. Its power is not rhetorical but actual, though metaphysical. His study of the etymology and usage of מַשָּׂא leads him to conclude that it was derived from נשא and served as a technical term for a particularly threatening kind of prophecy:

> The word as used in prophecy suggests the idea of catastrophe, destruction, threat, punishment, or the judgment of God and carries with it sublime ominousness....The מַשָּׂא came from God to the prophet, but it did not remain with the prophet. He in turn raised it or lifted it or laid it upon an individual or nation. This sense can be best brought out by *burden*, which reflects the etymology of the original and is an exact reproduction of it; at the same time the term

---

as an Oracle Title," paper read at the 83rd meeting of the Society of Biblical Literature and Exegesis, New York, NY, 29 and 30 December 1947, summarized in *JBL* 67 (1948) v-vi; M. Saebø, *Sacharja 9–14* (WMANT, 34: Neukirchen-Vluyn: Neukirchener, 1969) 137–40; F. Stolz, "נשא *nś'* aufheben, tragen," *Theologisches Handwörterbuch zum Alten Testament*, ed. K. Jenni and C. Westermann, vol. 2 (Munich: Chr. Kaiser, 1971–76); G. Tucker, "Prophetic Superscriptions and the Growth of a Canon," *Canon and Authority*, ed. G. Coats and B. Long (Philadelphia: Fortress, 1977) 56–70; Wilson, *Prophecy and Society*, 257–59.

[31]In this group, which seems to represent the dominant opinion, we should include the studies of de Boer, Saebø, Wilson and Stolz.

burden permits us to read into the word all that is implied in the Hebrew. (110, 120)

"Burden" is used to render מַשָּׂא in some modern translations. Gehman's study never mentions, however, whether the term refers to a special prophetic genre. He never addresses the question whether prophetic texts designated מַשָּׂא have any typical features that would distinguish them from other prophetic texts that lack the heading.

Scholars prior to Weis have agreed that מַשָּׂא is not a genre category, or that, at least in the literature we now possess, it defines no generically cohesive group of texts. Wilson thought that the term "may have designated a distinctive type of oracle associated with Judean prophets" but that the characteristic features of the type have been obscured over time: "If maśśāʾ ever had a distinctive structure, that structure must have degenerated by the time the extant oracles against foreign nations were produced. The examples that have been preserved contain a number of distinct prophetic speech forms and do not exhibit a common literary structure."[32] This conclusion stood uncontested until Weis's study.

Weis's dissertation deserves our close attention for two reasons. First, he concludes that the term מַשָּׂא designates a genre with specific and consistent features. Thus his description of the genre, should we accept it or parts of it, would provide crucial guidance for our interpretation of Isaiah 15–16. Second, he has written the entry at "oracle" for the recent *Anchor Bible Dictionary*, and his definition will gain a wide hearing, and very possibly acceptance.[33] His conclusions should be carefully tested, therefore, both by an examination of the method he uses to arrive at them, and by an analysis of the way he handles his primary data, the מַשָּׂא texts. The results of the present study of Isaiah 15–16 may prove useful in this respect.

The body of Weis's dissertation is divided into two sections: an examination of מַשָּׂא (1) at the level of the final form of the text

---

[32]Wilson, 257–59; cf. Stolz, col. 116.

[33]J. Brangenberg uses Weis's study as a foundation for his own work on the Isaianic OAN ("Reexamination," 11–17).

and (2) at levels earlier than the final form. His study of the final form is by far the longest part of the dissertation, and it is here that he develops most of his main proposals. The final form section is sub-divided into (1) an analysis of the semantics of מַשָּׂא in the HB, (2) an analysis of the texts in themselves, (3) an assessment of the form and intention of the texts, and (4) an analysis and assessment of the function of the texts in their literary contexts. The second section, in which he studies "levels earlier than the final form (tradition history)," consists of an attempt to reconstruct the tradition history of the term מַשָּׂא and an investigation of the tradition history of the typical aspects of the מַשָּׂא texts.

Weis begins his final form study by rejecting the etymological analysis of מַשָּׂא. He argues that the etymology of the term is not a proper starting point since etymology is not determinative of meaning (27–32). In its place Weis offers a two-pronged approach. First, he undertakes a semantic analysis of מַשָּׂא in the final form of the Hebrew Bible. He examines the use of the term both as it appears in headings to texts and as it occurs in the body of a few texts (especially Jer 23:16–40). He concludes,

> First of all a *maśśāʾ* is a definite prophetic speech or text unit, indeed, it is a genre name. It is not a *dābār* or a *ḥāzôn* although it seems to be related to or like them and appears to be connected with revelatory experience. A *maśśāʾ* is emphatically not a *dĕbār yhwh* although a *maśśāʾ* is probably based upon and derived from a preexisting *dĕbār yhwh*, and in any event is closely related to it. It is closely related to concrete, human historical entities—be they nations, groups or individuals, Hebrew or foreign—and situations. In particular these entities seem to be its topics. It may be either oral or written. It is preeminently a human composition and in some texts it is attributable to or attributed to a prophet. According to some texts it is not a prophetic messenger speech. According to some it is not a prophetic judgment speech as defined by Westermann (102).

At this point in his study he leaves a number of issues open, but the main outlines of his final conclusions are established and do not change: מַשָּׂא is a genre name for a prophetic speech unit consisting not of a divine word (though it may contain or refer to a divine word), but of a "human composition" related topically to political events and situations.

In his form-critical analysis of the final form of those texts to which מַשָּׂא is attached as a heading, Weis attempts to discern "typical formal aspects" among the texts as well as typical intentions. To accomplish this he examines the structure, rhetoric and intention of each of the מַשָּׂא texts. At the end of his analysis, he summarizes the formal aspects that typify the texts:

> We may say that in respect to form these texts are characterized by the absence of the prophetic messenger formula. They are also characterized by the absence of an accusation + announcement of judgment pattern except in occasional subordinate or peripheral roles. They are predominantly the speech of the prophet although the speech of YHWH is mixed in with this, sometimes clearly identified with tags, sometimes not. In some texts there are specially highlighted quotations or citations of some YHWH revelation or of YHWH's plan. These are particularly bound up in the process of connecting YHWH's acts and/or intentions with their manifestation in the human sphere. The addressee of the whole is never YHWH or the prophet, but rather the entity that constitutes the topic of the *maśśāʾ* or the prophet's own community.
>
> The texts are principally made up of descriptive (report or announcement) and/or ordering (command or prohibition) genres.... Seventy-five percent of the time a YHWH act is given with its human result....This connection between YHWH acts and their human manifestations or results emerged as the dominant and crucial infrastructural pattern (225–26).

This represents a near reversal of the view put forward by Gehman and others. Not only are the מַשָּׂא texts notably lacking in threat, they are not even primarily divine speech. The speech of the prophet predominates in these texts. They are not announcements of YHWH's word, but interpretations of it.

As did those before him, Weis finds that variety rather than unity predominates in the "superstructural aspects" of the texts (227). This diversity suggests that one should seek the unifying aspect of the מַשָּׂא texts in their intention rather than their form. Weis concludes that the intention of the texts is to explain how particular events reveal the divine will at work in human affairs (228). This intention points to a common situation behind the texts, a situation characterized by "indeterminancy" arising from the unfolding of events and the need to understand a previous word of the LORD in the new situation (229). For this reason, the מַשָּׂא has as its subject a previous YHWH revelation and often quotes this previous word. It is prophetic application and exposition of an accepted and authoritative דבר יהוה in the light of current events (224–25). As such, it is often delivered mid-event and not as an anticipation of the event. There is some evidence to suggest an even more specific situation. On the basis of Isa 14:32 and Isa 21:11b–12, Weis suggests that a מַשָּׂא was typically given as a response to an inquiry (230–31, 269). He offers "prophetic exposition (of YHWH revelation)" as the best translation for מַשָּׂא (276).

Thus the conclusions of Weis's semantic and form-critical investigations of the final form largely cohere. Weis balances them in the remainder of the dissertation with a traditio-historical examination of both the term itself (corresponding to his semantic analysis) and the typical aspects of the מַשָּׂא texts (corresponding to his form-critical analysis). He concludes from his traditio-historical study of the *term* that its use was limited in society to the Judahite prophetic movement (283–84). In his analysis of the מַשָּׂא *texts* he observes that texts from the eighth and seventh centuries B.C.E. "*all* contained within themselves a quotation or report of the revelation whose manifestation in human affairs they expounded" (347). In this period the prophets responded to an inquiry with a מַשָּׂא text that contained a YHWH revelation and then interpreted its "manifestation...in human affairs" in order to elicit the appropriate action from those involved. Weis concludes that the genre developed over time. Toward the end of its life (in the post-exilic period) it came to be used to respond to the perceived "failure of YHWH's revealed intention to manifest itself in human affairs in the expected way" (364–65). This later use was quite similar to the earlier use; the essential difference lay in the fact that "the locus of revelation had shifted from the living encounter of a prophet with YHWH to the recorded or remembered words of an earlier prophet who had had such an encounter" (365). Thus none of the מַשָּׂא texts from the sixth and fifth centuries quoted or expounded a divine word. Instead, they assumed knowledge of the content of previous prophetic texts and expounded these shared texts in light of events of the time. In this respect the later use of the genre מַשָּׂא is similar to the inner-biblical exegesis identified by M. Fishbane and points toward the shift from living prophecy to midrash, from revelation mediated by living persons to revelation mediated by texts.[34] While Weis's traditio-historical study offers insights into the late development of the genre, it does not at all change the definition of the term and the description of the genre that he developed in earlier chapters (351).

Weis does not attempt to reconstruct the tradition history of the texts themselves. His reasons for this are important to understand since his study is liable to criticism for this omission. He defends his decision to deal only with the final form of the text in two ways:

> On the one hand, we want to avoid, so far as possible, circular arguments...we want to refrain from assuming that we know what a *maśśāʾ* is at any stage prior to the final form of the text which is the only stage for which we can be certain that a given text is a *maśśāʾ*. Thus we should avoid using the evidence of reconstructed earlier stages of any of these eighteen texts which either envision a different internal composition for the text or a different literary context. On the other hand, some of the proposed tradition histories proper to the texts as individual texts are controversial and hardly a firm foundation for our work. Since those discussions have taken place without the definition of *maśśāʾ* that we have developed for the final form of the Hebrew Bible, the use of their results is further complicated. We simply do not have the space in this study to reopen and settle all the questions involved in the tradition histories of the individual texts (292–93, cf. 277).

Weis has other reasons for not undertaking traditio-historical analysis of the individual texts that become clear later in the dissertation. He conducts an extended study of the percentage of formulaic language in each of the מַשָּׂא in an effort to determine whether they were orally composed (297–320).[35] The results he obtains (13 to 22 percent formulaic) indicate that "the *maśʾôt* we have are written compositions, and that oral composition is in no

---

[34]M. Fishbane, *Biblical Interpretation in Ancient Israel* (Oxford: Clarendon, 1985).

[35]Weis uses the method pioneered by M. Floyd, "Oral Tradition As a Problematic Factor in the Historical Interpretation of Poems in the Law and the Prophets" (Ph.D. diss., Claremont Graduate School, 1980). Floyd's method is an adaptation and application of Parry and Lord's theories about oral, formulaic literature.

way constitutive for the genre as represented in the exemplars we have." He believes, however, that they were composed for oral delivery: "written composition and oral delivery—as in the reading out in some formal setting of what was written—would be a suitable explanation of the evidence" (319–20). Such a conclusion tends to weaken the foundation of previous traditio-critical studies of the מַשָּׂא texts since most of the studies presuppose oral composition and short original units (359). It also strengthens the case of those who, like Weis, look for large unifying literary patterns in the text.

As we have noted, Weis's study is susceptible to criticism primarily because he chose to deal exclusively with the final form of the individual texts. His literary analysis of the texts, an analysis that shows the influence of rhetorical criticism in many places (of the sort practiced by the Muilenberg school), seems to be responsible to a large extent for this decision. This becomes clear when he notes,

> In general, a traditio-historical explanation of some feature(s) of a text is resorted to when an adequate literary explanation is not to be found. That is to say, since the texts present themselves as wholes, we may posit a composite character for them only when they are not reasonably explicable as wholes. As we have seen, Isa 14:29–32 is explicable as a whole; it is structurally integral. A traditio-historical explanation is not required to explain the phenomena of the text (322).

In a similar vein he comments on Isaiah 15–16,

> This text is also structurally and rhetorically integral. Indeed, it is strikingly balanced and well formed. Although recent scholarship tends to see the text as a composite, most notably chapter 16, there is little reason to seek a traditio-historical explanation since most of the phenoma that have usually called forth such an accounting can be adequately interpreted from a literary point of view, as we have done (323–24).

Weis's literary analysis leads him to conclude in almost every case that the מַשָּׂא text is an original compositional unity. His starting point, the final form, and his reading method, rhetorical-structural analysis, predispose him toward this conclusion. As a method of reading, rhetorical-structural analysis tends to define large unities and point toward the literary integrity of texts. Thus his conclusion about the integrity of the texts is not surprising. Nor is it necessarily wrong. The fault in his analysis is that he never sufficiently confronts the evidence and arguments of those who have analyzed the texts as composites, as the product of multilayered redaction. He does not show why his reading of the texts is more valid than that of the form and redaction critics. This is a matter of great consequence for his study. The question whether the individual מַשָּׂא texts are original compositional unities or found their present unity only in a multilayered process of editing and glossing cannot be avoided or deferred if one wishes to define a genre used by the prophets themselves. Weis does not wish for us to agree only that he has produced an acceptable final form interpretation of the texts; he wants us to accept that his readings form a reliable basis for the delineation of genre as it was understood by the eighth and seventh century prophets. His method is synchronic/final-form as it pertains to the individual texts, but it leads him to diachronic/historical conclusions.

This is not to say that Weis's analysis of the texts is wrong in every case. But his interpretations of the texts in question are very often idiosyncratic, and this introduces a substantial element of uncertainty into his conclusions.[36] He is quite right to point out that the final form of the texts is the only form to which we have certain and direct access (33, 359), but his study is seriously weakened by the fact that he repeatedly concludes that the final form and the original form are the same. The reasons that he gives for equating the original and final forms vary from text to text, but typically they derive solely from his own rhetorical analysis. Several of his most important conclusions are substantially weakened if one accepts even the most conservative traditio-historical analysis of the מַשָּׂא texts. In fact, if only a few of the texts he treats can be shown to be redactional complexes, his thesis becomes suspect at key points. His reason for the decision not to

[36]See, for example, the summary of his interpretation of Isaiah 15–16 in my history of interpretation above and the critique of this interpretation given in the following chapter. This is but one example, but it is an important one since his analysis of these chapters is a crucial support for some of his conclusions.

grapple with the complex issues of tradition history in the texts—"We simply do not have the space in this study to reopen and settle all the questions involved in the tradition histories of the individual texts"(293)—suggests that he did not consider the omission methodologically significant.[37] But one suspects that, insofar as the study is based on interpretations that are in varying degrees idiosyncratic and that for practical purposes ignore the previous traditio-historical anaysis of the texts, it will struggle to find acceptance.

Finally, Weis's definition of מַשָּׂא suffers to some degree from a lack of practical specificity. Can his definition effectively exclude other prophetic texts not marked as מַשָּׂא? Prophetic texts frequently combine both divine word and prophetic exposition, but Weis's study offers no attempt to show on what grounds such texts might be distinguished from the genre מַשָּׂא.[38] Without a "superstructural" pattern(s) to mark the genre, the terms of Weis's definition tend toward generality and superficiality. If we had no מַשָּׂא headings to guide us, would the texts exhibit sufficient typicality to have caused us to notice that they form a set? It remains unclear to what extent the typical features pointed out by

---

[37]Weis does not discuss his methodological decision at any length. He cites only the comments of R. Knierim ("Criticism of Literary Features, Form, Tradition and Redaction," *The Hebrew Bible and Its Modern Interpreters* [ed. G. Tucker and D. Knight; Chico: Scholars, 1985] 155–56) in defense of his position (33, n. 73; 359, n. 4). Knierim, however, takes pains to emphasize the necessity of respecting the "historicality of the texts" and eschewing "methodological shortcuts attempting either to supply us with an uncomplicated historical picture or to offer a quick, direct hermeneutical access to the texts" (126). On the pages cited by Weis, Knierim suggests that the exegetical procedure focus "from the outset on the interdependence of larger redactional works and their smaller units," but it is clear that he thinks that this is only the first step in a multistep process (156).

[38]See studies cited by W. March, "Prophecy," *Old Testament Form Criticism*, ed. J. Hayes (San Antonio: Trinity University, 1974) 150–51. One would also like to know how Weis would explain the fact that all but one of the מַשָּׂא texts in Isaiah are found in the OAN collection. Clearly, Isaiah also entertained "inquiries" related to internal state affairs (assuming Weis is correct about the situation behind a מַשָּׂא). One would assume that these inquiries would have led on occasion to an exposition of a previously revealed word. Why, then, do all but one, very brief, מַשָּׂא text have as their subject the foreign nations rather than Judah?

Weis may be incidental and to what extent the texts may have been made to fit a predetermined pattern.[39] A genre must be identified from several distinct angles. As Gunkel warned, "...only where we can ascertain that definite thoughts in a definite form on a definite occasion were expressed have we the right to speak of a genre."[40] At the very least, texts grouped together as a genre must exhibit typicality in both their form and their content. Finally, if מַשָּׂא was a distinctive genre heading from as early as Isaiah's time and not a later redactional addition, it is surprising that the term appears in this capacity not at all in Jeremiah and only once in Ezekiel. One would expect an established genre, especially one with the utility suggested by Weis's definition of מַשָּׂא, to have been employed more frequently.

Despite its weaknesses, Weis's study does clarify certain issues of method and present some valuable observations and conclusions. First, Weis makes a good case for his contention that previous research has depended too much on etymology. His semantic approach is methodologically sound, even if occasionally flawed in its execution. Second, his thesis that מַשָּׂא refers to an identifiable genre marked more by its intention and the problem it addresses than by its superstructural form is a useful reminder that genre can be constituted in different ways and that the seach for similarity in the מַשָּׂא texts may have failed only because the wrong questions were asked. The similarities that he notes among the texts are important, even if they do not prove that מַשָּׂא is a genre. At the very least his conclusions suggest that if the heading

---

[39]As Kneirim notes, "The quest for verification [of genre exemplars] is decisive: in our search for exemplars in the texts, we have only the texts and cannot presuppose what must be found out (i.e., the problem of circular conclusions)" (140; cf. 139–44). T. Conley comments, "If the end is adjudicative criticism, the organization of discursive wholes into genera and species, no matter how 'empirical' its basis may be, tends naturally to assimilate itself to the deductive a priori" ("The Linnaean Blues," 65).

[40]Quoted in Hayes, "Form-Critical Study of Prophecy," 60–99. More recently G. Coats has outlined four elements that adequately define a genre: (1) a typical structure; (2) a typical vocabulary; (3) a typical setting; (4) a typical function ("Genres: Why Should They Be Important for Exegesis?" *Saga, Legend, Tale, Novella, Fable: Narrative Forms in Old Testament Literature* [JSOTS 35; Sheffield: JSOT, 1985] 11–13).

מַשָּׂא was sometimes added by a redactor, it may not have been applied blindly or without warrant (258–63, 361). Third, even though his study is liable to criticism because it depends on final form readings, the patterns of similarity that it highlights are often discernible in those layers usually thought earliest. Additionally, several of his observations pertain to what is commonly *lacking* in מַשָּׂא texts when compared to other prophetic texts, and these points are not invalidated if the original form is defined along more traditional lines. Specifically, five interrelated observations remain viable: (a) the prophetic messenger formula כה אמר יהוה almost never occurs in מַשָּׂא texts (204–205); (b) מַשָּׂא texts "are not characterized by the accusation and announcement of judgment pattern that Westermann showed to be the basic structural pattern of the prophetic judgment speech." Nor are they messenger speech (206, 212); (c) "Texts labeled *maśśāʾ* are never addressed as a whole to YHWH or to a prophet... The common presumption would be that the addressees are Judahite audiences" (214); (d) the speech of the prophet predominates in the מַשָּׂא texts (212); (e) descriptive and ordering genres—reports of past or present events, announcements of coming events, commands and prohibitions—predominate in the מַשָּׂא texts (215–22). Finally, Weis's analysis of the texts to determine if they were orally composed provides consistent results and suggests that oral tradition may have played a less significant role in the formation of this literature than has generally been supposed.[41]

Our investigation of OAN and מַשָּׂא texts has disclosed several characteristic features and themes of these texts that suggest broad guidelines for our interpretation of Isaiah 15–16. The similarities we have noted do not indicate that we are dealing with a fixed genre in either case. The OAN texts in particular exhibit a remarkable freedom in the way that they mix genres to accomplish various rhetorical goals, and whatever their original setting or settings may have been, the texts we now possess in the prophetic OAN collections do not indicate that these origins have had a determinative influence.

---

[41]See also Barstad, "No Prophets?" 56–60.

If the OAN are not defined by their genre, how are they defined? At least in Isaiah, the OAN seem to be a collection gathered under a common theme—"YHWH's plan concerning the arrogance of nations," or something similar. The same holds true for the Isaianic מַשָּׂא texts, but Weis's observations that מַשָּׂא texts are not cast as messenger speech and that they are often characterized by *particular* component genres suggests that some deeper commonality exists.

M. Fox has argued that messenger speech can be understood as a particular "rhetorical stance" taken by the prophet, an aspect of the prophet's rhetorical strategy. Weis's observations suggest that it might prove helpful to ask what rhetorical stance or strategy typifies the מַשָּׂא texts.[42] If we look at this for just a moment, we may note that the preponderance of descriptive genres suggests that the speaker of a מַשָּׂא takes the stance of "reporter" or "spectator" (Fox's terminology). This stance has the rhetorical effect of unobtrusively promoting the speaker's implicit arguments while maintaining the appearance of objectivity. It is as if he speaks from the point of view of the audience, and by speaking from this perspective "the rhetor makes his audience's point-of-view congruent with his own. The audience looks over the rhetor's shoulder and watches the event unfold from the same angle of vision. Alignment of perspective encourages alignment of belief."[43] This is somewhat the same strategy one observes in prophetic vision accounts where the spectator role of the prophet is clearly marked.[44] This rhetorical strategy occurs outside מַשָּׂא texts as well, and even within the מַשָּׂא texts the strategy is employed in various ways. Thus the מַשָּׂא texts no more point to a

[42]See Fox, "Ezekiel's Vision," 8–9, for a discussion of this concept. See also my discussion below.

[43]Fox, 9.

[44]In this regard, note the preface to the מַשָּׂא in Isa 21:1–10 (v 2) that specifies its origin as a vision experience. Although this מַשָּׂא does not proceed as a vision account, it does share some similarities with that genre. Note especially that it explicitly casts the prophet in the role of a divinely appointed spectator ("watchman," vv 6–10). Similarly, the prophet is cast in the role of a watchman in the following מַשָּׂא (21:11–12; see also 22:1). The vision aspect of מַשָּׂא texts is also clear in Isa 13:1, Hab 1:1, Nah 1:1 and Lam 2:14—all texts that connect מַשָּׂא with the term חזה.

single, well-defined rhetorical genre than they point to a literary genre.[45] The legitimacy of the application of this sort of rhetorical analysis does not, however, depend on a strict definition of usage since rhetorical strategies are usually thought to be used rather flexibly and adapted freely to new contexts. Form critical methodology, on the other hand, has traditionally adhered to more strictly defined categories.

IV. Form Criticism and the Study of OAN and מַשָּׂא Texts

The effort to apply form criticism to the OAN and מַשָּׂא texts has had limited success due in part to the nature of the texts and in part to problems that inhere in the method itself. While we cannot deal here with the entire range of issues in the debate over the presuppositions and methods of form criticism, it is necessary to discuss several issues that pertain directly to the method adopted for our own analysis. First, there is the issue of prophetic compositional practices and, hence, of the nature of original compositional unities in prophetic speech. The tendency prevalent among form critics to focus on short units, and, often, to ascribe to these short units an original independence in oral tradition has been noted frequently. The basic tenets of this approach are spelled out by S. Mowinckel:

> The result with which we shall have to rest satisfied, is that the relatively brief, in itself, complete and concluded, independent separate saying ("oracle") is the original and real form of prophet "speech", his message, and that this is also largely the case with the historically known prophets, "the scripture prophets" as they are generally, and misleadingly, termed. —These separate sayings have been transmitted by oral tradition in the prophet circles, partly unchanged, partly adapted to and revived in the new situations of new times; they have been living a *life* in tradition and have been serving a religious purpose within the circle; the tradition has not been static. —In the course of the history of the tradition there have arisen greater "tradition complexes" and collections out of these separate sayings, which again in their turn have been joined

---

[45]See W. Wuellner, "The Rhetorical Genre of Jesus' Sermon in Luke 12.1–13.9," *Persuasive Artistry: Studies in New Testament Rhetoric in Honor of George A. Kennedy*, ed. D. Watson (JSNTS 50; Sheffield: JSOT, 1991) 93–99, for a discussion of the distinction between literary and rhetorical genre.

> together to final collections of tradition. The latter may also have been handed on by word of mouth. Finally, however, they have been recorded; they have become "books". This written fixing may have started earlier, with the separate minor complexes, and the oral tradition may have continued side by side with the written one.[46]

Some interpreters of Isaiah have stated explicitly this preference for short, "authentic" units. G. Gray comments:

> The first thing to be remarked is that the prophecies are almost without exception poems or poetic fragments, and that these poems are short. Probably the longest poem is 9:7–10:4 and 5:26–29; and this, in Hebrew, scarcely exceeds 300 words. We have therefore no speech, sermon, oration (or whatever other term we may prefer to use) of Isaiah's that would have taken in its present literary form more than 4 or 5 minutes to deliver.[47]

For others it seems simply to be assumed as a well-accepted notion in need of no defense, part of the secure foundation upon which further scholarship might build. M. Greenberg notes how widely the basic assumptions of form criticism are shared:

> A universal prejudice of modern biblical criticism is the assumption of original simplicity. A passage of complex structure, or one containing repetition, or skewing a previously used figure is, on these grounds, suspect of being inauthentic. Another widespread prejudice equates authenticity with topical or thematic uniformity. A temporal vista that progresses from present, to penultimate, to ultimate time is considered an artificial result of successive additions to a single-time original oracle. Doom oracles that end with a glimpse of a better future are declared composites on the ground of psychological improbability. Such prejudices are simply a prioris, an array of unproved (and unprovable) modern assumptions and conventions that confirm themselves through the

---

[46]*Prophecy and Tradition: The Prophetic Books in the Light of the Study of the Growth and History of the Tradition* (Oslo: Jacob Dybwad, 1946) 60; quoted in J. Hayes, *Amos: the Eighth-Century Prophet: His Times and His Preaching* (Nashville: Abingdon, 1988) 35; cf. 34 for Hayes's summary of Gunkel's position.

[47]*Isaiah*, liv. Gray's division of the text into small poetic fragments is often based on considerations of poetic rhythm (see his discussion on lxvii-lxviii), but his view that prophetic poetry originated as oral composition and was later written down in condensed form is the most fundamental reason for his division throughout the analysis (liii-lv).

> results obtained by forcing them on the text and altering, reducing, and reordering it accordingly.[48]

Greenberg's criticism of this "prejudice" inherent in form criticism is not an entirely new or isolated opinion. One finds criticism of certain aspects of form critical method coming from several quarters in the scholarship of the last three decades.[49] Perhaps the most influential voice has been that of J. Muilenburg in his 1969 SBL presidential address.[50]

The question of the typical length of prophetic speech units is particularly acute in the case of OAN texts. Gunkel's idea that the OAN represented one of the earliest kinds of prophetic speech and that, therefore, they were very short in their original state does not correspond well with the length of some of the OAN we actually have. J. Hayes has called attention to this problem. After quoting two passages in which Gunkel asserts that the earliest kind of prophetic utterance consisted of "short enigmatic words" and that the OAN exhibit a style characteristic of the earliest prophetic speech, Hayes comments:

> It is difficult to see how Gunkel could understand the oldest prophetical style reflected in both the short, enigmatic words and the oracles against foreign nations. No reference is made to the possibility that oracles against foreign nations may have originally been only short, enigmatic words nor is any attempt made to explain the length and form of the foreign oracles except to say that

---

[48]M. Greenberg, *Ezekiel, 1–20* (AB 22; Garden City: Doubleday, 1983) 20.

[49]For example, see Greenwood, "Rhetorical Criticism and Formgeschichte," 418–26; A. Rofé, "The Classification of Prophetical Stories," *JBL* 89 (1970) 427–40; Knierim, "Criticism of Literary Features," 144–45, 155–56; Y. Gitay, "Reflections on the Study of Prophetic Discourse," *VT* 33 (1983) 208–212; E. Greenstein, *Essays on Biblical Method and Translation* (Brown Judaic Studies 92; Atlanta: Scholars, 1989) 3–51; J. Kugel, ed., *Poetry and Prophecy: The Beginnings of a Literary Tradition* (Ithaca, NY and London: Cornell University, 1990), see especially the first two essays by J. Kugel and A. Cooper.

[50]"Form Criticism and Beyond," *JBL* 88 (1969) 4–8. Muilenburg's criticisms of form criticism pertain mainly to its tendency to deal exclusively with the typical and general and to ignore the artistry and particularity of the text, its "literary features," and thus to "obscure the thought and intention of the writer or speaker" (4–5). Although he does not explicitly say so in this address, it is clear elsewhere in his writings that Muilenburg is also dissatisfied with form criticism's fragmentation of the text.

> only late examples have survived....I suggest that the use of these two examples (short, enigmatic words and oracles against foreign nations) reflect [*sic*] two unreconciled emphases in Gunkel's thought regarding the style of the earliest prophetic genre, namely the ecstatic and the futuristic. This seems to be the case in spite of his use of the term ecstatic with reference to oracles against the nations in two of his writings.[51]

Hayes observes that the notion that prophetic oracles in their original form consisted of short speeches derives from Gunkel's idea that the prophets received their messages in internal visions, auditions and, at times, in states of ecstasy.[52] The original short speeches that emerged from such experiences became, as we have seen, the standard for authenticity among form critics. Isolating such units became the prerequisite of any analysis. This gave methodological priority to form-critical questions and produced at the beginning of analysis a fragmented text. The next logical step is then clearly redactional analysis.[53]

Such a procedure makes sense only if we can be certain in all cases that short oracles underlie the text. The possibility of large unified compositions in which component genres are built together into a rhetorical whole would suggest another sort of procedure. At the very least, the possibility of large compositional unities (from a single author) suggests a different model of intention and artistry than would apply in the case of an editor dealing with disparate and potentially conflicting units of oral tradition. If long compositions are considered as a possibility, one must ask form-critical questions in such a way that the text is not immediately suspect because of its length and rhetorical complexity.[54] Knierim comments: "The time is passing rapidly in which one could prematurely jump to conclusions about oral tradition before

---

[51]Hayes, "Form-Critical Study of Prophecy," 64–65.

[52]"Form Critical Study of Prophecy," 63–66; see also Kugel, ed., *Poetry and Prophecy*, 16–18; 28–29; W. E. March, "Prophecy," *Old Testament Form Criticism*, 144–45.

[53]Knierim has recently questioned this priority on the basis that it tends to distort the results of analysis ("Criticism of Literary Features," 138, 144–45, 156).

[54]See M. Buss, *The Prophetic Word of Hosea* (Berlin: Alfred Töpelmann, 1969) 29–37.

doing what must be done first: the form-critical assessment of the written text itself."[55] This does not mean that one should stop with the analysis of the final form of the text, i.e., treat it purely and only synchronically. The investigation of possible compositional substrata is sometimes appropriate, but the warrants for such investigation must emerge from an assessment of the content and literary features of the text and not from an analysis based on assumptions about the typical length of prophetic speech units.

J. Barton has recently challenged the view that the classical prophets were primarily ecstatics. He sees the prophets as politically astute laymen whose theological expressions and interpretation of history functioned as rhetorical strategies in their struggle to persuade others to certain views and actions:

> If a prophet in the ancient world was essentially someone who reported non-rational experiences and premonitions and appealed simply to his divine authorization, not to the reason of his hearers, then the classical prophets were very far from being 'prophets' in this technical sense.... Far from being visionaries filled with a non-rational foreboding, they were clear-sighted commentators on the society of their day.[56]

Barton's study highlights an area of conflict between form criticism and the study of classical prophetic speech as rhetorical act. Form critics have usually downplayed the role of persuasion in prophetic speech and emphasized that the prophets' role was only to *announce* the divine word. In summarizing form critical conclusions on this matter, G. Tucker comments: "Most of the evidence supports the conclusion...that the prophets functioned primarily to announce the future as the word of God; they were not first of all preachers of repentance."[57]

If the prophets were primarily delivering the messages given to them by the deity, their own role in forming these messages into persuasive speech and the techniques that they used to this

---

[55]Knierim, 145. Similarly, see R. Melugin, "Muilenburg, Form Criticism, and Theological Exegesis," *Encounter with the Text*, ed. M. Buss (Philadelphia: Fortress; Missoula: Scholars, 1979) 93–94.

[56] "History and Rhetoric," 53, 63.

[57]"Prophecy and Prophetic Literature," *The Hebrew Bible and its Modern Interpreters*, 339.

end are of secondary interest. Indeed, too great an emphasis on the prophets' own shaping of the divine word compromises the idea that they were messengers who primarily announced the divine decision.[58] Some form critics, both in theory and in their actual exegesis, apparently favor stripping away the obvious elements of the prophets' own artistry in order to get to the divine word.[59] If, however, the prophets are seen as rhetors with certain views to promote, then messenger speech genres and the prophets' self-portrait as announcers of YHWH's word are analyzed as rhetorical strategies in the prophets' rhetorical arsenal. Primacy is given to the analysis of the prophets' own involvement in persuading others to accept a particular analysis of history, of YHWH's intentions and of what actions are appropriate in the present situation. Viewing the prophets as rhetors need not lead to cynicism about them or their message; it is unlikely that they were motivated primarily out of self interest since their message often led others to oppose or reject them (e.g., Jeremiah). They proclaimed a message to which they were deeply committed, a message that they believed correctly revealed YHWH's intentions and which they thought was in the nation's best interest. Their

---

[58]See the important study by J. Kugel ("Poets and Prophets: An Overview," *Poetry and Prophecy,* 1–25) tracing the development and influence of the equation of poetic and prophetic inspiration. Emphasis on inspiration has frequently led to a de-emphasis on the prophet's own role in shaping the message. In the same volume, see also the essay by A. Cooper, "Imagining Prophecy," 26–27, 42–44.

[59]This concern is inherent in G. Fohrer's description of the development of prophetic oracles through four distinct stages, from the "secret experience" of the prophet in "another sphere" to its initial articulation and exposition to an "intellectual revision" which "produces words spoken by the prophet in his own right, which he forms without any preceding secret experience on the basis of his certainty that he can speak as Yahweh's messenger" and, finally, to a stage of "artistic development" in which the message is adapted to a specific "rhetorical form" and is clothed "in metrical poetry." The delineation of this process serves in part to distinguish the original from elaboration; it is clear that the original is preferred: "This much can generally be said: the less mediation and rational revision a prophetical oracle betrays, the more tersely and unconditionally it proclaims God's will, the more clearly it preserves as its nucleus a primitive complex of sounds..., the closer we are to its origin.... (*Introduction to the Old Testament,* tr. D. Green [Nashville: Abingdon, 1965] 349–50).

claims to have received their message from YHWH are not merely convenient artifices; such claims probably reflect deep convictions. If one is convinced that one's views represent those of the deity, the various means one uses to communicate this conviction need be justified only in terms of their effectiveness.[60]

This view does not eliminate the possibility that prophetic oracles sometimes grew out of revelatory experiences or that the oracles sometimes consisted of short, orally composed units. It does suggest, however, that there is no reason to believe that this was the only, or even the predominant, means by which prophetic speech came into existence. As we have noted above, among the OAN we find long, complex speeches that originated as literary unities. Weis's contention that the מַשָּׂא texts are "prophetic exposition" of previously received divine words points to the importance in these texts of the prophet's own artistry and rhetorical involvement. Moreover, Weis's determination that the מַשָּׂא texts originated as written compositions suggests that attempts to distill oral substrata may be of limited value. Finally, in defense of the notion of long prophetic speech units, Weis notes that "Jer 21:4–24:10 is presented as one long speech of Jeremiah to Zedekiah's messengers. Whether Jeremiah actually delivered such a speech is beside the point for us. For the text to work it needs to

---

[60]See further C. Shaw (*The Speeches of Micah: A Rhetorical-Historical Analysis*, Ph.D. diss., Emory University, 1990 [Ann Arbor: University Microfilms, 1991] 12–14. Shaw argues that the Hebrew prophets functioned in somewhat the same way in society as did the Greek orators. Demosthenes summarizes the role of the orator as follows:

> But for what is he [the orator] responsible? To discern events in their beginnings, to foresee what is coming, and to forewarn others. These things I have done. Again it is his duty to reduce to the smallest possible compass, wherever he finds them, the slowness, the hesitation, the ignorance, the contentiousness, which are the errors inseparably connected with the constitution of all city-states; while on the other hand, he must stimulate men to unity, friendship, and eagerness to perform their duty" (*De Corona*, para. 246).

The prophets and the Greek orators clearly drew from very different tradition histories. In particular, the prophets' dependence on Hebrew moral law sets them apart. Nevertheless, this model is quite close to what Barton has suggested.

be verisimilar, thus for a prophet to deliver a speech of this length could not have been utterly implausible to the book's audience."[61]

The example of Jeremiah raises the question whether the prophets themselves sometimes wrote their message or whether their words were preserved in writing only by their disciples. We are told that Jeremiah dictated his prophecies in some organized fashion to his amanuensis, Baruch (36:2, 32), and we have a clear example of his written prophecy in the letter he sent to the exiles in Babylon (ch. 29).[62] Then, too, there are hints in other prophetic books that this practice was not unique to Jeremiah.[63] E. Davis has recently argued that the prophets often wrote their words. Her main thesis is that Ezekiel composed most of his speeches in writing, but she also contends that this practice did not originate in the exile:

> From the eighth century, writing was a feature of prophecy, not only for transmission and publication at scribal hands (Isa. 8.16; Jer. 36f), but also apparently as a means of illustration and emphasis within the original act of pronouncement (Isa. 8.1; Hab. 2.2; cf. Jer. 17.1).... The difference between Ezekiel and his predecessors with respect to their use of writing is not absolute: earlier prophets wrote or were closely associated with those who did.[64]

In addition to the hints scattered in the Hebrew prophetic texts, she notes evidence that Mesopotamian scribes and messengers frequently relied on written texts rather than oral tradition or

---

[61]Weis, 359–60.

[62]The command reported by Jeremiah in 30:2 makes no reference to Baruch's assistance, but we should probably assume that Jeremiah fulfilled the command to "write in a book all the words which I have spoken to you" with the help of an amanuensis.

[63]Other references to recording the prophetic word in writing include Isa 30:8 and Hab 2:2; in both cases the written text is to function as a validation of the prophetic word at some future time. This validating function derives from the fact that written language has a rhetorical and legal force that oral tradition cannot equal (cf. Jer 17:1). To the extent that prophetic discourse at times attained a quasi-legal status, the probability that it would have been written is increased: writing reifies indictment (see Isa 8:1, 16). On the significance of Ezek 2:9–10, see E. Davis, *Swallowing the Scroll: Textuality and the Dynamics of Discourse in Ezekiel's Prophecy* (Sheffield: Almond, 1989) 47–64.

[64]*Swallowing the Scroll*, 38–39.

memory.[65] To this we may add the recently published evidence from the Mari texts that supports the view that the practice of composing prophetic speeches in writing was not uncommon in the ancient world.[66] Thus, we may safely assume that writing was an available means of composing prophetic speeches, and certainly of preserving them, from as early as the eighth century. Whether a text was composed orally or in writing should be determined on a case by case basis, if the available evidence will support such a determination. In any case, oral composition cannot simply be assumed.

Long, integral written compositions pose something of a problem for form-critical analysis as it has traditionally been conceived, however. Much has been done in OT research to isolate and study texts composed of a clearly defined genre and a relatively specifiable *Sitz im Leben* (e.g., Psalms, legal texts). Few studies, however, have dealt with long compositions in which component genres are combined into a larger rhetorical whole. In such instances the lines of genre as they have traditionally been conceived are often blurred and breached. And just such a phenomenon often appears in prophetic speech, especially in the OAN.[67] Either form criticism must be employed in such a way that it can account for the borrowing, reshaping and combining of

---

[65]Ibid, 42.

[66]See the discussion of ARM 26/2, #414 in A. Malamat, "New Light from Mari (ARM XXVI) on Biblical Prophecy (III–IV)," in D. Garrone and F. Israel, eds., *Storia e tradizioni di Israele. Scritti in onore di J. Alberto Soggin* (Brescia: Paideia, 1991) 186–90. New evidence about the socio-political function of written prophecy is just now becoming available with the publication by S. Parpola of the State Archives of Assyria IX (forthcoming). This was brought to my attention in a paper presented by M. Nissinen ("Prophecy and Power Struggle in the Neo-Assyrian Empire," 1994 annual meeting of the Society of Biblical Literature, Chicago). The Assyrian oracles were committed to writing and saved as a means of legitimating the (contested) kingship of Esarhaddon and Assurbanipal.

[67]The complex mixing and distortion of genres in the OAN possibly indicates that they were composed in writing. E. Davis comments, "As a result of its greater inherent explicitness, and also its more luxurious relation to time (for both creation and assimilation), written language is less firmly bound to the common stock of ideas, stories, familiar phrases and patterns upon which oral speech largely depends for ready intelligibility to an audience and for manageability by a speaker or reciter" (33).

genres that is common in prophetic speech, or another, more appropriate method or combination of methods must be used.[68]

M. Fox has argued for an approach to genre that may be helpful in accounting for such mixing of genres and blurring of boundaries.

> No text has a single "right" genre. Every text is a member of numerous different sets, each one of which constitutes a different genre. A psalm (Ps 89, e.g.) can be a poem and a liturgical song and a hymn and a national lament and a royal psalm and a prayer for deliverance, and more—not because it is a "mixture" of originally "pure" genres, but because it belongs to overlapping and nested sets.[69]

He argues in a footnote to this comment that "Genres are in fact fuzzy sets. In fuzzy-set theory, an element may belong partially to a set, and there may be gradations of membership and blurred boundaries."[70] This complicates the idea of genre considerably and suggests that analysis of a text's genre must find ways adequately to represent the complexity of the text. Knierim deals with another aspect of the same issue, the overlapping of structural features in texts. He suggests that analysis might move ahead by finding a way to combine traditional methodologies:

> The attention to text structures has also opened the way, actually for the first time, for the correlation of the form critical method with the methods of rhetorical criticism and the criticism of literature. If one compares the text structures identifiable through the criteria of rhetoric, of literature, and of genre (form-critically speaking) with one another, the discrepancies in one and the same text are obvious. The acrostic or prosodic structure of a psalm, e.g., is very different from, and in principle independent of, the generic structure of the psalm. Evidently, each of these structures is intrinsic to the textual phenomenon, and it makes no sense for us to carry out a methodological warfare among these different approaches. Instead, a meth-

---

[68]This aspect of prophetic speech and the special challenge it presents to form criticism is discussed by J. Barton, "Form Criticism," 840–41.

[69]*Character and Ideology in the Book of Esther* (Columbia, SC: University of South Carolina, 1991) 142. Fox notes that Gunkel's concept of genre was distorted by his notion that genres originated as pure exemplars which then progressively degenerated.

[70]Ibid., n. 2. See also the arguments for a "morphological approach" in Buss, *Hosea*, 1–5. As is Fox, Buss is concerned to account for aspects of a text that cut across traditional boundaries of classification.

> odology is necessary that enables us to correlate these approaches in such a way that the interrelationship of the rhetorical, literary, and generic structures in the same texts can be determined.[71]

Knierim's chief concern is that method adapt itself to the text as much as possible. The diversity of OT texts raises the question "whether the same method and the same process are commensurate with each of these literary types" and suggests that method must be varied in accordance with the nature of the text under examination. What is needed is an approach to the texts that accords with their reality.[72]

A more complex understanding of genre suggests that we must also find more nuanced ways of thinking of the concept of *Sitz im Leben*. In long prophetic texts the notion of *Sitz im Leben* becomes problematic because frequently such texts are composed of component genres that have been loosened from their original settings and recast according to some new rhetorical purpose. In such cases, the original *Sitz im Leben* of the component genres is of doubtful interpretive value. As B. Long has noted,

---

[71]"Criticism of Literary Features," 144–45; R. Melugin advocates a method that combines form-critical analysis with the sort of rhetorical-critical analysis practiced by Muilenburg. He offers some guiding questions for exegesis: "Which elements are typical and which are unique? Does the particular formulation stay within conventions normally expected for the genre? Or has the author gone so far beyond the conventional options that the genre is no more than background in the formulation of the text? ("Muilenburg," 94).

[72]"Criticism of Literary Features," 134–35, 149, 155. M. Floyd has recently demonstrated the danger inherent in a method that focuses on traditional form-critical categories to the exclusion of a broader rhetorical analysis of the text ("The Chimerical Acrostic of Nahum 2:1–10," *JBL* 113 [1994] 421–37). He shows that the supposed acrostic in Nah 2:1–10 is a chimera, the creation of certain form-critical expectations that have been allowed to suppress and even modify the details of the actual text. The form-critical description that he thinks describes the text—"prophetic interrogation"—designates a combination of a scribal form of expression and a well-known prophetic technique, the "direct address rhetorical question." His study is form-critical in its method, but it has paid sufficiently close attention to rhetorical and literary structures to discern that the text had been forced into an ill-suiting category. His analysis provides a good example of the more flexible use of form-criticism that I am advocating here.

> A distinction ought to be made between original and transferred setting... genres of literature are freely available to a speaker or author. Hence, a literary type, originally at home in one setting, could be used rhetorically in different settings for other purposes... Our conception of *Sitz-im-Leben* must be loosened up considerably."[73]

The degree and manner of influence that the original setting of a genre exercises over the use of the genre in another setting and context are difficult to determine and perhaps not very useful for understanding the meaning of the text into which it is fused. There is a great deal of variety and variability in the way that genres are used in new settings, especially when they are combined with other genres having quite different origins. G. Coats comments: "The author's freedom to employ the genre in new and creative ways must not be overlooked...the task of the interpreter is not to foreclose on the creativity of an artist at any given point, the ability of an artist to use a genre in a new setting or to add elements of content that might conflict with the genre."[74] To return to the subject at hand, it is of less hermeneutical value to know that an OAN originated in the context of warfare or that it owes something to cultic genres and practices (if in fact such is the case) than it is to know the kind of "transferred setting" in which it was actually used and how its various parts functioned together as an act of communication, artistry and persuasion.

In summary, our survey of the work done on the OAN collections and the מַשָּׂא texts, as well as our discussion of the use of form criticism to analyze these texts have indicated that we should allow for the possibility of long, integral and complex prophetic compositions among the OAN collections. This is different from saying that long composition is *preferred* from the beginning, or

---

[73]B. Long, "Recent Field Studies in Oral Literature and the Question of *Sitz im Leben*," *Oral Tradition and Old Testament Studies* (*Semeia* 5; ed. R. Culley; Missoula: Scholars, 1976) 36, 44. This view is now becoming widespread; see Barton, "Form Criticism," 840–41; D. Knight, "The Understanding of 'Sitz im Leben' in Form Criticism," *SBL 1974 Seminar Papers* (Missoula: Scholars, 1974) 1. 105–25; R. Melugin, "Muilenburg," 95–96; Tucker, "Prophecy and Prophetic Literature," 338; Greenwood, "Rhetorical Criticism," 418–19.

[74]On this point see G. Coats, "Genres: Why Should They Be Important for Exegesis?" 10–11.

that the final form is the final stop on the journey of interpretation. It merely means that we must not at the outset assume that the text is composed of originally independent, short oracles later collected and edited into longer units. Moreover, we have argued that the OAN material suggests a strong interest in political questions and that, as a consequence, we should pay particular attention to the political elements and persuasive strategies in the texts.

CHAPTER 3

THE COMPOSITIONAL INTEGRITY OF ISAIAH 15–16

I. Introduction

In the previous chapter we have examined the characteristics of the two categories of texts (OAN and מַשָּׂא) to which Isaiah 15–16 belongs. In this chapter we shall examine in detail the question of the poem's compositional or literary integrity (whether, or to what extent, the poem is the product of multiple acts of redaction or authorship). As we have seen in our survey of the history of interpretation, the mixture of lament, threat and petition in the poem has provided the most influential evidence for dividing the poem into several compositional layers. Our study of the OAN and מַשָּׂא texts, however, suggests that such mixing of sub-genres is typical of this material, even in texts displaying clear signs of literary integrity. Thus the question must be examined again. The investigation of compositional integrity will lead us quite naturally into the question of irony in the poem (which will be covered in the following chapter) since the mixture of lament and threat is a problem only if the lament is intended straightforwardly.

II. Methodological Issues

The first task is to establish the literary integrity or compositeness of Isaiah 15–16. The issue is not whether the poem is "original" or "authentic"; the issue is to what extent the text is the product of a single act of composition by a single author and to what extent it is the product of multiple authors or redactors.

The distinction between the terms *author* and *redactor* is not entirely clear, nor is there very great clarity concerning the kind of literary activity that may be expected of each. At the end of his treatment of the formation of the Pentateuch, Eissfeldt gives an explicit definition for his use of the terms: "there is a distinction, for the most part clearly recognisable, between the author, organically shaping the material, and the redactor working mechanically."[1] This definition implies that the literary integrity of the text is to be determined by the presence or lack of mechanical (i.e., clumsy) additions to and manipulation of the text. Eissfeldt goes on to note, however, that his definition may be valid only for the narrative sources. Indeed, a very different sort of definition seems often to be at work in the application of literary-critical analysis to the prophetic books.

The prevailing view of the composition of the prophetic books has been that they consist of original, short orally composed units that were collected and later redacted into the books that we now have. How much of this process of collecting was the work of the original prophets and how much was the work of later hands is uncertain, but very often the prophet's disciples and later tradents receive the credit for shaping individual texts and the larger collections.[2] In this situation, the distinction between author and redactor is unclear, and it seems more appropriate to call the collectors and shapers of the various collections and of the final book "authors" than it does to use this term to refer to the prophets themselves. Our own view, that the prophets were not limited to short, oral compositions, but were, on occasion at least, responsible for fairly long and complex speeches, only complicates the problem of distinguishing authors and redactors since it attributes a degree of literary sophistication to the prophets similar to that often attributed to later redactors. This makes distinguishing a speech composed by the prophet from one composed by an editor a difficult enterprise.

What constitutes an act of authorship and how is this to be distinguished from redaction? R. Knierim comments:

---

[1]*The Old Testament: An Introduction*, 240.

[2]The previous consensus that the prophets collected "schools" of disciples appears now to have disintegrated. See J. Blenkinsopp, *Prophecy and Canon: A Contribution to the Study of Jewish Origins* (Notre Dame, 1977) 103–106, and A. Cooper, "Imagining Prophecy," 30.

> It can be observed in virtually all the publications past and present that verbs such as collect, compose, compile, combine, connect, assemble, and their respective nouns are used for the description of the activities of authors as well as of secondary redactors. It seems that this is not primarily the result of the fluctuating usage of words. Rather it indicates that...both authors and redactors can use *techniques* of collecting, composing, compiling, combining, and connecting. In other words, these activities as such constitute neither a difference between authors and redactors nor the activities of redactors alone...[3]

As noted in the preceding section, this problem is particularly acute in the case of the OAN. The length, rhetorical complexity and mixing of genres that often characterizes these texts suggests authorship of a type that is inherently difficult to distinguish from redaction. One cannot necessarily deduce from the presence of mixed traditions or genres the presence of a later redactor or redactors. Even when material has been borrowed (i.e., a clearly older tradition is incorporated) one cannot speak with certainty of a redactional addition. One may safely claim to have found a redactional addition only when one discovers a part of the text that is not rhetorically or literarily integral to the whole, i.e., when one finds some part (or parts) that is logically, historically or thematically inconsistent or wholly extraneous in its present context.[4] This is essentially no different from Eissfeldt's criterion

[3]"Criticism of Literary Features," 151; see 150–152 for his longer discussion of this issue, on which I am partly dependent.

[4]There are those who would question even the criterion of mechanical character. E. Greenstein comments, "Source criticism has always rested on Western presuppositions and standards about logical sequence, the unacceptability of logical contradiction, the aesthetic blemish of duplication or repetition, and the ideal of consistency. Studies of orally performed literature in preliterate societies, however, demonstrate that 'repetitions, doublets, false starts, digressions, rough transitions and the like so dear to the heart of biblical critics' tend to pervade oral literature. This means that the source critic's evidence of documentary difference may not represent difference at all. Without the discovery of independent documents attesting to the historical reality of sources, one simply is in no position to decide whether a discrepancy or duplication results from editorial splicing or a compositional sensibility that differs from the modern critic's. The source critic must in any event admit that the redactor found the end-result aesthetically acceptable. What was acceptable to an ancient redactor might also have been acceptable to an ancient author. For these and other reasons source critical conclusions

that one must distinguish between "the author, organically shaping the material, and the redactor working mechanically."[5]

Of course in some places we are confronted with redactional work that has been done quite skillfully and subtly and is not at all "mechanical." Unfortunately, there is no methodology that will allow us to differentiate such work with any degree of certainty. There is no clear way to distinguish between a skillful, theologically and literarily subtle redaction of pre-existing material and an act of authorship. The phenomenon of the "disappearing redactor" discussed by John Barton illustrates this quite well.[6] Barton shows that a redactional analysis that delineates a subtle and artistic redaction can effectively eliminate the original signs of disunity and composite character. They are consumed by the redactor's artistic conception, and the redactor "disappears" in the sense that the need to posit the redactor's existence has been taken away: "While it is undoubtedly sometimes possible to see that a redactor has tried with some success to bring order out of chaos, it is in the nature of the case impossible to identify a *perfect* redactor, since *ex hypotesi* his perfection would consist in having removed all the inconsistencies which enable us to know that he exists at all."[7] What is at stake here is not the validity of either source- or redaction-critical methodology per se, but rather the criteria by which we determine the literary integrity of a text. Signs of composite character must have sufficient force and distinctiveness that they cannot be convincingly explained as a part of a larger artistic scheme.

III. Delimitation of the Text

The broad delimitation of the text is, on the surface at least, a relatively straightforward task in the case of Isaiah 15–16. The

---

must remain indecisive" (*Essays*, 32–33). Greenstein's observations also underline the problem of distinguishing between a redactor and an author.

[5]M. Buss offers a similar principle: "Generally, one may postulate that a tight or rich connection indicates an originally intended continuity. A superficial, mechanical bridge probably reflects a later juxtaposition" (*Hosea*, 29)

[6]*Reading the Old Testament* (Philadelphia: Westminster, 1984) 56–58.

[7]Ibid., 58.

poem has a clear heading, משא מואב, and it is followed by another poem with the same type of heading, משא דמשק. All of the material between these two headings deals in one way or another with Moab and thus comprises a single, well marked thematic unity. Was it also an original compositional unity?

The first and most widely accepted sign of composite character appears in the final two verses of the poem. 16:13, "This [was] the word that the LORD spoke concerning Moab in the past [מאז]," suggests a temporal distance between these words and those that immediately precede them. The temporal distinction is emphasized in 16:14 by the temporal adverb "now" (עתה) which introduces a prediction of Moab's certain decline within three years. This clear differentiation between "then" and "now" has led most scholars to take 16:13–14 as a later addition to the poem.

Hayes and Irvine present an interpretation, however, that integrates 16:13–14 into the preceding material. We have discussed their interpretation in our history of interpretation, but we will summarize it here for convenience. They take 16:12–14 as an argument against aiding the Moabites. Verse 12 refers hypothetically to a situation in which the Moabites have been admitted to Judah and attempt to worship at the temple of YHWH. Such an attempt "would not be allowed [לא יוכל]" since "the word spoken in the past" specifically denied entrance to the Temple to the Moabites (i.e., Deut 23:3: "No Ammonite or Moabite shall enter the assembly of YHWH; even to the tenth generation..."). In favor of this interpretation is the fact that לא יוכל is seldom used in the HB to mean "to be unsuccessful in one's solicitations of the deity." The meaning "not be allowed" (i.e., be prohibited by agreement, custom or law), however, is a frequently attested use of the term.[8]

Hayes and Irvine's interpretation has several problems, however. First, "his sanctuary" (v 12b) refers most naturally to Moab's sanctuary; there is no indication in the context that the temple of YHWH is meant. Secondly, this interpretation leaves the reader uncertain upon which במה Moab is to weary itself. We must either assume that the במה mentioned in v 12 is YHWH's high place

---

[8] Gen 43:32; Deut 12:17; 14:24; 16:5; 17:15; 22:3; Judg 21:18. See further the note on 16:12 in the chapter on text and translation below.

or that the prophet first pictures Moab at its own במה and then switches the scene to YHWH's temple. Neither option seems promising, although the second one is possible. It is simpler and more natural to understand both במה and מקדשו as references to Moab's cultic center(s) (cf. 15:2). Thirdly, Hayes and Irvine must interpret כי as an unusual subjunctive particle, "should." It is more natural to understand it temporally, "when," or concessively, "although."

These difficulties suggest that the commonly accepted understanding of the passage should be affirmed, and along with it the traditional assertion that 16:13–14 were added at a later time.[9] One further observation supports this conclusion. B. Childs has noted that in second Isaiah the term "former" (מאז) is linked to the teachings of chapters 1–39.[10] Likewise, the term "now" (עתה) refers in second Isaiah to the later writer's own time in which YHWH was doing new things.[11] The wording of 16:13–14 suggests that it was added by a later writer who thought in just such terms. Perhaps the motivation for the addition lay in the fact that Isaiah 15–16 seemed not to have reached its full realization in the destruction of Moab, inasmuch as Moab was still thriving at this later date (cf. Ezek 25:9). The addition is an attempt to overcome this "cognitive dissonance" and revitalize the prophecy by announcing that Moab's true decimation lies in the very near future.[12]

---

[9]Other pieces of evidence that have been aduced to prove the disjuncture between the main poem and 16:13–14 include (1) the shift from poetry to prose; (2) the lack of any clear grammatical connection between 16:12 and 13; (3) the mathematical exactitude of the reckoning of Moab's demise suggestive of apocalyptic ideas.

[10]*Introduction to the Old Testament As Scripture* (Philadelphia: Fortress, 1979) 328–30.

[11]See Isa 43:1, 19; 48:6, 7, 16; 49:5, 19.

[12]See M. Fishbane, *Biblical Interpretation in Ancient Israel* (Oxford: Clarendon, 1985) 476, 509. On cognitive dissonance see Blenkinsopp, *A History of Prophecy in Israel*, 46 and sources cited there.

IV. Evidence of Composite Character

The text under investigation in this study, then, is delimited as Isa 15:1–16:12.[13] Three types of evidence have been offered as proof that the poem is a literary composite. The first and most widely mentioned evidence is the poem's combining of incompatible genres. Ewald's initial observations that 15:1–9 and 16:7–12, with its elegiac form, extensive use of paronomasia, and "tender expressions of feelings," stand in stark contrast to both the style and content of 16:1–6 led to further distinctions between the original, sympathetic lament (or laments) and later elements of threat. Thus it is common to find 15:9 and 16:12 designated as later additions of threatening prophecy. In the case of 15:9, the sudden and unexpected introduction of God speaking in the first person substantiates the contention that it was added later. Substantial variety in the analysis of 16:1–6 has resulted from the coupling of its designation as a later addition with its inherent difficulties of interpretation. Since v 6 strongly suggests that the petition was denied, if one includes it with the preceding material the whole petition section takes on a very negative tone . If, on the other hand, v 6 is grouped with the following material, 16:1, 3–5

[13]Although the idea that the text begins in 15:1 is universally accepted, matters are not quite as simple as they seem. It is possible that the immediately preceding verse, 14:32, has more to do with chapters 15–16 than it does with 14:28–31. The מַשָּׂא concerning Philistia does not mention or even hint at the sending or receiving of messengers, as commentators acknowledge, and its relation to what precedes it is unclear. The fact that 14:32 is placed immediately before a text that deals quite explicitly with foreign ambassadors who seek an answer raises the possibility that it might originally have followed the מַשָּׂא heading in 15:1a. If the מַשָּׂא headings were added sometime after the Isaianic OAN were collected together, it is possible that the one in 15:1 was misplaced, thereby creating both an odd ending to the Philistia speech and an abrupt beginning to the Moab speech. Of course chapters 15–16 are not the only instance in which the Isaianic OAN refer to other nations sending envoys in search of aid or alliance; this is also the case in 18:1–2 and is implicit in 19:11–12; 21:11–12 and 21:13–15. Perhaps the note in 14:32 is intended as a thematic question standing over all the subsequent OAN in the book. It highlights the theme of non-alliance with and isolation from other nations: "How should one answer the messengers of nations? That YHWH has established Zion, and in *it* [and no other] shall the needy of *his* people [and no other] find refuge" (translation mine).

(leaving aside v 2 for the moment) takes on the air of an eschatological promise of salvation. In either case, the style and content of 16:1, 3–5 (6) differ from those of the laments that surround it. Its genre is seldom specified precisely by scholars; it contains a summons to send tribute, a petition consisting of terse imperatives in rapid succession, something that sounds similar to the proclamation of the just rule of a king typical of an enthronement Psalm, and (if one includes v 6) a reflection on the pride of Moab. Many interpreters see the passage as a generic farrago resulting from the combination of two later additions.[14] It is generically distinct from the lament that surrounds it, or, to put it another way, it forms an interruption of the once continuous lament now found in 15:1–8, 16:7–11.

Alongside the evidence of generic incompatibility may be included the presence of ideas characteristic of a time later than the hypothesized original poem. Only once does such material present itself in the text. In 16:5 we read, "then a throne shall be established in steadfast love in the tent of David, and on it shall sit in faithfulness a ruler who seeks justice and is swift to do what is right." As we have seen, a number of scholars see in this verse ideas that they consider to be later than those expressed in the original lament (e.g., Marti, Fohrer, Kaiser, Wildberger).

A second kind of evidence was added to the discussion by Gray, who noted that "whereas almost the whole of 15:1–7a, 16:6–11 is quoted, or has left its trace, in Jer 48, no trace of the long intervening section is to be found there." Similary, he noted that 16:12 does not appear in Jeremiah 48.[15] This observation corroborated the emerging consensus that 16:1–5 and 12 had been added secondarily because their absence in Jeremiah 48 suggested that the later compositor used some form of the poem that lacked these verses.

The apparent geographical confusion in the poem contributed the third kind of evidence. A number of problems have been cited:

---

[14]Fohrer (191–92) maintains that 16:1, 3–4a is a *Kriegslied* interpreted in the light of eschatological theology by the addition of 4b–5, an interpretation followed also by Kaiser and Wildberger.

[15]Gray, *Isaiah*, 271. Gray's arguments were repeated and affirmed by others including Auvray, Rudolph and Wildberger.

(1) 15:1–8 depict mourning in the north over the destruction of Ar and Kir, cities south of the Arnon, and a subsequent flight southward. It is somewhat unclear in 15:2–4 if the territory north of the Arnon has been attacked or is only the scene of mourning, but most scholars conclude that the north was largely unaffected. Thus the sudden shift of geographical perspective to Dimon (=Dibon) on the northern plateau in 15:9 from a southward flight toward Zoar in 15:5–8, as well as the indication that some disaster has now taken place in the north ("the waters of Dimon are full of blood") suggests that 15:9 was added later, perhaps at a time when Dibon had come under attack. In the same way, 15:1–8 may be distinguished from 16:6–11; the first lament envisions destruction of only the southern cities of Ar and Kir, but the second lament primarily concerns a devastation of the territory north of the Arnon. Thus some scholars assume that two separate incidents lie behind the two laments.

(2) In 16:2 the Moabites are depicted at the "fords of the Arnon," but 16:1 and 3–5 indicate that the situation is an appeal for help made to the Judean king at "the mount of daughter Zion." A gathering of Moabites at the Arnon fits better either in the context of the description of the flight in 15:5–8 or in the context of Dibon's troubles depicted in 15:9. For this reason most commentators move 16:2 to a position immediately after 15:9.

(3) Wildberger argues for dividing 16:6–11 into two sources. He notes that while 16:6–7 mention Kir Hareseth, Moab's capital city south of the Arnon, 16:8–11 focus mainly on cities north of the Arnon.[16] He also notes a difference in tone: condemnation of Moab in vv 6–7 and extreme sympathy in vv 8–11.

---

[16]Wildberger (601–602) regards the mention of Kir Hares in 16:11 as a redactional device designed to bind the addition in vv 8–11 to the material in vv 6–7 which was already present in the text. Marti (139) argued in a similar manner that 16:11 is a variant of 16:7.

The first sort of evidence is in many ways the foundation of the argument for composite character, and we will look at it first. The argument that 16:1–6 is an "intrusion" into an original lament is based to a certain extent on the preference for pure genre in original composition and reveals a disinterest in what logical or rhetorical connection might exist between the two kinds of material. As argued above, this is not an adequate criterion for detecting a literary composite. But something more is at stake in this division of the poem on the basis of genre. There is no denying that a tension in the "tone" inhabits the poem. At times we find sympathy for Moab either implied by the lament genre itself or expressed explicitly in extreme language (16:9, 11), and at other times we find statements implicitly and overtly critical of Moab's past behavior (16:1, 6), threats and negative predictions (15:9, 16:12), and unfavorable depictions of the Moabites (16:2). This is precisely the type of logical conflict that does qualify as good evidence of a composite. The tone of the poem and its attitude toward Moab is not, however, a simple matter. Several aspects of the poem suggest that an ironic intention may be at work and that, far from a lament with expressions of deep sympathy, we are dealing with a bitter, sarcastic taunt. If this is the case, there is in the poem no conflict in tone that would suggest its composite character. The conflict is only apparent and the poem is in fact uniformly negative in its attitude toward Moab. The evidence for and against an ironic reading of the poem will be examined below.

Also in this category of evidence, but far less significant for determining the overall integrity of the text, is 16:5 with its references to the rule of a just king. It is clear that these ideas are not *necessarily* late, even if they do suggest an eschatological (though certainly not apocalyptic) concept. Procksch has noted that such ideas can be found in material generally regarded as coming from Isaiah himself (Isa 9:6–7). Isa 16:5 is certainly not dependent on 9:6–7, but the comparision does suggest that messianic hope in a general sense is not a late idea. As Gottwald has pointed out, the verse has some affinities with enthronement hymns (e.g., Ps 72). It goes beyond the available evidence, however, to claim as he does that the verse is "a quotation from an enthronement hymn."[17] Nothing about the content of the verse points conclusively to a time later than the rest of the poem. We shall treat the logical and rhetorical relationship between 16:5 and its immediate context in chapter six.[18]

The second kind of evidence of composite character derives from a synoptic comparison of Isaiah 15–16 and Jeremiah 48. The exact relationship of these two texts cannot be determined with absolute certainty. The studies of Gesenius, Auvray, Schottroff and Wildberger, however, have been successful in showing that it is highly improbable that the Isaiah poem is a condensed version of the poem in Jeremiah and that it is at least unlikely that the Isaiah and Jeremiah poems were drawn from a common source. The most likely hypothesis is that the composer of the Jeremiah poem borrowed freely of material from a variety of sources, including Isaiah 15–16.[19] Most agree that the composer of Jeremiah 48 used the Isaiah poem selectively and reworked rather freely what material he did borrow.

In light of this the question arises, Why was the material in 16:1–5 and 12 omitted? Several scholars have noted that one cannot legitimately argue that material missing in Jeremiah 48 must have been missing in whatever version of Isaiah 15–16 the later composer had before him, since the later composer omitted material found in sections of the poem thought to be original as

---

[17]Gottwald, *All the Kingdoms*, 175.

[18]Similarly, see the arguments of Rudolf, "Jesaja xv–xvi," 140.

[19]Wildberger comments: "Ähnlich wie Jer 51f. ist auch Jer 48 ein Konglomerat von literarischen Reminiszenzen und steht keineswegs bloß mit den beiden Jesajakapiteln in Beziehung....Der Verfasser is ein Kompilator, der ohne Hemmungen andere alttestamentliche Schriften als Steinbruch benutzte" (*Jesaja*, 605). The most obvious sources behind Jeremiah 48, other than Isaiah 15–16, are Num 21:28–29; 24:17; Isa 24:17–18b; 25:10; Jer 11:23b; 23:12b; 49:6, 36 (see the chart in Wildberger, 607–609). The comparison of Isaiah 15–16 and Jeremiah 48 offers a useful illustration of what we have said above about the use of the terms redactor and redaction to designate a "mechanical" combining of sources in which no coherent plan may be discerned. Jeremiah 48, in the estimation of most scholars, is a clear example of redaction betrayed by its clumsiness and by the mechanical way it has been assembled.

well as the material in 16:1–5.[20] One must distinguish, however, between omission of small pieces scattered here and there and the complete omission of a large section. For instance, it is less significant that 16:12 has been omitted in Jeremiah than it is that 16:1–5 is missing.

A more serious criticism of this evidence lies in the fact that hints of Isa 16:1–2 do in fact appear in Jeremiah 48:28.[21] The evidence for this is summarized in the following chart:

Isaiah 16:1–2	Jeremiah 48:28
שלחו־כר משל־ארץ	עזבו ערים
מסלע מדברה אל־הר בת־ציון	ושכנו בסלע ישבי מואב
והיה כעוף־נודד קן משלח	והיו כיונה תקנן
תהיינה בנות מואב מעברת לארנון	בעברי פי־פחת

Obviously, a sea change has been worked upon the Isaiah poem by the later compositor; nevertheless, the verbal and structural echoes are quite remarkable: (1) In Jer 48:29–36 we find the longest sustained example of material borrowed directly (with some alterations) from the Isaiah poem, material taken from Isaiah 16:6–11. Thus the position of 48:28 in the structure of the Jeremiah poem is the same as the position of 16:1–2 in the structure of the Isaiah poem, if we allow for the fact that Jeremiah 48 has omitted the material in Isa 16:3–5. (2) Syntactic, semantic elements are parallel both in the sense that the same word, grammatical form or idea is used and in the sense that these similarities occur in the same order. Both passages begin with an imperative. Semantic parallels include בסלע and מסלע, תקנו and קן, והיו כיונה and והיה כעוף, בעברי פי־פחת and מעברת לארנון. No one of these parallels would weigh very heavily as evidence of borrowing, nor would a few verbal similarities count for much if they were scattered in a random pattern. The accumulation, however, of structural and syntactic and semantic parallels makes it highly improbable that these similarities are merely coincidental. The compositor of Jeremiah

[20]So König, 192–93; Kaiser, 60.

[21]This has been pointed out by König, 190, n. 7.

48 must have had at least Isa 16:1–2 in his or her *Vorlage*.[22] Gray's argument, which has been repeated often, must be rejected.

One might still argue that 16:3–5 are not duplicated in Jeremiah 48, and that, therefore, these verses represent a later addition. This argument is not nearly so strong as when this claim could be made for the entire petition section, however. The omission of the actual petition (Isa 16:3–4) and the very difficult to interpret words concerning the establishment of a throne in faithfulness and justice (16:5) is readily explained. A later compositor who understood these verses as an inducement to offer aid to the fleeing Moabites might have deleted them because such an attitude seemed unthinkable (cf. Jer 48:26–27, 39, 42). Alternatively, if the verses were interpreted as a plea by the Moabites that is implicitly rejected in the poem, they might have been deleted as inapplicable in the current situation, or, perhaps, as inappropriate since during the time of Gedeliah's administration, Judeans reportedly sought refuge in Moab (Jer 40:11). In either case, the omission may be explained further by the tendency, evident throughout the poem, freely to delete material from the sources when it does not suit the compositor's purposes. Moreover, the argument that the poem was originally a pure lament and the argument that 16:1–5 has no parallel in Jeremiah 48 no longer coincide and mutually strengthen one another. The later compositor clearly did not have an earlier form of Isaiah 15–16 that consisted only of lament. Thus the argument that 16:3–5 was a later addition receives little support from the idea of an originally pure lament. Something further emerges from this analysis: the fact that Jer 48:28 indicates that Isa 16:2 followed Isa 16:1 in the later compositor's *Vorlage* substantially weakens the case of those who argue that 16:2 has been misplaced or added at a later time.

A similar argument may be made for the presence of Isa 16:12 in the *Vorlage* of the compositor of Jeremiah 48. Once again it is the structural pattern that transforms an otherwise banal corre-

[22]I use *Vorlage* here and below only as a convenience. The way the later compositor has used Isaiah 15–16 suggests a process somewhat looser than the duplication of a written scroll lying beside the writer. Perhaps he or she had memorized the poem in Isaiah 15–16 and thus had it in a form that could easily be molded and transformed.

spondence into a probable instance of borrowing. As noted, Jer 48:28–36 parallels Isa 16:1–2, 6–11. Some changes have been made: 16:6 has been expanded considerably (48:29–30); minor verbal changes have been made to the material in Isa 16:7–10 (48:31–33); material from Isa 15:4–6 has been inserted after the material borrowed from 16:10, apparently to expand on the theme of shouting and agricultural desolation (48:34). Isa 16:11 is paralleled by Jer 48:36 (to which material from Isa 15:7 has been added). This leaves only Jer 48:35 unaccounted for. Is this the compositor's own work? Or is it too borrowed from another source as is all the rest of this section of the poem? Jer 48:35 reads, "And I will bring to an end in Moab, says the LORD, those who offer sacrifice at a high place and make offerings to their gods." Let this be compared with Isa 16:12, the only verse in Isa 16:6–12 that the compositor appears not to have borrowed, "When Moab presents himself, when he wearies himself upon the high place, when he comes to his sanctuary to pray, he will not prevail." Both Jer 48:35 and Isa 16:12 refer to Moab's worship at its high place; both texts are threats against Moab. The order of 16:11 and 12 has been reversed in Jer 48:35–36, but this is not surprising given the compositor's free rearrangement of material elsewhere in Jeremiah 48—the order of Isa 16:8 and 9 is similarly reversed in Jer 48:32. The differences in the actual language of the two verses in question are quite obvious, of course, and we should have no reason to suspect that any borrowing took place if it were not for the structural parallel between the two passages and the fact that everything *except* 16:12 had been borrowed. But these facts suggest quite strongly that the similarity in content between Jer 48:35 and Isa 16:12 is not coincidental but the result of the fact that the later compositor had Isa 16:12 in the *Vorlage*.[23] We must conclude, therefore, that while elements of threat such as Isa 16:12 may have been added to an originally pure lament, the synoptic comparision of Isaiah 15–16 and Jeremiah 48 in no way supports the idea that such elements represent additions. Both Isaiah 16:2 and 16:12

---

[23]So too W. Rudolph, *Jeremia* (*HAT*; Tübingen: J. C. B. Mohr, 1968^{3}) 281; W. Schottroff, "Horonaim, Nimrim, Luhith und der Westrand des 'Landes Ataroth,'" *ZDPV* 82 (1966) 184.

were apparently in whatever form of Isaiah 15–16 that the later compositor used. Among the threatening elements in Isaiah 15–16, only 15:9 seems clearly to have been omitted by the later compositor.

What remains to be evaluated is the third kind of evidence offered to prove that the poem is a composite, the presence of geographical inconsistencies. The presumption that inconsistencies are present is based on three ideas: (1) that Kir is shorthand for Kir Hareseth and that this city is to be identified with modern Kerak which lies about eighteen miles south of the Arnon; (2) that Kir and Ar (also on the southern plateau) were the focus of the attack and destruction described in the poem; and (3) that 16:2 depicts the Moabites at the Arnon. The assumption that Kir and Kir Hareseth are the same place is problematic; there is no evidence to support the identification and some reason to doubt it.[24] In fact, it is not even clear that Kir (קִיר) is a place name. Both ער and קיר in Isa 15:1 may be taken either as common nouns or as place names; the context and syntax of the verse give us no help. More importantly, as has recently been shown, there are no grounds for identifying Kir Hareseth with modern Kerak; all the evidence available suggests that Kir Hareseth lies somewhere north of the Arnon.[25] Once it is recognized that Kir Hareseth was located north of the Arnon, all serious geographical inconsistencies disappear. The idea that there is a disruption in 16:2 likewise is based on mistaken evidence, in this case a doubtful translation. The NRSV renders 16:2, "Like fluttering birds, like scattered nestlings, so are the daughters of Moab at the fords of the Arnon." The final phrase of the verse, מעברת לארנון, is difficult to translate, but a more likely translation is "beyond the Arnon."[26] Having

[24]When two-element place names are abbreviated, the practice is always to retain the second element, not the first. We will give the evidence for this in a later chapter.

[25]See the present author's study, "In Search of Kir Hareseth: A Case Study in Site Identification," *JSOT* 52 (1991) 3–24. See also K. Smelik, *Converting the Past: Studies in Ancient Israelite and Moabite Historiography* (Leiden: Brill, 1992) 85–89, who independently came to the same conclusions as the present writer.

[26]So Gray, 290. See also my arguments below in the chapter on text and translation.

crossed the Arnon on their southward flight, the Moabites now dither about like frightened birds. Instead of presenting a geographical problem for the integrity of the text, this verse actually links its immediate context to what has preceded by reminding the reader of the situation described in 15:5–8, i.e., that the Moabites have fled south out of their heartland.

To summarize, the argument that the poem displays geographical inconsistencies was based primarily on a mistaken site identification. The observation that a major section of the Isaiah poem (16:1–5) is missing from Jeremiah 48 is inaccurate and misleading. Similarly, the assertion that the threatening elements found in Isaiah 16:2, 12 are shown to be late additions by their absence in Jeremiah 48 is doubtful. The only remaining evidence is the genre and content of the poem. The mixture of lament and whatever we are to call 16:1–6 is without parallel in the HB, though this fact alone is not determinative of composite character. More significant is the fact that the poem intermingles lament genres with threats, or, in terms of content, that it contains conflicting attitudes toward Moab. We shall address this issue below. First, however, it is necessary to examine the arguments for the integrity of the poem.

V. Evidence of Integrity

We may begin with the obvious fact that the poem has been preserved for us as a unity. There is at least some force in the simple fact that the whole poem appears under a single heading and thus comprised a sensible unit of prophetic speech to some ancient audience. In somewhat the same category is the fact of the poem's most basic thematic unity, the fact that it deals throughout with Moab. More than that, it deals with Moab in a state of distress and weakness. The consistency of this theme is accentuated by the occurrence of Moabite place names with great frequency and in even dispersion throughout the first and third major sections of the poem. This aspect of the poem is so remarkable that we must assume either that these two sections are an original, integral unity or that one of them (probably the second) was modeled in conscious imitation of the other.

Most arguments in the history of scholarship for the literary integrity of the poem have consisted of a defense of its rhetorical or logical consistency. Cheyne, König, Rudolph, Eichrodt and Hayes/Irvine have all argued for the unity of the poem on such grounds.[27] Their interpretations of the logical flow of the poem differ little from those proposed by Lowth, Eichhorn and Gesenius, scholars who pre-dated the division of the poem into historically distinct sources. All agree that the poem consists of a description of Moab's distress, a petition for help, a denial of this petition and a concluding lament as a response to this denial. Rudolph makes two observations that add further strength to the argument for the poem's unity: (1) 16:1 presents the Moabites sending envoys from Edomite territory and thus assumes information given in the preceding section. (2) 16:6 provides the answer to the petition in 16:3–5, but it also provides the grounds for the renewal of lamentation in 16:7–11, thus linking these to major sections.

The analysis of the poem presented in R. Weis's dissertation on the genre מַשָּׂא is a more narrowly focused, technical approach to the question of literary integrity. Weis argues that Isa 15:1–16:11 contains several repeated patterns and that these patterns demonstrate its unity. His analysis differs substantially from that of other scholars who have argued for the unity of the poem, which suggests that the supposedly repeated patterns he has pointed out are not easily perceived by a reader. Someone hearing the text read probably would have been even less able to perceive this structural repetition since its recognition depends to a great extent on having the written text immediately available.

J. Culler has pointed out a danger inherent in arguments based on the observation of patterns of repetition and symmetry:

> ...if one wishes to discover a pattern of symmetry in a text, one can always produce some class whose members will be appropriately arranged. If one wants to show, for example, that the first and last stanzas of a poem are related by similar distribution of some lin-

[27]Rudolph and Eichrodt exclude only 15:9; 16:2, 12 from the original poem.

> guistic item, one can always define a category such that its members will be symmetrically distributed between the two stanzas.[28]

This fact does not in itself invalidate evidence derived from symmetrical patterns; some texts have clear and widely recognized patterns of symmetry. The crucial question one must ask in such analysis is how *distinctive* and *perceptible* is a pattern or repetition. One cannot put the repetition of very common elements (e.g., conjunctions) on the same level as the repetition of highly distinctive vocabulary. Perceptibility is the key issue.[29]

Weis's arguments for the literary integrity of the text fail for at least this reason; if we are to judge from the history of interpretation, the patterns he has noticed are quite indistinct. Moreover, Weis has not taken into sufficient account the actual ideational content of the poem. To give but one example, he understands 16:6–11 in its entirety as a judgment speech of YHWH.[30] In this case we must imagine that the expressions of grief and sympathy in 16:9, 11 are expressed by YHWH rather than by the prophet. The idea that YHWH should express deep sorrow for an enemy of Judah and should employ terms so markedly anthropomorphic is difficult to accept. No analogy for this kind of expression of grief by YHWH is to be found in the HB.

The principal argument for the literary integrity of the poem is, then, the logical flow of ideas. This is both a positive argument for integrity and, of necessity, a negation of the strongest argument for composite character, that based on genre and content. The critical question is, Does Isaiah 15–16 make sense in the form we now have it, or does it display sufficient logical inconsistencies to warrant our hypothesizing an original composition to which additions were later made? It appears that, except at one point, there are insufficient grounds for claiming that it is a literary composite. The one aspect of the text that may suggest its com-

---

[28]*Structuralist Poetics* (Ithaca, NY: Cornell Univ., 1975) 57–58.

[29]A. Berlin offers a set of four guidelines for assessing "perceptibility and interestingness" (*The Dynamics of Biblical Parallelism* [Bloomington: Indiana University Press, 1985] 10, 130–35): (1) proximity of the components of the parallelism; (2) similarity of surface structure; (3) number of linguistic equivalences; (4) expectation of parallelism.

[30]Weis, 124–26.

posite character is the apparent conflict in its attitude toward Moab. For this reason, the determination of the literary integrity of the text depends partly on whether the expressions of sympathy for Moab were intended ironically or straightforwardly. Before we move on to that discussion, we shall look briefly at the question of author and date.

VI. Date and Author

The various proposals for date and author were summarized in our history of interpretation. Most scholars profess agnosticism on the question of authorship and offer only tentative guesses as to date.[31] The present study will offer no new proposal on these difficult issues. First, the evidence available to decide these questions—especially that of authorship—is not of a kind that yields a high degree of certainty. Secondly, the demonstration of our thesis does not rest in any way on the answers to these questions. Nevertheless, we shall define some boundaries within which we believe the answer must lie.

Regarding the date, the evidence provided by the poem's style and vocabulary is open to various interpretations. For example, Albright argued at one point that the style and vocabulary of the poem pointed to the mid-seventh century. Later, he retracted this suggestion and argued that Isaiah 15–16 was adapted from a "ninth-century prototype."[32] Style has led many scholars to agree with Albright's later position, and one often finds references to the poem's "archaic features." Poetic language may be intentionally archaicized, however, and for this reason late features of style are generally more reliable evidence than putative early features.[33] Perhaps all that should be said on the basis of style and vocabulary is that the poem shows no clear signs of having been composed late in Judah's history.[34]

---

[31]Wildberger's position is typical, see 603–605.

[32]W. Albright, *Yahweh and the Gods of Canaan* (London: University of London, Athlone, 1968) 21, n. 57.

[33]On the widespread tendency to archaicization in Hebrew poetry, see D. Robertson, *Linguistic Evidence in Dating Early Hebrew Poetry* (SBLDS 3; Missoula: Scholars, 1972) 135–147.

[34]The language of 16:5 is not necessarily late, as we have argued above.

More definite evidence comes from references to historical circumstances. The poem indicates that the disaster occurred during a time when Moab was relatively strong and prosperous, controlling territory as far north as Heshbon.[35] Moab apparently was enjoying a time of prosperity during which it could accumulate a "surplus" (Isa 15:7) and be accused of arrogance over its power and reputation (16:6, 8). Clearly, it is not subservient to Israel at the time of the attack; it seems to be experiencing a period of relative autonomy.

The fact that the appeal by Moab is made to Judah (16:1) suggests that Judah was strong enough at the time to offer help. If the event occurred when the state of Israel was still intact, however, one wonders why the appeal was not made to Israel; Israel appears to have dominated Judah, at times reducing Judah to the status of a client state, during most of the period Judah and Israel existed alongside one another.[36] Perhaps Israel no longer existed as a state when the poem was composed. Here, however, our evidence becomes thin. We may state only that the historical indications point away from periods in which Israel dominated Moab (the reigns of David, and probably Solomon; the reign of the Omrides until the later part of Ahab's tenure; probably some or all of the reign of Jeroboam II) and in which Judah would have been in no position to offer help or receive gifts of tribute (especially the exilic and post-exilic periods). One thinks of the eighth or seventh century, possibly after 722 B.C.E. The (uncertain) date at which Jeremiah 48 was composed forms the *terminus ad quem*.[37]

The limits set by date neither rule out the possibility that Isaiah of Jerusalem wrote the poem nor offer any substantial

---

[35]By the time Jeremiah 48 was composed, Moab no longer controlled Heshbon (Jer 48:2; cf. Isa 15:4; 16:9).

[36]See J. M. Miller and J. Hayes, *A History of Ancient Israel and Judah* (Philadelphia: Westminster, 1986) 233–34, 279, 307–11.

[37]The attack is made by an unidentified foe: "The destroyer," "the violent one," "the trampler" (16:4), "the lords of the nations" (16:8). Why no specific nation is named is not clear, although the designation "lords of the nations" was probably chosen for the sake of a double entendre (see below) and not to obscure the true identity of the attacker. In any case, we can derive no evidence for date from the identity of the attacker.

support for his authorship. The arguments that have been offered for and against Isaianic authorship are based primarily on considerations of style, diction and theological content. Some have claimed that these elements point decisively away from Isaiah, and others have claimed with equal conviction that the poem is pure Isaiah. These opposite interpretations result from the nature of the evidence as well as the analytical procedures used. First, it is questionable whether our sample of "genuine Isaiah" is a sufficiently broad specimen of either Isaiah's style or his thought to serve as a satisfactory standard of comparison. Secondly, the possible breadth of a single author's style and diction is not known with any certainty; nor is it clear that a prophet's theological and ideological positions remain stable throughout his or her life.[38] Uncertainties over how a particular author's style might have changed over time or in new rhetorical settings or under different generic constraints offer significant impediments to the determination of authorship by means of style. Attempts to answer the question of authorship through a statistical analysis of style have not successfully overcome these limitations and have produced doubtful results.[39] Nothing in the style, diction or theological content of the poem may yet be said either to prove or to disprove Isaianic authorship.

Regarding authorship, therefore, only the following observations can be made with confidence. First, the poem is grouped with other prophetic texts and bears sufficient similarities to such texts that we should probably assume that it was written by a

---

[38]See my article, "Isaiah 8.11 and Isaiah's Vision of Yahweh," *History and Interpretation: Essays in Honour of John H. Hayes*, ed. M. P. Graham, W. Brown and J. Kuan (JSOTS 173; Sheffield: JSOT, 1993) 145–59.

[39]S. Erlandsson's study of Isaianic style and authorship (*The Burden of Babylon: A Study of Isaiah 13:2–14:23* [ConBOT ser. 4; Lund: CWK Gleerup, 1970]) does not use a strictly statistical methodology, but it amasses a large amount of stylistic evidence to prove Isaianic authorship. More recently, J. Brangenburg has attempted to prove by statistical methods the Isaianic authorship of most of the material in Isaiah 13–23 ("Reexamination," 270–324). Erlandsson's arguments based on stylistic analysis have not found acceptance (see, e.g., G. Tucker's review, *JBL* 90 [1971] 486–88; R. Clements, *Isaiah*, 131). For an analysis and critique of statistical studies of style generally, see A. Dean Forbes, "Statistical Research on the Bible," *ABD* 6. 185–206; and D. Greenwood, "Rhetorical Criticism," 425–26.

prophet. Second, the fact that the poem appears to be designed to influence official disposition toward Moab suggests that the author had access to and influence at the court. Third, since the author apparently addressed the speech to the Judean court, he or she probably was a Judean. The fact that the text is designated a מַשָּׂא also indicates that the author was a Judean prophet, as do the assumptions and language of 16:5.[40]

Finally, it has often been argued that the "appendix" in 16:13–14 was written by Isaiah in order to adapt for his own use an older prophecy concerning Moab (some or most of 15:1b–16:12). The reuse of Mic 4:1–4 in Isa 2:2–5 is often cited as evidence that prophetical readaptation of earlier materials was a usual practice. We must also consider, however, the hypothesis that the appendix was added to the poem sometime after it was composed, perhaps after the speech had become part of the Isaianic OAN collection. The second possibility seems the more probable for several reasons. First, we have no evidence that Isaiah or any other prophet borrowed a complete speech from another prophet and adapted it for his own use. As Wildberger states, "Nie hat ein Prophet der vorexilischen Zeit Worte eines früheren Propheten zitiert und einfach für seine Zwecke uminterpretiert."[41] Second, the example of Isa 2:2–5 is not apropos. In Isa 2:2–5 a distinctive tradition, probably one which was well known, is quoted in the context of a larger speech unit. Isa 15:1b–16:12 has a quite different character, however. It is a situation-specific speech, and has nothing of the character of a distinctive tradition suitable for quoting. Moreover, Isa 15:1b–16:12 is not a quotation contained in a larger speech or rhetorical unit, as is Isa 2:2–5, but constitutes almost the entire speech unit. The idea that Isaiah himself borrowed the speech is especially problematic, since it is hard to imagine why Isaiah would have updated an older speech by some other prophet rather than composing his own speech germane to the occasion.

It would be very helpful for our investigation of the possibility of an ironic intention if we could know precisely who wrote the

[40]On מַשָּׂא as a peculiarly Judean mode of prophetic speech, see Wilson, 249; Weis, 344. On 16:5 see Petersen, 54, n. 66.

[41]Wildberger, 604.

poem. The evidence, however, will not support a specific attribution. We must proceed, therefore, with only an approximate idea of the date and authorship of the poem.

CHAPTER 4

THE QUESTION OF IRONIC INTENTION

I. Introduction

As the history of interpretation demonstrates, Isaiah 15–16 has been read ironically in whole or in part by several interpreters, but never have the grounds for such a reading been examined in detail. Our task in this chapter is briefly to establish a theoretical framework and a method for determining the presence of ironic intention in a text, and then to apply this method to Isaiah 15–16. First we must define what we mean by "irony" and related terms.

II. A Definition of and Method for Detecting Irony

The OED gives two definitions for irony: (1) "A figure of speech in which the intended meaning is the opposite of that expressed by the words used; usually taking the form of sarcasm or ridicule in which laudatory expressions are used to imply condemnation or contempt"; (2) "A condition of affairs or events of a character opposite to what was, or might naturally be, expected; a contradictory outcome of events as if in mockery of the promise and fitness of things."[1] These two definitions denote two distinct types

---

[1]*The Compact Edition of the Oxford English Dictionary*, vol. 1 (Oxford: University Press, 1971) 1484. Extended theoretical treatments of irony abound. I have found useful the following works: W. Booth, *A Rhetoric of Irony* (Chicago: University of Chicago, 1961); E. Good, *Irony in the Old Testament* (Sheffield: Almond, 1981[2]; Philadelphia: Westminster, 1965[1]) second ed. cited here, 13–38; G. O'Day, "Irony and the Johannine Theology of Revelation: An Investigation of John 4" (Ph.D. diss., Emory University) 1983, 63–103; P. Duke, *Irony in the Fourth Gospel* (Atlanta: John Knox, 1985) 13–23. Duke's discussion is particularly helpful. As is Duke, I am interested in "stable

of irony for which we shall use the terms (1) verbal irony and (2) situational irony.[2] The first definition implies that irony may be used as the heading of a general category under which we may list various kinds of ironic expression and technique such as satire, sarcasm, parody, understatement, and hyperbole. Satire often refers to the literary genre of an entire work ("the play was a satire on American politics"), and it fits least comfortably under the heading irony.[3] We shall use the term satire in the limited sense corresponding to the OED entry 2b: "The employment, in speaking or writing, of sarcasm, irony, ridicule, etc. in exposing, denouncing, deriding, or ridiculing vice, folly, indecorum, abuses, or evils of any kind."[4] Parody is ridicule through skewed imitation. Sarcasm is a heavy-handed form of verbal irony designed to ridicule an idea, person, custom or practice: "a bitter jibe or taunt" (OED).[5] Incongruity is a common element in all forms of irony.

The presence of verbal irony in a text is not easily proven. Indeed, it may often seem to some a "safer" choice to take a writer's words literally, as straightforward statements, than to risk the "overreading" or "reading between the lines" that is necessary to an ironic interpretation. As Gail O'Day notes, however, "signals of irony are often difficult to detect, because the essence of irony is to be indirect. A straightforward ironic statement would be a

---

irony," a term coined by Wayne Booth to indicate irony that is covert yet intended by the author, finite, and signalled in some way by the relation between the context (the situation be it historical, dramatic or narratival) and the text (Booth, 5–14).

[2]Similarly see Duke, 21–27. Duke also mentions "dramatic irony," an irony occurring when the reader/audience has knowledge that a character in a story lacks and can see that the character acts foolishly, ridiculously or tragically.

[3]Good notes that not all satire is ironic; an ironic satire is a specific kind of satire (28–30).

[4]Vol. 2, p. 2642. The flexibility of categories can be seen in the fact that here irony is listed as a kind of satire.

[5]M. H. Abrams lists sarcasm as a type of irony but limits its meaning to "the crude and taunting use of apparent praise for dispraise" (*A Glossary of Literary Terms*, fifth ed. [New York: Holt, Rinehart and Winston, 1988] 93). I employ the term somewhat more broadly to refer also to the use of expressions of feigned sympathy for gloating or scorn.

contradiction in terms."[6] In a similar vein E. M. Good asks: "Is not a source of irony's attraction and repellence alike that it may plausibly be taken literally, invites us to take it literally, makes a certain sense when taken literally?"[7] Irony is a subtle art that works by indirection. Thus, once the possibility of irony has been raised (by at least a few readers), a straightforward reading is not "safer" simply because it refuses to overread. The possibility of ironic intention in a text must be confronted directly; on the basis of the evidence available a reader must decide whether irony is present. Since it is in the very nature of irony to proceed covertly, the reader must risk reading between the lines if he or she is to avoid misreading.

But how does a reader become suspicious in the first place? Or, to ask the question from another perspective, How do authors signal their audience that they are speaking ironically? And, since ironic messages can be and often are mixed with straightforward ones, we must ask, How are we to distinguish between ironic and straightforward content within the very same text? We need some set of criteria by which we may evaluate the possibility of irony.

D. C. Muecke provides a helpful discussion of the markers of irony in a text.[8] He states that irony is marked by the presence of "some form of perceptible contradiction, disparity, incongruity or anomaly."[9] The contradiction, etc. may be set up between (1) text

---

[6]O'Day, 92.

[7]22. See also his comments on 151.

[8]D. C. Muecke, "Irony Marker," *Poetics* 7 (1978) 363–75. Booth offers a similar categorization of clues to irony: (1) Straightforward warnings in the author's own voice; (2) Known error proclaimed (something "simply incredible"); (3) Conflicts of facts within the work; (4) Clashes of style; (5) Conflicts of belief (49–76). In Isaiah 15–16, evidence of irony is limited to Booth's fourth and fifth categories. I have found Booth's book stimulating and very helpful, but Muecke's categories have proved more applicable for the present study.

[9]Muecke, 365. Quintilian's oft cited criteria for discovering irony are similar. He notes that irony "is made evident to the understanding either by the delivery, the character of the speaker or the nature of the subject. For if any of these three is out of keeping with the words, it at once becomes clear that the intention of the speaker is other than what he actually says" (*Institutio oratoria* 8.6.54; quoted in W. Booth, 49).

and context, (2) text and co-text, or (3) text and text. We shall take up these three kinds of contradiction in order.[10]

A text's *context* is the socio-cultural setting in which it was written, that body of knowledge, prejudices, values, assumptions and traditions (including literary) shared by the author and his or her audience. Ironic contradiction is usually limited to one shared value, assumption or piece of knowledge, and different ironic texts focus on different aspects of context as the means of signaling irony. One of the chief difficulties for detecting irony in ancient texts is our lack of knowledge of the ancient socio-cultural and political context. We must always guard against detecting irony on the basis of assumptions and values derived from our own socio-cultural *milieu*. The necessary hypothetical reconstruction of the ancient context adds an element of uncertainty to the decision whether the text is ironic or not. Ironic texts may exist for which we have insufficient knowledge of the context to enable us to detect the irony at work. Many times, however, we do have sufficient knowledge of the ancient context to catch an author's hints that he or she is speaking ironically. Fortunately, values and attitudes are not infinitely variable across cultures and time, and much is known or can be assumed with a fair degree of certainty. Care must be taken, however, to distinguish what is known, what can safely be assumed and what is only probable.

What we know about the author or speaker is also part of the context. Knowledge of the author's values and prejudices is very important in the determination of irony. When an author or speaker is known to think or feel a certain way and makes statements that flatly contradict this attitude (even if his or her audi-

---

[10]In the introduction to their recent collection of essays on humor and the comic in the HB, A. Brenner and Y. Radday deal with the problem of distinguishing the reader's response from the author's intent. They offer the following means of discernment: "(a) the degree to which the reader has thorough command of the writer's language in reading, writing and speaking; (b) the immediate and, later, wider context of the passage in question; (c) the overall tenor and purpose of the entire book interpreted" (*On Humour and the Comic in the Hebrew Bible* [JSOTS 92; Sheffield: Almond, 1990] 27). These "means" correspond primarily to Muecke's co-textual and intra-textual categories, and as such are best suited to narrative. When dealing with public discourse, the social and historical contexts provide crucial clues.

ence does not fully share this attitude), we must be alert for possible irony. In his discussion of the clues to the presence of irony in a text, Wayne Booth comments,

> Any one of the clues I turn to now can be stated in the form of an inference about an implied author's intentions: "If the author did not intend irony, it would be odd, or outlandish, or inept, or stupid of him to do things in this way." Every clue thus depends for its validity on norms (generally unspoken) which the reader embraces and which he infers, rightly or wrongly, that his author intends.[11]

Booth does not limit inferences to the "implied author" only; he unapologetically appeals to the actual author's intentions as a requisite for determining irony:

> For some critical purposes it thus makes sense to talk only of the *work's* intentions, not the author's. But dealing with irony shows us the sense in which our court of final appeal is still a conception of the author: when we are pushed about any 'obvious interpretation' we finally want to be able to say, 'It is inconceivable that the author could have put these words together in this order without having intended this precise ironic stroke.'[12]

Booth notes that discussion of irony in texts requires reference to the author's intentions.[13] Thus, the detection of irony in a text depends to a great extent on a reconstruction of the author's probable attitudes and values. Such reconstruction is unavoidable, even if it is fraught with uncertainties.

Futhermore, knowledge of an author's literary/rhetorical tendencies can provide helpful clues for the detection of irony. An author or speaker known to use irony is less likely to have his or her ironic comments misunderstood than is a speaker known to be straightforward. Moreover, the more we know of an author's typical literary modes, style and temperament, the better the

---

[11]Booth, 52–53.

[12]Ibid., 10–12.

[13]See Booth, 4, 19, 52–53, 80–82, 91, 120–23. Booth is aware that his work is susceptible to criticism that it indulges in the so-called "intentional fallacy." He argues, however, that the dangers involved have been overdrawn. He notes: "there is by now an enormous literature showing that we simply cannot get along without using inferences about intention, try as we will" (126, n. 13; cf. 11, 56).

position we are in to make judgments about the probability of irony in a particular text written by the author.[14]

Unfortunately, it is not possible to determine who wrote Isa 15–16 and as a result, we can know nothing about the attitudes or literary tendencies of the author of our text, that is, apart from the poem itself. Nevertheless, the poem is part of the Isaianic corpus, and it is possible to speak of the attitudes and tendencies of the corpus. In this way we can bracket out the question of actual authorship, although we cannot ignore the fact that our arguments will be much weaker than if we could speak of the author directly. At the very least, those who hold that Isaiah authored chapters 15–16 will find persuasive an argument from the tendency of the corpus.

Another, and to my mind more persuasive, angle of attack is to examine the tendency of texts similar to the one under investigation and the tendency of prophetic discourse generally. Here we throw the net more widely to include what we know of the rhetorical techniques of the Hebrew prophets and what we know of similar texts, particularly the OAN and מַשָּׂא texts, and texts that either consist of or contain the genre lament. Some kinds of speech and writing lend themselves to irony better than others. Legal codes are, by and large, straightforward texts; we will probably suffer society's correction if we take the Ten Commandments or government tax forms ironically. Narratives and political discourse, on the other hand, often contain irony. Thus we must determine whether irony is used by the prophets and whether it is typically present in texts similar to Isaiah 15–16. This will give us grounds for deciding whether Isaiah 15–16 is the kind of text in which irony is typically, or even sometimes, present.

Finally we may throw the net as widely as possible and ask about the values and opinions displayed in the Hebrew Bible as a whole. If an attitude or value can be shown to be widespread and long-lived in a society, it is probable that an unknown author

---

[14]The fact that a writer is known to use irony cannot, of course, function as first order evidence that a *particular* text is intended ironically. It would, however, offer supporting evidence if other indications were present. The detection of irony necessarily depends on an accumulation of clues and weak probabilities, no one of which may be said to present decisive evidence.

from that society shared it. For this reason, values and attitudes that are well-attested and consistent throughout the HB corpus, especially those that are represented in sources of varying historical provenance, may be assumed to have been shared by our unknown author. The attitude toward Moab expressed in the HB is, then, crucial evidence for deciding whether the expressions of sympathy for Moab in Isaiah 15–16 are genuine or ironic.

In summary, if we are to argue successfully that Isaiah 15–16 is ironic, it will be important to show that the Hebrew prophets used irony (of the specific kind supposed to exist in Isaiah 15–16), that irony is present elsewhere in Isaiah, that irony occurs in the OAN and מַשָּׂא texts, and that the lament form is elsewhere used ironically. It will also be important to demonstrate that a conflict exists between the apparent opinions and values expressed in the poem and those we construe to have been typical of the Judeans around the time the poem originated. Specifically, we will need to determine as well as we can what attitude toward Moab and the Moabites was generally held by the people.

Contradictions between a text and its *co-text* are those created by the author within the wider literary context. If the author is unsure that his or her audience will understand the irony from context alone, he or she can build a context around the ironic element that will signal the ironic intention. In the case of Isaiah 15–16, we have no wider literary context of material by the same author. Uncertainties about authorship leave us with essentially an isolated poem. As was the case with contextual clues, we may argue from the co-text of the Isaianic corpus in its final form and from the co-text of the HB. To some extent this represents a synchronic determination of irony, or, to put it another way, it locates the ironic intention at the level(s) of redaction. Such final form arguments are not without value for historical understanding. The attitudes and values of the later collectors and editors are interesting in themselves, and they are at least occasionally continuous with the attitudes and values of the original author. In our effort to determine whether Isaiah 15–16 was *originally* intended ironically, however, we must treat all co-textual evidence of irony tentatively.

Finally, contradictions between a *text and text* are "those which indicate a disparity within different levels of the particular text itself."[15] We shall call these intratextual contradictions. These include certain uses of paronomasia, abrupt change of style or tone, syntactic and semantic ambiguity, understatement and overstatement, parody, paradox, repetition, and metaphor.[16] For example, it has frequently been observed that a certain degree of irony is present in the statement, "For the waters of Dimon are full of blood [דם]" (Isa 15:9). Irony at the level of the intratext often consists of isolated *bon mots* strewn here and there, but their presence sometimes signals a larger ironic intention.

No one indicator suffices to prove the presence of irony. A probable argument for ironic intention is necessarily based on an accumulation of clues. In our study of Isaiah 15–16, it will be most convenient to leave the analysis of intra-textual indicators until the chapter in which we offer a reading of the poem. In what follows we shall limit our investigation to the clues provided by contradictions at the level of context and co-text. This investigation will be divided into two parts. First, we shall look at the question of literary tendency in texts similar to Isaiah 15–16. We shall examine to what extent irony is used in prophetic literature, in the OAN and in Isaiah. Most importantly, we wish to know if there exist other texts in which lament (or closely related genres) is employed ironically. Fortunately, some of the investigative work has been done already, and we need only summarize the findings of the pertinent studies and look at a few of the leading examples of prophetic irony. We shall also examine those texts in which apparently genuine sympathy is expressed for foreign nations, since such texts offer evidence against an ironic reading of Isaiah 15–16. Secondly, we shall reconstruct the ancient context insofar as it pertains to the question we are investigating. We need

---

[15]O'Day, 96.

[16]O'Day, 96. See Muecke, 368–73 for a more detailed analysis of this third category. Also included here are clues available only in real life encounter—a wink, an elbow in the ribs, a raised or nasal voice tone or other affectation of speech style, pauses, etc.—as well as those clues found in modern typography: changes of character size or shape, scare quotes, various marks of punctuation, unusual text alignment.

not survey a wide range of attitudes and values to accomplish our purpose. Only one attitude is of much importance to us: the attitude toward Moab and the Moabites in the HB and in Isaiah. The questions we must ask are, How were the Israelites, and, more specifically, Isaiah and his audience, disposed toward the Moabites? How are the Moabites generally treated in the literature? What is the tenor of the traditions, images and themes attached to this close neighbor of Israel? This investigation will allow us to decide whether the sympathy expressed for the Moabites in the poem should be accepted at face value or interpreted ironically.

III. Irony and Satire in Prophetic Literature

No thorough study of irony in prophetic literature yet exists.[17] Currently, the best treatment of the topic available is found in E. Good's book, *Irony in the Old Testament*. Good devotes a long chapter to prophetic irony.[18] Significantly for our investigation, he chooses Isaiah as the prophetic book most suitable for illustrating irony. He finds irony of various kinds in a great many places in the book, both within that material generally considered to be

---

[17]We could begin our investigation by asking to what extent irony is used in the HB. But the usefulness of such a query is very limited for the present argument. On irony in the HB generally see E. Good, *Irony in the Old Testament*; L. Klein, *The Triumph of Irony in the Book of Judges* (JSOTS 68; Sheffield: Almond, 1988); Y. Radday and A. Brenner, eds. *On Humour and the Comic in the Hebrew Bible*; as well as other sources cited below.

[18]Good, chapter 5, 115–167. This is by far the longest chapter in Good's study. Passages often cited as examples of irony in Isaiah include Isa 1:2–3; 2:6–22; 5:1–6, 18–19; 7:7–9; 8:6–8; 9:7–9 [8–10]; 10:5–15; 22:1–2, 5; 23:7–8, 15–16; 28:1–4, 7–13; 30:15–17; 34:13–17; 37:22–29 [=2 Kgs 19:21–28; cited by Eissfeldt, *Introduction*, 94, as attributable to Isaiah at least in its original form]. Several of these texts offer examples of verbal irony; 28:7–13 has been called "bitterly ironic" (A. Brenner, "On the Semantic Field of Humour, Laughter and the Comic in the Old Testament," *On Humour and the Comic*, 56). J. G. Williams ("Irony and Lament: Clues to Prophetic Consciousness," *Semeia* 8 [1977] 51–74) examines prophetic irony in Isaianic laments introduced by "alas-utterances." On the ironic tone in Isa 29:9–14, see C. Exum, "Of Broken Pots, Fluttering Birds and Visions in the Night: Extended Simile and Poetic Technique in Isaiah," *CBQ* 43 (1981) 347–50. For further examples see Stinespring, "Irony and Satire," *IDB*, 2. 727–28.

genuine and within the material thought to have been added by later hands. His examples do not all illustrate irony with equal clarity, and occasionally one wishes to object that he has forced irony upon a particular text. On the whole, however, he successfully demonstrates that Isaiah (both the prophet and the book) frequently uses irony. Below, we shall examine a few pertinent examples of ironic expression in Isaiah. First, however, we must narrow and define our topic more precisely.

We are not interested in a broad range of ironic expression. It is more to the point in the present case to ask if examples of irony in prophetic literature can be found that are similar in some way to the kind of irony supposed to be present in Isaiah 15–16. Thus we must define that kind of irony. Precisely what kind of irony does Isaiah 15–16 exhibit? For the sake of convenience, we shall accept for the moment the ironic interpretation offered by Luther, Calvin, and Hayes and Irvine. Accepting this interpretation as our model, we note that the irony of the poem consists chiefly in the inverting of the intention of the lament genre. On the surface the poem seems to lament the troubles suffered by the Moabites; its true intention, however, is to mock the suffering of the Moabites. Several times the author utters expressions of seemingly profound sympathy for the plight of the Moabites. These expressions are, however, intended as biting sarcasm, gloating mockery over the well-deserved suffering of an enemy. As a whole, the most appropriate designation for the poem would be *satiric lament*. The poem is a satiric attack on Moab that employs irony to whet its blade.

To what extent does prophetic literature employ satire, and especially *ironic* satire? W. Booth notes, "...irony is used in some satire, not in all; some irony is satiric, much is not. And the same distinctions hold for sarcasm."[19] The introduction of the category of satire into our investigation is a logical necessity; although not all irony is satiric, if Isaiah 15–16 is ironic, it is also satiric. Examples of ironic satire will provide the closest analogy to our poem and hence the best evidence that such rhetorical strategies were used by the prophets.

---

[19]Booth, 30.

Scholars have often commented (mostly in passing) on the fact that the prophets employ satire with great effect.[20] Two studies have recently been published that address this topic in detail: D. Fishelov, "The Prophet as Satirist"; and T. Jemielity, *Satire and the Hebrew Prophets*.[21] Both authors argue that satire is a regular feature of prophetic literature. Jemielity, for instance, notes,

> Often indistinguishable from the prophetic message itself, satire serves as a major weapon in the arsenal of the Hebrew prophets, whose careers and writings strongly buttress the Psalmist's confidence: "He that dwelleth in heaven shall laugh them to scorn; the LORD shall hold them in derision" (Ps 2:4).[22]

This evaluation is echoed by R. P. Carroll who finds "caustic wit and sardonic expression...throughout the prophetic collections."[23] Of Isaiah he says, "There is a strong sense of the ridiculous in many of the sayings in Isaiah.... Satire and kaleidoscopic irony remain the dominant thrusts of the book...[24] Carroll goes on to note that such techniques are particularly prominent in the OAN collections found in each of the major prophets and singles out Isa 14:4–21 as an especially noteworthy example. Jemielity's examples of satiric technique are numerous and include Isa 1:2–3; 3:16–25; 14:4–21; Jer 2:20–24; 3:1–2, 9; 4:30; 5:7–8; 10:3–5; 13:26–27; Ezek 7; 16; Joel 1:5; Amos 4:4–5; 6:1, 4–7; 8:5–7; and Hab 2:18–19.[25] He

---

[20]Especially noteworthy treatments include J. Chotzner, *Hebrew Humour and Other Essays* (London: Luzac, 1905); idem, *Hebrew Satire* (London: K. Paul, Trench, Trubner, 1911); C. Randall, "Satire in the Bible" (Ph.D. diss., Hebrew Union College, 1969); H. Wolff, *Amos the Prophet* (Philadelphia: Fortress, 1973) 6–54.

[21]D. Fishelov, "The Prophet as Satirist," *Prooftexts* 9 (1989) 195–211. T. Jemielity, *Satire and the Hebrew Prophets* (Louisville, KY: Westminster/John Knox, 1992). Jemielity's study is by far the most extensive. See also R. Alter, *The Art of Biblical Poetry* (New York: Basic Books, 1985) 137–62. Alter lists three principal modes of prophetic poetry: "(1) direct accusation; (2) satire; (3) the monitory evocation of impending disaster" (141).

[22]Jemielity, 85.

[23]"Is Humour Among the Prophets?" *On Humour and the Comic in the Hebrew Bible* , 177.

[24]Ibid., 182–183.

[25]These represent only part of Jemielity's examples, most of which are found in his chapter 3.

argues that the book of Hosea as a whole is an ironic satire.[26] Fishelov's article examines satirical techniques in Isa 3:16–4:6; 14:4–23; 47:7–11; Jer 3:6–18; Ezek 23; 27; 28; 29:3–5; and Amos 4:1–5.[27] To these examples we should add Nah 2:8–12 and 3:1–19 as well as the book of Jonah, which is often regarded as both ironic and satiric.[28] Thus we are presented with satire in nearly every prophetic book, and in many texts it is the dominant mode of address.

Jemielity's study deserves close attention, both because it is the most thorough study of the topic to date and because it makes several points that have a direct relevance for our study. He takes as his thesis that Hebrew prophecy shares a number of features with the genre *satura* employed by Roman writers in the first century B.C.E. and that *satire* is an appropriate designation for much of prophetic literature. He is careful to avoid anachronistic argument:

> I do not claim that satire and prophecy are always interchangeable or formally equivalent terms. However, I do claim that Hebrew prophecy often displays the nature, qualities, techniques, themes and patterns of satire, but, more to the point, I do not argue that the satire of Hebrew prophecy is a conscious literary device. In the present state of biblical knowledge, no one can assert that those responsible for preserving, amplifying, and passing down the prophetic text deliberately wrote satire. Nor is such an affirmation essential to any argument. If, as I believe, literary qualities and patterns can appear unconsciously, then the critical impulse and prompting as central to prophecy as to satire can, not surprisingly,

---

[26]See 110–116. His interpretation depends heavily on the recent *Anchor Bible* commentary on Hosea by Andersen and Freedman.

[27]198–209. Ezek 32:2–16 should be mentioned as well. On Ezekiel's satire of the downfall of Tyre, see C. Newsom, "A Maker of Metaphors: Ezekiel's Oracles Against Tyre," *Interpreting the Prophets* (ed. J. Mays and P. Achtemeier; Philadelphia: Fortress, 1987) 188–199, esp. 192–94. For other examples of satire, especially that found in the OAN, see J. Smith, "Destruction of Foreign Nations," 169–70.

[28]See Good, 39–55; D. Rauber, "Jonah—The Prophet as Shlemiel," *BToday* 49 (1970) 29–37; J. Holbert, "Deliverance Belongs to Yahweh: Satire in the Book of Jonah," *JSOT* 21 (1981) 59–81; J. Ackerman, "Satire and Symbolism in the Song of Jonah," *Traditions in Transformation: Turning Points in Biblical Faith* (ed. B. Halpern and J. Levenson; Winona Lake: Indiana University, 1981) 213–46.

> anticipate the deliberate artistic fashioning of ridiculing judgment called satire (24–25).

The similarity that Jemielity sees is a product of the similar social function of prophet and later satirist, and the generic similarities are the natural outgrowth of a similar rhetorical goal: "to praise and to blame" (15).[29]

Jemielity constructs his argument primarily on three points of comparison. First, he notes the pervasive use of shame in both prophetic literature and satire. Both "function in a society where ridicule looms large as a humiliation to be avoided or as an especially satisfying form of punishment for one's enemies." In this respect, prophecy "shares with satire a very rhetorical character" (15). Shame itself functions in both prophecy and satire as a punishment, and both the prophet and the satirist assume, therefore, "a judicial authority" in their rhetorical condemnations of their people (23–24).

Secondly, he shows that both satire and prophecy borrow, mix and ironically invert genres.

> Critical analyses of satire and prophecy recurrently point to the mixture of speech forms as a major feature of both, a fertile field for the appearance of all sorts of forms, each a form of forms using and subverting the shape of language familiar from other discourse and from other walks of life (58; see 58–61).[30]

Jemielity does not address the question to what extent the mixing of genres in prophetic texts is the result of redactional activity, and his point is weakened by this omission. His observation does, however, caution us against hasty assumptions of redactional activity in prophetic texts that appear to involve satire. An as-

---

[29]An interesting correspondence exists between one of the original *Sitze im Leben* proposed for the OAN and the origin of satire as proposed by R. Elliott in his *The Power of Satire: Magic, Ritual, Art* (Princeton University, 1960) 66–78. Elliott argues that satire evolved out of curse in much the same way that the OAN are thought to have evolved, in part, out of prophetic curse against enemy nations in time of war.

[30]On the mixing of forms in satire, see L. Guilhamet, *Satire and the Transformation of Genre* (University of Pennsylvania, 1987): "Satire is by its nature a borrower of forms.... this appropriation of other forms is unique to satire and is one of its chief identifying characteristics." (13, 16; cf. 165).

sessment of possible rhetorical strategies in texts that mix genres with apparent caprice is a necessary first step in analysis. When we consider that a number of examples of satire are found among the OAN texts and that these very texts typically exhibit genre mixing, the force and relevance of Jemeility's point becomes clear.

Thirdly, Jemielity focuses on one particular device common to both prophecy and satire: the use of sexual and excremental imagery.

> As one of satire's devices, invective requires literary talent to be successful, a talent specifically described by Frye as including "a sense of rhythm, an unlimited vocabulary and a technical knowledge of the two subjects which ordinarily form the subject matter of swearing, one of which is theology." The other, I assume, is anatomy or physiology, at least sexual and excremental. At any rate, the appearance of even this one satiric device in prophecy demonstrates how prophecy and satire comprise a common rhetorical market across whose borders the individual critic can easily and profitably pass. Whenever the prophet joins humor to his attack, whenever he ridicules as well as criticizes, the prophet dons the satirist's mantle.
>
> . . . .
>
> Nowhere do satire and prophecy prove more outrageously shocking and more outrageously funny than in their use of the ordinarily tabooed subjects of sex and excretion (87, 98; see also 98–107).[31]

The instances of prophecy that employs such imagery to ridicule behavior and opinion are many. Leading examples of the use of sexual imagery include Isa 1:21; 3:16; Jer 3:1–2, 9; 4:30; 5:7–8; 13:26–27; Ezekiel 16; and much of Hosea ("scatalogical, sexual, and irreverent punning and insult pervades the book of Hosea" [115, cf. 110]). The use of excremental imagery is less frequent; examples include Isa 25:10–11; 28:8[32]; Hos 5:11[33]; and, if we may include prophetic legenda, 1 Kgs 18:27. Both kinds of imagery are designed to shock and offend as well as to arouse shame in the

---

[31]On the use of such imagery in satire, see N. Frye, "The Mythos of Winter: Irony and Satire," *Anatomy of Criticism: Four Essays* (New York: Atheneum, 1968) 234–36.

[32]On the excremental nature of the imagery in 28:8, see B. Halpern, "The Excremental Vision: The Doomed Priests of Doom in Isaiah 28," *HAR* 10 (1986) 109–21, esp. 114–16.

[33]See Jemielity, 115.

victim. The shame that is usually attached to illicit sexual conduct and inappropriate toilet manners is metaphorically transferred to whichever practice of the victim the satirist or prophet aims to condemn. This strategy is not without its dangers; satirist and prophet alike have often aroused in their victims more anger than shame. Indeed, it is doubtful that the satirist intends to reform his or her victim. As is the case with the OAN texts, the true audience of satire is not the subject of the attack but some part of the wider society which the satirist wishes to join him in condemning the subject's folly.

On the whole, Jemielity does an excellent job of maintaining his thesis. The prophets frequently assumed the satirist's voice. Thus, we may safely assume that the satiric mode was available to the author of Isaiah 15–16 and that such an attitude would not have been unusual or unexpected.

Are there other examples of ironic satire in prophetic literature? One frequently used technique in the OAN material is the "sarcastic imperative," a device found most often in prophetic satire of the foreign nations.[34] By means of expressions such as Flee! Turn Aside! Hide! Go down and mourn! Sit in the dust! the prophets highlight the pointlessness of resisting the coming judgment. For example, in Nah 3:14–15 sarcastic imperatives are part of a call to defense that is clearly intended ironically:

> Draw water for the siege,
>   strengthen your forts;
> trample the clay,
>   tread the mortar,
>   take hold of the brick mold!
> There the fire will devour you,
>   the sword will cut you off.
>   It will devour you like the locust.

In the same vein, we find in Jeremiah exhortations to Egypt:

> Prepare buckler and shield,
>   and advance for battle!

---

[34] I take this term from Smith, "Destruction of Foreign Nations," 122–128. This technique is also discussed in Fishelov, "The Prophet as Satirist," 200–201.

Harness the horses;
mount the steeds!
Take your stations with your helmets,
whet your lances,
put on your coats of mail!

. . . .

Advance, O horses,
and dash madly, O chariots!
Let the warriors go forth

. . . .

Go up to Gilead, and take balm,
O virgin daughter Egypt!
In vain you have used many medicines;
there is no healing for you.

. . . .

Pack your bags for exile,
sheltered daughter of Egypt!
For Memphis shall become a waste,
a ruin, without inhabitant.
(46:3–4, 9a, 11, 19)[35]

Such imperatives not only ironically underline the inevitability of defeat and the pointlessness of resistance, they also are a part of the intention to satirize the subject. Jer 46:17 makes this abundantly clear: "Give Pharaoh, king of Egypt, the name 'Braggart who missed his chance.'" There is often a "gloating" quality in passages using sarcastic imperatives; the speaker's *real* audience (his or her own group) is invited to join with the speaker in mocking the fate of another nation. Such satire also offers implicit comfort and, at times, direction to the in group. This is clearly the case in Isa 8:9–10:

Band together, you peoples, and be dismayed;
listen, all you far countries;
gird yourselves and be dismayed;
gird yourselves and be dismayed!
Take counsel together, but it shall be brought to naught;
speak a word, but it will not stand,
for God is with us.

[35]Other examples include Jer 48:6, 9, 28; 49:8, 30; Joel 1:5; Nah 2:2; 3:14.

Israel and Judah are, like the nations, sometimes the subject of sarcastic imperatives. For example, the mixture of irony and satire is apparent in Amos 4:4–5:

> Come to Bethel—and transgress;
> to Gilgal—and multiply transgression;
> bring your sacrifices every morning,
> your tithes every three days;
> Bring a thank-offering of leavened bread,
> and proclaim freewill offerings, publish them;
> for so you love to do, O people of Israel!

Similar examples include Isa 6:9, "Keep listening, but do not comprehend; keep looking, but do not understand;"[36] and Isa 29:9, "Stupefy yourselves and be in a stupor, blind yourselves and be blind! Be drunk, but not from wine; stagger, but not from strong drink!" While it is not entirely clear that the subject of these attacks and the intended audience are the same, it is clear that the prophets did not expect that anyone would take the exhortations straightforwardly. The intention is obviously ironic, and the mode is pointedly satiric.

The sarcastic imperative shows that the prophets employed *ironic* satire. But we are after something even more specific. We

---

[36]The irony involved in the following verse, 6:10, is more complicated. The prophet is the subject of the imperative. He is given an ironic task. Instead of turning the people away from the impending disaster, he is commanded to encourage them down the path of destruction. Various theological ruminations on this perplexing text may be found in the commentaries. Jemielity suggests that this ironic result of the prophet's message is one shared by the satirist: "The new society will come only at the cost of painful self-awareness. But little in the prophetic or satiric text provides the comfort or expectation of precisely such a conversion. Indeed, if the two are measured against the historical circumstances which seem tied to their origin, prophecy and satire are discourses about great moral failure. Prophets and satirists repeatedly complain about their ineffectiveness" (68; see also 66–71). Indeed, it would seem that both prophecy and satire actually harden the resolve of those they reprimand and arouse in them an attitude of defensiveness (the Ninevites' repentance at Jonah's preaching is probably the exception that proves the point; we are supposed to be surprised when the Ninevites don sackloth). On the irony involved in Isa 6:9–10, see also Good (136–37) who argues that "The command is the counterpart of the ironic quotation in ch. 5:19, where the people sarcastically express their eagerness to see and hear."

should like to know if they ironically inverted the lament genre in order to satirize their victims.

To begin with, Jeremiah 48 presents a clear and unmistakable satiric attack on Moab and yet retains the elements of lament found in Isaiah 15–16. It begins as a lament (vv 1–6), and has fragments of lament spread throughout (vv 17–20, 31–33a, 34, 36–39). But this lament is ironically inverted by interruptions that call attention to Moab's former ease (v 11–12), its pride (vv 14, 29–30, 42), its gloating over Israel's troubles (v 27). The theme "How the mighty have fallen" is sung over Moab's crushed corpse: "Mourn over him, all you his neighbors, and all who know his name; say, 'How the mighty scepter is broken, the glorious staff'" (v 17; cf. vv 2a, 7, 18, 26). In the context, the irony oozes thickly around the edges of the genre's usual intention. The ironic quality of the lamentation in vv 31–32 is equally unmistakable, preceded as it is by the excoriating condemnation in vv 26–30:

> Make him drunk, because he magnified himself against the LORD; let Moab wallow in his vomit; he too shall become a laughingstock. Israel was a laughingstock for you, though he was not caught among thieves; but whenever you spoke of him you shook your head!
>
> . . . .
>
> We have heard of the pride of Moab—
> he is very proud—
> of his loftiness, his pride, and his arrogance,
> and the haughtiness of his heart.
> I myself know his insolence, says the LORD;
> his boasts are false,
> his deeds are false.
> Therefore I wail for Moab;
> I cry out for all Moab;
> for the people of Kir-heres I mourn...

The compositor of the Jeremiah poem used the same structure as is found in the comparable section of Isaiah 15–16, but he or she strengthened the criticism of Moab and inserted a pointed reminder of Moab's hateful taunting of Israel. The ironic inversion of the lamentation is now obvious. The later compositor who borrowed so much from Isaiah 15–16 either saw an ironic intention at work in the poem or, at the very least, thought it well suited as a vehicle for his or her own ironic and satiric intention.

O. Eissfeldt offers a helpful treatment of ironic and satiric lamentation in his discussion of "mocking sayings" and the "mocking songs."[37] The mocking saying, according to Eissfeldt, is referred to as a משל in the HB and is connected with popular proverbs that also go by this name. To be a "proverb" among the people usually indicates that one is the object of mockery (Deut 28:37; Ps 69:12). The mocking song, also called a משל (e.g., Isa 14:4; Mic 2:4; Hab 2:6), often served as a powerful political weapon, in a manner similar to modern newspaper propaganda.[38] Eventually the mocking song was replaced by the prophetic threats against the foreign nations. Such threats are to be found "in considerable quantity in the books of Isaiah, Jeremiah, Ezekiel and Zechariah, and other books such as Obadiah, Nahum and Habakkuk are entirely made up of them" (93).

> Just like the mocking songs at an earlier stage, so now these prophetic threats against foreign nations were an instrument of foreign policy, and when we consider that in both cases the word itself is thought to have dwelling within it a power which shapes reality, the difference between the two is, at least in this respect, not very great, quite apart from the fact that these threats against foreign nations very frequently contain motives from the mocking song (Isa. xxxvii, 22–29; xlvii). (93)

In addition to the two examples mentioned in the quotation, Eissfeldt lists Num 21:27–30;[39] Judg 5:15–17, 28–30; Isa 23:15–16; and 44:12–20. A further development of the genre, according to Eissfeldt, is the "'prophetic' mocking song," a song "composed with reference to an event which still lies in the future, and which is represented as if it had already occurred" (94). Eissfeldt cites Isa 37:22–29 [=2 Kgs 19:21–28] as the leading example of this form.

---

[37]*Introduction*, 66, 92–94.

[38]Eissfeldt notes that the power of the mocking song as conceived among the inhabitants of ancient Arabia reached beyond its rhetorical force into the realm of magic (*Introduction*, 66, 92 and sources cited there). For further discussion of this important topic see below.

[39]Introduced by "therefore say the משלים" indicating that there existed a defined role for those who created and performed mocking songs. The fact that the compositor of the ironic lament in Jeremiah 48 quotes the mocking song from Numbers 21 suggests that the intention of the song was compatible with his or her own.

Eissfeldt also notes an ironic use of the genre "funeral dirge:"[40]

> In the prophets there is to be found another type of usage of this prophetic *qinah*, and this is by far the more common, namely where it is used in a mocking sense. It is noteworthy that this mocking dirge is almost invariably directed against an external non-Israelite entity—a people, a city or a king. What the prophet feels at their downfall is not sympathy and distress, but the opposite, the bitterest scorn and the most joyful satisfaction (96).

As principal examples of this ironic use of the funeral dirge, he cites Isa 14:4–21; Ezek 19:1–14; 27:2–10, 25b–36; 28:12–19; and 32:2–16. Ezekiel's ironic inversion of the lament genre in the speeches on the foreign nations is widely acknowledged.[41]

The most striking example of this ironic use of the funeral dirge is Isa 14:4–21. Eissfledt calls this poem "the most powerful prophetic dirge which we possess in the Old Testament." This dirge is full of "bitter irony. This ironical use of a motif of mourning produces a tremendous heightening of the bitterness of the poem's mockery..." (97, 320). Kaiser describes the genre of 14:4–21 as a "taunt in the form of a lament." As evidence that it was intended ironically he notes: "A people will lament at the death of its heroes, but hardly for the end of an oppressor and the affliction he has caused."[42] The dominant theme of the poem is the contrast between Babylon's former pride and glory and its present abasement. An unmistakable tone of gloating permeates the poem:

---

[40]See also Christensen, *Transformations*, 139–40. He tentatively groups Isaiah 15–16 in this genre category: "Nonetheless, it should be noted that Isaiah 15–16 is without parallel within the formal collections of OAN material in Amos, Isaiah and Jeremiah. The closest comparison would be that of the OAFR [oracles against foreign rulers] material, the mocking dirges directed against foreign rulers who will be felled by the axe of the Divine Warrior because of their insolence in challenging the suzerainty of Yahweh."

[41]Cf. L. Boadt's list of "mocking laments" in Ezekiel ("Ezekiel, Book of," *ABD* 2. 717). Boadt includes also 26:15–18. See also discussion in Jemielity, 94.

[42]*Isaiah*, 29, 34. See also the fine poetic analysis of this poem in Alter, *Art of Biblical Poetry*, 146–50. Alter calls it a "sarcastic-triumphal 'elegy.'"

How the oppressor has ceased!
How his insolence has ceased!
The LORD has broken the staff of the wicked,
the scepter of rulers,
that struck down the peoples in wrath
with unceasing blows,
that ruled the nations in anger
with unrelenting persecution.
. . . .
How you are fallen from heaven,
O Day Star, son of Dawn!
How you are cut down to the ground,
you who laid the nations low!
You said in your heart,
"I will ascend to heaven;
I will raise my throne
above the stars of God;
I will sit on the mount of assembly
on the heights of Zaphon;
I will ascend to the tops of the clouds,
I will make myself like the Most High."
But you are brought down to Sheol,
to the depths of the Pit. (vv 4b–6, 12–15)

The ironic intention is quite obvious. The twice-uttered expression "How" glistens with ironic venom,[43] and the poet's vicious satisfaction with the destruction of Babylon is apparent throughout the poem. Probably no one would mistake the author's meaning and suppose that he or she really felt sympathy for the fallen tyrant (see esp. vv 20–21). The purpose of the poem is to provide the formerly oppressed with a focus for rejoicing and to highlight the reasons why the mighty one is now sunk to Sheol.[44]

The relevance of Isa 14:4–21 for the present investigation is obvious. The poem is one of the Isaianic OAN; it precedes and is separated from Isaiah 15–16 by only eleven verses. It presents a clear case of the ironic inversion of genre, specifically the ironic

[43]The exclamation איך (vv 4, 12) carries several different shades of meaning. In lamentation the sense is "How sad it is that...," an expression of sympathy (Smith, "Destruction of the Foreign Nations," 111–12). The use of this exclamation in Isaiah 14 is similar to the ironic expressions of sympathy supposed by some to be present in the following two chapters.

[44]For other treatments of this ironic dirge, see Good, 163–67; Fishelov, 198–99; Jemielity, 94–96.

use of dirge, a genre that shares many features with lament.[45] Thus Isa 14:4–21 provides an important co-textual indication that an ironic motive may be at work in Isaiah 15–16, and it demonstrates the use of ironic satire and of the ironic inversion of genre in a prophetic text, indeed, within the Isaianic corpus itself.[46] It is clear, therefore, that prophetic literature offers evidence of the attitudes and techniques of ironic and satiric discourse.

Admittedly, the prophets present no obvious examples of ironic first-person expressions of sympathy, while straightforward, first-person expressions of sympathy do occasionally occur. Gesenius uses this fact to argue against the idea that the expressions of sympathy in Isaiah 15–16 are ironic. He notes that the prophets now and then express sympathy in threatening prophecies and gives as examples Isa 16:11; 21:2–4; 22:4; Mic 1:8; Jer 23:9; and 48:36. Yet some distinctions need to be made. Isa 16:11 and Jer 48:36 should be set aside since both are susceptible to ironic interpretation and derive from the text in question. Both Isa 22:4 and Jer 23:9 are expressions of personal grief over the fate of the prophet's own nation, not over the fate of a foreign nation. Similarly, Mic 1:8 expresses a Judean prophet's grief over the disaster that overtook Israel and now threatened his own group. In situations such as these, it is not surprising to find genuine grief intermingled with threats; such mixed moods are especially common in Jeremiah (e.g., 8:18–9:1). This leaves only Isa 21:2–4 as a possible comparable example of a prophet expressing grief for a foreign nation.[47]

---

[45]Auvray has suggested that Isaiah 15–16 finds a close generic cousin in Isaiah 14 (*Isaïe*, 175, cf. 168–69).

[46]The influence of this co-textual signal in the final form of the book should not be underestimated. The studies of Good and Williams are particularly significant in this regard. Once a reader's expectation of irony is aroused by a clear instance of irony, the reader becomes suspicious and looks closely for irony in whatever follows. This is especially true if irony of a kind similar to that already experienced is encountered. Perhaps the placement of the speech about Moab immediately after the sarcastic dirge in ch. 14 is designed to alert the reader to the less obvious irony at work in the latter poem.

[47]Hayes and Irvine suggest that the expressions of grief in these verses may have been spoken ironically (275). The difficulty of the text does not allow for even relative certainty on this point, however, and it would be all too convenient an interpretation for us to accept in the present case.

Therefore my loins are filled with anguish;
pangs have seized me,
like the pangs of a woman in labor;
I am bowed down so that I cannot hear,
I am dismayed so that I cannot see.
My mind reels, horror has appalled me;
the twilight I longed for
has been turned for me into trembling. (vv 3–4)

Unfortunately, this text is notoriously difficult to interpret.[48] Without attempting a full interpretation, we can make the following observations. First, the prophet says that a "stern vision" (חזות קשה) has been given to him.[49] The text is marked by vivid imagery that is not so much *described* as *reported*. This sort of reporting is typical of vision accounts, a significant fact since descriptions of severe psychic disturbances are elsewhere found in vision accounts (e.g., Ezekiel, Daniel). Such descriptions are not intended to communicate the prophet's sympathy with the subject of his vision; they function rather to lend credence to the prophet's vision by dramatizing his visionary experience.[50]

Secondly, the prophet's reaction to the vision seems to be related to its sternness or severity. Apparently, what is taking place in the vision displeases or disturbs him, although it is not clear why this is so. It is certainly not the kind of sympathetic reaction we find in Isaiah 15–16. The initial indication is that the prophet is distressed over the continued malfeasance of "the

---

[48]See, for example, the comments of Kaiser, 120–122.

[49]This is the only example of this specific idiom in Isaiah. The unusual form חזות appears in the HB only here and in 28:18; 29:11; and Dan 8:5, 8. In 28:18 it designates an "agreement" or a "pact" made with Sheol. Thus it is not entirely clear that it refers to a vision in 21:2; one could translate the first line of the verse "A harsh agreement has been disclosed to me." This translation is supported by the fact that the following references to one who betrays and deals treacherously belong to the same semantic field of meaning dealing with broken agreements. Nevertheless, the vision-like quality of what follows and the use in 29:11 suggest that "vision" is also a legitimate translation.

[50]I do not mean to imply that these visionary experiences were fabrications. I mean only to point out their *rhetorical function* in the text. Such experiences are related for a rhetorical purpose, not simply because the prophet thought them interesting.

betrayer/the destroyer" who has caused "sighing" (v 2a).[51] The text goes on, however, to tell us that this betrayer will be "brought to an end," apparently by Elam and Media (v 2b). Both "the betrayer's" betrayals and its destruction are told in v 2. This means that the "therefore" (על־כן) at the beginning of v 3 has no clear logical antecedent; it may be taken to refer either to the actions of the "betrayer" or to the destruction of the "betrayer." We do not know if the prophet is distressed because "the betrayer betrays" or because it will be (has been?) destroyed. The derogatory epithets "the betrayer" and "the destroyer" make it unlikely that the prophet's consternation is caused by sympathy for this doomed power. Equally improbable is the idea that he is distressed over its treachery since the destruction of "the destroyer" is envisioned in the immediate context. Perhaps the prophet is distressed at the sheer violence that will be released when these Titans unsheath their swords. This would make some sense of the line, "the twilight I longed for has been turned for me into trembling." The longed-for destruction of the tyrannical world power, when it is actually at hand, causes deep distress. The foundations of the world tremble during such events.

Whatever the reason for the prophet's distress in Isa 21:2–4, there is little reason to suppose that it is caused by concern for another nation. Not a single explicit expression of sympathy is found in the text. It would appear, therefore, that the prophetic corpus does not in fact contain first person expressions of sympathy for foreign nations, that is, unless we read the expressions of sympathy in Isaiah 15–16 straightforwardly rather than ironically.[52]

---

[51]This motif is repeated in the book; cf. 24:16; 33:1. The identity of this entity or person is never made clear, and it may in fact serve simply to identify an archetype in the later texts.

[52]This is different from saying that the foreign nations are nowhere treated positively in prophetic literature. While not common, positive treatments do appear. For example, the portrayal of the eschatological coversion of Egypt and Assyria in Isa 19:18–25 is exceedingly positive (cf. Mic 4:1–3; Isa 2:2–4; 25:6–8; 56:6–7; sometimes the tradition of the pilgrimage of the nations is recast so that the the nations appear in a less favorable light: Isa 45:14–16; 49:14–23; 60; Jer 3:17; Hag 2:6–9; Zech 8:22). Similarly, the portrayal in Jonah of the Ninevites is positive.

In summary, irony and satire, as well as ironic satire, are well attested in prophetic literature. The mockery of foreign nations is prevalent and pointed in the prophets, the book of Isaiah being no exception. More specifically, there are examples of the ironic use of the funeral lament genre in both Ezekiel and Isaiah, Isa 14:4–21 providing the most important example. The compositor of Jeremiah 48 rendered the subtle irony of Isaiah 15–16 obvious and unmistakable in the recasting of the poem, and this may suggest that he or she recognized the presence of intended irony. Gesenius's contention that expressions of sympathy for foreign nations are common in prophetic literature does not hold up under close examination; expressions of grief and sympathy for foreign nations are unattested elsewhere in prophetic literature. An ironic reading of Isaiah 15–16 is, therefore, supported by the techniques and practices of prophetic literature, especially those typical of the OAN collections. Our next task is to seek out positive contextual indications of irony.

IV. Moab in the Hebrew Bible

The principal clue that Isaiah 15–16 is intended ironically is the conflict between the negative attitude toward Moab expressed nearly everywhere in the HB and the deeply sympathetic attitude expressed in Isaiah 15–16. All the foreign nations are, with but a few exceptions, portrayed negatively in the HB. Moab, however, is cast in an *exceptionally* negative light, as will be apparent in the following survey of those texts in the HB that mention Moab.[53]

Evidence of hostility is often noted in the Genesis account of Moab's origin (Gen 19:30–38), which portrays the birth of Moab's

---

[53]This survey of texts relating to Moab includes texts that I have deemed significant for understanding those traditions, images and themes related to Moab. In selecting the texts, I have made every effort to include all texts pertinent to the question we are investigating. See L. Handy ("Uneasy Laughter: Ehud and Eglon as Ethnic Humor," *SJOT* 6 [1992] 238–40) for a survey aimed at highlighting the Israelites' derisive attitude toward Moab. J. Levenson similarly notes that the Moabites are presented negatively throughout the HB ("Is There a Counterpart in the Hebrew Bible to New Testament Antisemitism?" *Journal of Ecumenical Studies* 22 (1985) 251. For a full survey of the texts dealing with Moab, see van Zyl, *The Moabites*, 5–29.

eponymous ancestor as the result of drunken stupor and incestuous relations in a mountain cave. This etiological story probably dates from before Isaiah's time.[54] After the destruction of Sodom and Gomorrah, according to the story, Lot and his daughters flee to Zoar but live in a mountain cave outside of the town "for he was afraid to stay in Zoar." Living in isolation, Lot's daughters fear that "there is not a man on earth to come in to us after the manner of all the world" and they agree to "preserve offspring through our father." They accomplish this by getting him drunk and having sexual relations with him while he is nearly unconscious and cannot tell "when she lay down or when she rose." The childern born of these unions are Moab ("from [my] father) and Ben-Ammi ("son of my people"), both names being etymological puns on the incestuous origins of the children. Most scholars agree that this story is intended to deride the Moabites and Ammonites, that it is a vicious insult.[55] As seen above, the use of

---

[54]Traditions of this sort are extremely difficult to date. It is generally thought to predate the J writer who is responsible for its inclusion. Eissfeldt attributes it to the earliest stratum of the Pentateuch, his L source (*Introduction*, 194).

[55]See A. Brenner, "Semantic Field," 41. Brenner notes that this interpretation goes back to Gunkel. I agree with van Zyl (*The Moabites*, 5–6) that it is unlikely that the story was ever used by the Ammonites and Moabites in a positive way, as some have suggested (e.g., G. von Rad, *Genesis: A Commentary*, tr. J. H. Marks [London: SCM, 1963[2]] 218–19). The story of Tamar and Judah in Genesis 38 also portrays a woman plotting to preserve offspring by means of a close male relative. In the book of Ruth this story is implicitly linked to the story of Lot's daughters by virtue of the fact that Ruth is a Moabite and Boaz is a direct descendant of Perez, the son of Tamar, a fact highlighted in the genealogy at the end of Ruth. In the story of Judah and Tamar, the action of the woman is seen positively and no stigmatic name is given the twins born of the union. Does this suggest that the story of Lot and his daughters should be interpreted positively? Probably not. The story of Lot and his daughters is set in a mountain cave where Lot hides in fear, an inauspicious setting for the birth of a nation (cf. the birth of Isaac that follows in ch. 21). There may be a greater stigma attached to incest with one's own father than that committed with one's father-in-law, though this is difficult to determine with certainty. Both stories, however, assume that the women's action is reprehensible. This is clear in the Tamar and Judah story, and in the story of Lot's daughters, the fact that they must make their father sufficiently drunk that he does not know what is happening shows that their actions are unacceptable, at least to their father. Unlike the Tamar and Judah story, there is no focus on the larger issue of the just treatment of a woman according to

sexual imagery and themes is common in the satiric abuse of enemies. The story of Lot skulking in a cave until his own daughters contrive incestuous measures to carry on the family line is intended to evoke a knowing smile from every Israelite when the name Moab or Ammon is spoken.

In Num 21:27–30 we encounter a "mocking song" directed against Moab.[56] The narrator suggests that the song is a traditional piece, part of the continuing repertoire of the "taunt makers" (יאמרו המשלים; cf. Isa 14:4; Mic 2:4; Hab 2:6). It celebrates some past calamity suffered by Moab. Moab is depicted as destroyed and its population deported by the Amorite king Sihon. Many questions of interpretation vex this text, but it is sufficient for our purpose simply to note Israel's negative attitude toward Moab in this mocking song and the fact that this attitude is depicted as originating very early and continuing to the writer's own time.

The longest entry narrative dealing with the conflict between Israel and another nation follows in the next chapter. Numbers 22–24 describes the attempt by Balak, king of Moab, to curse Israel by means of the great Babylonian imprecator, Balaam, son of Beor. The story relates how Balaam repeatedly attempted to curse Israel but failed each time. Instead of cursing, he could only bless Israel.

> God who brings him out of Egypt,
> is like the horns of a wild ox for him;
> he shall devour the nations that are his foes

---

law and custom (cf. 38:26). Instead, the problem is that Lot's daughters are totally isolated from society (by their father's bad choices and fear, the story suggests). For these reasons it is quite probable that the story of the origins of Moab and Ammon is intended derogatorily. See further below in our discussion of Ruth.

[56] O. Eissfeldt, *Introduction*, 92–93. He declares the song "ancient," but we have little way of judging just how ancient it may be. The discussion of this text is extensive and has reached no consensus on questions of date and origin. See, for example, van Seters, "The Conquest of Sihon's Kingdom: A Literary Examination," *JBL* 91 (1972) 182–97; *idem*, "Once Again—the Conquest of Sihon's Kingdom," *JBL* 99 (1980) 117–19; J. Bartlett, "The Historical Reference of Numbers 21:27–30," *PEQ* 101 (1969) 94–100; *idem*, "The Conquest of Sihon's Kingdom: A Literary Re-examination," *JBL* 97 (1978) 347–51; W. Sumner, "Israel's Encounters with Edom, Moab, Ammon, Sihon and Og according to the Deuteronomist," *VT* 18 (1968) 216–28.

and break their bones.
He shall strike with his arrows.
He crouched, he lay down like a lion,
and like a lioness; who will rouse him up?
Blessed is everyone who blesses you,
and cursed is everyone who curses you (24:8–9; cf. 24:17).

Ironically, the last two lines imply a curse against Moab because it had hired Balaam to curse Israel. In a subsequent oracle (probably a late addition to the text), this malediction takes explicit shape.

I see him, but not now;
I behold him, but not near—
a star shall come out of Jacob,
and a scepter shall rise out of Israel;
it shall crush the borderlands of Moab,
and the territory of all the Shethites (24:17).

Running throughout the Balaam narrative is the theme of Moab's fear of Israel and the poetic justice that will overtake Moab when they attempt to hurt Israel. We may surmise that Moab's supposed fear is a wishful projection by the later writer. Israel's fear and hatred of the Moabites is here expressed in inverted form; the narrative seeks to defuse the anxieties of a later time. At the very least, the narrative testifies to the powerful rivalry and hostility between the two nations, an attitude of significance sufficiently strong and abiding to have been recorded and preserved at length in the foundational traditions of the nation.

A subtheme in the narrative is the danger posed by Moab's cultus. The failed attempts to curse Israel take place at Moab's high places, and Balaam's oracles are preceded by sacrificial rites. We encounter anxiety of a similar kind in the pericope that follows the Balaam narrative. In this account, Moab's cultus and women prove seductive to Israelite men with the result that "Israel yoked itself to the Baal of Peor" (Num 25:1–9). Anxieties about the danger of Moab shimmer below the surface of the narrative.[57] Similar anxiety is also apparent in the strange note at

[57]The narrative probably derives ultimately from a quite early tradition (cf. Hos 9:10). In its present form it appears that P has reworked an original J account on the basis of the tradition found in Ps 106:28–31 (P. Budd, *Numbers* [WBC; Waco: Word, 1984] 275–79).

the end of 2 Kings 3 stating that when the king of Moab sacrificed his firstborn son to repel an Israelite and Judean attack, "a great wrath came upon Israel, so they withdrew from him and returned to their own land" (3:27). This note is unique in the HB by virtue of the power it indirectly attributes to a foreign deity. All three of these narratives disclose an attitude of fear toward Moab, fear of its power, both religious and political.

The Balaam tradition and the tradition of Moab's inhospitality toward Israel when the Israelites came from Egypt provide the basis for the exclusionary law in Deut 23:4–7 [3–6]: "No Ammonite or Moabite shall be admitted to the assembly of the LORD. Even to the tenth generation, none of their descendants shall be admitted to the assembly of the LORD, because they did not meet you with food and water on your journey out of Egypt, and because they hired against you Balaam son of Beor, from Pethor of Mesopotamia, to curse you.... You shall never promote their welfare or their prosperity as long as you live" (vv 4–5, 7). The law excludes Ammonites and Moabites from any involvement in the community of Israel, and it prohibits Israel from any friendly relations with Moab and Ammon whatsoever.[58] It suggests a vehement hatred for the Ammonites and Moabites such as is seldom directed toward any other nation in the HB. If this law predated Isaiah 15–16, it would have provided a clear directive for denying sanctuary to the Moabites when they petitioned Judah, as Hayes and Irvine have noted.[59] The context of the Deuteronomy text is significant. The exclusion of these two nations born of incest immediately follows the law specifying that "Those born of an illicit union shall not be admitted to the assembly of the LORD" (23:3 [2]). The editor in this way makes clear yet a third reason that Ammonites and Moabites must not be admitted: they are nations born of "an illicit union." In its present context, this law sums up the attitude toward Moab expressed throughout the Pentateuch; it reminds the Israelites that the Moabites are the ill-

---

[58]The language of the final prohibition is from the semantic domain of treaty making and probably prohibits any treaty relationship between Israel and Moab. See P. C. Craigie, *The Book of Deuteronomy* (NICOT; Grand Rapids: Eerdmans, 1976) 298.

[59]Hayes and Irvine, 246.

mannered, vicious spawn of incest, a people with whom one should have nothing to do.

Amos contains arguably the earliest prophetic reference to Moab. The judgment speech against Moab in 2:1–3 mentions a specific sin of Moab: "he burned to lime the bones of the king of Edom." The meaning of this act is not entirely clear, but obviously it was a grave offense. At the very least, the act was a powerful means of showing disrespect for one's enemies.[60] Moab's punishment is a case of poetic justice: "So I will send a fire on Moab, and it shall devour the strongholds of Kerioth, and Moab shall die amid uproar, amid shouting and the sound of the trumpet; I will cut off the ruler from its midst, and I will kill all its officials with him." Having burned the bones of the king of Edom to lime, Moab itself will now endure the burning of its fortifications and the loss of its king and its high officials. If the act of burning bones to lime constitutes a kind of sorcery, we have yet another instance of Israel's incipient anxiety about the prowess of Moab to inflict harm by magical means.

In Isaiah, Moab is mentioned twice outside of chapters 15 and 16. Isa 11:11–16 designates Moab along with Edom, Ammon and the Philistines as the enemies of Israel and Judah that will be vanquished on "the day of the LORD."[61] Isa 25:9–12 also portrays the destruction of Moab as an eschatological hope, and Moab alone is singled out as the enemy to be destroyed in this case. The text is often dated quite late.[62] Textual difficulties preclude any precise understanding, but the general sense is clear:

---

[60]Cf. 1 Kgs 13:2; 2 Kgs 23:16. Perhaps the import of the action extends beyond insult into the realm of actual damage to the dead person. Mistreatment of the bones of the dead is mentioned in Jer 8:1–2 as a punishment. See F. Andersen and D. Freedman, *Amos* (AB; New York: Doubleday, 1989) 288–89. Belief in the king's role in the afterlife is attested at least in Egypt, and the integrity of the physical remains apparently played an important part in the king's enjoyment of this role. Burning a king's bones to lime might conceivably have been an attempt to deny him a role in the afterlife.

[61]This grouping of Israel's enemies—Moab, Edom and Philistia (but not Ammon)—is found also in Pss 60:10 [8]; 108:10 [9].

[62]See Kaiser, 178–79; 202–04. Van Zyl dates the passage to ca. 582 B.C.E., but his reasons for dating the passage early center around his belief that Isaiah 15–16 reflects a positive attitude toward Moab and that therefore a distinction should be made between an earlier positive attitude (i.e., of

> For the hand of the LORD will rest on this mountain. The Moabites shall be trodden down in their place as straw is trodden down in the dung-pit. Though they spread out their hands in the midst of it, as swimmers spread out their hands to swim, their pride will be laid low despite the struggle of their hands. The high fortifications of his walls will be brought down, laid low, cast to the ground, even to the dust.

The writer begins the depiction of Moab's fall with a comparison between "this mountain," that is, Zion, the mountain of YHWH where the eschatological banquet is to be held (cf. 25:6), and Moab. He or she imagines Moab as a person lying prostrate in a pool of water and manure,[63] flailing about to find a way out.[64] The words "despite the struggle of their hands" may also be translated, "despite the skill [ארבות] of their hands."[65] In the metaphor of the struggling swimmer, the "skill of their hands" serves to keep them afloat. The tenor of the metaphor, however, refers to the Moabite's skill at surviving the disasters that overtook their neighbors, especially their prowess at building "high fortifications" (v 12, cf. Jer 48:1). But their skill will provide no help on the day when the LORD rests his hand on Zion; then "the struggle/skill of his hands" and "the high fortifications of his walls" will be trampled in the muck. Why Moab is singled out in a

---

Isaiah) and the much later strong hatred (*The Moabites*, 25–29). Hayes and Irvine date the text to Isaiah's time, at the very end of the eighth century (294–310). There is in fact very little solid evidence to date these verses. If one will allow that Isaiah could have thought and expressed himself in an eschatological mode, the early date of Hayes and Irvine is possible.

[63]The word for manure pile, מדמנה, may be a word play either on Madmen, a place name mentioned in Jer 48:2 (if the Jeremiah text can be trusted), or on the important Moabite city Dibon. Cf. Isa 15:9.

[64]W. von Soden ("Ist im Alten Testament schon von Schwimmen die Rede?" *ZAH* 4 [1991] 165–70) has argued that swimming is mentioned nowhere in the OT and that the phrase in Isa 25:11a, כאשר יפרש השחה לשחות, does not refer to swimming. He proposes reading הַשֹּׁחֶה instead of הַשֹּׂחֶה. If this change is accepted, we should translate the line something like, "Though they spread out their hands in the midst of it, just as the supplicant spreads out (his hands) to do homage, their pride will be laid low despite the struggle [skill?] of their hands." Little is gained for the present argument in deciding this question; either translation indicates a similarly negative attitude toward Moab.

[65]So Wildberger, *Jesaja*, 971.

context otherwise marked by a universal tone is hard to guess. Perhaps Moab serves as the archetype of all Judah's enemies; perhaps some historical circumstance caused the writer to focus on Moab.[66] Whatever the reason, the hatred expressed for Moab in this text is quite remarkable.

Jeremiah 48, already discussed above, shares with Isa 25:10–12 a focus on the strength of Moab's fortifications and its pride in this achievement. In 48:1–2 the writer rejoices that the "lofty stronghold" of Kiriathaim has been destroyed, and for this reason "there is praise for Moab no longer" (cf. vv 18, 41). Moab has trusted in its "own achievements and treasures"; it is depicted as a people who have never suffered serious destruction from foreign invasion (v 11), but it will go into exile along with its god Chemosh and "all his priests and princes" (48:7).[67] Another similarity between the two texts is the use of excremental imagery; the humbling of Moab is likened to the humiliation of the drunkard wallowing in his own vomit (48:26). This picture of Moab's descent into filth and its counterpart, the recalling of Moab's former might and arrogance (48:25–29, 39, 42), are part of the hubris theme that dominates the OAN texts. In 48:27 the arrogance takes on a particular form especially prominent in the texts relating to Moab and Ammon; Moab is accused of ridiculing Israel: "Israel was a laughingstock for you, though he was not caught among thieves; but whenever you spoke of him you shook your head!" Moab and Judah clearly were involved in a war of insults around the time of the exile, and some of Moab's verbal attacks must have been keenly felt.[68]

---

[66]B. Dicou (*Edom, Israel's Brother and Antagonist: The Role of Edom in Biblical Prophecy and Story* [JSOTS 169; Sheffield: JSOT, 1994] 182–97) has recently challenged the view that Edom was Israel's foremost adversary in the pre-exilic period. He argues that the portrayal of Edom as the prototypical enemy of Israel developed after the exile.

[67]The judgment of Moab's *rulers* is a repeated theme in the HB; see Jer 48:45; Num 21:28; 24:17; Amos 2:3.

[68]The brief prophetic speech on Ammon in Jer 49:1–6 contains geographical problems that E. A. Knauf ("Jeremia XLIX 1-5: Ein Zweites Moab-Orakel im Jeremia-Buch," *VT* 42 [1992] 124–28) has suggested result from the fact that originally the speech was directed against Moab and that a redactor reworked it to apply it to Ammon. He argues that (1) the reference to

The book of Zephaniah's prophecy against Moab (2:8–11) dwells on many of the same themes as do the prophecies against Moab found in Jeremiah and Isaiah:[69]

> I have heard the taunts of Moab
> and the revilings of the Ammonites,
> how they have taunted my people
> and made boasts against their territory.
> Therefore, as I live, says the LORD of hosts,
> the God of Israel,
> Moab shall become like Sodom
> and the Ammonites like Gomorrah,
> a land possessed by nettles and salt pits,
> and a waste forever.
> The remnant of my people shall plunder them,
> and the survivors of my nation shall possess them.

Malcom/Milcom, the Ammonite god, in v 1 should be read instead as "their king;" (2) vv 1 and 6, which mention Ammon are redactional additions; (3) the fact that the LXX lacks "sons of Ammon" in v 2 suggests that it is likewise a secondary addition; (4) the LXX has replaced "Gad" with "Gilead" because Ammonite-Gadite conflict is an unlikely idea (it is unattested in the HB); (5) both Heshbon and Ai (v 3aα) are Moabite, not Ammonite cities; (6) "Rabbah" in vv 2 and 3 refers to the Moabite city Rabbah (Rabbathmoba, modern *er-Rabbe*).

If Knauf's thesis could be proved, we should add this text to our survey. His arguments are not, however, convincing. First, Jer 48:2 indicates that Heshbon is held by an enemy of Moab: "In Heshbon they planned evil against her [Moab]." Who are "they"? The most likely candidate, given the geographical realities and the history of the post-monarchic period, is Ammon. Thus it seems that 48:2 supports the idea that Ammon controlled Heshbon in the exilic or post-exilic period. Secondly, if Ammon was extending itself southward during this time, as their control of Heshbon would suggest, then conflict with the Gadites is understandable. Thirdly, Rabbah is well-known in the HB as a city of Ammon, but not as a Moabite city. Neither the long catalogue of Moabite cities in Isaiah 15–16 nor that in Jeremiah 48 mentions a Moabite Rabbah, nor does the Mesha Inscription mention the name (especially significant since Knauf dates the original oracle to the 9th century BCE.). In fact, the name Rabbathmoba cannot be traced back beyond Josephus (he gives it in the apparently garbled form "Arabatha" [*Ant.* 14.1.18]); all evidence suggests that it is the coinage of the Persian or Hellenistic period (See further J. M. Miller, ed., *Archaeological Survey of the Kerak Plateau* [ASOR Archaeological Reports 01; Atlanta: Scholars, 1991] 65–66). These considerations substantially weaken Knauf's position.

[69]Sons of Ammon" apparently designates both the Moabites and the Ammonites by the late seventh century. Cf. Ezek 25:10.

> This shall be their lot in return for their pride,
> because they scoffed and boasted
> against the people of the LORD of hosts.
> The LORD will be terrible against them;
> he will shrivel all the gods of the earth,
> and to him shall bow down, each in its place,
> all the coasts and islands of the nations.

Here again we encounter the theme of Moab's arrogance and of its taunting of Israel (vv 8, 10). Indeed, Moab's taunting and pride is the *only* offense of which it is accused, unless "boasts against their territory" refers to a territorial encroachment. Zephaniah prophesies that Moab will suffer the fate of Sodom and Gomorrah, becoming a dry and infertile desolation (v 9). It is YHWH's plan to win the submission of the nations by "shriveling" or "making lean" their protective deities. The threat of infertility and leanness relates closely to a theme we will encounter again, that of Moab's substantial agricultural resources. The vindictive attitude exhibited here is typical of the defeated whose sworn enemies have gloated over their misfortune, and perhaps even taken advantage of it.

The final prophetic text requiring examination is Ezekiel's prophecy against Moab in 25:8–11:

> Thus says the Lord GOD: Because Moab said, The house of Judah is like all the other nations, therefore I will lay open the flank of Moab from the towns on its frontier, the glory of the country, Beth-jeshimoth, Baal-meon, and Kiriathaim. I will give it along with Ammon to the people of the East as a possession. Thus Ammon shall be remembered no more among the nations, and I will execute judgments upon Moab. Then they shall know that I am the LORD.

In the verses preceding this text, the sin of Ammon is detailed: "Because you said, Aha!" over my sanctuary when it was profaned, and over the land of Israel when it was made desolate.... Because you have clapped your hands and stamped your feet and rejoiced with all the malice within you against the land of Israel..." (25:3, 6). This picture of the reaction of Ammon and Moab to the misfortunes of Judah is consistent with that in Zephaniah. Apparently, a great wave of taunting, derision and hatred poured out of Ammon and Moab when the exiles were carried off and their temple and capital city were destroyed. Moab is specifically accused of ridiculing Judah's claim to be a people set apart from the other nations by divine election. The verse suggests that the Moabites were aware of some of Judah's theological claims. Moab's punishment is that its "flank/shoulder" [כתף] will be opened up. כתף refers to a line of three border cities crucial to Moab's defense, Beth-jeshimoth, Baal-meon and Kiriathiam. These cities, "the glory of the land," are to be taken away from Moab, and as a result, the land itself will be given over to the "people of the East," the nomadic tribes from the desert fringe. Here again we encounter the themes of Moab's verbal arrogance and taunting of Israel and of its strong defenses based on its fortified cities. Apparently, these cities still offer Moab effective protection in Ezekiel's time. The prophet expresses the people's sense of personal injury as well as their desire for revenge against their powerful neighbor.

Several references to Moab in the Deuteronomistic history suggest a protracted struggle between Moab and Israel. In Judges there is the story of Eglon, the king of Moab, in coalition with the Ammonites and Amalekites, taking over Jericho and exacting tribute from the Israelite settlers (Judg 3:12–30). Several commentators have noted that the story has a strong humorous element intended to heap scorn on the obese king of Moab. L. Handy states succinctly: "the story of Ehud and Eglon is not history, but rather ethnic joke...it was composed and edited precisely because it was insulting to the Moabites while simultaneously being an example of the cleverness of the Israelites."[70] As Handy argues, the humor consists of the depiction of Moab's king as a fat (3:17,

[70]"Uneasy Laughter," 233; see p. 234, n. 3 for other treatments of the story as humorous. R. Alter calls the story "a satirical vision, at once shrewd and jubilant" (*The Art of Biblical Narrative* [New York: Basic Books, 1981] 37–41, quotation is from 39). A. Brenner refers to the story as an example of "low comedy" ("Semantic Field," 41). The emphasis on Eglon's obesity may hint at Moab's self-satisfied prosperity, a theme we have noted elsewhere. As J. M. Miller has argued ("Moab and the Moabites," *Studies in the Mesha Inscription and Moab* [ed. J. A. Dearman; Atlanta: Scholars, 1989] 31–34), Eglon should not be thought of as the king over the entire territory north of the Arnon. He was probably only a local ruler who briefly made Jericho his base for exacting tribute from the surrounding villages, if he existed at all (see Handy, 245).

22), stupid (3:20), cow-like man (his name may be the invention of the author since it seems quite likely that it is a pun on the word "calf"). The mention of Eglon's obesity serves to satirize him, and the description of his death, with a sword buried in his fat belly[71] and his bowels spilling forth, heaps multiple insults on him at the moment of his death. The assumption of his servants, that the king is taking a long time behind closed doors because he is sitting on the toilet, lampoons not only the king (cf. 1 Kgs 18:27) but also his rather stupid servants whose delay allows Ehud time to escape. Indeed, the fact that 3:29 relates that all the Moabites were fat (כל־שמן) emphasizes that all the Moabites, not just the king, are the butt of the joke.[72] With short, bold strokes the author of this story depicts the Moabites as fat, stupid and weak. The narrative assumes that its audience shares a cohesive negative attitude toward the Moabites. It offers the Judeans an occasion to laugh at the common enemy and revel in their own superiority.[73]

The great warrior king David is said to have subjugated Moab, treated its population rather brutally and exacted annual tribute (2 Sam 8:2). This harsh treatment is, however, difficult to reconcile with two other things we are told elsewhere about David: (1) that while he was on the run from Saul, David requested that the king of Moab grant sanctuary to his parents (1 Sam 22:3–4); (2) that David's paternal grandfather was half Moabite (Ruth 4:18–22). Perhaps the traditions of David's amicable and familial relationship with Moab were somewhat of an embarrassment to the

---

[71]The Hebrew term is בטן which can mean "belly" or "womb." There may be a subtle feminizing of Eglon in the narrative: his name suggests a female animal; Ehud's sword penetrates Eglon's "womb"; and the king is pictured at ease in a cool upper chamber (vv 20, 24), hardly the scene of vital action (the cultural biases I here assume are those common in the ancient world; I do not mean to endorse them). See Alter (*Art of Biblical Narrative*, 137–62) who argues that both sexual and scatological elements enter into the Ehud narrative.

[72]Is there in this story a suppressed jealousy of a neighbor whose land produced sufficient food that its people appeared well-fed to the Israelites?

[73]Ethnic humor supposes a cohesive attitude among its audience toward the object of the joke, and it is intended to reinforce this attitude and strengthen group cohesion. See Handy, 234. Of course history suggests that this narrative is, on the whole, a case of wishful thinking; Moab proved throughout most of its shared history with Israel and Judah that it was anything but fat, stupid and weak.

deuteronomistic historians, and the story of David's harsh treatment of the Moabites is their attempt to overcome this. This thesis would allow us to make better sense of the fact that in the next generation Solomon is reported to have built a high place for the worship of Chemosh on the mountain east of Jerusalem (1 Kgs 11:7, 33; 2 Kgs 23:13), an action suggesting that Solomon entered into a parity treaty relationship with Moab.[74] Thus, although the time of David and Solomon is depicted as a time when Israel/Judah held power over Moab, serious doubts about this picture arise when the narrative is examined closely. It is possible that the power in the relationship, at least by Solomon's time, was more or less evenly divided and that the relationship was somewhat amicable.

2 Kings 3 tells the story of a military campaign against Moab undertaken by a coalition consisting of Israel, Judah and Edom.[75] According to the story, the campaign was launched in response to Moab's rebellion against Israelite control and refusal to send the customary tribute.[76] The coalition routed Moab until the Moabite king took refuge in one of his fortified cities. There he sacrificed his firstborn son on the wall in order to invoke divine help (presumably Chemosh's) to defeat the combined forces (2 Kgs 3:21–27). We are told that "there came a great wrath against Israel" (v 27), and the coalition was forced to abandon the attack. This narrative plays on themes we have already encountered: the strength of Moab's fortified cities (v 25) and the powerful threat posed by Moab's cultus. L. Handy has suggested that in 3:23–24

---

[74]See Miller and Hayes, *History*, 214.

[75]The narrative in 2 Chr 20:1–30 describing Jehoshaphat's campaign against Moab, Ammon and Mount Seir was held by Wellhausen and Kautzsch to be a literary reworking of 2 Kings 3. More recently, this view has been called into question (see J. Myers, *II Chronicles* [AB 13; Garden City, NY: Doubleday, 1965] 114). In any case, 2 Chronicles 20 offers little evidence for or against the present thesis and has, for that reason, been omitted from this investigation.

[76]The bare fact of a rebellion by Moab against Israelite control at approximately the time suggested by 2 Kings 3 (after King Ahab's death) is corroborated by the Mesha Inscription (see esp. lines 4–9). The details of the conflict and the relative success of the opposing sides as related in the biblical history and in the Mesha Inscription differ considerably, however.

the story also evokes the theme of the Moabites' stupidity; the Moabites are fooled into a hasty attack on the coalition armies because they mistake the red glare of sunrise on pools of water for a sign that the enemy armies had turned against one another.[77]

In the latter part of the ninth century, it would appear that power had shifted decisively in Moab's favor. We are told that Moab was able to send raiding bands across the Jordan apparently without fear of significant reprisals (2 Kgs 13:20). In the final chapter of Judah's life as a state, we again find an account of Moabite raiding parties nibbling away at her strength (2 Kgs 24:2). This situation comports well with the attitudes we have observed in Isa 25:10–12, Jer 48, Zeph 2:8–11 and Ezek 25:8–11. While it is not possible to give a detailed account of the history of relations between Moab and Israel/Judah, the evidence suggests that from the end of the Omride dynasty Moab maintained its independence from Israel and Judah, and that on occasion it was the stronger power and acted aggressively against its neighbors to the west.

Turning now to the Psalms, we find Moab mentioned in a short, nationalistic poem designed to emphasize YHWH's sovereignty over the neighboring nations (Ps 60:8–10 [6–8]= 108:8–10 [7–9]):

> God has promised in his sanctuary:
> "With exultation I will divide up Shechem,
> and portion out the Vale of Succoth.
> Gilead is mine, and Manasseh is mine;
> Ephraim is my helmet;
> Judah is my scepter.
> Moab is my washbasin;
> on Edom I hurl my shoe;
> over Philistia I shout in triumph."

This poem, which exults in YHWH's ownership (and protection) of Israel and Judah, ends in bathos; Ephraim and Judah are exalted in status as YHWH's "helmet" and "scepter," but Moab and Edom are belittled by being symbolized as humble parts of YHWH's domestic life. Probably, the metaphor is intended to denote

---

[77]Handy, 239.

YHWH's ownership of all the places mentioned while at the same time stressing the lower, even comical, status of Moab, Edom and Philistia in this group.[78] It is not clear whether the poem alludes to a historical circumstance or a nationalistic hope, though the latter seems the more likely idea since the whole poem falls under the rubric of "promise" (60:8).

In Psalm 83:6–9 [5–8], Moab appears along with Edom, the Ishmaelites, the Hagrites, Gebal, Ammon, Amalek, Philistia, Tyre and Assyria as a nation that has conspired to destroy the people of YHWH. The coalition is described as "the strong arm of the children of Lot" indicating that Ammon and Moab are the instigators of the action.[79] It is unclear what historical conspiracy, if any, occasioned this Psalm.[80] We have elsewhere met the theme of Moab and Ammon plotting against Israel, and this aspect of the text is very plausible, even if the membership of the coalition seems inflated beyond the realm of possibility.[81] Perhaps we have here a fear of "the sons of Lot" that has deepened into a mild paranoia.

Ruth alone among all the texts in the HB has been construed as presenting Moab, or at least the Moabite woman Ruth, in a positive light.[82] Such an interpretation of the story probably misses the point, however. Part of the narrative tension in Ruth derives from the danger involved in Elimelech's family seeking

---

[78]Christensen (*Transformations*, 125–27); A. Anderson, *The Book of Psalms*, Vol. 1 (NCBC; Grand Rapids: Eerdmans, 1972) 445. Cf. Ruth 4:7; Deut 11:24.

[79]Christensen (*Transformations*, 117) comments, "On the basis of the observed use of the phenomenon of poetic inclusion [in Psalm 83], one can conclude that the dominant party in the conspiracy is Moab."

[80]Ibid., 117–118. After noting that "It is not possible to date the historical situation recalled in this poem with any degree of certainty," Christensen suggests that the situation behind this Psalm is the same as that behind Isaiah 15–16, 2 Kings 3, 2 Chr 20:1–30, and the description of Mesha's campaign against Horonaim (what may have been the description of such a campaign is contained in a section of the Mesha Inscription that, except for the opening line, has been lost). That such an hypothesis may be proposed and meet no contradicting evidence demonstrates only the meagerness of the evidence for dating the mentioned biblical texts.

[81]So A. Weiser, *The Psalms: A Commentary* (London: SCM, 1962) 562–64.

[82]See the examples and discussion in D. Fewell and D. Gunn, *Compromising Redemption: Relating Characters in the Book of Ruth* (Louisville: Westminster/John Knox, 1990) 11–13.

refuge in Moab during a famine and the even greater threat presented when Elimelech's two sons marry Orpah and Ruth, Moabite women. These dangerous decisions bear fruit when not only Elimelech, but also his two sons, die in the land of Moab. Moreover, the narrator subtly calls to mind the Moabite primal scene of origin (Gen 19) in his account of Ruth lying down by the drunken Boaz on the threshing floor (Ruth 3).[83] Quite probably the story assumes and plays upon the contempt the Israelites felt toward the Moabites.[84] At the very least, the story presents a complex picture, as difficult to interpret as it is intriguing. It does not, however, give any solid evidence of a positive attitude toward Moab and in no way suggests that amicable relations existed between the nations at the time it was written.

Ruth's depiction of a Judean family seeking refuge in Moab during a Cisjordan famine lends credence to the "fat Moabite" theme found in Judges 3. The story assumes that Moab is a land blessed with a plentiful food supply. Judeans may be scraping the bottom of their grain jars, but in Moab there is still food aplenty, even enough to share with sojourners. Topographical and climatological facts suggest that this theme has its basis in historical reality.[85]

---

[83]The second genealogy at the end of the book seems also to do this by tracing Boaz's lineage back to Perez, the scion of the Judah-Tamar incest. Thus King David descends from two oddly conjoined lines, both of which began in incest.

[84]So Fewell and Gunn, 25–28, 69–70, 72–74. L. Handy argues that "Even the character of Ruth is derived from the contempt in which the Israelites held the Moabites" (239). The assessment of the Moabitess Ruth in later Jewish tradition was often very positive, of course; see J. Neusner, *The Mother of the Messiah in Judaism: The Book of Ruth* (The Bible of Judaism Library; Valley Forge, PA: Trinity International, 1993).

[85]The Medeba plateau, especially toward the north, receives sufficient rainfall and has soil sufficiently porous and able to hold water to enable successful agriculture. Rainfall at the northern end of the plateau where Heshbon and Elealah were located approaches 20 inches per year, and all the territory north of the wadi Mujib receives at least 10 to 15 inches per year (H. G. May, ed., *Oxford Bible Atlas* [New York: Oxford University, 1984^3] 51). The rolling plains are very attractive for pasturing flocks both today and, as is shown by Num 32:1 and 2 Kgs 3:4, in ancient times. On the agricultural productivity of this area see further J. M. Miller ("Moab and the Moabites," 2).

One source outside the HB must also be included in this study. The Mesha Inscription reports King Mesha of Moab's struggle to overcome the Omride domination of his kingdom.

> Omri was king of Israel, and he oppressed Moab for many days because Kemosh was angry with his country. His son succeeded him, and he also said, "I will oppress Moab." In my days he said th[is]. But I prevailed over him and over his house, and Israel utterly perished forever. Now Omri had taken possession of a[ll the lan]d of Mehadaba...but Kemosh returned it in my days.[86]

Mesha unmistakably considers the Israelites to have been Moab's principal enemy. His inscription records at length how he succeeded in driving the Israelites out of Moab, fortifying his strongholds and building his royal city at Qarḥoh. In the process of accomplishing all this, he did several things that no doubt deeply angered the Israelites. He used Israelite captives as forced laborers to build his royal city (lns 25–26); he killed "the entire population" of the Israelite city ʿAṭarot as "a satiation for Kemosh and for Moab," and took some cultic object ("the altar hearth of its DWD") from the city to present it before his own god (lns 11–12); and he killed all the Israelites who lived in Nebo, seven thousand, he claims, and took its holy vessels to present before Kemosh (lns 14–18). We may assume that Mesha was a very successful ruler and left Moab much stronger at his death than when he took the throne. He left Moab in a position of strength vis-á-vis Israel and Judah that it seems to have enjoyed up to and beyond the exile.[87]

---

[86]Lines 4–9. All citations are from the translation found in A. Dearman, ed., *Studies in the Mesha Inscription and Moab*, 97–98.

[87]Jer 48:11; 2 Kgs 13:20; 24:2. It is hard to know what to make of 2 Kgs 10:32–33. The implication that Israel is still in control of the area north of the Arnon during the reign of Jehu flatly contradicts the Mesha Inscription. Mesha probably still controlled the area from Heshbon southward at this point. Can we then assume that 2 Kgs 10:32–33 means that Syria took control of this area shortly after Mesha had so brilliantly recaptured and fortified it? (so Miller, "Moab and the Moabites," 40). It seems more likely that 2 Kgs 10:32–33 is a simplification of how Israel lost control of the Transjordan during this period. The Syrians receive all the credit, but 2 Kgs 3 and the Mesha Inscription suggest that the Moabites were responsible for Israel's failure to retain its hold on Moab.

The Assyrian records mention that Moab rendered tribute to Tiglath-pileser, Sargon, Sennacherib, and Esarhaddon. Ashurbanipal used Moabite

The general picture of the shift of power from Israel to Moab in the last half of the ninth century is common to both the Mesha Inscription and the HB. Quite probably this shift had a great deal to do with Moab's conquest and subsequent fortification of key cities along the border between the two countries. Many of the steps that Mesha took to free his land of Israelite domination were no doubt considered great atrocities by the Israelites. These atrocities together with the "bragging rights" Moab won through the successful fortifying of its cities and securing of its territory are sufficient in themselves to account for the hatred and longing for revenge that we have found throughout the HB. The Mesha Inscription thus reveals what are surely some of the most significant events underlying the strong animosity between the two nations, perhaps even the events that gave rise to the hatred. In any case, friendly relations between the two states were unlikely after the middle of the ninth century.

In summary, we may safely assume that Israel's and Judah's attitude toward Moab in most periods of their history was very negative. They hated the Moabites and longed for their destruction. Indeed, it appears that in the pre-exilic period Israel and Judah's hatred of Moab exceeded their hatred of other neighboring enemies. Consider that two of the primary instances of derisive humor found in the HB, the story of Ehud and the story of Lot and his daughters, concern Moab.[88] Both satirize the Moabites by means of sexual and/or scatological imagery, a technique we have observed also in Isa 25:10–12 and Jer 48:26. This testifies to a widely shared delight in deriding Moab with

---

soldiers in his battles with Egypt and in his campaigns against the Arabian king Uate' (J. M. Miller, "Moab and the Moabites," 25). But the Assyrians never conquered the land of Moab; nor for that matter did the Babylonians. Apparently, Moabite kings successfully negotiated a safe passage through the tumultuous political times of the eighth and seventh centuries and preserved their kingdom intact. On this history see J. Bartlett, "The Moabites and Edomites," *Peoples of Old Testament Times* (ed. D. Wiseman; Oxford: Clarendon, 1973) 229–44; J. M. Miller, "Moab and the Moabites," 24–26.

[88] A. Brenner cites these two stories as leading examples of the comic in the HB ("Semantic Field," 41–42).

low humor.[89] Israel's fear and hatred of Moab is obvious in the Baalam and Baal Peor narratives and is even enacted in law in Deut 23:4–7 [3–6]. When we add to these examples the "mocking song" found in Num 21:27–30 and the extremely negative treatment of Moab in late prophetic texts, we have considerable evidence for a long-lived Israelite tradition of hatred for Moab. Even the Ammonites, who are sometimes reviled alongside the Moabites, are abused less frequently. What other nation among the neighboring enemies of Israel and Judah is singled out for the intense hatred and abuse heaped on Moab?

We have seen that the Mesha Inscription reveals at least some of the reasons behind the hatred. Mesha won for Moab (at Israel's expense) a position of strength and security that meant that Moab was never "emptied from cup to cup" as were Israel and later Judah (Jer 48:11). Deriding the Moabites with tales and poems of low humor was probably a popular outlet for the frustration and anger the Israelites and Judeans felt over the loss of territory they suffered at Mesha's hand and over the subsequent contrast between their own vulnerability and Moab's relative security.

This frustration and anger was no doubt made acute by the derision aimed at Israel and Judah by the Moabites. Several times in the prophets Moab is portrayed as arrogant and boastful—taunting Israel and Judah, laughing at their neighbors' vulnerability and misfortunes. The fear of the Moabite cultus implicit in several texts in the HB (Numbers 22–24; 25; 2 Kings 3) perhaps expresses the anxiety and jealousy caused by Moab's success and security: is Chemosh more powerful than YHWH after all? The Israelites could only comfort themselves with the belief that justice would prevail and Moab would soon be punished. But though the longing for judgment against Moab was strong, apparently it was never fully satisfied during the history of the states of Israel and Judah.

---

[89]See Handy, 240–41, on "low humor."

V. Conclusion

The foregoing analysis of the Israelite and Judean attitude toward Moab provides a context in which to read Isaiah 15–16. Reading the chapters in that context, we are confronted with an obvious anomaly. These chapters alone include verses which display a positive attitude toward Moab. Given the evidence presented above, however, including the prominent use of ironic satire in prophetic texts and the co-textual indication provided by Isa 14:4–21, the most likely explanation for this anomaly is that the verses in question were intended to be heard or read as irony.

The decision to read Isaiah 15–16 ironically suggests at least two things further. First, it suggests that the poem has literary integrity. The one real obstacle to reading the poem as an integral unit is removed when its ironic intention is perceived. Second, it suggests that, while the poem appears to be *sui generis*, it belongs in the same general category as the *mašal* in Isa 14:4b–23, that of taunt or mocking song. The poem is satiric; it is a mocking song based on an ironic use of the lament genre.

Why then have so many commentators either missed or dismissed the irony in Isaiah 15–16? W. Booth comments,

> Every reader will have greatest difficulty detecting irony that mocks his own beliefs or characteristics. If an author invents a speaker whose stupidities strike me as gems of wisdom, how am I to know that he is not a prophet? If his mock style seems like good writing to me, what am I to do? And if his incongruities of fact and logic are such as I might commit, I am doomed.[90]

Booth's observations suggest that past interpreters have missed and dismissed the irony in the poem because of certain of their own "beliefs or characteristics." What beliefs and characteristics have led interpreters to miss the irony? Or, to put this another way, What beliefs or characteristics are we required to assume in order to catch the irony? First, we are required to assume hatred for the Moabites.[91] If we fail to agree with the writer that the

---

[90]Booth, 81.

[91]In reading an ancient text, one is required to align oneself as closely as possible with the ancient audience. One need not actually agree with their

Moabites are indeed odious, an arrogant people who have treated us badly, then we shall miss the irony. Secondly, we must believe that satire of the Moabites in their hour of need is acceptable, indeed, that it is desirable and good. Thirdly, we must believe that the speaker or writer is both temperamentally and artistically capable of ironic satire. Fouthly, we must be capable of detecting irony, we must have an ear for it (this characteristic is not inherent in human nature, though it is typical of it).

Considering these requirments, it is easy to guess why modern interpreters have been inclined to miss, or dismiss, biting irony in Isaiah 15–16. The image of Israel's prophets as great theologians and examples of piety has influenced scholars and laity alike. The notion that the prophets should engage in biting satire and damning vitriol does not fit well with this image. In his article on "Irony and Satire" in the *Interpreters Dictionary of the Bible,* W. F. Stinespring comments:

> The outstanding example [of satire] in the Bible is the prophets' bitter criticism of the corrupt society in which they lived. The terrific impact of this satire is often avoided or evaded by readers or exegetes who wish to see the Bible as a book entirely of sweetness and light (e.g., the many absurdly sentimental interpretations of the life and theology of Hosea). In general, the extent of satire in the Bible is probably unknown to many.[92]

Similarly, David Fishelov has noted the tendency of biblical critics "to regard biblical satire and mockery as 'inferior' to the prophecies that express sublime anger and visions of redemption." This, he supposes, results from the concern that an image problem might develop if the satirical element in prophecy were highlighted: "this emphasis might produce the effect of casting the prophet in the role of a perpetual railer, a bothersome person who hurls his satirical arrows on surrounding society: thus, the aura of

---

views, but to project one's own views onto the ancient audience destroys historical exegesis.

[92]Vol. E-J, p. 727.

the prophet as a medium of God's solemn pronouncements would run the danger of being sharply diminished."[93]

To these observations we may add two others. First, it appears that the Christian ideal of love for one's enemy has influenced some interpreters. This is not to claim that love always typifies Christian practice, especially in the area of international politics, but that the idea that simple hatred for an enemy should be expressed in the Bible presents a problem for Christian interpreters.[94] What place in sacred scripture can there be for expressions of sarcasm and gloating at the misfortunes of another? The Christian doctrine of inspiration (in its many nuanced forms, not entirely limited to conservative scholars), as well as the idea of poetic inspiration (a similar idea, but one more acceptable among "liberal" scholars, e.g., Gunkel), imply that the words of the

---

[93]Fishelov, 196. Fishelov's observations about the negative image of the satirist are confirmed in L. Feinberg's *Introduction to Satire* (Ames, Iowa: The Iowa State University Press, 1967). "Satire bears a bad name," says Feinberg, and he proceeds at length to describe the distastefulness and deficiencies of satire and satirists (263–272). Of particular interest is his note that "satire is, or is generally regarded as being, cruel. Caustic people are not popular, for even those who laugh at the satirist's quips are uncomfortably aware that his next jibe may be at their expense. They prefer to avoid him. Since superiority and aggression are basic elements in the satiric process, there is much that is cruel in the satirist's method" (267). He quotes the psychologist E. Bergler as saying that satire is "a pseudoaggressive mechanism by means of which the neurotic satirist works off some of the conflicts within his masochistic personality" (270). This negative attitude toward the satirist is found among the ancients also. Aristotle comments, "We feel shame with respect to those whose chief occupation is with the failings of their fellow men; satirists, for example, and comic poets—for these are, in effect, evil-speakers and tale-bearers" (*The Rhetoric of Aristotle* [Englewood Cliffs, NJ: Prentice-Hall, 1932] §2.6; p. 115). While not all biblical scholars will have held such an extremely negative attitude toward satire and the satirist, many of them will have had an attitude sufficiently negative to discourage them from imagining the prophets as satirists. In this regard it is interesting to note that the most comprehensive study to date of satire in the prophetic literature was produced not by a biblical scholar, but by a professor of English (T. Jemielity).

[94]Compare in many of the commentaries the struggle that Christian interpreters have with the story of Jesus's rebuke of the Syro-Phoenician women in Mark 7:27. Perhaps the fact that Jewish interpreters are prominent among those who have led the way in finding satire in the prophets is significant in this regard.

biblical prophets communicate a message of unique status. Is hatred and invective the stuff of inspiration? The anxiety interpreters feel over such sentiments is especially noticeable in connection with the Psalms, where the straightforward (and therefore unavoidable) communication of strong hatred for enemies has elicited many explanations. This problem can be avoided more easily in Isaiah 15–16. One may even interpret the prophet's unique attitude toward Moab as a sign of great piety and identification with the suffering of God over the sin of the nations.

The effect of these presuppositions and values is obvious in many of the treatments of Isaiah 15–16, especially those written by conservative scholars. It shows itself, for example, in the way J. Alexander takes Calvin to task for his ironic reading of the poem:

> Calvin adopts this general view of the meaning of the verse, but interprets it ironically..., and understands the Prophet as intending to reproach the Moabites sarcastically for their cruel treatment of the Jewish fugitives in former times. This forced interpretation, which is certainly unworthy of its author, seems to have found favour with no other. It is not the first case in which Calvin has allowed his exposition to be marred by the gratuitous assumption of a sarcastic and ironical design.[95]

Barnes's comment on the expression of sympathy in 15:5 reveals an ethic in which love for an enemy represents not a conflict but an example of prophetic (and Christian) virtue:

> ...here, the phrase is designed to denote the deep compassion which a holy man of God would have, even when predicting the ills that should come upon others. How much compassion, how much deep and tender feeling should ministers of the gospel have when they are describing the final ruin—the unutterable woes of impenitent sinners under the awful wrath of God...![96]

---

[95]Alexander, 323. Cf. 315.

[96]A. Barnes, *Notes: Critical, Explanatory, and Practical on the Book of the Prophet Isaiah* (2 vols; Boston: Crocker & Brewster, 1840) 1. 290. In a similar vein, E. Young (*The Book of Isaiah* [3 vols; NICOT; Grand Rapids: Eerdmans, 1965–72] 1. 455; cf. 458, 466–67) comments: "Isaiah enters into the suffering of Moab, for his own heart is painfully affected and grieved by what he knows must come to pass. What a picture of the true evangelist!" Cf. Delitzsch, 322;

Elsewhere we find comparisons between the deep empathy expressed in the poem and that found in Jeremiah's laments.[97] Occasionally, one finds also among higher-critical scholars an acknowledgement of the conflict. W. Rudolph notes: "Bemerkenswert ist, daß kein Haß gegen Moab vorliegt, beim Propheten sogar Mitleid, das man nicht für scheinheilig und ironisch halten darf."[98] Wildberger's concluding comments on the chapters have an affinity with those of the more conservative group:

> Aufs Ganze gesehen hat die Stimme des Mitleidens mit Moab das Übergewicht und muß ernst genommen werden. Das theologische Zentrum, schon durch den Aufbau der beiden Kapitel als solches gekennzeichnet, ist 16[1.3–5], die "messianische Weissangung", die unbeholfen tastend für das vielgeplagte Moab ein Tor der Hoffnung zeigt. Eines Tages wird Druck und Vergewaltigung vorüber sein und Moabs so durchdringende Klage verstummen.[99]

On the whole, however, the higher-critical redactional analysis and reattribution of authorship alleviates the conflict in the poem sufficiently that these scholars feel little need to comment on the expressions of sympathy. Still, one suspects that, at least occasionally, higher-critical scholars have also been influenced by the preconceived image of the prophets as examples of piety and morality.

In light of the interpretation of commentators in the last two centuries, Luther and Calvin's acknowledgement of the irony and sarcasm in the poem seems surprising. Far from being embarrassed by the poem's irony, Luther positively delights in the sarcasm. Perhaps the historical circumstances of the two great reformers explain this. For them, religion and politics were inex-

---

H. Leupold, *Exposition of Isaiah* (2 vols.; Grand Rapids: Baker, 1963–1971) 1. 289.

[97]See, for example, Oswalt, 346 (Oswalt's approach to the problem has been summarized above in our history of interpretation), and Gesenius, 160.

[98]Rudolph, "Isaiah xv–xvi," 143. Similarly, see Wildberger, *Jesaja*, 617–18, and Fohrer, 193.

[99]632. See also his comments on 16:9 where the extreme expressions of sympathy lead Wildberger to conclude that either a different author is speaking or the same author *aus einer andern Stimmung* (628; similarly, see his comments on 16:11, p. 594).

tricably intertwined, and as a result both men experienced personal and international strife and hatred profoundly. Indeed, their revolutionary ideas and political struggles several times caused their very lives to be threatened by powerful foes.[100] They knew at first hand what it was to attack and be attacked in the service of God, and they would have been predisposed to accept that this was an acceptable mode of behavior among God's prophets of old. Indeed, Luther is well known to have possessed a caustic wit, and freely to have satirized those he considered enemies.[101]

On the whole, the most prominent "beliefs or characteristics" responsible for causing interpreters to read the poem straightforwardly, even while acknowledging the contradiction this entails, are those widely prized virtues of respect, restraint, tolerance, and even love for one's enemies—in some cases the *imitatio Christi*. These are no doubt worthy values, ones which many people hold. If we are to read the poem ironically, however, we must accept an image of the prophet as a satirist, even as a "perpetual railer, a bothersome person." If we are to place ourselves among the poem's original audience (in so far as this is possible), we must be ready to hate the Moabites, to wish them destroyed, to rejoice and gloat over their misfortune. Then we shall be suitably prepared to catch the poet's meaning in the confession, "My bowels growl like a lyre for Moab" (16:11).

---

[100]W. Walker, *A History of the Christian Church* (New York: Charles Scribner's Sons, 1970[3]) 301–57.

[101]M. Hodgart (*Satire* [New York: McGraw-Hill, 1969] 53–54; cf. 24–25; 49) comments, "All the early reformers were vigorous pamphleteers, and masters of abuse, lampooning and crude satirical techniques....Luther commissioned Cranach to make obscene drawings of the Pope."

CHAPTER 5

TEXT AND TRANSLATION

The text of Isaiah 15 and 16 has suffered corruptions in the process of its transmission; this is widely agreed. A number of issues of text and translation require discussion more extensive than may conveniently be given in a footnote. These include problems found in 15:1, 15:2, 15:3, 15:5a, 15:9 and 16:1 and are treated in a series of short essays at the beginning of this chapter. The essays are followed by our translation of the chapters together with endnotes that treat the less cumbersome issues.

Textual criticism is not separable from syntactic analysis nor can it be entirely separated from interpretation, especially when one intends to produce a translation. We have attempted in what follows to keep the discussion of textual variants and syntax from wandering too far into interpretation, but some overlap is unavoidable.

15:1

BHS מַשָּׂא מוֹאָב

כִּי בְּלֵיל שֻׁדַּד עָר מוֹאָב נִדְמָה

כִּי בְּלֵיל שֻׁדַּד קִיר־מוֹאָב נִדְמָה׃

A number of unusual features mark this verse and make its interpretation difficult. Two of them drew comment from the Masoretes. They noted that the expression בְּלֵיל occurs only here in all the HB and that נִדְמָה occurs only four times—twice in 15:1 and twice in Hos 10:15. The most unusual characteristic of the verse, however, is that, apart from the heading, it consists of two nearly duplicate lines.[1] There is no other instance in the HB of a prophetic speech beginning in this manner. The possibility of a scribal duplication is exceedingly small since the versions are unanimous in their support of the MT.

Adding to the challenge presented by these unique features is the syntactical ambiguity of the lines. Is כי causative or asseverative? Is בליל to be taken as a construct form or repointed as an absolute? Are ער and קיר to be connected with מואב as compound place names, to be taken separately from מואב as the proper names "Ar" and "Kir," or to be taken separately as the common nouns "city" and "wall"? If the compound names are read, of which verb are they the subject, שדד or נדמה?

Scholars have wrestled to resolve the problem. Very early there was preference for dividing Ar and Kir from Moab and assigning each verb its own subject. Examples of translations based on this strategy include:

Lowth
Because Ar is utterly destroyed, Moab is undone
Because Kir is utterly destroyed, Moab is undone.[2]

Gray
Because in a (single) night ʿAr has been spoiled, Moab is undone;
Because in a night Ḳir has been spoiled, Moab is undone.[3]

Driver
For in the night when Ar was sacked
Moab was brought to nought;
for in the night when Kir was sacked
Moab was brought to nought.[4]

---

[1]For other examples of duplicate or nearly duplicate lines see R. Lowth, *Lectures on the Sacred Poetry of the Hebrews*, tr. G. Gregory (London: S. Chadwick & Co., 1847) 212–213.

[2]R. Lowth, 225. Lowth's translation is based on his emendation of the beginning of both lines to read כִּי כָּלִיל. He interpreted the expression כָּלִיל as "utterly."

[3]Gray, 273.

[4]S. R. Driver, "Isaiah I–XXXIX: Textual and Linguistic Problems," *JSS* 13 (1968) 44.

Other commentators have preferred to read the compound form of the names:

Gesenius
Ja! in der Angriffs-Nacht wird's mit Ar-Moab aus,
ja! in der Angriffs-Nacht wird's mit Kir-Moab aus.[5]

Kaiser
Truly, laid waste in a night,
undone is Ar-Moab.
Truly, laid waste in a night,
Undone is Kir-Moab.[6]

Wildberger
Wahrlich, über Nacht wurde verheert,
wurde vernichtet Ar-Moab,
wahrlich, über Nacht wurde verheert,
wurde vernichtet Kir-Moab.[7]

There are good reasons for reading ער and קיר with מואב as either compound names or construct chains. Both the masora of the MT and the versions suggest reading the terms this way,[8] and Num 21:28 and 22:36 (emended) attest either the construct or a compound name ער מואב.[9] But reading the compound names results in difficult rhythm and syntax. Making the two verbs share the subject, ער מואב or קיר מואב, is by no means impossible, but it is unusual and disrupts the rhythm. A further problem, not often acknowledged, arises from the fact that the gender of the compound names does not agree with either of the verbs as they are pointed in the MT.[10]

---

[5]Gesenius, 37.

[6]Kaiser, 57.

[7]Wildberger, 588.

[8]The cantillation marks in 15:1a group שדד ער מואב together as a unit, and the *māqqēp̄* draws קיר מואב together emphatically. The LXX and other Greek translators dropped ער and rendered Moab with a single term, ἡ Μωαβῖτις, "the Moabite land" (see H. Smyth, *Greek Grammar* [rev. ed.; Cambridge, MA: Harvard University, 1956] §844), and קיר מואב they understood as a common noun and a gentilic in construct, τὸ τεῖχος τῆς Μωαβίτιδος, "the wall of the Moabite land." The Syriac and Targum translate both ער and קיר as common nouns in construct with Moab.

[9]Wildberger, 611.

[10] שֻׁדַּד is *puʿal* pass. 3ms; נִדְמָה is *niph* 3ms from נדה. The genders of Ar Moab and Kir Moab must be determined by inference and probability because the gender of Ar (Moab) is not indicated in the other contexts in which it is found

Solving the gender agreement problem may provide the key for understanding this verse. If נִדְמָה (√דמה, niph. pf. 3ms., "be cut off, destroyed") is repointed as נָדַמָּה (√דמם, niph. pf. 3fs.), the gender problem is half solved. The most common meaning of דמם is "to be silent," but a second sense is also attested: "to lament, wail."[11] Frequently, the sense "to lament" is as acceptable in a given context as "to be silent."[12] In the context of Isaiah 15 and 16,

---

(Num 21:15, 28; 22:36 [emended]; Deut 2:9, 18, 29), and Kir Moab occurs only here. The proper noun מואב is normally masculine, but its gender is not determinative because the gender of compound names is determined by the first or "head" element (Waltke-O'Connor, *An Introduction to Biblical Hebrew Syntax* [Winona Lake: Eisenbrauns, 1990] 6.4.1 c-d). Most city names have עִיר (n. f.) as an assumed head element (i.e., "city of ____;" for examples of names with עִיר as articulated head element, see BDB, 746). For this reason city names are usually feminine. Thus, since most interpreters assume that עָר is related to עִיר, it is most probable that Ar is a feminine noun.

The gender of קִיר may be determined with greater certainty since it is used as a head element in a context which clearly indicates the gender of the name. In 2 Kgs 3:25 קיר חרשת is twice the antecedent of a feminine pronoun. The Mesha Inscription uses קיר in lines 11, 12, 24, and 29 as a common noun meaning "city," but its gender is never clearly indicated by the context (see Dearman, 111; Dearman tentatively takes it as a feminine noun). The well-attested Hebrew term קִיר, "wall" is masculine, but both Hebrew and Moabite usage suggest that קִיר, "city," is to be kept distinct from קִיר, "wall." Thus, whether one understands ער מואב and קיר מואב as place names or as common noun + proper noun, the gender of the composite term is most probably feminine.

Gray (281) notes the gender problem and suggests that either ער "is, exceptionally, masc." or that שֻׁדַּד (and נִדְמָה?) has a hidden subject and that ער functions as an accusative after passive (cf. GKC § 130d). The latter is an improbable solution given that two verbs are involved.

[11]Wildberger (853, 855) translates דמם this way in Isa 23:2, giving as evidence the Akkadian word *damāmu*, "wail," and the arguments of M. Dahood ("Textual Problems in Isaiah," *CBQ* 22, 400–403). Dahood argues convincingly from a Ugaritic parallel that the Hebrew root *dmm* carries the meaning "to mourn." He cites Isa 23:3; 38:10; Lam 2:10; and Ps 4:5 as instances in which *dmm*, "to mourn" is the most appropriate translation. The first meaning of דמם has prevailed among translators of 15:1 largely, one suspects, because no secure line of argument for the second meaning had been offered. BDB (198–99) gives the definition "wail" under meaning II but lists only one instance, and to this it attaches the caveat, "most, however, assign this to [meaning] I."

[12]Wildberger, 855, notes that the meaning "lament, wail" is appropriate where דמם is used in Pss. 4:5; 31:18; Lam 2:10. All occurrences of the Niph.

the meaning "to lament" is very fitting. When translated "...Ar/Kir Moab laments" the first verse makes sense as a general heading for the rest of the poem, a poem devoted primarily to a description of Moab's lament. The pointing נָדַמָּה thus has the double advantage of solving part of the gender agreement problem and of establishing a very sensible thematic connection between 15:1 and the following description of lamentation.

Several of the versions support the pointing נָדַמָּה. The LXX has ἀπολεῖται twice in 15:1a and b, but it appears that ἀπολεῖται translates שדד and that נדמה has simply been dropped.[13] Aquila, Symmachus and Theodotion likewise translate שדד with ἀπολεῖται, but they render the second occurrence of נדמה with either ἐσιώπησεν (α and θ) or ἐσιωπήθη (σ), "to be silenced." This would indicate that they derived נדמה in 15:1b from דמם rather than from דמה.[14] The same is true of the Syriac which has *ʾtbzzt*, "to destroy," for שדד, and *wtmhw*, "to be numb, speechless," for נדמה. Targum Jonathan renders נדמה with רדימין, "they slept," most likely reading דמם. Finally, the Vulgate translates נדמה as *conticuit* (has become

---

easily bear the meaning "to lament" (1 Sam 2:9; Jer 25:37; 49:26; 50:30; 51:6. On this reflexive sense of the Niph. see Waltke-O'Connor, 23.3c). For example, in Jer 25:37 the verse fits much better with the context when translated:

> Hark, the cry of the shepherds,
> and the wail of the lords of the flock!
> For the Lord is despoiling their pasture,
> and the peaceful folds *lament* [RSV: "are devastated," emending],
> because of the fierce anger of the Lord.

All occurrences of *dmm* in the HB should be reexamined. What we know of mourning in the ancient Near East would suggest that it is characterized by loud cries, not silence (Dahood, 402). Where *dmm* occurs in contexts of lamentation the meaning "mourn" or "lament" should be preferred over "be silent" unless there is good contextual reason to suppose that the reaction described is one of stunned silence.

[13]Isa 15:1, LXX: Τὸ ῥῆμα τὸ κατὰ τῆς Μωαβίτιδος. Νυκτὸς ἀπολεῖται ἡ Μωαβῖτις, νυκτὸς γὰρ ἀπολεῖται τὸ τεῖχος τῆς Μωαβίτιδος. All LXX citations, both here and subsequently, are from the Göttingen edition.

[14]According to Hatch and Redpath, the LXX translates דמם six times with σιωπάω, but only once does it use σιωπάω to translate דמה (Lam 3:49). Cf. Wildberger, 590.

silent). The MT alone points the verb as נִדְמָה; the versions are uniformly on the side of the pointing נָדַמָּה.

Repointing נדמה does not, however, completely solve the gender problem. The first term, שדד, also presents a problem when pointed as in the MT (*puʿal* pf. 3ms). The gender agreement conflict presented by שֻׁדַּד may also be resolved by repointing, but before assaying possible alternatives one must consider the question of the preceding term, בליל, a rare construct form.[15] The construct form is often dismissed as impossible, but if one repoints שֻׁדַּד as שֹׁדֵד (Qal ptc.) and translates "Indeed, in the night of [the] destroyer...", a solution emerges that both makes sense of the construct form and solves the gender agreement and rhythm problems.

What justification exists, other than the need for gender agreement, for pointing שדד as a substantive participle and translating it "destroyer"? In Isa 16:4 the enemy of Moab is denoted in the phrase מִפְּנֵי שׁוֹדֵד "before the destroyer."[16] Jeremiah 48 also refers to "the destroyer of Moab" (שֹׁדֵד מוֹאָב v 18) and "the destroyer" (שֹׁדֵד vv 8, 32). Elsewhere in the HB the substantive use of the Qal ptc. of שדד is well attested.[17] Obad 5 is particularly intriguing because it shares several elements with Isa 15:1:

---

[15]Gray (281) and Wildberger (590) both reject this construct form; Driver (44) reads the construct with the following perfect verb and cites GK, § 130d, as support. Q gives the form בלילה, but the MT has the more difficult text, and the text of Q is plausibly explained as an attempt at improvement. Thus the MT is to be preferred. Though the construct form of לילה is indeed rare, it does occur in Exod 12:42, לֵיל שִׁמֻּרִים, and Isa 30:29 (cf. non-construct instances in Isa 16:3; 21:11; Prov 31:18; Lam 2:19). For comparable references to attack "in the night," see Jer 6:5; 49:9; Isa 28:19.

[16]This term may again designate the enemy in Isa 16:9c; the parallel Jer text (48:32) has שדד instead of הידד, and it is possible that the הידד in 16:9c was mistakenly copied back from the end of Isa 16:10. The Targum has בזוזין נפלו, "destroyers have fallen," reflecting a Hebrew *vorlage* of שדד נקל. See also the use of this term in Isa 21:2 and 33:1.

[17]It is especially common in Jeremiah: 6:26; 12:6, 12; 15:8; 25:36; 47:4; 51:48, 53, 55, 56. On the other hand, the *puʿal* 3ms is only attested twice in Jeremiah, 48:15, 20. Other instances of שֹׁדֵד include Job 15:21; Isa 21:2; 33:1; Obad 5.

אִם־גַּנָּבִים בָּאוּ־לְךָ֙ אִם־שׁוֹדְדֵי לַיְלָה
אֵיךְ נִדְמֵיתָה הֲלוֹא יִגְנְבוּ דַּיָּם
אִם־בֹּצְרִים֙ בָּאוּ לָךְ הֲלוֹא יַשְׁאִירוּ עֹלֵלוֹת׃

If thieves came to you,
if plunderers by night
—how you have been destroyed!—
would they not steal only what they wanted?
If grape-gatherers came to you,
would they not leave gleanings?

The expression שׁוֹדְדֵי לַיְלָה אֵיךְ נִדְמֵיתָה has striking similarities to Isa 15:1. The construct relationship is reversed, but merely the linking of לילה and שדד when coupled with the fact that נִדְמֵיתָה appears in the very same line suggests that Obad 5 and Isa 15:1 both draw on a common poetic idiom or that there has been influence, either direct or mediated by a common source. Note also the metaphor employed in 5b; the loss Edom is to suffer is compared with the loss of viniculture. This resonates with the plight of Moab as described in Isa 16:8–10. While the nature of the relationship between these two texts is uncertain, the comparison suggests the appropriateness of the Qal ptc. pointing of שדד in Isa 15:1.

The expression "night of the destroyer" is unique in the HB, but it is not without analogy. One has only to think of the frequent term "day of Yahweh," or other such "day of..." expressions that frequently refer to military destruction (e.g., Isa 9:4; 17:11; 22:5; 27:8; 30:25; 34:8). Also significant is the expression found in Jer 15:8, שֹׁדֵד בַּצָּהֳרָיִם, "A destroyer at noonday," which provides an example of the substantive ptc. of שדד used with time expression. Thus, several good analogies for the translation "night of the destroyer" exist. Repointing the text as here proposed creates a phrase that is entirely clear and appropriate to the context; it solves the gender, construct form, and rhythm problems; and it requires no change of the consonantal text. For these reasons it should be preferred.

One question remains: Are עָר מוֹאָב and קִיר־מוֹאָב proper place names or construct chains formed on the pattern common noun +

proper noun? A good deal of uncertainty attends this question.[18] Does "the city of Moab" refer to Dibon, Mesha's primary residence and center of power (see MI lines 1–2, 21, 28)? Does it refer to another chief city named "Kir"? Is Kir an abbreviation of a longer name such as Kir Hareseth, Kiriathaim or Kerioth? Does 15:1a designate the city usually referred to as "ער" (Num 21:15; Deut 2:9, 18, 29)?

Two assumptions have guided most translators. First, it has been assumed that Ar and Kir were singled out in the thematic heading to the poem because they were Moab's most prominent cities. Kir is usually equated with Kir Hareseth on the assumption that it is a shortened form of that name. The context of 2 Kings 3 suggests that Kir Hareseth was Mesha's chief stronghold, and the position of Kir in Isa 15:1 suggests that it too was a principal city. As for Ar, the fact that it is mentioned relatively frequently in the HB (seven times) and the fact that it sometimes seems to be a territorial designation or even a synonym for Moab (Deut 2:9) suggests its prominence.

A second assumption has been that Isa 15:1 reports the destruction of both Ar and Kir. Those who translate "Because Ar/Kir is destroyed, Moab is undone" usually understand the verse to be saying that because Moab's defense depended on these two essential places, their destruction signals the downfall of Moab.[19] Those who translate "Truly, laid waste in a night, undone is Ar/Kir Moab" usually suggest that the destruction of these two principal cities is a metonym for the destruction of the whole land.[20] In either case, it is assumed that 15:1 refers to the destruction of two principal cities.

The first assumption is weak for several reasons. It is unlikely that Kir is a shortened form of Kir Hareseth or any other Moabite name beginning with the קיר element. When two-element place names of this type are apocopated, the first element—the generic

---

[18]See Schottroff, "Horonaim, Nimrin, Luhith...," 179–81; J. M. Miller, "The Israelite Journey Through (Around) Moab and Moabite Toponymy," *JBL* 108 (1989) 590–92.

[19]For example, Lowth, *Isaiah*, 226; Gray, 274–75; Oswalt, 334, 336–37.

[20]For example, Eichhorn, 247–48; Ewald, 144–45; Gesenius, 127–32; Kaiser, 57, 65–66.

term—is dropped, not the second, significant element.[21] The head element, in this case קיר, would not appear by itself as the truncation of a longer name. We might, of course, suppose that קיר is the full name (not a shortened name) of a prominent Moabite city. Such an idea presents us with a new problem; neither the Mesha Inscription nor the HB ever mentions a place named "Kir." One would expect a prominent city to appear more than once in these texts, containing as they do such an unusually large number of Moabite place names. This argues against the idea that the proper name Kir is a designation of a prominent Moabite city. Another possibility is to suppose that "Kir Moab" should be understood as an appellative for Moab's capital, "the city of Moab," another name for Dibon, for instance.[22] This suggestion is not without problems. One is still confronted with the peculiarity that this appellative designation for Moab's capital appears nowhere else in the HB or the Mesha Inscription, and the poetic parallelism of 15:1 is diminished when the appellative phrase, "the city of Moab," is paralleled with a proper place name, "Ar Moab."

---

[21]Waltke-O'Connor, §§ 6.4.1c-d; 13.4b; 13.6a; GKC §125h. Examples from the HB include Beth Nimrah (Num 32:36; Josh 13:27) and Nimrah (Num 32:3); Beth Baal-meon (Josh 13:17; Num 32:38) and Baal-meon (1Chr 5:8; Ezek 25:9); for other examples see W. Borée, *Die alten Ortsnamen Palästinas* (Leipzig: Eduard Pfeiffer, 1930) 75–98, esp. 97–98. Proper names, especially geographical appellatives, occasionally exhibit the opposite behavior, e.g., Ramoth-gilead is referred to as both הרמה (2 Kgs 8:29; 2 Chr 22:6) and רמות גלעד (1 Kgs 22:3, 4, 6, 12, 15, 19; 2 Kgs 8:28; 9:1, 4, 14). But the appellative force of names such as this is typically marked by the addition of the definite article when only the first element is given (e.g., הרמה, הגבעה; cf. territorial descriptors such as המישור, השפלה, etc.; see BDB 207). GKC notes that "When nouns which the usage of the language always treats as proper names occasionally appear to be connected with a following genitive, this is really owing to an ellipse whereby the noun which really governs the genitive, i.e. the appellative idea contained in the proper name, is suppressed" (§125h). In the case of רמות גלעד the ellipse would be Ramoth (the city of) Gilead. The same applies to non-appellative names such as Dibon-Gad (Dibon [the city of] Gad). In this instance, which represents a rare type, the head element does occur alone without an article. This is no doubt due to the fact that Dibon is a true proper noun. We may conclude, therefore, that while קיר מואב is a possible place name, the idea that קיר by itself is a place name or an abbreviation of a place name is highly improbable.

[22]Kaiser, 65–66.

Of course the parallelism would make sense if "the city of Moab" denoted Ar. But what do we know of Ar? Ar's role in Moab's political structure is unclear. Even its location is uncertain. Recently, J. M. Miller has argued for identifying it with Kh. Balūᶜ, a site on the main north-south roadway where it ascends to the plateau from the Wadi Mujib (at this point, Wadi el-Bālūᶜ) canyon.[23] Regardless of whether one locates Ar at er-Rabba, Kh. ᶜArāᶜir or Kh. Balūᶜ, its location near or south of the Mujib makes it an unlikely candidate to be singled out in the heading of the poem describing an attack focused on territory located primarily north of Medeba. Its strategic value in such an attack would be minimal.

The question of the location of Ar and Kir may be beside the point. The terms may well be only common nouns. The versions unanimously translate קִיר as a common noun.[24] The evidence is even more compelling in the case of עָר. 1QIsa[a] has עיר, "city," in both 15a & b.[25] The versions also suggest that we should read common nouns. It is helpful to survey the versions' treatment of ער in all occurrences in the HB. The evidence is summarized in the following table:

[23]Miller, "Israelite Journey," 590–95. Miller (and others) have noted that the Iron Age road across the Arnon would not have ascended the steep south canyon wall as does the modern highway; it would have followed the path along the Wādī el-Bālūᶜ.

[24]The LXX and Greek fathers give τεῖχος, "wall"; the Targum translates לחיית, "fortress"; the Syriac has *šwryh*, "the wall."

[25]Num 22:36 also refers to עיר מואב, and Wildberger (612) has suggested that perhaps all instances of ער in the HB should be pointed as עִר. He bases this idea on the observation that Moabite does not give the internal *matres*, a fact that might have confused a later scribe.

	Num 21:15	Num 21:28	Deut 2:9	Deut 2:18	Deut 2:29	Isa 15:1
LXXA	ἤρ	ἕως (= עד)	ἀροηρ	ἀροηρ	ἀροηλ	dropped out
LXXB	ἤρ	ἕως	σηειρ	σηειρ	ἀροηρ	dropped out
Other Gk	σηιρ, σιηρ, σιιρ, etc.	ἕως	ἀροηρ, σηειρ	σηειρ	ἀροηρ	πολις (Sym. and Aq.)
Syriac	ʿd	ʿd	dropped out	ʿd	ʿd	qrytʾ[26]
Sam Pent.	עיר	עד	ער	ער	ער	
Targum	לחיית	לחיית	לחיית	לחיית	לחיית	לחיית

The versions recognize ער as the place name "Ar" only once, in the case of the LXX translation of Num 21:15. Frequently, the LXX translators understood ער to refer to Aroer (ערער). This would suggest that although some of the ancient translators knew a little about Moabite toponymy (the LXX translators knew about a city in Moab named Aroer), a city named "Ar" was unknown to them. The various manuscripts of the LXX tradition are unanimous in dropping ער altogether in Isa 15:1; ἡ Μωαβιτις is used to translate Hebrew מואב, not ער מואב as is often supposed.[27] Had the LXX translated ער it would presumably have rendered it in one of the three ways it does elsewhere—as Aroer, as Seir, or with a transliteration. The Targum renders ער with לחיית, "fortress," and the

[26]It is significant that the Syriac translates Hebrew קיר with *šwryh* (√*šwr*) "city wall" (see J. Smith, *A Compendious Syriac Dictionary* [Oxford: Clarendon, 1903] 568). The translator has understood both ער and קיר as common nouns.

[27]See, for example, Kaiser, 66; Schottroff, "Horonaim, Nimrim, Luhith...," 181; Wildberger, 611. Against this view, note that the LXX translates מואב with ἡ Μωαβιτις in 15:1b, 2b, 4b, 5a, 8a, etc., which indicates that ἡ Μωαβιτις is the usual translation for מואב alone (Gray pointed this out also, *Isaiah*, 279; see also E. Grohman, "A History of Moab" [Ph.D. diss., Johns Hopkins, 1958] 116–17). The LXX translation is often elliptical in this chapter, and there is nothing unusual in the fact that it simply drops ער.

Syriac translated it with *qryt'*, "city"; both these versions have read the common noun עיר and not a place name. Thus the versions do not support the translation of either ער or קיר as the proper name of a city.[28]

There are indications in the content of Isaiah 15 and 16 that also point to the conclusion that ער and קיר should be translated as common nouns and not as proper names. First, Isaiah 15 and 16 is a litany of the important cities of Moab. In the traditional understanding of 15:1, Ar and Kir Moab function as leading examples of the destruction of the cities of Moab. Since these two cities are found in the heading and since they are usually considered to be the principal cities of Moab, one would expect to find them mentioned elsewhere in the body of the poem. No other mention is made of them, however, even though cities such as Heshbon, Elealeh and probably Dibon are mentioned twice.

The best solution to the problem of Ar and Kir Moab is to read common nouns rather than proper names and to understand them as collectives:

> Indeed, in the night of the destroyer
> the cities [Israelite term] of Moab lament
> Indeed, in the night of the destroyer
> the cities [Moabite term] of Moab lament.

The context of the poem supports this translation.[29] The poem begins by portraying the lamentation of various Moabite cities. The Moabites ascend Dibon's high place to weep; on the high places of Nebo and Medeba they wail; the cry of Heshbon and Elealeh is heard as far as Jahaz. Moab's lamentation continues as a recurring theme throughout the poem (see 15:8; 16:7). The reason for lamentation is not the destruction of Moab's *cities*, as is usually thought, but the destruction of its *agriculture*. No city is actually

---

[28]The reference to ער מואב in Num 21:28 probably should also be translated as a common noun in construct with Moab, "the cities [collective] of Moab." The context of the verse suggests this. Reading the collective "cities" makes better sense of the parallel between ער מואב and בעלי במות ארנן; the "cities of Moab" in 21:28c are further defined in 28d as "the lords of the heights of the Arnon." BHS suggests emending ער to ערי apparently for the same reason, but there is no need to emend the text if ער is understood as a collective term.

[29]This will be discussed more fully below in chapter six.

said to have been destroyed or even attacked; the lamentation is prompted exclusively by the loss of the agricultural productivity of the land (cf. 15:6–7; 16:7–10).[30] The heading as it is translated above is very appropriate to the poem's content: the lamentation of Moab's cities after a nocturnal destruction of its fields and vineyards. The parallelism of the Hebrew and Moabite terms for city is a part of the rhetoric of the poem designed to remind the hearer that the "Kirs" in which the Moabites now lament were once "ʿIrs" belonging to the Israelites.

To summarize: both the rhythm and the gender problems can be overcome by repointing שֻׁדַּד and נִדְמָה as שֹׁדֵד and נָדַמָּה. In this way, 15:1 becomes a fitting thematic heading for the poem, a poem describing the lamentation of Moab in its various cities.

15:2

BHS עָלָה הַבַּיִת וְדִיבֹן הַבָּמוֹת לְבֶכִי
עַל־נְבוֹ וְעַל מֵידְבָא מוֹאָב יְיֵלִיל
בְּכָל־רֹאשָׁיו קָרְחָה כָּל־זָקָן גְּרוּעָה׃

Problems of text and translation are found in all three lines of Isa 15:2, but the perplexities of 15:2a & c are sufficiently serious to require an extended discussion.

15:2a

Regarding 15:2a, Wildberger comments, "עלה הבית ודיבן ist unverständlich."[31] The text of the MT, if translated literally, reads, "The house and Dibon have gone up to the high place to weep." The coupling of "the house" and "Dibon" is strange; one expects two place names in parallel, Dibon and Beth Diblathaim for instance. This has led several commentators to read הבית as an abbreviated place name.[32] Another way to deal with the problem is to understand "Moab" as the implied subject of עלה and translate the text

---

[30]Compare Jer 48, which has the destruction of Moab's *cities* in view: 48:1, 8, 18, 41.

[31]590, essentially quoting Duhm's pronouncement: "הבית ist unverständlich" (99).

[32]See examples cited in Gesenius, 133; BDB, 110; and Wildberger, 590.

"He [Moab] has gone up to the house (temple), and Dibon to the high place to weep."[33] In this instance הבית is logically parallel with הבמוה, and it is easily interpreted as a reference to the Moabite temple or the royal palace at Dibon.[34] The NRSV also understands הבית and הבמוה as parallel elements, but it makes Dibon the subject of עלה. Finally, with some textual emendation it is possible to take הבית in construct with דיבן and translate either "The (royal) house of Dibon has ascended the high place to weep" or "The daughter of Dibon has ascended the high place to weep."[35] In the first instance one need only drop the *waw* before Dibon and the *heh* before house/daughter.[36] In the second case, it is also necessary to change עלה to עלתה to obtain gender agreement.

The emendations required by these last two options find some support in the versions. The Targum has סליקו לבתיא דדיבון, "They go up to the houses of Dibon...," and the Syriac has *lsqw lbytʾ ddybʾn*, "They go up to the house of Dibon."[37] Both assume a construct relationship between הבית and דיבן and either ignore the *waw* before דיבן or lacked the *waw* in their *Vorlage*. The Vulgate, on the other hand, has *ascendit domus et Dibon...*, "(the) city and Dibon has gone up...."

Unfortunately, the LXX offers a translation of 15:2a that is either confused or very free: λυπεῖσθε ἐφ' ἑαυτοῖς, ἀπολεῖται γὰρ Λεβηδων· οὗ ὁ βωμὸς ὑμῶν, ἐκεῖ ἀναβήσεσθε κλαίειν: "You are grieved for yourselves, for Lebedon is destroyed; where your altar is, there you go up to cry out" (translation mine). The initial

---

[33]For example, König, 189; NJPS translation.

[34]So Gesenius, 132 (citing Kimchi). In this case it would be a shortened form of בית המלך (e.g., 1 Kgs 9:1, 10; 10:12; over 60x) or בית + DN (e.g., 1 Kgs 6:1ff.; 9:1, 10; over 78x) which appear elsewhere in the HB in an abbreviated form (e.g., "palace": Jer 22:14; 2 Sam 5:11; 1 Kgs 5:5; 2 Kgs 11:6, 11; "temple": 2 Sam 7:5; 1 Kgs 3:2 [versus high places]; 2 Kgs 12:6–8).

[35]The second option is preferred by Duhm, 99; Gray, 273, 279; Kaiser, 57; Wildberger, 588, 590.

[36]The versions may simply have ignored the anomaly of the determination of the *nomen regens*. For other examples of this anomaly see GKC, § 27 f 4 (a); Waltke-O'Connor, § 13.6. It is significant that it occurs frequently in the case of constructs formed with a place name as the *nomen rectum*, Num 21:14; 2 Kgs 23:17; Gen 31:13; Isa 36:16; etc.

[37]Also attested in the Syriac is *lsqw lbytʾ drybʾn*, "They go up to the house of Rîbʾan."

phrase is probably a simple addition to the original. The phrase עלה הבית has apparently been translated by ἀπολεῖται. One can only guess what the translators had in mind; perhaps they read עלה as "burnt offering" and applied it metaphorically to Lebedon; perhaps they read בתה, "end, destruction" (see BDB, 144; Isa 5:6) instead of הבת. In the case of Λεβηδων the manuscripts attest a wide variety of readings.[38] The *lambda* may indicate the presence of a *lamed* before Dibon in the LXX's *Vorlage*; it is unlikely that a *waw* before Dibon would have been read as a *lamed* since this is not a common graphical error. Several manuscripts attest the *waw* before Dibon as we have in the MT.

In summary, the versions present ambiguous evidence in the case of Isa 15:2a. The evidence is split on whether a *waw* is to be read before Dibon. The fact that Syriac and the Targum both support deleting it must be set against the fact that some of the manuscripts of the LXX support keeping it. On one point the versions agree; none supports the reading "the daughter of Dibon." Significantly, 1QIsa[a] has the same text as the MT, and this fact, coupled with the fact that the versions generally appear to be attempting to "improve" a difficult text, cautions against emendation.

Those who favor reading "daughter of Dibon" usually cite Jer 48:18: בת־דיבון. But the context of this verse is unrelated to Isa 15:2, and the evidence it provides is indirect.[39] Both the lack of versional support for this reading and the number of emendations required to create it argue against it.

We are left then with the "unverständlich" syntax of the unemended MT. One solution to the problem may be eliminated immediately. As we have argued above, two element place names are not typically abbreviated by the removal of the second element. In the case of place names formed with "Beth," there is no evidence that such an abbreviation is possible. Thus we must

---

[38]It appears as λαιβηδων (A′, Alexandrian group; 26[c]; V; 770), δαιβηδων (S*), λαιδηβων (710; 407*), λεδηβων (233), λεδημων (410), και δηβων (S[c]; B-oI; 46; Eus.); και δεβων (L[1]; 93; 91-490; 403′; 407[c]).

[39]Instead of comparing Jer 48:18 with Isa 15:2, one should compare Jer 48:17–18 with the themes and language of Isa 14:4–21. In any case the phrase in Jer 48:18 is ישבת בת־דיבון, not בת־דיבון, and it is the subject not of עלה, but of ירד.

reject the translation "Beth(-Meon, -Diblatain) and Dibon have gone up...."[40] This leaves us with only three options: (1) the solution offered by the NRSV, "Dibon has gone up to the temple..."; (2) a literal translation of the unemended MT with a compound subject for עלה: "the house and Dibon have gone up..."; or (3) a literal translation of the unemended MT with the subject of עלה unspecified: "He (or it = Moab) has gone up to the temple, and Dibon...."

The linking of "Dibon" and "the temple" as if the terms were metonyms for two distinct groups would be very peculiar, and this argues against option two. Option three, which requires that we supply "Moab" from 15:1 as the subject of the verb, is awkward. These two translations are possible and cannot be ruled out, but they strain sense and syntactical probability. The NRSV translation finds support in a recent article by W. B. Barrick. Barrick offers two suggestions:

> [1] *habbayit* and *habbāmôt* could be in synonymous apposition.... [2] the poet...may have deliberately broken up a compound phrase by distributing its elements between the first and second members of the hemistich. If we are dealing with a broken compound phrase, the reference would be to a sanctuary building—a beth-bamoth—in Dibon for the worship of Kemosh.[41]

The *waw* preceding Dibon, he notes, may be understood as pleonastic (or vocative) and is designed to emphasize the subject.[42] Barrick's suggestions lead to the same rendering; both support the NRSV translation, "Dibon has gone up to the temple, to the high

---

[40]So Vitringa, Rosenmueller and Ewald; see Gesenius, 133.

[41]"The Bamoth of Moab," *Maarav* 7 (1991) 80–82. For arguments in favor of the second proposal, see M. Dahood, "The Moabite Stone and Northwest Semitic Philology," *The Archaeology of Jordan and Other Studies* (ed. L. Geraty and L. Herr; Berrien Springs: Andrews University, 1986) 437–38, n. 48. See also E. Z. Melamed, "Break-Up of Stereotype Phrases as an Artistic Device in Biblical Hebrew," *Scripta Hierosolymitana* 8 (1961) 115–153; and J. Gray, *I–II Kings* (2d. ed.; OTL; Philadelphia: Westminster, 1970) 278. Gray has argued that *bāmôt* is often an abbreviation of *bêt bāmôt*.

[42]This suggestion has been made by both P. Wernberg-Møller ("'Pleonastic' Waw in Classical Hebrew," *JSS* 3 [1958] 324) and M. Dahood ("The Moabite Stone," 437–38, n. 48). See also M. Pope, "'Pleonastic' *Waw* before Nouns in Ugaritic and Hebrew," *JAOS* 73 (1953) 95–98.

places to weep." Consequently, there is little reason in the present context to decide between the two. Both represent economical and elegant solutions to this old problem. The phrase portrays the Moabites going to their temple to seek help from their deity in a moment of great need.

15:2c

The statement in 15:2c of the MT that בְּכָל־רֹאשָׁיו קָרְחָה, "On every head is baldness" has led several commentators to suppose that this phrase contains a punning reference to Qarḥoh, a place usually thought to be the royal quarter of Dibon.[43] The name never occurs in the HB, but the Mesha Inscription mentions קרחה, "Qarḥoh," as the place where Mesha built his palace and a high place.[44]

Recently, E. Easterly has argued that 15:2c contains more than a punning allusion to Qarḥoh. He believes that the Hebrew text originally referred to the city of Qarḥoh and that the text was subsequently corrupted in such a way that Qarḥoh was read as a common noun.[45] Easterly bases his arguments on a reconstruction of the LXX's *Vorlage*. The LXX reads ἐπὶ πάσης κεφαλῆς φαλάκρωμα πάντες βραχίονες κατατετμημένοι, "On every head is baldness, all arms are cut in pieces." He argues that the LXX translators did not fully understand the Hebrew text, and in particular, that they failed to recognize קרחה as a place name. The original Hebrew he reconstructs as follows:

MT:	בכל־ראשיו קרחה כל־זקן גרועה
Reconstruction:	בכל ראשי קרחה כל זרע גדוע
Translation:	Among all the leaders (heads) of *qrḥh*, every descendant is cut off.

[43]See, for example, F. M. Abel, *Géographie de la Palestine* (2 vols.; Paris: Gabalda, 1938, [3]1967) 2. 418; J. A. Dearman, "Historical Reconstruction and the Mesha Inscription," *Studies in the Mesha Inscription and Moab*, 170; Kaiser, 67; Donner and Röllig, *Kanaanäische und Aramäische Inschriften* (Wiesbaden: Harrassowitz, 1963) 2. 172.

[44]Lines 3, 21–25. Various vocalizations have been proposed for קרחה. See K. Smelik, *Converting the Past*, 88.

[45]"Is Mesha's *qrḥh* Mentioned in Isaiah XV 2?" *VT* 41 (1991) 215–19.

He sees the LXX translation emerging in the following manner. Since the translators failed to recognize קרחה as a place name, they misread it as the noun קָרְחָה, "baldness." This misinterpretation led them to translate ראשי as "heads" rather than as "leaders." Together, these misreadings suggested to the translators that the verse was describing mourning rituals. When they came to כל זרע גדוע, therefore, they understood זרע not as "descendant" but as "arm" (זְרֹעַ, translated by the LXX as βραχίονες), the cutting of the arm being a sign of extreme mourning.

As support for his thesis Easterly makes several points: (1) the proposed reconstruction of the Hebrew original is entirely idiomatic as can be seen when it is compared to 1 Sam 2:31: וגדעתי את־זרעך ואת־זרע בית אביך, "I shall cut off your descendants and the descendants of your father's house."[46] The verb גדע is easily read instead of גרע .(2) A place name would fit well at this point in the structure of Isaiah 15. (3) The LXX translation βραχίονες reflects a *Vorlage* of זרע, not זקן, as the MT has it. (4) The evidence of the Hebrew manuscripts suggests that there was a good deal of confusion over ראשיו; ראש (= LXX), ראשו, and ראשם are all attested. The graphic confusion between *waw* and *yod* may have contributed to the corruption of the original ראשי. (5) The initial preposition בְּ is more idiomatically translated as "among" than as "on."

Easterly has defended his position very well, but several of his arguments are unconvincing. First, he bases his reconstruction of the Hebrew solely on his reading of the (reconstructed!) LXX and ignores other important evidence. Jer 48:37 parallels Isa 15:2c (probably a direct borrowing), and it supports the text of the MT; the Qumran text of Isaiah supports the MT;[47] the Syriac and the Targum both support the MT of 15:2c. In fact, except for the word βραχίονες, the LXX supports the MT. When one looks at all the versional evidence, it seems simpler to explain the LXX's

[46]Easterly (219, n. 9) follows Kyle McCarter's emendation of the MT of this verse. On the basis of the LXX McCarter emends MT "arm" to read "seed."

[47]It adds a *waw* before the second *kol*, a fact that offers further evidence against Easterly's suggestion.

βραχίονες as a misreading of זקן than to emend the MT to support the LXX.

Easterly's reconstruction is unlikely on contextual grounds also. It suggests that the descendants of "all the leaders" were killed. But this is not the usual practice. On occasion members of the royal blood line of a conquered nation were killed, but there was nothing to be gained from a full scale purge of the leading families. Moreover, the poem does not depict the sort of conquest that would have led to the systematic elimination of even the royal line. The attack seems to have been aimed at destroying the agriculture of the land. If there had been a slaughter, especially a slaughter of the families of a number of important officials, one would expect some more explicit mention of it.

The text of 15:2c is perhaps awkward, but it is not impossible; radical emendation is both unwarranted and unnecessary. The parallel text in Jer 48:37 has ראש with neither the pronominal suffix nor the marker of the plural. The LXX and the Syriac reflect a *Vorlage* with ראש, as do a few Hebrew MSS, but both 1QIsa[a] and the Targum support the majority of MT MSS (Targ. has בכל רישיהון). The MT's בכל ראשיו, "On all its heads," is slightly awkward since 2cβ has the singular כל־זקן, "every beard," which upsets the parallel. Jer 48:37 and the versions probably represent attempts to remove this awkwardness. The expression itself is, however, completely idiomatic as is shown by Ezek 7:18: ובכל־ראשיהם קקרחה. This example demonstrates the appropriateness both of the ב to mean "on" and of the plural of ראש. Both Ezek 7:18 and the context of Isa 2cα suggest that we should read "baldness," at least at the literal level. Various traditional expressions of mourning are listed in verses 2–3, and baldness is clearly one of these expressions.[48] In light of these considerations, it seems best to follow the MT.

---

[48]Many examples could be cited. Other than Ezek 7:18, however, we will mention only Isa 22:12, a catalogue of actions appropriate to mourning, as especially significant:

וַיִּקְרָא אֲדֹנָי יְהוִה צְבָאוֹת בַּיּוֹם הַהוּא לִבְכִי וּלְמִסְפֵּד וּלְקָרְחָה וְלַחֲגֹר שָׂק׃

In that day the Lord GOD of hosts called to weeping and mourning, to baldness and putting on sackcloth.

15:2cβ presents another difficulty. Whether one reads גְּרוּעָה or גְּדוּעָה, the verb is, as far as can be determined, not being used idiomatically.[49] One should take into account, however, that poetry frequently employs unusual or archaic idioms. The fact that emending the MT to גדועה results in neither an idiomatic improvement nor a significant change in the sense suggests that it is best to follow the MT, "every beard is cut off."

15:3

BHS בְּחוּצֹתָיו חָגְרוּ שָׂק עַל גַּגּוֹתֶיהָ
וּבִרְחֹבֹתֶיהָ כֻּלֹּה יְיֵלִיל יֹרֵד בַּבֶּכִי׃

Three problems trouble this verse: the change of gender in the pronominal suffixes; the brevity of and apparent lack of a verb in 3aβ; and the difficult expression כלה יילל ירד בבכי. The change in the gender of the pronominal suffixes strikes a reader immediately. A 3ms suffix is appended to "streets," apparently referring back to Moab in v 2c, but as one reads on one encounters 3fs suffixes on both "housetops" and "squares," presumably with the same antecedent. Gray assumes that the change of gender in the suffixes is due to some textual corruption and emends them all to 3ms.[50] Wildberger also emends the suffixes to 3ms, noting that Moab as a people is the object of the suffixes and that יֹרֵד is masculine.[51] He suggests that the 3fs suffixes arose because the masculine suffixes were originally written as *heh*, as they are in the Mesha Inscription.

All solutions offered to date for the agreement problem leave the verse lacking a clear antecedent for the suffixes. Furthermore,

---

[49]A cognate to the term גרועה is common in Syriac and Aramaic with the sense of cutting hair (Gesenius, 135; Gray, *Isaiah*, 281), and it is very possible that this usage was a correct idiom of which we have only the examples in Isa 15:2 and Jer 48:37. This verb does not occur sufficiently often in the HB to warrant dogmatism about the subtleties of its usage. See also Wildberger, 591.

[50]See Gray, 273, 281.

[51]Contra Gesenius (135–36) and others who explain the gender variation as a reflection of a changing object: Moab as a land (fem.) and Moab as a people (masc.).

it is more natural for a particular city to be the antecedent of "its streets" than for the antecedent to be the land or people of Moab.[52] But if a particular city, which city? It is unlikely that we should look as far back as Nebo or Medeba in 2bα for the antecedent. In addition to their distance from the problematic suffixes, they would be quite confusing for several reasons: they are not the subject of their clause but the objects of prepositions; an entire line intervenes in 2c in which the Moabites as a people are the subject; both Nebo and Medeba are mentioned, and this makes it unclear which would be the antecedent; finally, most cities are treated as feminine nouns, and thus the 3ms suffix on "streets" would be anomalous. Clearly, the gender shift is only part of the problem. Neither Moab nor a previously mentioned city works well as the antecedent of the pronominal suffixes in 15:3. None of the emendations suggested solves the whole problem.

There is, however, a solution that brings clarity to the verse. With very minor emendation one can read בחוצת יחגרו שק, "In Huzoth they gird on sackcloth." "Huzoth" would be an abbreviated form of the full name "Kiriath Huzoth," a Moabite city mentioned in Num 22:39.[53] This emendation involves the deletion of a *waw* and a redivision of the text. It assumes a corruption that occurred when the preformative *yōd* of the imperfect יחגרו was read as a *waw* and taken as a 3ms suffix on חוצת, perhaps under the

---

[52]Cf. Jer 48:38, כל־גגות מואב וברחבתיה, "On all the housetops of Moab and in its squares...." But here the *land* of Moab is the subject, and the 3fs pronominal suffix is correctly used. H. Olivier ("Archaeological Evidence Pertaining to a Possible Identification of Ar-Moab and er-Rabbah," *NedTTs* 30 [1989] 185) thinks this expression odd but explains it in another way. He holds that "Moab" refers to a city: "From the parallel section to Is 15:3 in Jer 48:38 reference is made to 'all the roofs of Moab...and her plains/streets'..., clearly indicating a *city* named Moab... What else could be indicated by words such as streets, plains, roofs?" I will deal with Olivier's suggestion in detail below; briefly, I am unconvinced that Moab is a city name, and I think Jer 48:38 is more easily explained as an attempt to improve 15:3.

[53]On the common practice of apocopating place names see the discussion above on 15:1. The versions offer several alternatives to קרית חצות in Num 22:39. The Targum has *lqrjt mḥwzwhj*, some MSS of ⅏ read חיצות, and the LXX has πόλεις ἐπαύλεων (= קִרְיֹת חֲצֵרוֹת). The term קִרְיַת is the construct form of קִרְיָה, "town" or "city," a synonym in Hebrew for עִיר. The term חֻצוֹת refers to "streets" or "bazaars."

influence of ראשיו in the preceding line. The influence of ראשיו may also account for the addition of the *yōd*. If we emend the text in this way, the 3fs suffixes in 3aβ and 3bα clearly have a city as their antecedent, and the 3ms suffix is eliminated. Furthermore, emending to read יחגרו brings the verb into aspectual agreement with the parallel verb ייליל and with the present tense description throughout this section. The poet uses imperfects and a present participle to create a vivid depiction of the Moabites in their distress. Quite understandably none of the versions recognized חוצת as a place name since it frequently occurs as a common noun in Hebrew and only one other time as a place name.[54] Indeed, the LXX translators failed to recognize Kiriath Huzoth as a place name in Num 22:39 also; there they translated the name πόλεις ἐπαύλεων, "city of streets." Apparently, (Kiriath) Huzoth was a place unknown to them. For this reason the lack of versional support presents no problem for the proposed emendation.

As noted above, the brevity of 15:3aβ and its supposed lack of a verb have bothered many commentators. Duhm supplies a word at the end of 3aβ, מִסְפֵּד, "lamentation," on the basis of the parallel text in Jer 48:38 and the LXX's κόπτεσθε.[55] Rudolph (followed by Kaiser) prefers to supply יִנְהוּ or נָהוּ since it is difficult to explain the loss of מִסְפֵּד given the present state of the MT in 3aβ.[56] Wildberger observes, "Der zweite Hemistich der ersten Verszeile ist zu kurz, es fehlt ein Verb, denn die Gassen liegen nicht auf den Dächern."[57] The translation proposed here clears up Wildberger's second objection, and his claim that the line is too short is questionable. The BHS division of the verse does not fit the poetry or the sense;

---

[54]The versions and 1QIsa[a] support the MT. The LXX has the aorist verb περιζώσασθε for חגרו in most MSS; a few MSS, however, have the future περιζώσεσθε. This may reflect an effort to match the tenses of the verbs חגרו and ייליל. 1QIsa[a] smoothes out the pronominal suffix gender problem by changing the 3ms suffix on "streets" to 3fs: בחוצותיה.

[55]Duhm, 99.

[56]Rudolph, "Jesaja xv–xvi," 134; Kaiser, 57. Presumably Rudolph means to find the source of the corruption in the suffix attached to גגותיה. Driver (44) offers another way to supply a verb; he suggests that the verb was lost due to haplography and that we should supply קעו (from Syr. *qʿâ*, "raise a clamour") and read "<*qāʿū*> *ʿal gaggûteyhā* 'they screamed on her roof-tops.'"

[57]Wildberger, 591.

it separates the two prepositional phrases that logically should go with the second line. The Masoretic pointing, however, puts the major break after שק, creating a short line followed by a long line. While the syllable or foot count is thrown off by this division, it appears doubtful that such counting is a reliable means for dividing Hebrew poetry.[58] Metrical variation of this sort should not, in any case, be used as the sole ground for textual emendation.[59]

The versions do provide some support for emending the text of 15:3aβ by adding a verb. The LXX has ἐν ταῖς πλατείαις αὐτῆς περιζώσασθε σάκκους <u>καὶ κόπτεσθε</u>, which suggests that it may have had an additional verb in its *Vorlage*. The verb κόπτω, "to beat one's breast" (in mourning), frequently translates Hebrew ספד, "to lament," or the noun מספד, "lamentation."[60] Significantly, Jer 48:38 reads על כל־גגות מואב וברחבתיה כלה מספד. It is tempting on this basis to supply יספדו in 3aβ. Neither 1QIsa[a] nor any of the other versions supports the reading of the LXX, however, and this suggests caution. The LXX reading may plausibly be explained as a harmonization of Isa 15:3 and Jer 48:38, but it is more probably a simple semantic reflex.[61] The terms κόπτω, περιζώννυμι, and

---

[58]If one is inclined toward syllable counting, one might understand Isa 15:3 as an example of the "double-duty modifier" that M. Dahood has pointed out in the Psalter ("A New Metrical Pattern in Biblical Poetry," *CBQ* 29 [1967] 574–79). 15:3 would then scan as follows:

In Huzoth they put on sackcloth;	בחוצת יחגרו שק
on its rooftops and in its plazas	על גגותיה וברחבתיה
everyone wails, drowning in tears.	כלה ייליל ירד בבכי

The second line functions according to Dahood's description: "This double-duty modifier is a phrase...suspended between the first and third cola of a verse and simultaneously modifying both of them" (574). Whether or not one accepts Dahood's metrical reasons for division, one can accept the poetics of this clever tricola. For an example of a similar device used in the poem, see below on 16:8.

[59]See J. L. Kugel, *The Idea of Biblical Poetry: Parallelism and Its History* (New Haven: Yale University, 1981) 287-304; M. O'Connor, *Hebrew Verse Structure* (Winona Lake, IN: Eisenbrauns, 1980) 29–54.

[60]See for example Isa 32:12; Jer 4:8; 16:4, 5, 6; etc. (plus 24 times).

[61]Gray points out that the word order in the LXX of 48:38 is very different from that in Isa 15:3 and judges it unwise to emend the latter on the basis of the former. He suggests that the LXX was influenced by Jer 4:8 and 49:3 (LXX

σάκκος are all part of the same semantic domain. Περιζώννυμι and σάκκος are frequently paired in the LXX, and κόπτω often occurs with them (2 Kgs 3:31; Joel 1:13; Isa 32:11–12; Jer 4:8; 30[49]:19; 31[48]:37). For this reason the phrase "gird on sackcloth" may have led the translator to add "and lament" in much the same way that "weeping and wailing" might cause an English speaker to add "and gnashing of teeth."[62] Thus it seems best to leave 15:3aβ as it stands in the MT.

Finally, a brief word must be said about the phrase ירד בבכי, translated here as "sinking in tears." This expression is unusual. The verb ירד several times denotes the flow of tears. For example, Ps 119:136 (similarly Lam 3:48) has פלגי־מים ירדו עיני, "Streams of water run down my eyes"; Lam 1:16 reads עיני ירדה מים, "my eyes are streaming water"; and Jer 9:17 has תרדנה עינינו דמעה, "our eyes stream tears" (similarly Jer 13:17; 14:17). In all these cases either "eye(s)" or "tears/water" is the subject of the verb. In Isa 15:3, however, the subject of the participle יֹרֵד is the people, "everyone" (כֻּלֹּה). This syntax is unique. The LXX has no equivalent for ירד. 1QIsa[a] and the Syriac (*wnḥt* = ירד) both have it, but they put a *waw* before it and must, for this reason, have read ירד as a perfect. The Targum has מצוחין ובכן "shrieking and weeping" in the final phrase, reading both the final terms as participles.

The commentators usually refrain from emending the MT here. Rudolph understands the expression to indicate the extreme nature of the mourning: " ירד ב heißt nicht 'hinabsteigend (auf die Platze) unter Weinen'..., sondern ist prägnante Ausdrucksweise: während sonst das 'Hinabsteigen im Weinen' vom Auge ausgesagt wird, ist es hier direkt auf die Person bezogen, also: 'zerfließend in Tränen.'"[63] Gray translates the phrase "Running

---

30:19). The pairing of the terms in Jer 49:3 is highly significant since the verse is dealing with Moab.

[62]On the psycholinguistic basis for this phenomenon, see A. Berlin, *The Dynamics of Biblical Parallelism*, 65–80.

[63]He is followed by Kaiser, 57; cf. similarly Keil and Delitzsch, 325, and Wildberger, 591.

down (?) with weeping," which leaves the subject of the participle unclear and fails to produce idiomatic English.[64]

The context suggests that the writer intends the phrase to convey a sense of complete and utter grief; throughout the town the people mourn, and their loud cry is heard far away. It is unlikely that ירד describes the people's descent from the roofs and plazas (can one descend from a plaza?). Rather ירד emphasizes the extremity of their grief. Thus it is best to translate the phrase "sinking in tears." While it is true that בכי usually denotes the act of weeping rather than its natural product, tears, the two ideas are so closely connected that one can be used as a metonym for the other (e.g., Ps 102:10). Furthermore, there is no precedent for translating ירד as "dissolving," as most commentators have done. There are, however, several texts that use ירד to denote sinking or drowning in water (Exod 15:5; Jonah 2:7; Ps 107:26). It would appear, then, that the writer uses this unusual expression to paint a picture of people sinking into a pool of their own tears.

15:5a

BHS לִבִּי֙ לְמוֹאָ֣ב יִזְעָ֔ק בְּרִיחֶ֖הָ עַד־צֹ֑עַר עֶגְלַ֣ת שְׁלִשִׁיָּ֑ה

Two problems in this verse require extended comment. The first concerns the meaning of בריחה. 1QIsa[a] has ברחוה, "they will flee her," which appears to be a correction of the more difficult MT. The LXX and Theodotion read the *yod* as a *waw* and translate "in itself/its spirit" (similarly the Syriac), while Symmachus and Aquila support the MT with μοχλος αυτης, "its bar." The roughly parallel text in Jer 48:34 lacks the word. Driver has argued that there has been a haplography, and he reconstructs the text "[*bārᵉḥû*] *bᵉrîḥehā*, 'her nobles [fled].'" His suggestion, however, is unsupported by manuscript or versional evidence. A simple repointing of the MT yields a tolerable sense. With most commentators and the BHS note, we choose to read a substantive adjective

[64] *Isaiah*, 273.

with a 3ms suffix, בָּרִיחֹה, "its fugitives."[65] Thus, 15:5a provides a fitting heading for the flight description that follows.[66]

A second problem complicates our understanding of 15:5a. Eglath Shelishiyah is commonly held to be an explanatory gloss of some kind, probably an appositional explanation of Zoar. Jer 48:34 has מצער עד־חרנים עגלת שלשיה in a similar, though not strictly parallel, context. The versions translate the apparent place name as a reference to a three-year-old heifer. A wide variety of explanations have been offered for why the text would refer to such an animal in this context, but the probability that the phrase is a gloss on Zoar suggests that we should take it as a proper name.[67] Since Jeremiah 48 also attests the name, the gloss must predate the

---

[65]So Gesenius, 137-38; Duhm, 100; Kaiser, 57; Wildberger, 591. Gray holds that the five words of 15:5aβ "do not constitute a sentence, appear to have no relation either to what precedes or to what follows them, are scarcely intelligible, and are probably corrupt." He deletes them entirely. The first three words of this clause are surely not so hopeless; only the gender of the suffix presents a real problem. Chapters 15 and 16 are consistent in referring to Moab with 3ms suffixes and in using 3ms verbs (15:2b, 2b-c, 4b, 5c, 8b; 16:6b-7a) except where the land is clearly meant (גבול מואב followed by 3fs suffixes in 15:8). The 3fs suffix on בריחה either refers to the land of Moab (which is not clear) or it is anomalous.

[66]One other intriguing possibility exists. בָּרִיחֹה may be a corrupt form of a place name. The idiom ...מן...עד frequently describes the extent of an area by referring to places on opposite borders (e.g., Gen 10:19; Deut 2:36; Amos 6:14; cf. BDB, 581). If we assume that the initial ב in 5aβ was originally a מ, we can read "from ריחה to Zoar," understanding the phrase as a general summary of the flight across the southern plateau (alternatively, we might avoid emendation if we take the ב to mean "from," a rare but possible meaning; cf. Ps 18:9). Thus, ריחה may be a place name; perhaps it is a variant spelling of the name Jericho. Perhaps the name is preserved in the name of modern Ariḥa, a city located on the northeastern extremity of the southern plateau, nine km. north of Kh. el-Baluᶜ (E. A. Knauf, "Toponymy of the Kerak Plateau," *Archaeological Survey*, [ed. J. M. Miller] 286). This suggestion is no more than a possibility, but in light of the difficulty of reading the text as it stands, such a possibility warrants consideration.

[67]The best summary of explanations for the mention of a heifer may be found in Gesenius, 138-40. Delitzsch (324) offers a cogent defense for understanding the term "three-year-old heifer" as a reference to Zoar's vitality; he compares it to similar expressions in Jer 46:20 and 50:11 (but these are applied to nations, not individual cities). Along a completely different line, Hvidberg (*Graad og Latter in det Gamle Testamente* [1938] 108-09; mentioned in Rudolph, 134) argues that עגלת is a reference to the goddess Anat, and שלש is to be taken as a verb (based on a Ugaritic cognate).

writing of that chapter.[68] Thus, it is probable that the name Eglath Shelishiyah provides geographical information from a relatively early time. Unfortunately, the meaning of this information has yet to be deciphered.

15:9

BHS כִּ֣י מֵ֤י דִימוֹן֙ מָ֣לְאוּ דָ֔ם כִּֽי־אָשִׁ֥ית עַל־דִּימ֖וֹן נוֹסָפ֑וֹת
לִפְלֵיטַ֤ת מוֹאָב֙ אַרְיֵ֔ה וְלִשְׁאֵרִ֖ית אֲדָמָֽה׃

Robert Lowth comments on this verse, "The reading of this verse is very doubtful; and the sense, in every way in which it can be read, very obscure."[69] In a similar vein Gray comments, "In so corrupt and obscure a passage it would be easier to multiply guesses than to justify them."[70] Indeed, the guesses have multiplied. Perceived corruptions involve דימון, אריה, לשארית and אדמה. The shift of speaker in 9aβ is also suspect, for here Yahweh speaks for the first time in the poem, as some suppose, suddenly and unexpectedly.

Two typical attempts to correct the text are found in Rudolph and Kissane. Rudolph emends only 9b: אריה he reads יִרְאָה, אדמה he reads אֵימָה, and to שארית he adds a 3ms suffix שְׁאֵרִיתוֹ—"Ja, die Wasser von Dimon sind voll Blut, doch ich füge zu Dimon noch Weiteres hinzu: für die Geretteten Moabs Angst und für seinen Rest Schrecken."[71] Kissane's emendations affect both 9a and 9b. In 9a he emends אשית to read שָׁאוֹת, and נוספות to read נִסְפּוֹת; and in 9b he emends אריה to read אֲנִיָּה, and אדמה to read אֵימָה. He translates, "Because the waters of Dimon are full of blood, Because disasters are multiplied over Dimon, For the escaped of Moab there is sorrow, For the remnant terror."[72] The mention of a lion at this

---

[68]Of course one could claim that it was a gloss in both places, but this is unlikely since in Jeremiah the gloss is attached to Horonaim, a strange variation if the work of a glossator.

[69]*Commentary*, 227.

[70]*Isaiah*, 287. Gray refuses to translate the words he deems corrupt beyond repair and presents his readers with ellipses rather than guesses.

[71]*Jesaja XV–XVI*, 132, 135.

[72]E. Kissane, *The Book of Isaiah* (2 vols.; Dublin: Browne and Nolan, rev. ed., 1960; orig. 1941–43) 1. 178, 180, 183. His reasons for emending include the fact

point in the poem bothers both interpreters. Rudolph comments, "...9b mit der sonderbaren Stellung von אריה is kaum richtig.... Aber was soll hier überhaupt ein Löwe (trotz 2 Reg. xvii. 25f.)?" Likewise, they both emend the difficult reference to "the land" because it makes little sense in the context.

All of the proposed emendations suggested for 15:9, with the exception of changing דימון to דיבון, are based solely on contextual considerations. The versions substantially support the text of the MT. The LXX translates, τὸ δὲ ὕδωρ τὸ Ρεμμων πλησθήσεται αἵματος· ἐπάξω γὰρ ἐπὶ Ρεμμον Ἄραβας καὶ ἀρῶ τὸ σπέρμα Μωαβ καὶ Αριηλ καὶ τὸ κατάλοιπον Αδαμα, "But the waters of Remmon will be full of blood. For I will send Arabs against Remmon, and I will remove the seed of Moab and Ariel and the rest of Adama." The translation is free and interpretive at points. The verb אשית has probably been read as a 1cs impf. of נשא; the translator may have supplied it a second time in 9b to fill a perceived gap, hence "I will remove."[73] "Arabs" is probably a midrashic translation of נוספות, perhaps under the influence of 15:7b where the LXX has translated ἐπάξω γὰρ ἐπὶ τὴν φάραγγα Ἄραβας. Perhaps there is historical knowledge of the eventual fate of Moab in this translation. "The seed" has no correlative in the Hebrew (certainly not פליטה); apparently it is a simple addition. Note well, however, that the LXX tends to support the MT at two points. First, since Αριηλ is quite probably a free translation of אריה, it warns against adventurous emendations of אריה.[74] In particular, neither Rudolph nor Kissane has proposed a reconstructed *Vorlage* that adequately accounts for the LXX translation. Secondly, Αδαμα almost certainly attests אדמה.[75] The Targum is likewise quite free, but it tends to support the MT.

---

that "Dimon cannot endure further trials for it is destroyed" and a resemblance between 15:9aβ (as he emends it) and Deut 32:23.

[73]The verb שית is translated with ἐπάγω nowhere else in the LXX; נשא is by far the most common term so translated. A *taw* in the oldest scripts could have been read as an *aleph* by a later translator. Frequent also is the translation αἴρω for נשא. Symmachus and Aquila have προσθησω γαρ επι διμων προσθεματα το διασωσματι απο μωαβ λεοντα = MT.

[74]In his translation of Isa 21:8, Theodotion renders אריה with Αριηλ.

[75]Aquila and Symmachus have χθονος = אדמה.

Admittedly, the text presented in the MT is difficult. To begin with, the phrase, "I will place upon Dimon additions" is not a common idiom for indicating further calamities. The substantive Niphal participle נוספות is elliptical in the context; we must wait for the next line to discover in what these "additions" consist. But as Gesenius has noted, ellipses in the case of the verb יסף are found elsewhere.[76] Gray's comment that neither the verb nor its object in 9aβ suggests calamities is true in part;[77] both terms have a fairly broad semantic spread, and neither is negative *per se*. On the other hand, שית על is used to denote a penalty or judgment laid upon an offending party (Exod 21:22; 21:30; Num 12:11), and יסף is frequently found in the oath formula יעשה אלהים לך וכה יוסיף "May God do to you and more [if you do/do not...]" (e.g., 1 Sam 3:17; 14:44; 20:13; 25:22; 1 Kgs 2:23; 19:20; 20:10; 2 Kgs 6:31). With these usages in mind, it requires no great effort to understand 9aβ as a threat that the LORD will require of Dimon further suffering.[78]

As noted above, there is textual evidence for reading דיבון rather than דימון.[79] Most MSS of the LXX and Targum attest the spelling דימון, but 1QIsa[a] has דיבון both times in 15:9. The Vulgate has *Dibon* and the Syriac *rybwn*. Certainly, דימון is *lectio difficilior* since it is easier to explain דיבון as a replacement of an otherwise unknown place name with one both more familiar and immediately at hand (15:2) than it is to explain how דיבון became corrupted to דימון. Strictly on text critical grounds, therefore, דימון is the preferred reading.

---

[76]Gesenius (145) cites Job 20:9; 34:32; Num 11:25.

[77]Gray, *Isaiah*, 286.

[78]I find unconvincing E. Power's argument that "additions" refers ironically to additions to the territory of Dimon (=Dibon): "The irony would consist in regarding the neutral territory [=Judah] and the land of the invaders [=Edom], where the surviving Dimonites now dwell, as additions made to the city of the slain" ("The Prophecy of Isaias against Moab," 436). Aside from its rather forced reading of 9aβ, his interpretation requires that we emend both אריה and אדמה.

[79]For a thorough evaluation of the textual evidence see H. M. Orlinsky, "Studies in the St. Mark's Scroll," *IEJ* 4 (1954) 5-8. Orlinsky argues persuasively that the MT has the best reading.

The question is not only a text-critical one, however.[80] Most commentators have suggested that "Dimon" is a slight modification of "Dibon," either a dialectical variant or an intentional perversion, and that this modification is designed to create a pun with the following word דם (blood): "The waters of דימון are full of דם."[81] This line of reasoning leads to the conclusion that "Dimon" and "Dibon" refer to the same place.[82] Of course, given the nature of the argument, the identification of Dimon and Dibon on this basis can never be proven. Indeed, some have rejected this widely asserted equation.[83] At most it is a possibility rendered more or less probable depending on how one evaluates the rhetoric of the poem. We should be clear, however, that paronomasia is present

---

[80]This question of דמון/דבון is traditionally placed among other text-critical issues. However, it is primarily an issue of interpretation and historical geography. I include a treatment of it here in order to follow the tradition and to avoid dividing the present discussion among several different chapters.

[81]See, for example, J. Koppe, 242; Gesenius (145: "In v. 9 it [Dibon] is written דימון, with the common interchange of מ and ב."); Delitzsch, 329; Gray, *Isaiah* (285: "Dimon may be an error for Dibon, or possibly a dialectic variation, like Mecca and Becca, adopted to gain an assonance with *dam, blood*."); Rudolph (135: "Bei dem häufigen Wechsel von *m* und *b* kann kaum bezweifelt werden daß Dimon = Dibon (so D.S.) wegen des Wortspiels mit דם."); Van Zyl, 80; Schottroff, "Horonaim, Nimrim, Luhith...," 188 and nn. 113–14; Wildberger, 592. See Orlinsky, 6, n. 3 for others who have argued this way.

[82]Jerome records that Dimon and Dibon were alternate spellings for the name of a single place: "Usque hodie indifferenter, et Dimon et Dibon, hoc oppidulum dicitur" (J. Migne, *Patrologia Cursus Completus, Series Latina*, 221 vols. [Paris: Venit Apud Editorem, 1844–1864], 24:170); of course this may only reflect a harmonizing of the text. The alteration of *beth* to *mem* is found again with this name in Josh 15:22, "Dimonah" and Neh 11:25, "Dibon"—both apparently refer to the same place in Judah (Wildberger, 592). Elsewhere in prophetic literature pejorative overtones in city names serve as the basis of derisive puns (cf. Beth Aven, Amos 5:5; Hos 4:15; 10:5; Lo Dabar, Amos 6:13). Mic 1:8-16 is a leading example of the use of this technique; we shall discuss this important text more fully in chapter six.

[83]Orlinsky (6) rejects the idea that "Dimon" is a pun on Dibon on the basis that names are not changed elsewhere in the chapter, or indeed in the HB, to underscore a pun. O. Procksch (214) contends that only places south of the W. Mujib are in view in 15:5–9 and concludes that Dimon must lie south of this boundary and thus be a different place from Dibon. For a defense of Dimon as a pun name see I. M. Casanowicz, *Paronomasia in the Old Testament* (Boston: Norwood, 1894; reprint ed., Jerusalem: Makor, 1970) 43.

whether we decide "Dimon" refers to Dibon or to some other city; the question concerns only whether the writer skewed a well-known place name for the sake of the pun. What is needed if the equation of Dimon and Dibon is to be defeated is a likely candidate for the site of Dimon; apart from some confirmation that a city named Dimon once existed the idea that Dimon is a corruption or variant of Dibon will remain an attractive possibility.

Several scholars have found just such confirmation in the modern site of *Kh. ed-Dimna(h)*, a village located two and a half miles northwest of er-Rabba near the western edge of the plateau lying south of the W. Mujib. A. Musil long ago suggested that *Kh. ed-Dimna* was to be identified with Dimon.[84] Others have followed him and developed arguments to support his suggestion.[85] The primary reasons given for equating Dimon and *Kh. ed-Dimna* are the similarity between the names and the fact that an impressive wadi runs near *Kh. ed-Dimna*. The building of the modern village and cultivation of the surrounding fields have destroyed most of the ceramic evidence for reconstructing the occupational history of the site, but Worschech and Knauf discovered, just southeast of the village at about 800 feet below the plateau, an area of building ruins (800' x 500'; foundations only) among which was scattered substantial ceramic evidence of Iron II occupation.[86] This lower city they suggest is the Iron Age site of Dimon. The present location of Kh. ed-Dimna may be explained on the supposition that

---

[84]*Arabia Petraea: I Moab* (Kaiserliche Akademie der Wissenschaften; Wien: Hölder, 1907) 157 and 170, n. 1 (cf. 15, 19, 374).

[85]F.-M. Abel, *Géographie de la Palestine*, 2. 372; J. Simons, *The Geographical and Topographical Texts of the Old Testament* (Leiden: Brill, 1959) §1261; Kaiser, *Isaiah*, 69. The most extended arguments are those presented in U. Worschech and E. A. Knauf, "Dimon und Horonaim," *BN* 31 (1986) 70–75; and U. Worschech, *Die Beziehungen Moabs zu Israel und Ägypten in der Eisenzeit. Siedlungsarchäologische und siedlungshistorische Untersuchungen im Kernland Moabs (Ard el-Kerak)*; (Ägypten und Altes Testament. Studien zu Geschichte, Kultur und Religion Ägyptens und des Alten Testaments 18; Wiesbaden: Harrassowitz, 1990), 49–53. See also J. M. Miller, ed., *Archaeological Survey of the Kerak Plateau*, 53. Apparently, neither Wildberger (592) nor Watts (227) was aware of this suggestion; both assert that no Moabite town named Dimon is known.

[86]Worschech and Knauf, 70–72; Miller's survey team found only one LB and one IR sherd at *ed-Dimna* (Miller's site #64, p. 53).

the name was at some time transferred (migrated) to the present site atop the plateau.

Two considerations should caution us against immediately adopting this identification. First, we have only one reference to Dimon in the HB.[87] This seems strange in view of the fact that the context of Isa 15:9 suggests that Dimon was a major city of Moab. Indeed, the poet uses Dimon as a synecdoche for all Moab, just as Dibon is used as a synecdoche for Moab in 15:2. This being the case, one would assume that Dimon designates a principal city of Moab, if not its capital. Is it possible that such a city would be mentioned only once in the HB and never at all in the Mesha Inscription? If we should allow that this has happened, would the size and type of site represented by *Kh. ed-Dimna* (or Worschech and Knauf's suggested site) be appropriate as a candidate for such a city? Both ideas appear unlikely. The prominence of Dimon implied in Isa 15:9 has been one of the primary reasons that commentators have suggested the Dimon = Dibon equation.

This leads to a second consideration. The poem mentions only places north of the W. Mujib in the description of Moab's lamentation in 15:1–4. In 15:5–7 the flight of the Moabites southward to Zoar is depicted. The cities mentioned in these verses are not described as belonging to Moab; they are places the fugitives pass through on their search for a place of refuge. At 15:8 the poet returns to the theme of Moab's lamentation in "the territory of Moab," and in 15:9 specifies some further judgment to come on Dimon/ Moab.[88] The sense of 15:9a is that Dimon is to receive punishments added to those already described in the immediately preceding context. All the calamities so far described in the chapter have affected only cities north of the W. Mujib, among which we must logically include Dimon. As we have argued above, Isaiah 15–16 indicate that the attack on Moab affected only the territory north of the W. Mujib, and there is every reason to believe that this was the Moabite heartland at that time. The fact

---

[87]Unless one identifies Madman in Jer 48:2 with Dimon, as do F. Buhl (*Geographie des alten Palästina* [Freiburg and Leipzig: Mohr, 1896] §135) and others. This suggestion is based primarily on the LXX translation of Jer 48:2 which has παῦσιν παύσεται (דְּמוֹם) suggesting a *Vorlage* containing דמם.

[88]On the difficult phrase אשית על דמון נוספות see below.

that Dimon (as a representative of Moab) is singled out for some added punishment suggests that it lies north of the W. Mujib, not south as does *Kh. ed-Dimna*.

The similarity of the names Dimon and *Dimna* is admittedly striking, but what little we can glean about the city from Isaiah 15 suggests that we should reject this identification. The fact that there is a strong wadi nearby does little to substantiate the identification since the reference to "the waters of Dimon" is vague at best, and one can point to many possible sites with nearby water sources (such is a requirement for a city of any size in that dry climate). In the end, the similarity of the names is the only evidence in favor of the identification. Thus, the suggestion that Dimon is either a variant form or a deliberate perversion of Dibon remains valid. When we consider that Dibon was, at least in Mesha's time, the capital of Moab, and that Isa 15:9 uses Dimon as a synecdoche for all of Moab, the suggestion appears quite probable.

Let us return now to the more strictly text-critical issues in 15:9. As we have seen, the versions generally support the text of the MT. Where they depart from the MT, their translations appear to be merely interpretive and never suggest a *Vorlage* that qualifies as a serious alternative to the MT. In this situation, we should be cautious about emending the text. Wildberger thinks that the safest approach is to emend in only one place; he replaces אדמה with אימה (terror).[89] This emendation yields a better sense, but there is no versional support for it. If the lion in 15:9bα is a metaphor for an enemy nation rather than a terror typically faced by fugitives, then it would be equally possible in the context to emend the text to read "Edom" (אדם > אדמה) as the parallel element: "For the fugitives, a lion, and for the remnant, Edom."[90]

---

[89]Wildberger, 592.

[90]For other examples of the lion as a symbol for an enemy nation see Isa 5:29 (= Assyria?) and Jer 4:7 (= Nebuchadnezzar); cf. the similar phenomenon in Isa 46:11. J. Reider ("Contributions to the Scriptural Text," *HUCA* 24 (1952/3) 87–88) argues that the syntax of 9b suggests that there should be a noun at the end of the line following אדמה to parallel אריה. His suggestion that שחל, "lion," fell out of the text through haplography is plausible. There is, however, no evidence to support this emendation in the versions. Thus it must be considered only an attractive possibility. Furthermore, the syntax of

This suggestion, like Wildberger's, is only one among several possibilities.

Such possibilities, having no versional support, should not be placed above the text of the MT itself, if, that is, the MT can be given a plausible interpretation. Two plausible readings of the consonantal text of the MT are possible. First, we may take ולשארית אדמה as a ballast variant: "For the fugitives of Moab, a lion, as well as for the remnant of the land." This appears to be how the Masoretes understood it. Secondly, we may repoint אֲדָמָה to read אַדְמָה, i.e., the place name "Admah": "For the fugitives of Moab, a lion, and for the remnant, Admah" (alternatively, "For the fugitives of Moab, a lion, as well as for the remnant of Admah").[91] Reading "Admah" is attractive since it requires no emendation of the consonantal text and since the LXX also reads אדמה as a place name (Αδαμα). At least by the time of Hosea, Admah had attained a proverbial status alongside Zeboiim, Sodom and Gomorrah as a place of aridity, desolation and divine judgment. The proverbial desolation that Admah typifies fits well with the description of what the Moabites encounter on their flight (15:6–7), and the fact that Admah is traditionally associated with divine punishment renders it a suitable means by which to reinforce the message of punishment explicit in 15:9a. Additionally, the suggestion that the Moabites have fled to Zoar (15:5) makes the epithet "remnant of Admah" singularly appropriate.[92] In the end, we must decide between "land" and "Admah" on strictly contextual grounds. We

---

9b does not necessarily suggest that another noun is needed; שארית can be read either as an absolute or as a construct, there being no formal difference (the cantillation mark, a *Ṭip̄ḥā*, indicates that it is an absolute form). The Masoretic reading is perfectly sensible. One need only recognize that the line is "gapped." "Moab" in 9bα has no corresponding element in 9bβ after לשארית (i.e., "Moab" repeated, or some poetic equivalent). Alternately, if שארית is read as a construct, אריה is gapped in 9bβ. In either case, the line offers no exception to normal poetic form.

[91] Admah is mentioned in Gen 10:19; 14:2, 8; Deut 29:22 [23]; and Hos 11:8. Among those who repoint to read "Admah" are Duhm, 101; Fohrer, 181; Kaiser, 58; and Oswalt, 335.

[92] Note that Admah is presented as a city near Zoar in the biblical narrative (e.g., Gen 14:2, 8; cf. Gen 19:17–38).

have chosen to repoint the MT to read "Admah" based on our understanding of the rhetoric of the poem.

We may wonder, however, why Admah would have been chosen over equally possible cities such as Sodom, Gomorrah and Zeboiim, or, if we read with the Masoretes, why אדמה would have been chosen over another possible word such as ארץ. Perhaps the author's choice was guided by the desire to create a play of sounds and meanings. The sound pairing in 9aβ and 9bβ is easily perceived: *ʿal dîmōn* is paired with *ʾadmāh*, and *ʾăšîth* with *lišʾērîth*. We may have in this sound pairing a reason for the seemingly difficult syntax and diction of the verse. When a poet chooses words for the sake of the sound pairing, common idiom may be strained.

16:1

BHS שִׁלְחוּ־כַר מֹשֵׁל־אֶרֶץ
מִסֶּלַע מִדְבָּרָה אֶל־הַר בַּת־צִיּוֹן׃

A literal translation of this verse as pointed by the Masoretes would read something like, "Send a lamb, the ruler of the land, from Sela in (or, the rock of) the wilderness to the mount of the daughter of Zion."[93] A number of emendations to this verse have been proposed. The BHS notes suggest adding a *waw* at the beginning of the sentence and reading a Qal pf. 3mpl instead of the MT's imperative. Indeed, a number of emendations have been proposed for the initial verb: שְׁלְחוּ, אֶשְׁלַח, שָׁלְחוּ, אֶשְׁלְחָה.[94] The singular form כר occurs only here; elsewhere in the HB it is always plural. This has led some to read כר as either a plural or a collective.[95] The appositional phrase משל־ארץ is unusual since the context leads one

---

[93]By means of the *maqqef* connecting both "Send a lamb" and "ruler of the earth," the Masoretes suggest that we not read one long construct chain "the lamb of the ruler of the earth" (contra Kissane, 184; Gray, 287; E. Power, 440) but that we take the "ruler of the earth" in apposition to "lamb," apparently as a further designation: "Send a lamb, a ruler of the land…,".

[94]See Wildberger, 592.

[95] The plural of כר occurs 11 times; the only possible example of a singular usage is the place name Beth Kar mentioned in 1 Sam 7:11. The BHS note suggests reading the term as a collective (so too NRSV; Gesenius, 146; Procksch, 215; König, 190; Rudolph, 135). Gray (*Isaiah*, 290) states that the reading of כר as a collective is improbable, but he gives no reason.

to expect either a vocative or the indirect object at this point. For these reasons a number of interpreters add a *lamed* and translate "to the ruler of the land."[96] Finally, the expression מסלע מדברה presents a problem because of the presence of the locative *heh* and because סלע can be understood either as a common noun or as the place name Sela.[97]

The versions provide some help. The LXX offers an intriguing instance of a completely different, yet nearly possible, construal of the consonantal text. It reads Ἀποστελῶ ὡς ἑρπετὰ ἐπὶ τὴν γῆν· μὴ πέτρα ἔρημός ἐστι τὸ ὄρος Σιων; "I will send, as it were, serpents upon the land. Is the mount of Zion a desert rock?" (= אשלח כ רמש לארץ סלע מדבר לא הר ציון). An *aleph* is added, a *waw* is deleted and the letters of אל are transposed. This reading, however, receives the support of no other version and makes little sense. As for the Syriac, it translates rather freely, but the *Vorlage* it suggests diverges from the MT only in that it reads an article before "wilderness." This probably reflects an attempt to smooth out a difficult expression. The Targum translates even more freely than the Syraic and is of little help in the present case. It is noteworthy,

[96]The phrase can not be read as one long construct chain. Doing so creates a semantic ambiguity, for the genitive may be objective or subjective (i.e., the "ruler of the land" could be either the Moabite or the Judean ruler). Moreover, the determination or nondetermination of both "lamb" and "ruler" presents a problem. We may translate either "*the* lamb of *the* ruler of *the* land" or "*a* lamb of *a* ruler of *a* land." We may not translate, however, "a lamb of the lord of the land" (so Oswalt, 340) since this would require a circumlocution involving the addition of a lamed to משל. "*The* lamb of *the* ruler of *the* land" suggests that a particular lamb (or kind of lamb) is meant, but no reason for this specificity is apparent (Kaiser [72] reads this way and suggests that *the* lamb is "a technical term for a gift handed over on the occasion of submission [cf. II Kings 3.4] or a request for protection." But there is no evidence for the existence of such a technical usage.) "*A* lamb of *a* ruler of *a* land" presents an indeterminacy that is completely impossible in the context. Both readings of the construct chain are less preferable than either emending the text so that "ruler of the land" becomes the indirect object or reading the epithet as a vocative.

[97]Rudolph, 135, drops the locative *heh* from "wilderness" and adds to the word a definite article. Wildberger (593) notes that the MT may be understood as "from the rock in the wilderness" in accordance with GKC §90d. Koppe (244) notes that סלע and הר are in parallel and chooses to read סלע as a common noun. He thinks that "the rock of the wilderness" is a poetic name for the whole destroyed territory of Moab.

however, that it understands מסלע as a verb and translates it with דתקיף "who prevailed" (= מסלה? מסלל?). Both the Syriac and the Targum contain messianic interpretations of the text, arising we may suppose because of the mention of משל־ארץ, "the ruler of the land."

The evidence of the versions does not support any probable emendation of the MT. The Isaiah scroll from Qumran, on the other hand, contains one very significant difference from the MT; instead of מסלע it has מסלה. This gives a sensible meaning: "Send a lamb, O ruler of the land, [by way of] the wilderness highway to the mount of the daughter of Zion." The mention of a "highway" (מְסִלָּה) in contexts dealing with the flight of exiles or refugees is quite natural.[98] The text of 1QIsa[a] is not without problems, however. Most importantly, 1QIsa[a] would need a preposition before מסלה in order to read smoothly— ב or על one would suppose. The reading of 1QIsa[a] could well be a correction designed to clarify the meaning of the line; the very appropriateness of the mention of a highway in a context pertaining to the sending of a gift probably suggested the change. One might even suppose an aural error by a copyist, the gutturals in LBH having been weakened. The MT's reading סלע offers a sense more unique (whether "rock" or "Sela") than that found in 1QIsa[a]. And, finally, the evidence of the LXX and the Syriac (*k*ʾ*p*ʾ, "the rock") both support the MT. For these reasons, the MT is to be preferred.[99]

Given the lack of versional evidence to support emendation, we would do well to follow the MT at the beginning of the verse as well. We could interpret משל־ארץ as a vocative, "O ruler of the land."[100] This reading requires no emendation of the MT, and it

---

[98]It is especially common in prophetic material dealing with flight from or return to a homeland; see Isa 11:16; 19:23; 40:3; 49:11; 59:7; 62:10; Jer 31:21.

[99]As we have argued above, Isa 16:1 is found in Jer 48:28 in a severely condensed and highly altered form:

עזבו ערים ושכנו בסלע ישבי מואב והיו כיונה תקנן בעברי פי־פחת	Leave the towns, and live on *the rock*, O inhabitants of Moab! Be like the dove that nests on the sides of the mouth of the gorge.

Thus, Jer 48:28 also supports the text of the MT at Isa 16:1.

[100]The Masoretic cantillation suggests either that משל־ארץ is a vocative or that it is in apposition with כר.

provides a sensible reading. The fact that the imperative verb is plural makes this reading difficult, however. This may be explained on the supposition that משל is collective term for a group of Moabite leaders. Or we might suppose that a *yod* dropped out of the text after משל, or, less easily, that a *waw* was appended to the main verb.[101] In favor of the first idea is the fact that the following petition presumably is delivered by a group of leading Moabites come as supplicants, and this group might be the subject of the imperative (16:2). None of these suggestions is fully satisfactory, however. One would normally expect that the call to send a present would be directed to Moab's king, not to a group of Moabite chiefs or princes. Note, however, that the problem is inherent in the verb, and unless one emends שלחו, one must contend with a plural subject for the imperative.

Wildberger favors emending the MT as little as possible. He rejects the various emendations proposed for שִׁלְחוּ by earlier commentators: "Trotz großer Bedenken wird man sich an 𝔐 zu halten haben."[102] He does, however, tentatively emend the MT by adding a *lamed* to משל and reads "ruler of the land" as the indirect object of the verb (his translation and his text-critical notes do not entirely agree at this point). Rudolph suggests a plausible means by which the *lamed* dropped out. He hypothesizes that the text originally read כָּרִים לְמ׳ and that a copyist's eye skipped from one *mem* to the next ("*aberratio oculi*") with the result that both a *mem* and a *lamed* were lost. This understanding of the text leads to the translation "Send lambs to [the] ruler of the land...," i.e., to the Judean king. The poetic parallelism of the verse lends support to this suggestion. If we add a *lamed* before משל, 16:1aβ and 16:1bβ correspond very nicely, both indicating the recipient of the gift: "to the ruler of the land" // "to the mount of daughter Zion." While this does not offer an indisputable solution to the knotty problems in 16:1a, it appears to be the best solution available.

The phrase מסלע מדברה also presents a problem, in part because it is syntactically ambiguous. As mentioned above, it is not clear whether סלע is the common noun "rock" or the place name Sela.

---

[101]Cf. Isa 28:14.

[102]Wildberger, 593. Similarly, see Rudolph, 135.

Jer 48:28 probably picked up the word סלע from 16:1, and in Jeremiah it clearly means "rock." The Syriac and the LXX also understood it as "rock." The context, however, suggests that a specific place is meant: the idiom שלח...מן...אל leads one to expect a place name.[103] Many of the older commentators have understood סלע as a place name. Sela was commonly identified with Petra, the Nabatean fortress city lying about 55 miles south of the Dead Sea.[104] The description of the Moabite flight in Isaiah 15 would not lead one to think, however, that the Moabites fled so far south as Petra. The geographical indications in 15:5–7 suggest that the fugitives were headed for the area just south of the Dead Sea; 15:5 implies that their goal was Zoar. Another site at which the name Sela is preserved lies about three miles north of Buṣeira (about 16 miles south of the Dead Sea). The name designates an unusual rock formation. The site shows signs of habitation (it is strewn with pottery, some of which is Iron Age) and is quite a bit closer to the area in which Zoar is usually located. If סלע is an Edomite place name, this Sela must also be considered as a candidate. A place named Sela is also mentioned in Judg 1:36 and 2 Kgs 14:7. This city is apparently located somewhere at the south end of the Dead Sea, near an area referred to as "the valley of salt" (cf. 2 Sam 8:13; 1 Chr 18:12). Perhaps it is identical with the Sela near Buṣeira.[105] While the phrase may be taken as either an epithet for some unspecified location, i.e., "a/the rock toward the wilderness," or as a place name, it seems most likely that "Sela" מדברה ("toward the wilderness") distinguishes this Sela from another city or cities of the same name.[106] It seems best, then, to under-

---

[103]Gray, *Isaiah*, 290. Gray thinks that סלע מדברה "may well be a corruption of some single phrase of place."

[104]E.g., Gesenius, 146–49; Duhm, 101; Barnes, 294. Against this see the more recent commentaries of König, 190; Kissane, 184; Kaiser, 58; Wildberger, 589.

[105]The evidence we possess allows no certain conclusions to be drawn. See Bartlett, *Edom and the Edomites* (JSOTS 77; Sheffield: JSOT, 1989) 51–52; W. Fanwar, "Sela," *ABD*, 5. 1073–74.

[106]Cf. 1 Chr 12:8, מצד מדברה, "the wilderness fortress," and 1 Chr 5:9. Contra Wildberger (589, 93) and Kaiser (58) who both take סלע as a common noun. Even if one translates "the rock" one must acknowledge that it appears some specific rock is meant. Why else would מדברה be used to further designate

stand סלע מדברה, "Sela (the one) toward the wilderness" as a reference either to the Sela near Buṣeira or to some as yet unidentified Sela in the region immediately south of the Dead Sea.[107]

סלע? If the writer had merely intended to compare some desolate location with mount Zion, why would not the phrase סלע המדבר or סלע במדבר have been chosen? We also consider improbable Alexander's suggestion (322) that we take the directive *heh* to mean "*from Petra to the wilderness* (and thence) *to mount Zion*." This would represent an unusual use of the locative *heh* (cf. GKC §90 c, d; Waltke-O'Connor §10.5).

[107]N. Glueck (cited in Bartlett, 52) notes that, "There must have existed during the Early Iron Age in eastern Palestine numerous sites built on more or less isolated prominences and known by the name 'Selaʿ.'"

Translation of Isaiah 15 and 16

15

1 Massah[1] concerning Moab
Indeed, in the night of the destroyer the cities of Moab lament.
Indeed, in the night of the destroyer the cities of Moab lament.

2 Dibon has gone up to the temple, to the high places to weep.
On[2] Nebo and on Medeba Moab wails.
On every head is baldness, and[3] every beard is shorn.

3 In Huzoth they put on sackcloth.
On its rooftops and in its plazas
everyone wails, sinking in tears.

4 Heshbon and Elealah cried out;
unto Jahaz their voice was heard.
Therefore the loins[4] of Moab cry out; his whole being quivers.[5]

5 My heart cries out for Moab;
His fugitives [flee] as far as Zoar (Eglath Shelishiyah).
For the ascent of Luhith[6] they ascend with tears;
For on the road of Horonaim they raise a shattering cry.[7]

6 For the waters of Nimrim are a desolation;
For the grass is withered, the young grass is finished,
nothing green remains.

7 Therefore the surplus it acquired and their stockpile[8]
they carry over the Wadi of the Willows.

8 For the cry has encompassed the territory of Moab.
Unto Eglaim its wailing; unto Beer Elim its wailing.[9]

9 Because the waters of Dimon are full of blood,
indeed, I will place upon Dimon additional [woes],
for the fugitives of Moab a lion,
as well as for the remnant of Admah.

16

1 Send a lamb to the ruler of the land,
from Sela toward the wilderness
to the mount of maiden Zion.[10]

2 And it will come to pass:[11]
Like fleeing birds, like scattered nestlings[12]
shall be the daughters of Moab beyond[13] the Arnon.[14]

3 Give counsel![15] Assume responsibility![16]
Cast your shadow as the night at high noon!
Hide the displaced! Do not betray the fugitive!
4 Let Moab's displaced sojourn among you.[17]
Be a shelter to him from the destroyer.
When[18] the violent one[19] has ceased, destruction has ended,
the trampler has vanished[20] from the land,
5 then a throne will be established in faithfulness,
and one will sit on it in truth.
In the tent of David[21] a judge and a seeker of justice
and an expert[22] in righteousness.
6 We have heard about the majesty of Moab,
the exceedingly proud one.[23]
About its hauteur and its haughtiness and its arrogance—
his boasting is not right.[24]
7 Therefore let Moab howl;
As for all Moab, let it howl.[25]
On behalf of the raisin-cakes[26] of Kir Hareseth
you will groan,[27] utterly stricken.
8 For the fields of Heshbon languish;[28]
as for the vine of Sibmah, the lords of the nations
its choicest vines have smitten.[29]
They extended to Jazer; they wandered [to] the wilderness.
Its shoots spread out;[30] they crossed the sea.
9 Therefore I weep with the weeping of Jazer
[for] the vine of Sibmah.[31]
I drench[32] with my tears Heshbon and Elealah.
For on your fruit harvest[33] and on your grain harvest
fell the victory shout,[34]
10 Joy and rejoicing have been taken away
from the garden land,[35]
And in the vineyards no cry rings out and[36] no one cheers.
No treader treads[37] wine in the vats.
I have brought an end to the victory shout.[38]
11 Therefore, my bowels growl like a lyre for Moab
and my innards for Kir Hares.[39]
12 And it will come about that although he presents himself,
although Moab exhausts himself upon the high place[40]

and enters his sanctuary to pray,
he will not succeed.[41]

[Later addition]

13 This is the word that Yahweh spoke formerly[42] concerning Moab.

14 But now Yahweh says, "In three years, like the years of a hired hand,[43] the glory of Moab will be shamed along with all the great population—(they will be) but a remnant, a very few, not many.[44]

---

[1]As noted above, the traditional translations of מַשָּׂא, "oracle" and "burden" are misleading. Weis's suggestions ("Definition," 276), "prophetic interpretation" and "prophetic exposition (of YHWH revelation)," are based on arguments we find problematic. Since מַשָּׂא appears to be some sort of technical term, we have chosen simply to transliterate it, as is the common practice with terms such as Maskil, Shiggaion and Miktam found in the headings of Psalms. Even if we come to agree on what מַשָּׂא means, it would still make sense to treat it as a proper noun.

[2]An ellipsis for "on (the high place of) Nebo." So most commentators, e.g., Rudolph, 134; Wildberger, 590 (who cites in agreement Delitzsch, Orelli, Marti, Dillmann, Gray, Duhm, Steinmann, Eichrodt, Young, Kaiser. But the latest edition of Kaiser has "concerning," 57; see 67 for comment).

The grammatical and idiomatic evidence tends to favor the meaning "on." In instances where יליל is followed by על elsewhere in the HB, על means either "on" (Hos 7:14, "on their beds") or "concerning" (Jer 48:31; 51:8; Joel 1:5, 11; Mic 1:8). In favor of "on" we may note that in Isa 16:7a&b יליל is followed by ל rather than על to obtain the sense "let everyone wail *concerning* Moab" (cf. Ezek 30:2). Isa 16:12 refers to Moab's activity על־הבמה, and the HB frequently uses על with במה when referring to mountain (often mythic) high places (2 Sam 1:19, 25; 22:34; Isa 14:14; 58:14; Amos 4:13; Mic 1:3; Job 9:8; Hab 3:19). See W. B. Barrick (80, n. 64) for counter arguments.

The context suggests the meaning "on" because the object of Moab's lament is elsewhere in the poem its agriculture, never its cities. On this point there is a striking difference between Isaiah 15–16 and Jeremiah 48. Jeremiah specifically indicates that many cities have been destroyed (see vv 1–2, 8, 18, 21–24, 41); Isaiah never once indicates that a city has been destroyed, not in 15:1–2 (assuming the correctness of our translation) and certainly not in the rest of the poem. Note, finally, that 15:2a refers to a plurality of high places (הבמות) to which Dibon (here a synecdoche for all Moab, cf. 15:2bβ, 9) has ascended to mourn. In 15:2a the poet has in mind more than just the high place at Dibon; it is the high places of the land collectively which Moab is depicted as ascending. The ellipsis of "the high place of" in 15:2b depends on this fact.

[3]Following a number of MSS, 1QIsa[a], the Syriac, and the Targum (Reuchlinianus).

[4]MT has חֲלֻצֵי, "warriors," and the Targum follows the MT. NRSV, Kaiser, Wildberger, et al., repoint חַלְצֵי. This pointing is supported by the LXX (ὀσφύς) and the Syriac.

[5]The verb רוע usually refers to war cries or shouts of victory or joy (cf. Isa 16:10); only one other time does it refer to a cry of distress (Mic 4:9, but the text is uncertain). The versions support the reading of the MT, and there is no reason to emend. The unusual choice of verb may have been dictated by poetic considerations, i.e., to create a sound pair with the following verb, יָרִיעוּ/יָרְעָה (see Berlin, *Dynamics*, 103–108). יָרְעָה, "quiver," is a *hapax legomenon*, and its meaning is derived from Arabic cognates meaning "timidity" and the Hebrew word יְרִיעָה, "curtain."

[6]הלשחית. The determination of this name probably indicates that it is an appellative place name (cf., e.g., הרמה, הגבעה; see BDB 207).

[7]"They raise"—MT has יְעֹעֵרוּ, which most commentators emend to read יְעַרְעֵרוּ (see GKC, § 72cc; Gesenius, 141; Gray, *Isaiah*, 285), pilpel of עור, "arouse, awaken." The first *resh* may have been read as a *waw* and subsequently written defectively as a *holem*. The versions betray their own confusion at this unusual expression: the LXX seems to support the MT with σεισμός = סערה (supposing a confusion of an original *ayin* with a square script *samek*; not ורעש as Gray suggests, 285); the Syriac has *nʿbdw*, perhaps reading יעשו (so Gray). Here again the poet may be playing on a Moabite place name with the choice of words; in this case the allusion is to Aroer (עֲרֹעֵר; a suggestion also made by Cocceius and noted with approbation by Gesenius, 141).

[8]Despite the sudden change of person with פקדתם, the MT should be retained. The LXX has ἐπάξω, suggesting פקדתי and thus פקדתו, so it is possible that the 3mpl suffix should be emended to 3ms, but the recurrence of the 3mpl suffix in the following line (ישאום) argues against this (contra Driver, "Linguistic and Textual Problems: Isaiah I–XXXIX," *JThSt* 38 [1937] 40; 1QIsa[a] supports the MT in both places where Driver wants to emend). The meaning "stockpile" (Gesenius, 143, "hoarded treasures") is not well attested (see only Ps 109:8), but the related word פקדון, "deposit, store" (Gen 41:36; Lev 5:21, 23), lends support to translating פקדתם in this way.

[9]None of the emendations proposed in BHS for this verse is warranted. As noted above, the 3fs suffixes are used because the subject here is the land of Moab, a feminine idea (the גבול [8aβ]defines the ארץ), rather than the people, as elsewhere. The non-repetition or "gapping" of עד is a perfectly acceptable poetic ellipsis; the fact that the LXX supplies it reflects a tendency among the ancient translators to fill out and clarify the text. The repetition of יללתה is found in all MSS and versions except the Syriac. Even though it might easily have entered the text through a copyist's error, there is insufficient evidence to warrant its removal. The verb נקף conveys the idea of the repetition of a cycle (cf. Isa 29:1) or the closing of a perimeter (Josh 6:3, 11); the repetition of "its wailing" perhaps serves to emphasize the idea of the verb.

[10]On the translation, "maiden Zion," see W. Stinespring, "No Daughter of Zion," *Encounter* 26 (1965) 133–41; E. Follis, "The Holy City As Daughter,"

Directions in Biblical Hebrew Poetry (ed. E. Follis; JSOTS 40; Sheffield: JSOT, 1987) 173–84.

[11]On והיה as a consequential link as here translated, see Weis, "Definition," 118, and GKC §112x-y. Cf. Gen 4:14 and Isa 3:24.

[12]With Gray, *Isaiah* (288) and Driver (*JSS* 13 [1969] 44). See Deut 32:11 for the meaning "nestlings" for קֵן.

[13]Following Gray, *Isaiah* (290; see there for further arguments) we emend to read מֵעֵבֶר לְאַרְנוֹן (or מֵעֶבְרַת, see Gray) "beyond the Arnon," for MT לְאַרְנוֹן מַעְבָּרֹת, "[at] some fords of the Arnon" (the MT takes the *lamed* as a circumlocution for the construct and thereby leaves "fords" indefinite; cf. GKC § 129c). The MT reading presents a grammatical construction found nowhere else in the HB; the locative accusative is "all but confined to cases in which the acc. is followed by a noun in the genitive" (Gray, 290; see GKC, § 118g). מַעְבָּרוֹת occurs eight times in the HB; elsewhere it always has the full spelling and is never once followed by *lamed*, the construct being elsewhere formed in the normal way (cf. Judg 3:28; 12:5, 6). The expression מֵעֵבֶר לְ (most often followed by the name of a river), on the other hand, is found frequently in the HB (20x; see, e.g., Isa 18:1; Num 22:1) and makes perfect sense in the present context. The flight of the Moabites as depicted in ch. 15 has already proceeded beyond the Arnon, and it would be strange to picture them now at the ford (as many commentators have noted). Wildberger (593) and Rudolph (136) choose instead to read במעברת assuming a haplography of a *beth* (Syriac = *bmʿbrtʾ*), but this does not finally solve the problem of the unidiomatic presence of the *lamed*.

The evidence of the versions is split. The LXX is very free but probably read מֵעֵבֶר (so Goshen-Gottstein, ed., *The Book of Isaiah* [Jerusalem: Magness Press, 1975], *s.v.*). Symmachus has πέραν (= מֵעֵבֶר), but Aquila and Theodotion have διάβασις (= מַעְבָּרוֹת). The Targum reads a hophal participle (מגיזין = MT consonants). The Syriac has *bmʿbrtʾ dʿrnw*, in agreement with the MT except for the addition of the preposition בְּ. 1QIsa[a] = MT.

[14]Duhm, 101; Kissane, 184; Rudolph, 136; Kaiser, 70; et al. move 16:2 before 16:1 in order to connect it with 15:9. They offer two reasons: (1) both 15:9aβ-b and 16:2 have a future orientation (Rudolph calls 16:2 an "Orakel"; Gray [*Isaiah*, 288] refers to it as "predictive") and (2) 16:1 deals with the south whereas 16:2 again mentions the Arnon. The future times to which 15:9 and 16:2 refer are not, however, necessarily the same (see our chapter on the interpretation of the poem). Rearranging verses solely on the basis of a apparent coincidence of genre or tense is a dangerous procedure, especially if the text can be rendered sensible in its present state by less drastic means. The present translation eliminates the problem of the mention of the Arnon since the Moabites are pictured not *at* but rather *beyond* the gorge.

[15]K הביאו, Q הביאי = impv. 2fs as are the other verbs in this section; the subject of the 2fs imperatives is daughter Zion (so Lowth, *Isaiah*, 227). The verb is apparently similar in meaning in this context to [עצה] יהב, "give [counsel]," cf. Judg 20:7; 2 Sam 16:20. 1QIsa[a] has הביו reading the less difficult √יהב. Some corruption is at work to be sure. Probably it resulted from the

difficulty presented by the unexpected feminine imperative. It is best to read the Qere (הביאי) which has some MS and versional support as well as the favor of the Masoretes; the sense is clear even if the wording is not completely idiomatic. Instead of "counsel," (√יעצ) Driver translates "firmness, resistance" (√עצי) since "The last thing that a bewildered group of fugitive women, huddled on the bank of a river, will want will be to receive advice or have judgement done—and judgement on what matters?" (*JSS* 13 [1968] 45). But the "daughters of Moab" should not be taken literally, nor should we think of the plea being made on the banks of the Arnon. The request for "counsel" is nothing but a polite beginning to what finally becomes a request for asylum (contra Gray, *Isaiah*, 288).

[16]Emending עשו to עשי in accordance with a number of MSS, LXX[a], Syriac, Targum, Vulgate and the general sense of the passage. The *hapax legomenon* פְּלִילָה is a term from the legal sphere probably denoting legal responsibility or guardianship. For this interpretation see A. Berlin, "On the Meaning of *pll* in the Bible," *RB* 96 (1989) 345–51, esp. 348. The closely related form פְּלִילִיָּה is used in Isa 28:7 with reference to the official activity either of priests or of prophets.

[17]Emending נִדָּחַי מוֹאָב, "my fugitives, O Moab" or "my fugitives. As for Moab...." Two MSS, the LXX (οἱ φυγάδες Μωαβ), and the Syriac (*mbdrʾ dmwʾb*) suggest נִדְּחֵי מוֹאָב, "the fugitives of Moab." Gesenius (152) argues that the MT pointing (but not cantillation) should be retained and read as a pleonasm: "my outcasts, i.e. Moab." But the MT pointing probably reflects an eschatological interpretation (so Kaiser, 58; Wildberger, 593). Attaching "Moab" to the following line (following cantillation; so Oswalt, 340, 43) wreaks havoc on the rhythm and sense of the verse (Gray, *Isaiah*, 289–90). Rudolph (136) thinks "Moab" is a gloss since it disturbs the meter, but this is not at all clear.

[18]It makes a great deal of difference for interpretation how one understands the syntax of this *kî* clause. I take the *kî* to mark the protasis for which v 5 is the apodosis (...וְהוּכַן). For this construction see Waltke-O'Connor, § 32.2.1b (so also Duhm, 102; Procksch, 217; Rudolph, 136; Kaiser, 58–59; Wildberger, 593; and Oswalt, 340). See also interpretation chapter.

[19]MT reads הַמֵּץ, "oppressor" (√מיץ), a *hapax legomenon*. Duhm (102) suggested חָמֹץ, and this is now supported by 1QIsa[a] which has חמוצ (not המוצ as in M. Burrows, *The Dead Sea Scrolls of St. Mark's Monastery, vol. I* [New Haven: The American Schools of Oriental Research, 1950], pl. XIII, ln. 21. A careful examination of the photograph reveals that Burrows has misread the letter; on this see E. R. Rowlands, "Mistranscriptions in the Isaiah Scroll," *VT* [1951] 228). The Targum has מעיקא, "oppressor"; the LXX ὅτι ἤρθη (אפס?) ἡ συμμαχία (המץ? אסף?) σου, "For your alliance has been removed." Reading חָמוֹץ also has the advantage of eliminating the article from the substantive to bring it into harmony with the other substantives in the verse (so Gray, *Isaiah*, 290; or one can add an article to שד, as does Wildberger [593] on the assumption of a haplography, but the tendency of the poem is toward anarthrous substantives). The parallel between a concrete and an abstract term in 4b is not so

difficult as to require emendation to harmonize the two terms (contra Driver [*JThSt* 38] 40; Wildberger, 593; Kaiser, 58).

[20]The MT verb is plural (תַּמּוּ), which is possible before a singular participle used collectively (Gray, *Isaiah*, 291; GKC § 145d). The other verbs in the verse are singular, however, and this suggests that we should emend to read with 1QIsa[a]: תם (so Wildberger, 593). There is little at stake here, finally.

[21]Wildberger (593) and Kaiser (59) hold that באהל דוד is metrically excessive and therefore a gloss. There is, however, no evidence other than the supposed excessive metrical length that we are dealing with a gloss; this "gloss" is attested in all the versions. If the expression is put at the beginning of 5b, the meter is more acceptable (so Rudolph, 136). The expression is a *hapax legomenon*. The only comparative example is Amos 9:11: סכת דויד, "the booth of David." F. Cross ("The Priestly Tabernacle in the Light of Recent Research," *Temples and High Places in Biblical Times* [ed. A. Biran; Jerusalem: Keter, 1981] 177, n. 31) notes:

> Amos 9:11 and Isaiah 16:5 preserve memories of the Davidic Tent of Yahweh. The expression *sukkat David* in Amos 9:11 refers on the surface to the Davidic Dynasty to be restored. This "rebuilding" may refer to the rule again over the North (and the old empire).... [The prophet] is drawing on the typology between the dynasty and the dynastic shrine—the Tent of Yahweh.

Amos 9:12 makes clear the point that the rebuilding of the "booth of David" is linked to the re-establishment of David's control over neighboring nations: "in order that they may possess the remnant of Edom and all the nations who are called by my name...." This text is not necessarily late, as some have supposed (see the arguments of S. Paul, *Amos* [Hermeneia; Minneapolis: Fortress, 1991] 289–92). The mention of "the tent of David" in Isa 16:5 may, therefore, contain an allusion to the hegemony David once established over Moab, an allusion entirely appropriate to the context as we shall argue in our interpretation chapter.

[22]On "expert" see E. Ullendorff, "The Contribution of South Semitics to Hebrew Lexicography," *VT* 6 (1956) 195. H. L. Ginsberg, "Some Emendations in Isaiah," *JBL* 69 (1950) 54–55, suggests emending מהר to שחר and translating, "a judge (and one) who seeks justice and searches for righteousness." He notes that elsewhere in the HB מהר is used only in the absolute state and always as an epithet for "scribe." But the attestation of the word is too light (4x) to allow firm conclusions, and if one admits evidence based on the usage of the verbal form, Isa 5:19 presents an example of the use of the root to refer to divine alacrity in carrying out justice (cf. Ps 69:18; 79:8; 102:3; 143:7).

[23]MT גא is a *hapax legomenon*; Jer 48:29 and 1QIsa[a] both have גאה (adj., "proud"). The meaning and translation is the same whether or not we emend, so there is little to be gained in deciding. Here it is rendered as a substantive in apposition to Moab. Cf. Wildberger's colorful translation, *der hochtrabend einherkommt* (589).

---

[24]Hebrew בדיו can also mean "his power" (see D. Dimant, "Targum Jonathan to Isa. XVI. 6 and Jer. XLVIII. 29f.," *JSS* 18 [1973] 55–56; C. Rabin, "Hebrew *Baddim* 'Power,'" *JSS* 18 [1973] 57–58). The Vulgate has *fortitudo*. The context, however, suggests the meaning "vain, idle talk" (cf. Job 11:3; Isa 44:25; Jer 48:30; 50:36). On this translation of the expression לא־כן see Gen 48:18; Deut 18:14; 2 Kgs 7:9—all contexts in which improper behavior is condemned; cf. GKC §152a, n. 1; Gray, *Isaiah*, 294. 1QIsa[a] has לכן, perhaps under the influence of the following verse.

[25]So A. Berlin (*Dynamics*, 70) who points out an ABBA pattern here. למואב is often deleted as a scribal error (so Gray, *Isaiah*, 294; Procksch, 220; Wildberger, 594), but exact repetition of this kind is well attested in Hebrew poetry (Berlin, *Dynamics*, 69–71). The LXX has the phrase, and Jer 48:31, though substantially different, attests it.

[26]Jer 48:31 has אנשי, "men," instead of אשישי. So too the Targum and, probably, the LXX = τοῖς κατοικοῦσιν. But the MT makes sense here, especially since "raisin cakes" fits with the theme of agriculture in the context, and 1QIsa[a] also supports the MT (though the text is somewhat broken at the point of the second *shin*). "Raisin cakes" are also mentioned in Hos 3:1; 2 Sam 6:19; Cant 2:5.

[27]The 2mpl verb תֶּהְגּוּ comes unexpectedly here, and some, supposing a dittography of the final *taw* of the previous word, emend the text to read the 3mpl יהגו or the m. pl. imperative הגו (e.g., Wildberger, 594). These emendations smooth out the text, and the suggestion יהגו is supported by the Targum (יימרון) and one of the MSS in Kennicot's collation (יהגו). In addition, Jer 48:31 (יהגה, but perhaps אהגה, following one MS and Q[Or]) offers some support for reading the third person. The LXX supports the MT, however, with μελετήσεις (= תהגי or, less likely, תהגה). If we suppose a straightforward dittography, we must explain why הגו is attested nowhere. Or, if we supposed that the 3mpl was obscured by a dittograpy, we must explain what became of the *yod*. Thus, the dittography suggestion is less probable than it might seem at first glance. The 3mpl in the Targum and one MS may be explained as attempts to smooth out the reading found in the MT. More difficult is the idea that the MT's 2mpl is a corruption of an original 3mpl. On "mutter" cf. Isa 8:19; behind this word often seems to be the sense of "talking under one's breath" as a part of internal reflection, hence "to meditate" (Josh 1:8; Ps 1:2; 63:7), "to devise" (Ps 2:1; Prov 24:2), and "to groan, growl" (Isa 38:14; 59:11).

[28]The subject, "fields" (plural), and the verb, "languish" (3ms), do not agree. The LXX reproduces this agreement problem exactly. The Targum has its own interpretation, ארי אתבזיזא משרית חשבון אתקטלא סיעת שבמה, "For the armies of Heshbon are plundered, the companies of Sibmah are killed," but אתבזיזא suggests that the translator read שדמות as a verb, perhaps a form of שדד (so BHS note). 1QIsa[a] has אמללה (cf. Isa 33:9). Lowth, *Isaiah*, (228–29) attaches the last two words of v 7 to the beginning of v 8, and reconstructs אך נכלמו שדמות חשבו (similar to LXX). The agreement problem may be explained, however, on the basis that "fields" is a collective idea as is the case in Hab 3:17 (so GKC §145h, k, u). N. Wyatt ("A New Look at Ugaritic *šdmt*," *JSS* 37 [1992] 149–53)

argues that שדמה can designate a part of a plant, most probably the shoot from which the fruits (particularly grapes) grow (he cites as examples Deut 32:32; Isa 16:8; Hab 3:17 and Isa 37:27). This intriguing possibility suggests we translate, "For the tendrils of Heshbon languish...."

[29]The verb הלמו is unusual in the context since it refers elsewhere to pounding (with a hammer: Judg 5:26; Isa 41:7; Ps 74:6; of hooves: Judg 5:22; fist/hand: Ps 141:5; Prov 23:35). But the fact that Isa 28:1 uses the same verb to describe drunkenness from wine (cf. Prov 23:35) suggests that we should not conclude too much about the semantic possibilities of the word from such a few occurrences. Certainly we should not conclude from such a small sample that the verb could not refer to the destruction of vines (cf. especially Ps 74:6; contra Wildberger, 594). Many commentators under the influence of Isa 28:1 took "its vines" as the subject of the verb, i.e., the lords of the nations were "smitten" by the vines, בעלי גוים standing as a *casus pendens* (so Cocceius, Vitringa, Lowth, Eichhorn, Hitzig, Knobel, Hendewerk, Delitzsch, Dillmann, Marti, Duhm, Eichrodt, Gray, Procksch). The consensus changed after Procksch; according to Kaiser, "The former widespread rendering of 8aαα2 as 'whose grapes once forced (i.e. intoxicated) the lords of the nations'... seems more recently to have been generally abandoned" (73, fn. c). But Rudolph (137) and, most recently, Wildberger (594) have again championed this interpretation. The ambiguity of the verse is irresolvable. On the one hand, the intoxicating-vines interpretation does not suit the preceding context which has mentioned mourning for the faded fields of Heshbon, nor does it prepare us for the weeping over the vine of Sibmah in verse 9. On the other hand, 8b recounts the previous *success* of the vine of Sibmah, not its present destruction. Thus the context does not give us much help. Perhaps a double meaning is intended. C. Gordon has pointed out a poetic device he names "Janus parallelism" that "hinges on the use of a single word with two entirely different meanings: one meaning paralleling what precedes, and the other meaning, what follows" ("New Directions," *BASP* 15 [1978] 59; quoted in A. Ceresko, "Janus Parallelism in Amos's 'Oracles Against the Nations,'" *JBL* 113 [1994] 486. See Ceresko's article for examples and analysis). The present translation reflects an attempt to reproduce in English the syntactic ambiguity found in the Hebrew.

[30]"Its shoots," שלחותיה, is a *hapax legomenon*. There may be some continued paronomasia affecting the poet's word choice; the verbal forms of √שלח and its related nouns all have metaphorically related semantic domains referring to the shooting forth of tendrils (Jer 17:8; Ezek 31:5; Ps 80:12) and to weapons, "shooters" (e.g., Josh 2:8; 1 Sam 20:20; Neh 4:11, 17). Perhaps it is significant that another nominalization from this stem appears in Isa 11:14 (משלוח), a context dealing with Moab. The suitability of the verb נטשו in the context is illustrated by the related form נטישה, n.f., "twig, tendril of vine" (Isa 18:5; Jer 5:10).

[31]The meaning of the phrase בבכי יעזר, "with the weeping of Jazer" is obscure. Are we to think of the people of Jazer as those in whose (imagined) company the writer weeps? The LXX apparently read כבכי (ὡς τὸν κλαυθμὸν

Ιαζηρ), probably a misreading of the *beth*. G. Landes ("The Fountain at Jazer," *BASOR* 144 [1956] 30–37) has suggested emending to read מבכי, "fountain, spring" (and similarly in Jer 48:32a). The root is either נבך or מבך and is attested in both Hebrew and Ugaritic with this meaning (see esp. Job 38:16). Landes's suggestion has found acceptance among scholars (see Bright, *Jeremiah* [AB; Garden City: Doubleday, 1984[2]] 321; Rudolph, *Jeremia*, 282; R. Carroll, *Jeremiah* [OTL; Philadelphia: Westminster, 1986] 790), and it makes good sense in the context. The syntax of the verse is difficult, since one would expect a preposition (על or ל) before "the vine of Sibmah." Landes's suggestion creates new difficulties by taking מבכי יעזר as a vocative: "O fountain of Jazer." If one decides to emend, it would probably be better to assume that a *mem* was dropped between the two *beths*, either a haplography of the *beth*-like *mem* or a correction of the text to "improve" it (i.e., to make it read more conventionally, מבך/נבך being uncommon). In this case one might emend to read כמבכי and translate, "I will weep like (following LXX) the fountain of Jazer (for) the vine of Sibmah." This expression, while unusual, would parallel the next line nicely; weeping like a fountain for Sibmah's vine would correspond to the tear drenching Heshbon and Elealah receive. Such an adventurous emendation is, however, against the the best text-critical principles since there is no MS or versional evidence to support it. It must remain only a tantalizing possibility.

[32]The MT אֲרַיָּוֵךְ is an impossible form. 1QIsa[a] has ארזיך; the *zayin* is probably a misreading of the *waw*, and so we may emend the MT and read אֲרַוֵּךְ, a reading proposed by commentators pre-DSS (See BDB, 924; GKC §75 dd).

[33]Jer 48:32 has בציר, "vintage" rather than קציר, "fruit harvest." All of the important versions, however, support the MT: the Targum and Syriac both have *ḥdd*, "reaping, harvest," and the LXX has θερισμῷ, "harvest," (contra Lowth, *Isaiah*, 229). Moreover, this line and the two following each contain alliterative word pairs: קיצך/קצירך, הכרמל/בכרמים, ידרך/הדרך. If we emend on the basis of Jer 48:32, we lose the alliteration.

[34]NRSV translates "for the shout over your fruit harvest and your grain harvest has ceased." This requires taking נפל in an unusual, but by no means impossible, sense. When connected with על, this verb usually refers to something ominous or disastrous befalling someone (cf. Josh 11:7; Isa 47:11; Eccl 9:12; Gen 15:12; Josh 2:9). Jer 48:32 is parallel to this verse, but instead of הידד, "victory shout," it reads שֹׁדֵד, "the destroyer," taking נפלעל as a reference to an attack. Note too that הידד, while it is used of the shouts of those treading out the grape harvest (16:10; Jer 48:33; Jer 25:30), is also used of a victory shout at the defeat of an enemy (Jer 51:14; cf. הד in Ezek 7:7). The two meanings are related metaphorically; just as one cheers both the defeat of one's enemies and the treading of vintage, so too one treads (דרך) both enemies and grapes (see BDB 202). Probably the double sense of the word is part of the continuing word play.

As for Jeremiah's שדד instead of הידד, the possibility that שדד is the original reading cannot easily be dismissed since the Targum (בזוזין) and Syriac (*dywšʾ*; cf. v 4) both attest it. Unfortunately, the LXX is unclear (καταπατήσω, reading

הדרך, hiph. pf. or inf.? But see the next verse where the LXX simply drops this word). 1QIsa[a] has the same text as the MT. The textual evidence opens the possibility that at least some (nonextant) MS(S) contained שדד in this verse, but neither context nor syntax points definitely to one or the other. We should note three things, however. First, the MT's הידד presents the more difficult (i.e., more distinctive, less conventional) reading. Secondly, הידד offers "a fine paronomasia," paronomasia being a tendency of the writer (so Gesenius, 159). Thirdly, Jeremiah uses שָׁדַד frequently (6:26; 12:6, 12; 15:8; 25:36; 47:4; 48:8, 18, 32; 51:48, 53, 55, 56—13 of the 18 occurrences in the HB), and this suggests the possibility that the change reflects only a preference for a favorite expression. Thus we should probably read הידד, although possibly we are confronted with an irreducible variant.

[35]Gesenius (159) takes this as an appellative place name. But where else are Moab's agricultural lands referred to by this name?

[36]Reading a *waw* here with BHS suggestion on the basis of 1QIsa[a], a number of MSS, the Targum and Vulgate.

[37]The LXX has no corresponding word for הדרך, but a cognate participle of this sort is easily dropped in free translations such as that of the LXX in this verse. The Targum and Syriac support the MT, and the MT's alliteration is lost if we delete this word (contra BHS note; Wildberger, 594; *et al.*).

[38]The shift from impersonal passive and 3rd person to first person discourse seems jarring to many interpreters. The LXX has πέπαυται, "it has ceased," which suggests a *Vorlage* with השבת (Hophal 3ms). But the Hophal of this verb would be a *hapax legomenon*, and the other versions and 1QIsa[a] support the MT. J. de Waard ("The Interim and Final HOTTP Reports and the Translator: a Preliminary Investigation," *Tradition of the Text: Studies Offered to Dominique Barthélemy in Celebration of his 70th Birthday* [ed. G. Norton and S. Pisano; OBO 109; Freiburg, Switzerland: Universitätsverlag; Göttingen: Vandenhoeck and Ruprecht, 1991] 280–81) notes that the LXX has made "some kind of translation technical operation such as an active-passive transformation...for syntactical reasons...many of these transformations can be found in Isaiah." Thus it is not clear that the LXX *Vorlage* differed at all from the MT. It is best, therefore, to leave the text alone and explain the intrusion rather than delete it.

[39]Procksch (222) thinks that we should add to the end of v 11 כחלילים יהמה, on the basis of Jer 48:36 (so too Kaiser, 59). Wildberger (594–95) also favors adding to the line, but he posits a haplography and supplies יהגה (cf. v 7). The gap in the second line of 11 is, however, acceptable poetic form, and no emendation is necessary (so Rudolph, 137) or supported by the versions. Kir Hares (קִיר חָרֶשׂ) is spelled in various ways in the HB: Isa 16:7 קִיר חֲרֶשֶׂת; Jer. 48:31, 36 קִיר חֶרֶשׂ; 2 Kgs 3:25 קִיר חֲרָשֶׂת (קִיר חֲרֶשֶׂת in several MSS and editions). It is possible that for some reason the *taw* was dropped in this second occurrence of the name, but this leaves Jeremiah's usage unexplained. It is easier to assume a dittography in 15:7 that subsequently influenced the spelling in 2 Kgs 3:25. Thus, this verse and Jeremiah 48 probably attest the correct spelling.

---

[40]1QIsa[a] has בא instead of נלאה, perhaps under the influence of בא at the beginning of 12b. Many commentators delete either כי־נלאה or כי־נראה as a dittography (so Gray, *Isaiah*, 293; Rudolph, 137; Wildberger, 594; BHS note). Some, however, think that these words are conjoined in this context as paronomasia (Gesenius, 160; Procksch, 222; Oswalt, 344). The versions do not fully support the MT. The LXX has καὶ ἔσται εἰς τὸ ἐντραπῆναί σε, ὅτι ἐκοπίασε Μωαβ ἐπὶ τοῖς βωμοῖς, "and it will come about to shame you for Moab has become weary on the high place...," probably reflecting כי(נ)כאה rather than כינראה. The Targum has אדייהלי, also probably reflecting כיכאה. Syriac has *wmʾ djnʾ* which reflects כיראה (so too Vulgate). All the versions and 1QIsa[a] support the actual presence of two separate terms, however, and lacking any other real support, the dittography hypothesis should be rejected. Wildberger (595) would delete נראה on the basis of usage, but against his position see BDB, 908, Niph., 1.b. The subject "Moab" is delayed until 12aβ, and no indirect object is explicitly stated.

[41]As we have discussed in chapter three, Hayes and Irvine (246) suggest "not be allowed" (i.e., be prohibited by agreement, custom or law), which is an attested use of the term (Gen 43:32; Deut 12:17; 14:24; 16:5; 17:15; 22:3; Judg 21:18). Although לא יכל is an unusual way to express the failure to gain help from one's deity, there are several comparable usages. Gen 32:29 [28] and Hos 12:5 [4] refer to Jacob "prevailing" with God to gain a blessing, and in Isa 47:11–12 the writer declares to Babylon, "But evil shall come upon you, which you cannot charm away; disaster shall fall upon you, which *you will not be able to ward off* (לא תוכלי כפרה)....Stand fast in your enchantments and your many sorceries, with which you have labored from your youth; perhaps *you may be able to succeed....*" While the context of these examples is somewhat different, the basic idea is very similar: the ability or inability to succeed in gaining the help of one's deity. Isa 47:11–12 is particularly significant since cultic and magical strategies play a part (cf. Zeph 1:18). These examples demonstrate the suitability of לא יכל to denote Moab's failure at its high place.

[42]Heb. מֵאָז can refer to the remote past (Ps 93:2; Prov 8:22) or to the recent past (2 Sam 15:34); cf. the frequent use of the term in Second Isaiah (44:8; 45:21; 48:3–8). There is no way to determine the time span here indicated.

[43]Or "like the years of a mercenary" as in Jer 46:21 (so Duhm, 103–104, *et al.*). The meaning of the phrase is obscure. Wildberger (631) notes that there is no article before שנים and suggests that the point of the comparison is not the time of duration (in three years, i.e., as the years of a hired worker), but the drudgery of the life of a hired worker (in three years, years as of one who does day labor; cf. Job 7:1–2). Still, the exact reckoning "three" leads one to think of quantity or of a method for determing quantity, not quality. The number is apparently not random; the nearly parallel expression in Isa 21:16 reads "within yet a year, as years of a hired worker." Deut 15:18 records that three years was a standard period of service for a שכיר ("for in six years he has given you double the service of a hired man" NJPS translation). This standard of service is probably the source of the "three years" in the present text. Kaiser's suggestion (74) that the specificity of the time owes to apocalyptic

thinking is, therefore, unnecessary. Lev 25:53 may indicate that one year was another standard length of hire. The equation in Job 7:1–2 between day labor and drudgery must be balanced against the proscriptions in Lev 25:39–40, 50, 53 against treating a שכיר as one treats a slave. Hired workers are to be well treated. Of course, this does not rule out drudgery, but if the writer wished simply to emphasize the drudgery of Moab's remaining time, a comparison to forced servitude rather than paid labor might have been more appropriate. Finally, the mention of the hired worker may be an allusion to the displacement of the Moabites depicted earlier in the poem. Apparently, the role of hired worker was one frequently assumed by displaced persons, "sojourners" (Lev 25:40; Jer 31:16; cf. Gen 30:25–36).

44"A remnant": the LXX has καταλειφθήσεται = ונשאר. The sense is the same as the MT, but the LXX has apparently smoothed out the syntax.

"A very few": or "in just a little while"; cf. temporal use of מעט מזער in Isa 10:25; 29:17.

"Not many": 1QIsa^a has כבוד rather than כביר, and the LXX has ἔντιμος (= √כבד). The letters involved are easily confused, but it is more likely that 1QIsa^a and the LXX were influenced by כבוד earlier in the verse than it is that an original כבוד in the MT was misread as כביר.

CHAPTER 6

A RHETORICAL ANALYSIS OF ISAIAH 15–16

I. Introduction

Two points that deeply affect the interpretation of the poem in Isaiah 15–16 have been argued in previous chapters. First, it has been maintained that the poem is ironic, an example of prophetic satire. The expressions of sympathy in this putative lament are in fact spoken ironically, as sarcastic taunts. Secondly, it has been shown that the poem has literary integrity and that previous redactional analysis was led astray by assumptions which were either incorrect or unnecessary and by a mistaken construal of evidence, both textual and geographical. The present chapter offers an interpretation of the poem premised both on its integrity and on the presence of an ironic intention. In the course of this interpretation, it offers further evidence to support both of these premises. The danger of circular argumentation in this endeavor is obvious. One should note, however, that no interpretation avoids entirely a certain degree of circularity.[1] The history of interpretation of Isaiah 15–16 contains many examples of this fact.

II. The Method of Rhetorical Analysis

The reading method employed in this chapter is a synthetic one. It owes much to Rhetorical Criticism, both as practiced by J. Muilen-

---

[1]This is especially true of decisions about genre which, in fact, constitute pre-judgments; see J. Barton, *Reading the Old Testament*, 17–18, 65–66. On the hermeneutical circle as an inescapable part of intepretation, see A. Thiselton, *The Two Horizons. New Testament Hermeneutics and Philosophical Description* (Grand Rapids: Eerdmans, 1980) 104–110, 163–68, 194–97.

burg and his students and as practiced by those oriented to the classical model, e.g., G. Kennedy, W. Wuellner, and Y. Gitay;[2] it uses the close-reading practices characteristic of the literary approaches to the Bible published in the last two decades;[3] and it is based, in part, on insights derived by means of traditional historical-critical method. Several caveats and words of explanation are necessary.

First, the present study is "rhetorical" to the extent that it examines the nature and quality of the text's persuasive strategies.[4] It assumes that the poem was composed for oral delivery in a specific situation and that the author had specific rhetorical goals in mind. The structure of the poem, the genres it employs, its various artistic touches, and the possible historical antecedents of the traditions upon which it draws will be examined for the sake of discovering how the poem persuades an audience to act or think in certain ways. One practical result of this focus is that artistic devices will be evaluated according to their rhetorical effect, not merely according to their elegance. For this reason the question of perceptibility, i.e., the probability that an audience would notice a device or technique at first hearing, is of crucial importance. Structural patterns and markers are particularly at issue here. That which the audience misses, misses the audience; it offers nothing to either persuasion or meaning.[5]

---

[2]For an overview and discussion of each of these lines of rhetorical criticism see C. Black, "Keeping up with Recent Studies. XVI. Rhetorical Criticism and Biblical Interpretation," *ET* 100 (1988–89) 252–57; T. Dozeman, "Rhetoric and Rhetorical Criticism. OT Rhetorical Criticism," *AB* 5. 712–15; and P. Trible, *Rhetorical Criticism* (Minneapolis: Augsburg Fortress, 1994) 25–62.

[3]For a thumbnail sketch of these, see Trible, 76–80.

[4]Rhetorical study of the Bible has a long history. For example, Augustine in *On Christian Doctrine* compared the rhetoric of the Bible with that of classical rhetoricians, and during the Renaissance, Judah Messer Leon produced a lengthy study of the rhetoric of the HB entitled *Sēpher Nōpheth Ṣūphīm* (*The Book of the Honeycomb's Flow*). On these and many other early rhetorical studies, see Trible, 13–18.

[5]The method used in the present study is based on a perspective similar to, and in part, borrowed from, that expressed by Fox in his article "The Rhetoric of Ezekiel's Vision of the Valley of the Bones." On the question of the perceptibility of structural elements, see Fox, 3–4.

The appropriateness of this method of analysis for the text under investigation has been adumbrated in chapter two. M. Kessler has argued that OAN texts in general lend themselves to rhetorical analysis because of their length, content and original function.[6] While the present study of Isaiah 15–16 will employ a method of analysis somewhat different from the rhetorical criticism advocated by Kessler, it proceeds from the same acknowledgement that the method of analysis must conform to the nature of the material under examination. Indeed, prophetic texts in general lend themselves to rhetorical analysis. Studies similar to the present one have examined prophetic texts almost exclusively.[7] Perhaps it is not too much to say, as Fox does, "The prophets offer excellent subjects for rhetorical criticism, for by any definition prophecy is rhetoric."[8]

Secondly, our analysis of the text will have both synoptic and sequential components. Sequential analysis is important because persuasive oratory moves its audience from one disposition or opinion to another over the course of its performance. This performance is, of necessity, sequential. The audience does not

---

[6]Noting the multiplicity and creative mixing of genres in the OAN, Kessler argues that rhetorical criticism offers an appropriate corrective to the atomistic tendencies of form criticism "by giving primary attention to the larger rhetorical usage, where a number of various literary forms may be adapted to new purposes by a given author" ("Oracles Against the Nations: Jeremiah 50 and 51" [a paper read at the annual meeting of the Society of Biblical Literature, Toronto, November 19, 1969]; quotation is from D. Christensen's summary of the paper [*Transformations*, 9]).

[7]For example, the studies of Y. Gitay have dealt mainly with texts in Isaiah (*Prophecy and Persuasion* [Forum Theologicae Linguisticae 14; Bonn: Linguistica Biblica, 1981]; "Isaiah and His Audience," *Prooftexts* 3 [1983] 223–30; "Reflections on the Study of the Prophetic Discourse; The Question of Isaiah I 2–20"). Fox, "Ezekiel's Vision," deals with Ezekiel. Here too we should include Hayes and Irvine's commentary on Isaiah and C. Shaw, "The Speeches of Micah." R. Duke's work on Chronicles is an exception to this trend (*The Persuasive Appeal of the Chronicler* [Sheffield: Almond, 1990]). Gitay's application of his method to biblical narrative ("Rhetorical Criticism," *To Each its Own Meaning* [ed. S. McKenzie and S. Haynes; Louisville: Westminster/John Knox, 1993] 143–44) fails to produce an analysis distinguishable from narrative-critical study. His summary statement that "The Hebrew Bible is oratorical in nature" is unsustained and, probably, unsustainable (if we take "oratorical" in a literary and not theological sense).

[8]Fox, "Ezekiel's Vision," 4.

know at the outset where the speaker will lead them (though they may have the means to guess the speaker's goal). The beginning, middle and end unfold in time. Sequential analysis respects this phenomenon by virtue of a reading procedure congruent with the nature of the text.[9] Synoptic analysis is also important. It affords an opportunity to analyze the larger structures of persuasion and to discuss more theoretically and at greater length those strategies inhabiting the poem as a whole. Separating these two components prevents the sequential analysis from becoming mired in extended analysis when it should be moving with the rhythm of the discourse.

Thirdly, our investigation of the persuasive strategies in the text will proceed inductively and will neither identify the poem with one of Aristotle's three species of rhetoric nor analyze the poem's rhetorical techniques and strategies according to the traditionally prescribed list. Those in biblical studies who use the classical model usually deal with texts containing prose oration or an epistolary variation thereof.[10] Classical rhetorical theory deals effectively with such genres and situations; it was conceived for just such speech acts.[11] Its suitability for the analysis of Hebrew prophetic poetry is, however, questionable. Aristotle's three species of rhetorical address, in particular, have limited applica-

---

[9]On the importance of respecting the dynamic of the process by which a text unfolds itself, an insight deriving from reception theory, see M. Perry, "Literary Dynamics," *Poetics Today* 1 (1979) 35. See also Ch. Perelman and L. Olbrechts-Tyteca, *The New Rhetoric: A Treatise on Argumentation* (Notre Dame: University of Notre Dame, 1969) 491–95, 502–508; and Fox, "Ezekiel's Vision," 3–4.

[10]Most of these scholars focus their efforts on the New Testament, e.g., H. Betz, R. Jewett, G. Kennedy, W. Kurz, D. Watson, and W. Wuellner. See B. Fiore, "NT Rhetoric and Rhetorical Criticism," *ABD* 5. 717–18; and C. Black, 255.

[11]Aristotle's *Rhetoric* was not, however, intended as an exegetical methodology. Aristotle primarily sought to teach correct and effective rhetoric rather than to describe actual rhetorical practice. E. Black notes that rhetorical analysis of the neo-Aristotelian kind "is probably alien to the conceptions of Aristotle, since there is no evidence in the *Rhetoric* that its generalizations were intended for the appraisal of rhetorical discourses" (*Rhetorical Criticism: A Study in Method* [New York: Macmillan, 1965] 92).

bility,[12] and his focus on discursive modes of speech raises the question whether or in what way his insights might be applied to poetry.[13] Using the categories of classical rhetoric to describe prophetic poetry risks distorting the true nature of the rhetoric involved.[14] Doubtless, we shall find similarities between the

---

[12]The extent to which these categories are derived from practices common in the Greek city state is obvious in Aristotle's introduction to the topic. There he derives the three species of rhetoric from the three kinds of hearer—the mere observer (or critic), the judge and the juror—and the corresponding situation in which each is addressed (*Rhetoric*, § 1.3). For analysis and critique of this aspect of the *Rhetoric*, see Ch. Perelman and L. Olbrechts-Tyteca (19–23) who reject the classification as it pertains to the study of argumentation; and W. Wuellner ("The Rhetorical Genre of Jesus' Sermon in Luke 12.1–13.9," 94–97), who advocates giving an inductive reading of the text priority over an analysis of either its literary or its rhetorical genre.

[13]G. Kennedy, (*New Testament Interpretation Through Rhetorical Criticism* [Chapel Hill and London: University of North Carolina, 1984] 10–11) argues that Aristotle's rhetoric has universal applicability: "Aristotle's objective in writing his *Rhetoric* was not to describe Greek rhetoric, but to describe this universal facet of human communication." We must ask, however, to what extent Aristotle (and those after him) was successful in abstracting a completely universal system. The rhetorical practice in different societies varies markedly, and although any technique or practice may be fit into Aristotle's scheme given sufficient ingenuity, the danger of distortion is very real. In the case of Isaiah 15–16, we are dealing with a text both poetic and prophetic. Aristotle's *Rhetoric*, however, treats prose oration exclusively. He explicitly excludes poetry as a proper mode for persuasion (due to its artificiality, see §§3.2, 3.3). His negative attitude toward the "ambiguous" language of "diviners" gives further evidence that he does not intend his system to encompass all modes of persuasion (§3.5). Prophetic texts are primarily involved in *persuading* (by playing on the prejudices, shared symbolic world, and opinions of a particular audience) rather than *convincing* (by appealing to rational proofs). (On persuading and convincing, see Perelman and Olbrechts-Tyteca, 26–31). The *Rhetoric*, however, privileges rational and discursive modes and warns against techniques "too poetical" (see, e.g., §3.3 [4]). Whatever analytical model is applied to prophetic rhetoric, it must be appropriate for the analysis of persuasive appeals operating at highly symbolic levels and finely tuned to the particularity of the audience.

[14]C. Black comments, "While rhetorical models may function as heuristic guides, particular texts often resist preset patterns....we should beware of rhetorical analyses that mask characteristics of Jewish or Christian discourse peculiar to their distinctive cultures" (255, 257). In his introduction to Judah Messer Leon's *Sēpher Nōpheth Ṣūphīm* ([*The Book of the Honeycomb's Flow*] Ithaca and London: Cornell University, 1983), I. Rabinowitz criticizes Leon's failure to take into account the cultural specificity of the "nature and powers of words" used in the HB, and particularly Leon's assumption that Greek

rhetorical techniques described by Aristotle and those used by the prophets, and our analysis would be poorer if we ignored this resource. We shall not, however, allow classical categories to rule the interpretation. Instead, we shall proceed inductively and imaginatively, drawing on whatever analogies and resources seem appropriate to the text we actually have before us.[15]

Fourthly, the present study depends on the diachronic analysis presented in the preceding chapters. It is not strictly synchronic and intrinsic, although it uses many of the analytical techniques typical of these methods.[16] As we have seen, the fact that we are interested in the function of irony in our text has led us unavoidably to focus on intentionality. We have argued that it is important to know, so far as is possible, the historical situation of the poem, i.e., the context in which it was written including: the opinions, beliefs and values of both the author and the audience, the situation that motivated the writer to make the poem, and the setting in which the poem was used. Much of this we cannot know with certainty. Nevertheless, the very nature of the text—e.g., its assumption that the audience is aware of a specific attack on Moab and its litany of Moabite city names—invites, perhaps even requires, a reconstruction of the situation. At the very least, one will need to inquire into the historical geography of Moab. The hypothetical reconstruction of the historical background and

---

and Latin rhetorical art was a suitable model for analysis. He concludes, "A valid rhetorical understanding of the Hebrew Bible is still...a prime desideratum of biblical scholarship," lxv).

[15]E. Black comments, "We have not evolved any system of rhetorical criticism, but only, at best, an orientation to it. An orientation, together with taste and intelligence, is all that the critic needs. If his criticism is fruitful, he may end with a system, but he should not, in our present state of knowledge, begin with one. We simply do not know enough yet about rhetorical discourse to place our faith in systems, and it is only through imaginative criticism that we are likely to learn more" (*Rhetorical Criticism*, 177).

[16]On the question whether rhetorical criticism is a diachronic or a synchronic method, see P. Trible, 49–50, and T. Dozeman, 714. Trible's refusal to confine her own method to synchronic questions (see esp. 93–94) and her insistence that the particularity of the text dictate the extent to which diachronic issues enter interpretation is similar to the present author's approach.

context, therefore, forms part of the horizon of understanding for the kind of rhetorical criticism we shall employ.

Fifthly, the relationship between the "historical situation" and the "rhetorical situation" requires clarification. "Rhetorical situation" is a concept frequently employed in rhetorical criticism as it is practiced by those scholars of biblical texts who use the classical model.[17] The term was coined and defined by L. Bitzer. His definition states that the rhetorical situation is "a complex of persons, events, objects, and relations presenting an actual or potential exigence which can be completely or partially removed if discourse, introduced into the situation, can so constrain human decision or action as to bring about the significant modification of the exigence." An "exigence" he defines as "an imperfection marked by urgency; it is a defect, an obstacle, something waiting to be done, a thing which is other than it should be."[18]

Bitzer's formulation has been widely influential in scholarship pertaining to both secular and religious texts.[19] The article first appeared as a manifesto for the journal *Philosophy and Rhetoric*.[20] G. Kennedy gives it a prominent place in his influential six-step model for rhetorical analysis, and rhetorical critics who apply Kennedy's method to HB texts almost universally depend on

---

[17]E.g., G. Kennedy, Y. Gitay, C. Shaw, R. Duke, J. Hayes and S. Irvine.

[18]L. Bitzer, "The Rhetorical Situation," *Philosophy and Rhetoric* 1 (1968) 6; reprinted in *Rhetoric: A Tradition in Transition* (ed. W. Fisher; Ann Arbor: University of Michigan, 1974).

[19]The concept of *situation* has received considerable attention among theorists of rhetoric. J. Kinneavy ("Contemporary Rhetoric," *The Present State of Scholarship in Historical and Contemporary Rhetoric* [ed. W. Horner; rev. ed.; Columbia and London: University of Missouri, 1990]) observes that "one of the most overpowering concepts in contemporary rhetoric, obvious in many different disciplines, is the notion that a piece of discourse must be judged against the situational and cultural contexts in which it was produced and in which it is being interpreted" (192). Other theorists construct situation quite differently from Bitzer (see Kinneavy, 193–94). Bitzer is important to us here, however, because his definition has been chosen over other available ones by those analyzing biblical texts in a mode similar to the one employed in the present study.

[20]See J. Kinneavy, 193.

Bitzer's definition.[21] For these reasons, his concept deserves our close attention.

Bitzer is concerned in the article to place rhetorical study among the genuinely "scientific" and practical methods that deal with "objective reality":

> ...rhetoric as a discipline is justified philosophically insofar as it provides principles, concepts, and procedures by which we effect valuable changes in reality. Thus rhetoric is distinguished from *the mere craft of persuasion* which, although it is a legitimate object of scientific investigation, *lacks philosophical warrant as a practical discipline*" (14, emphasis mine).

As a "practical discipline" rhetorical study must focus only on "real situations" in which there exists an exigence that may be removed or modified by means of discourse. Speeches delivered in fictive situations, in a novel for instance, are not properly the subject of rhetorical study (11). "The exigence and the complex of persons, objects, events and relations which generate rhetorical discourse are located in reality, are objective and publicly observable historic facts in the world we experience, are therefore available for scrutiny by an observer or critic who attends to them" (11). Moreover, not all situations or exigences in the real world are properly rhetorical (susceptible to change) nor are all audiences properly rhetorical since not all audiences are capable of mediating change. Discourse directed to situations, exigences or audiences insusceptible or incapable of change is not truly rhetorical nor properly the object of rhetorical analysis (6, 8, 10). Situation, and not the form or content of a discourse, thus determines whether a speech is rhetorical and whether rhetorical analysis is appropriate. To drive this point home, Bitzer offers the following illustration:

> Imagine a person spending his time writing eulogies of men and women who never existed: his speeches meet no rhetorical situations; they are summoned into existence not by real events, but by his own imagination. They may exhibit formal features which we consider rhetorical—such as ethical and emotional appeals, and

---

[21]Kennedy, 34–37. HB rhetorical critics using the definition include R. Duke, M. Fox, Y. Gitay, J. Hayes and S. Irvine, C. Shaw.

> stylistic patterns; conceivably one of these fictive eulogies is even persuasive to someone; yet all remain unrhetorical unless, through the oddest of circumstances, one of them by chance should fit a situation. Neither the presence of formal features in the discourse nor persuasive effect in a reader or hearer can be regarded as reliable marks of rhetorical discourse: A speech will be rhetorical when it is a response to the kind of situation which is rhetorical (9–10; see also 2).

So dominant is the rhetorical situation that it dictates the very form of the rhetorical response: "A situation which is strong and clear dictates the purpose, theme, matter, and style of the response.... One might say metaphorically that every situation prescribes its fitting response; the rhetor may or may not read the prescription accurately" (11). Thus situation determines discourse, and knowledge of the rhetorical situation is the foundation of a rhetorical analysis.

Seen in the context of his whole article, Bitzer's definition takes on a more definite shape than it has when it is quoted in abstract, as is usually done. The more definite shape of the definition raises a number of problems, however, and these problems have led us to reject this definition in the present study. A number of critiques of Bitzer's position have been published already,[22] and we will offer only a few observations sufficient to explain our own reluctance to use his terminology. To begin with, Bitzer defines rhetorical situation quite narrowly. He excludes from it the

---

[22]See, e.g., K. Wilkerson, "On Evaluating Theories of Rhetoric," *Philosophy and Rhetoric* 3 (1970) 82–96; R. Pomeroy, "Fitness of Response in Bitzer's Concept of Rhetorical Discourse," *Georgia Speech Communication Journal* 4 (1972) 42–71; R. Vatz, "The Myth of the Rhetorical Situation," *Philosophy and Rhetoric* 6 (1973) 154–61; S. Consigny, "Rhetoric and Its Situations," *Philosophy and Rhetoric* 7 (1974) 175–86; J. Patton, "Causation and Creativity in Rhetorical Situations," *Quarterly Journal of Speech* 65 (1979) 36–55. Kinneavy comments about Bitzer's program, "At its extreme, the obsequiousness of text to situational context can reduce rhetoric to history and dismiss language as an insignificant echo of political or economic action" (193). Bitzer's response to this barrage of critique is found, in part, in "Functional Communication: A Situational Perspective," *Rhetoric in Transition: Studies in the Nature and Uses of Rhetoric* (ed. E. White; University Park: Pennsylvania State University, 1980) 21–38.

"meaning-context" of the discourse.[23] It seems unlikely, however, that such a separation can be maintained. The exigence in a given situation often arises as much out of the meaning context as it does out of the historical event matrix. Indeed, one is hard pressed to imagine how mere events could give rise to an exigence apart from a meaning context; events obtain their meaning, and hence their significance, from the social and cultural setting. Apart from the meaning context events lack significance.[24]

Bitzer's argument that the rhetorical situation "prescribes its fitting response" (11) is equally problematic. He supports this assertion by appealing to highly tradition laden situations, such as Kennedy's assassination, a presidential inauguration speech and a primitive tribe's fishing excursion (4–5, 9, 13). It is inevitable that the situation will compel very predictable responses in these kinds of situations. But can we as easily predict the response in situations less constrained by tradition? Many situations are open to a number of quite varied responses, and these responses are conditioned more by the individual biases of the speaker and the available resources in the "meaning-context" than by "situation" as Bitzer defines it. Situation does not "prescribe" the appropriate response except in the most tradition-bound situations. Indeed, many situations are quite vaguely defined until rhetorical discourse enters to shape the situation and clarify thought and action.[25] This fact enables a skilled rhetor to define a vague or confusing situation in terms compatible with his or her rhetorical objective and, thereby, to convince the audience that the response desired by the rhetor arises from a necessity inherent in the situation.

---

[23]Bitzer offers little definition of "meaning context," but his discussion suggests that this term designates the shared linguistic and symbolic traditions of the audience and speaker (see "Rhetorical Situation," 3). He seems to contradict himself when he argues that one of the constituents of the rhetorical situation is its "constraints," which include "beliefs, attitudes, documents, facts, traditions, images, interests, motives and the like" ("Rhetorical Situation," 8). Are not such "constraints" a part of the "meaning context"?

[24]One may go further and affirm that, to a significant extent, rhetoric creates the meaning context. Vatz comments in arguing this point, "Meaning is not discovered in situations, but *created* by rhetors" (157; cf. 156–60).

[25]See Perelman and Olbrechts-Tyteca, 460.

Bitzer's contention that unless an audience is capable of mediating change, they are not "a genuinely rhetorical audience" is also questionable (8, 12). This aspect of his theory suggests that for discourse to be rhetorical, the speaker must find an audience with certain capacities and that, if the audience is not genuinely rhetorical, then neither is the discourse rhetorical. Very often, however, we cannot be sure if an audience is or was capable of mediating change. In such cases we could not know whether a discourse was rhetorical or not, by Bitzer's definition. This confuses genre and effect. The failure to distinguish between genre and effect weakens Bitzer's theoretical construction and leads him to questionable conclusions such as, "A speech will be rhetorical when it is a response to the kind of situation which is rhetorical" (10). In addition to being theoretically problematic, this narrow definition presents an insurmountable impediment to the rhetorical analysis of many ancient texts. We often do not know very much about the original situation of an ancient text, and anything we do know, we have usually derived from the text itself. If we were to accept Bitzer's criteria for defining rhetorical discourse, many ancient texts could not be considered rhetorical and hence would not properly be the subjects of rhetorical analysis.

Those scholars of biblical texts who quote Bitzer's definition of rhetorical situation apparently have not understood it as he intended. The rather abstract phrasing of the definition seems to have enabled scholars to fill it with their own meaning and use it in their own way. Kennedy and others using his method appear to assume that the rhetorical quality of a text inheres in its form and content. They do attempt to reconstruct the situation behind the text as best they are able, but never as a means of determining whether a text is rhetorical. Historical reconstruction serves primarily to establish a context or setting in which the text can be intepreted. This is, to our way of thinking, an entirely sensible approach.

We must ask, then, In what way is Bitzer's definition applicable to the rhetorical analysis of biblical texts? How is it helpful? In order to answer these questions, it is useful to locate Bitzer on the intellectual map. Although Bitzer does not say so explicitly in the article, he is attempting to define rhetorical analysis by clearly separating it from intrinsic criticism (primarily New Criticism) in which the text is given autonomy. His strong emphasis on situation as the determinative factor is intended to refocus critical attention on elements extrinsic to the text. Correspondingly, he is part of a group of scholars who are reacting against the stylistic focus of traditional rhetorical criticism, and especially against neo-Aristotelian approaches.[26] The significance of these facts for biblical rhetorical analysis is obvious. Bitzer's program is inherently at odds with the rhetorical criticism proposed by Muilenburg, especially as this criticism was in fact practiced by his students.[27] Not surprisingly, no one in this branch of biblical rhetorical criticism appeals to Bitzer. Those who appeal to Bitzer belong to the school which, for convenience's sake, we may designate the Kennedy school. Kennedy and his followers use a classical rhetorical model for analysis. This fact suggests that this group of scholars uses "rhetorical situation" quite differently from Bitzer, since the classical mode of analysis followed by Kennedy is part of the critical construction against which Bitzer is reacting. Indeed, it appears that members of the Kennedy school quote Bitzer's definition but share few of the perspectives that underlie it. For example, Kennedy includes the determination of "species of rhetoric" (i.e., judicial, deliberative, epideictic) in the same category and step with the determination of rhetorical situation.[28] Bitzer opposed such categorical abstractions and would not have equated the concrete and the typical in this way. Even more significantly, Kennedy reconstructs the rhetorical situation for the speeches in Acts and Jesus's farewell discourses in John's gospel, texts generally regarded as fictive.[29] Bitzer, as we have seen, explicitly

[26]Kinneavy, 206.

[27]See Dozeman, 714–15.

[28]Kennedy, 36. Kennedy comments earlier in the chapter, "[rhetorical situation] roughly corresponds to the *Sitz im Leben* of form criticism." The implicit link between the concept of *Sitz im Leben* and Aristotle's three species of rhetoric demonstrates to what extent Kennedy has reinterpreted Bitzer's "rhetorical situation." Kennedy does not share Bitzer's emphasis on particularity but focuses equally on the universal and the typical.

[29]See Kennedy (77–85, 114–40). Kennedy readily acknowledges that the speeches in Acts are fictive, but he is not hindered by this fact in his recon-

excludes fictive speeches from rhetorical analysis. On the whole, Kennedy and his followers typically use "rhetorical situation" not as Bitzer intended, but to designate those aspects of the historical situation that have to do with persuasion, those which have formed both the occasion and the situation (broadly defined) for the discourse.[30] "Rhetorical situation" is, in this case, a shorthand expression used to focus attention on those aspects of situation that pertain most directly to persuasive discourse, what motivates it and what shapes it.[31]

Definitions of the "persuasive" or "argumentative" situation more applicable to the rhetorical analysis of biblical texts may be found in other standard treatments of rhetorical criticism. For example, T. Sloane defines the rhetorical context as "[the] attitudinizing conventions, precepts that condition (both the writer's *and* the reader's) stance toward experience, knowledge, tradition, language, and other people."[32] Perelman and L. Olbrechts-Tyteca treat the argumentative situation primarily as a complex of elements inhering in the audience:

> Every social circle or milieu is distinguishable in terms of its dominant opinions and unquestioned beliefs, of the premises that it takes for granted without hesitation: these views form an integral part of its culture, and an orator wishing to persuade a particular audience

---

struction of the rhetorical situation. Similarly, see Gitay ("Rhetorical Criticism," 144–45) on Hushai's speech before David (2 Sam 17:1–14).

[30]See Kennedy, 34–35. Fox quotes Bitzer's definition but redefines it in his own way. Fox ("Ezekiel's Vision," 5–7) divides rhetorical situation into "objective" and "subjective factors." Objective factors include date, place and external conditions. Subjective factors consist of the speaker's view of the situation, i.e., his or her attitude toward circumstances based on his or her values, beliefs and judgments. Both of these must be reconstructed as part of the rhetorical analysis. It is hard to see why "historical situation" as traditionally conceived is not an adequate term to denote all of these factors. See also Shaw (22) who follows Fox in this division.

[31]W. Wuellner ("Where is Rhetorical Criticism Taking Us?" *CBQ* 49 [1987] 450, cf. 455–56) notes, "The rhetorical situation differs both from the historical situation of a given author or reader and from the generic situation or conventions of the *Sitz im Leben* of forms or genres in one point: the rhetorical critic looks foremost for the premises of a text as appeal or argument."

[32]Quoted in Wuellner, "Where?" 450; T. Sloane, "Rhetoric: Rhetoric in Literature," *The New Encyclopaedia Britannica*, 15th ed. (1975) 15. 802–803.

> must of necessity adapt himself to it. Thus the particular culture of a given audience shows so strongly through the speeches addressed to it that we feel we can rely on them to a considerable extent for our knowledge of the character of past civilizations (20–21, cf. 460, 491).

Both statements point to the importance of delineating the rich symbolic world in which a particular discourse was written. Situation as defined in them corresponds to the category "context" in our genre and composition chapter and provides further grounds for our detailed treatment there of the symbolic rendering of Moab in the culture. Although rhetorical analysis requires some knowledge of the symbolic world behind the text, this requirement is not unique to rhetorical analysis. The introductions to most scholarly Bible commentaries treat symbolic aspects of situation, and redaction critical studies often display a high degree of focus on just such elements. It is usual in these studies to use the term "historical situation" to include a number of facets of situation: events, social structures, power structures, and symbolic matrices. And this term has served adequately.[33] When additional specificity is needed, one may define one's meaning more accurately with a short description of the aspect of the historical situation under consideration than with a term such as "persuasive situation," for which no clear, univocal meaning has yet emerged.

In summary, Bitzer's definition, taken as he intended it, is both inherently flawed and of questionable value for the kind of rhetorical analysis practiced by biblical scholars. Those who have used his definition have not demonstrated in what way their particular application of his concept is fundamentally different from existing, well-accepted terminology. "Historical situation" is conceptually adequate for the practice of rhetorical analysis, and may be specified further when the need arises. In the present study, therefore, we have rejected the term "rhetorical situation" and chosen to speak in terms more commonly found in historical exegesis.

---

[33]The special term "tradition history" (*Traditionsgeschichte*) is warranted by virtue of the fact that this mode of analysis focuses on the evolution of a symbolic construction through time, rather than on its particular form at a fixed moment in time.

Our method, then, will be to analyze by close reading the persuasive strategies of the poem. We will begin with a synoptic analysis of several aspects of the poem's rhetoric. Then we will offer a sequential reading of the poem in which we will hypothetically reconstruct the effect of the poem on the audience. Our goal is to understand both the author's intention in the poem and the means by which he or she conveyed this intention to his or her audience and sought to win its assent.

III. The Rhetoric of Depiction and Rhetorical Stance

Isaiah 15–16 employs extensively what we may call *depictive rhetoric*. With the exception of two brief lines, chapter 15 is devoted entirely to a depiction of the lamentation and flight of the Moabites. The petition in 16:1–5 consists entirely of depiction, although here the picture includes quotation. In the last section of the poem, depiction is mixed evenly with other modes. Depiction is a technique used with great frequency in prophetic texts, and one of its effects is to vivify and enliven discourse, as has often been noted. But it does something more than this.

M. Osborn's article "Rhetorical Depiction" suggests several of the less obvious effects of depictive rhetoric.[34] Osborn lays out a scheme for analysis designed for modern media and its powers of visual depiction. He highlights the power of images to affirm or change the pre-intellectual mythos that grounds attitude and behavior. His approach offers one means by which we may move beyond classical rhetorical analysis and develop an analytical model suited to prophetic rhetoric. Rational argument, even when it uses stories and examples, is often less powerful for certain audiences than depiction. Osborn states:

> Therefore depiction may function as "allegory in miniature," to borrow George Campbell's happy description of significant metaphor. Its full rhetorical implications wait to be articulated in the ongoing text of discourse that preoccupies humankind. Yet its reverberating meanings can be influential even before they have been fully realized by either speaker or audience. Thus depiction is a

---

[34]"Rhetorical Depiction," *Form, Genre and the Study of Political Discourse*, 79–107.

> key to synchronic, multiple, simultaneous meanings in rhetoric, just as enthymeme is the elemental model for diachronic or linear demonstrations. The reason for the peculiar power of depiction is that it often possesses its audience at the moment of perceptual encounter, just as they are being introduced to a subject, and when they are especially vulnerable. Depiction may provide a benign moment of sharing, as rhetors overcome abstraction to disclose the world as it is revealed to them. Or depiction can be a cynical hoax, a manipulative vision that poses as disclosure for the sake of exploitation. It can insinuate itself into our consciousness, where it becomes difficult to dislodge.[35]

The purpose of Isaiah 15–16 is nowhere spelled out discursively. The depiction itself is designed to move the audience to view the situation in a certain way, to take a particular attitude toward the Moabites. Part of the benefit of this strategy is that it allows the speaker to influence the audience without appearing to be coercive. His or her intentions are subtle and hidden, especially at the outset. Through the writer's depiction, the audience is allowed to see for itself the nature of the situation and to decide accordingly what must be done. The speaker controls this vision absolutely; he or she directs all the action and specifies every camera angle. But this fact is not immediately apparent to the audience. The effect is that the attitude of the audience is modified almost without its awareness.

This modification takes place at levels both rational and prerational. The threats in 15:9 and 16:10, the rejection of the petition in 16:6, and, to a lesser extent, the pronouncement in the final verse persuade by rational, if somewhat indirect, appeals. As we shall see in our reading, however, the greater persuasive power of the poem lies in its use of metaphors and images designed to evoke negative feelings toward the Moabites. This mode of symbolic discourse subtly "insinuates itself into... consciousness," and evokes a response that will seem to the audience to be based on opinions already held. This is accomplished by a depictive conjoining of attitudes and feelings attached to traditional symbols with the subject of the discourse, in this case negative ones.

---

[35]Osborn, 80.

The author thus predisposes his or her audience against the Moabites.

Satire is well-known to use depiction in this way, especially in the case of parody. The audience's attention is fixed on the actions, thoughts, and experiences of the victim of the satire. Extraneous subjects are carefully avoided. Where this technique is employed in prophecy, one naturally finds few references to Yahweh. In Isaiah 14:4–21, for example, Yahweh is mentioned only once (v 5). This is the case even though there are a number of opportunities for the prophet to name Yahweh as the one who brought Babylon to its knees (see vv 11–12, 15, 19). In these places, the prophet chooses passive verbs and leaves unnamed the agent of Babylon's reversal. In Isaiah 15–16, Yahweh is never mentioned by name. Only twice—at the end of the depiction of Moab's lamentation and flight and at the end of the sarcastic lament—do we hear a voice we assume to be Yahweh's (15:9b; 16:10bβ). Throughout, the focus is not on the work of Yahweh (as it is, for instance, in second Isaiah) but on the humiliation of the enemy. This corresponds to the satiric intention of the poem.

The technique of depiction draws attention to the fact that every rhetor must take a particular "stance" relative to his or her audience. Rhetorical stance is an idea similar to that of point of view in the study of narrative; it defines the rhetor's relation to his or her audience. M. Fox identifies several possible stances a speaker may choose:

> (1) "one of the people," in which he seeks to convince the audience that he shares their position in life and their outlook on the world.... (2) the "father" role, in which he speaks to... [the audience] from a position of superior knowledge and moral wisdom.... (3) The "preacher" role, in which he claims that his propositions are deduced directly from the will of a higher, unquestioned authority (not necessarily God).... (4) the role of "reporter," in which he pretends neutrality in the issue at hand in order to enforce his implicit arguments with the appearance of objectivity.... (5) [the role of messenger, in which] the prophet claims to do nothing but transmit verbatim a message received from God.... (6) [the spectator

> role, in which] the prophet simply tells what he saw and heard [as in a vision account].[36]

Fox identifies Ezekiel's stance in the case of the vision of the dry bones as that of spectator. He notes that this stance derives its effectiveness in part from the fact that it "gives an impression of objectivity." The audience is invited to look over the prophet's shoulder, as it were, and experience with him or her the unfolding drama. The prophet is not required to make any direct claims regarding the truth or even meaning of the vision; these seem to inhere in the vision (which is, by genre, its own touchstone of authenticity) and are communicated to the audience without the apparent mediation of the prophet. "Alignment of perspective encourages alignment of belief."[37]

Much the same effect attaches to the stance taken by the author of Isaiah 15–16, that of "reporter."[38] In the first two sections of the poem, the prophet appears to relate an objective account of the lamentation, flight and petition of the Moabites. We trust the depiction because of its objective tone and vivid detail. For the original audience, there may be the additional fact that the author's account contains some objectively verifiable facts, the direction of the flight, for instance. Nevertheless, the account is not objective retelling. As M. Osborn points out, the author focuses our attention on certain places and events; other aspects of the situation are suppressed. We see only what the author chooses to show us. Moreover, we see everything in images selected by the author. Our vision is not only preselected, it is also shaped and colored by the specific words and images chosen.

Awareness of the degree of control exercised by the speaker over his or her audience suggests several things for analysis. First, we must attempt to assess the emotional effect of the images and symbols employed in the speech. Secondly, we must attend to the manner in which the author orders images and events, for order

---

[36]Fox, "Ezekiel's Vision," 8–9.

[37]Ibid., 9.

[38]Elsewhere in the Isaianic OAN we find this stance employed, notably in Isa 14:4–21 and 21:2–10.

greatly influences perception.[39] Thirdly, we may wish to examine what is *not* shown or told and what this might indicate about the author's rhetorical objectives. We shall direct our attention to these aspects of persuasion in our reading.

IV. The Rhetoric of Irony

Irony is one of the most important rhetorical strategies employed in the poem, and some general comments about the mechanism and effect of irony are in order. We may begin by noting the process by which an audience or reader becomes aware of a speaker or author's ironic intention. W. Booth defines four steps that a reader goes through in the process of recognizing irony: (1) "The reader is required to reject the literal meaning." This is something forced upon the reader because of "some incongruity among the words or between the words and something else that he knows." (2) "Alternative interpretations or explanations are tried out." In this step the reader tries to overcome the incongruity and naturalize the text. Various options are available: "it is a slip, or he is crazy, or I missed something earlier, or that word must mean something I don't know about." (3) "A decision must therefore be made about the author's knowledge or beliefs.... No matter how firmly I am convinced that a statement is absurd or illogical or just plain false, I must somehow determine whether what I reject is also rejected by the author, and whether he has reason to expect my concurrence." (4) "Having made a decision about the knowledge or beliefs of the speaker, we can finally choose a new meaning or cluster of meanings with which we can rest secure."[40] These steps are not necessarily, or even typically, ones of which the audience is conscious. Usually, the awareness of an ironic intention grows from hunch to realization in the mind of the audience, quickly and without much cognitive effort. There is

---

[39]See Perelman and Olbrechts-Tyteca, 490–507.

[40]Booth, *A Rhetoric of Irony*, 10–13. The mixing of "author" and "speaker" are inherent in Booth's treatment. Although there may be significant differences between written and spoken irony (e.g., a speaker has a greater range of options to signal an ironic intention), the process by which both a reader and a hearer come to recognize irony is essentially the same.

always, however, a moment of transition during which the audience senses the incongruity (or the accumulation of small incongruities) and passes from confusion to hypothesis to realization. It is common for a speaker to prolong this moment, to tease the audience with a certain amount of misdirection about his or her intention. The effect of such a prolongation is an intensification of the experience of realization and a concomitant intensification of alignment with the speaker's own viewpoint. This aspect of irony underlines the need for sequential analysis in the case of Isaiah 15–16. As we shall see, the intra-textual clues to irony are sparse in the first half of the poem and come rather more thickly toward the end.

We may also profitably examine certain sociological aspects of irony. All communication proceeds to a large degree on the basis of many commonly held assumptions, views, prejudices, pieces of factual knowledge, and experiences. In the case of ironic communication, this fact is both obvious and important. Without a shared horizon of perception, an audience would not be able to "catch" a speaker's irony. Incongruity would never become apparent since there would be no normal background against which the odd or disjunctive could stand out in relief. This much we have discussed already. What we should like to call to attention here is the fact that when an author or speaker states something ironically, he or she subtly calls attention to this shared horizon, and, indirectly but powerfully, to his or her identification with the audience, to those common opinions, values and knowledge that define the speaker and the audience as a community. Irony establishes both an "us" and a "them." Adherence to the views of the ingroup (as defined by the implications of the speaker's irony) is cemented primarily by the manner in which irony characterizes the views of the outgroup as ridiculous and stupid. The members of the audience are drawn into a self-congratulatory frame of mind arising from the delight in having caught the speaker's irony and the affirmation that their opinions and values place them securely among the community. Booth notes this community-building power of irony and comments,

> We need no very extensive survey of ironic examples to discover...that the building of amiable communities is often far more important than the exclusion of naive victims. Often the predominant emotion when reading stable ironies is that of joining, of finding and communing with kindred spirits.... Even irony that does imply victims, as in all ironic satire, is often much more clearly directed to more affirmative matters. And every irony inevitably builds a community of believers even as it excludes.[41]

Booth also points out that irony draws in a wider circle of assenting auditors than would have a non-ironic statement.[42] Irony allows hearers to agree in their own way and to only the degree with which they feel comfortable. By stating an opinion implicitly and covertly, the ironist does not risk having the opinion rejected simply because listeners have been put off by a too explicit formulation. In this manner, a speaker may create a sense of greater agreement among the audience than may in fact exist. Addtionally, since one can reveal gradually an ironic intention, one can avoid becoming overcommited. It is possible to feel one's way ahead and carefully gauge the level of assent that an opinion is likely to receive. If an opinion delivered ironically receives a negative response, one can always retreat behind the defense that one's words have been misconstrued. Booth notes that irony is "a powerful and potentially deceptive tool," and offers an apt metaphor for the devious aspect of irony when he speaks of the reader "being caught in a net of collusion cast by the skillful author."[43]

The fact that irony depends on a body of shared assumptions, beliefs, values, etc. highlights an apparent contradiction in our study: If the Judeans truly despise the Moabites, as we have argued, why would a speaker consider it necessary to persuade the Judeans to reject Moab's plea? One possible answer is that irony is used in the poem not in order to persuade but for the sheer joy of mocking a neighboring bully. E. Rosenheim, Jr. says of this use of irony, "No new judgment is invited; no course of action is urged; no novel information is produced. The audience,

---

[41]28, cf. 13–14.
[42]Ibid., 29.
[43]Ibid., 30.

rather, is asked chiefly to rejoice in the heaping of opprobrium, ridicule, or fancied punishment upon an object of whose culpability they are *already* thoroughly convinced."[44] No doubt this is a part of the function of the poem. The mocking of enemies in their troubles is a common topos in prophetic literature, probably because it enjoyed great popularity with audiences. Isaiah 15–16, however, does more than ridicule Moab. The petition and its rejection in 16:1–6 suggest that a decision is involved; either Judah will grant the Moabites aid or it will refuse them. Quite probably, the purpose of the poem is to influence this decision. Thus, the original question remains, why is persuasion necessary if the Judeans are already ill disposed toward Moab?

The answer to this question lies, in part, in the very nature of irony. Perelman and Olbrechts-Tyteca note that "Irony cannot be used if there is uncertainty [among the audience] about the speaker's opinions. This gives irony a paradoxical character: using it implies that argumentation is necessary; but in order to be able to use it, a minimum of agreement is required."[45] They go on to attribute this paradox to the "social character" of irony, its dependence on a web of commonly held beliefs.

Having noted this paradox is, however, different from having explained it, and we still must ask, Why, or in what situation, is argumentation both necessary and unnecessary? The answer to this question must lie in the fact that public opinion is often ill-defined and changeable. Indeed, the "fickleness" of public opinion is well known. What "we all agree on" changes day by day. Irony serves to solidify public opinion on issues and to evoke a desired response. To take a familiar example, Mark Antony in Shakespeare's *Julius Caesar* is well aware that public opinion on the murder of Caesar might move in several possible directions. The crowd is confused and lacks essential information. Maybe there are reasons why Caesar should have been murdered. Then, too, they know that Brutus is a man of integrity and honor, and his actions must have some explanation. What are they to think? Mark Antony attacks at the point of greatest confusion: the doubts

---

[44]*Swift and the Satirist's Art* (Chicago: University of Chicago, 1963) 13.
[45]Perelman and Olbrechts-Tyteca, 208.

raised by the fact of Brutus's honor. He assumes that all agree that regicide is a heinous crime. He seems at first to bring forward Brutus's honor as a mitigating factor in the situation. As he continues to speak, the irony in his references to this honor becomes progressively more obvious until no one among the crowd can doubt that his true opinion is that Brutus is a scoundrel, an opinion toward which many of the crowd would have been inclined in the first place. By at first appearing to assert a novel opinion, that regicide is acceptable in the present case, Mark Antony establishes the conflict underlying his ironic intention. Then, slowly, he shows the audience why this opinion is ridiculous and why they must agree that Brutus should be put to death for his crime. He risks appearing to assume the attitude he wishes to condemn so that his condemnation of the attitude will sound all the louder in the ears of his audience.

A similar situation obtains with Jonathan Swift's essay, "A Modest Proposal." Swift wrote the essay at a time when most people agreed that the level of squalor to which the Irish poor had been reduced was a great shame and that something should be done to alleviate the suffering. Swift's proposal was that the yearling children of the poor be purchased and eaten by the wealthy, thereby providing income for the poor and food for the wealthy. With but few exceptions, the irony in Swift's essay was obvious to all. His true intention was equally obvious; he wished to solidify public opinion and motivate those in power to act. In both examples cited, it is the weakness of public opinion, its maleability and enervation, that creates the occasion for irony. The audience agrees with the speaker, but it must be both persuaded to act and protected against rhetoric recommending a course of action to which the speaker is opposed.[46]

---

[46]In this respect, irony has a function similar to that described for epideictic oratory by Perelman and Olbrechts-Tyteca:

> ...the argumentation in epidictic discourse sets out to increase the intensity of adherence to certain values, which might not be contested when considered on their own but may nevertheless not prevail against other values that might come into conflict with them. The speaker tries to establish a sense of communion centered around particular values recognized by the audience, and to this end he uses the whole range of means available to

Isaiah 15–16 uses irony to solidify opinion and to secure a decision against Moab. The ill feeling toward Moab among the Judeans probably varied in intensity; it is probable that some Judeans had relatives among the Moabite population. Perhaps there were even those who would have been willing to offer help to this old enemy in its hour of disgrace. After all, a certain kind of revenge could be derived from the paternalistic and condescending attitude with which Judah would give the aid. It is also possible that some would recommend helping Moab because of the political expedience of doing so or out of fear that Moab would eventually retaliate if aid was not given. Whatever the case, the irony of the poem is deployed in order to ridicule any person or group that might advocate acting sympathetically toward Moab. The speaker's ironic lament with its extreme expressions of sympathy effectively caricatures such a sympathetic attitude, perhaps before it has even been voiced. In this way, the poem gathers and focuses public opinion and insures that it is sufficiently cohesive and energetic to support a continued hostile and isolationist stance toward Moab.

Up to this point, we have looked only at the effects of irony on the poet's audience. There may be a certain degree of distortion in this focus, especially since the irony involved in Isaiah 15–16 functions satirically. Satire affects both audience and victim. In the ancient (and parts of the modern) world, satire was conceived of as a powerful weapon, able to inflict real damage. Perhaps the richest and most extensive analysis of this belief is that of R. C. Elliott.[47] Elliott argues persuasively that satiric and ridiculing verse had its origins in magic. He shows with numerous examples drawn from ancient Greece and Arabia that such verse was thought to inflict real damage on an enemy.[48] Arabic poets had an important function in time of war; they composed satire or *hijá* against the enemy. A *hijá* was an "extemporized verse, employed

---

the rhetorician for purposes of amplification and enhancement (51).

[47]*The Power of Satire*. His first two chapters are especially helpful, and my discussion here is drawn from them.

[48]Ibid., 3–18.

humor, ridicule, and sometimes obscenity, and was designed to attack the enemy's honor."[49] The power of the *hijá* was believed to surpass that of spears and arrows.

Elliott's study suggests that we should not underestimate the political and social power that the prophets wielded by means of their poems. The insults, ridicule and satire that the Moabite and Israelite prophets traded back and forth across the Jordan, even those that never reached the ears of the enemy, were probably considered powerful weapons in the ongoing struggle for identity and survival.[50] The irony and satiric barbs in Isaiah 15–16 may have had a dual purpose: to harm the Moabites by casting shame and derision on them and to assure that the Judean court was aligned behind the policy of rejecting Moabite pleas for aid. At the very least we should remain open to the possibility that the prophets intended real, direct harm by means of their satiric lampoons.

V. The Rhetoric of the City Names

One of the most remarkable features of Isaiah 15–16 is the astonishing number of city and place names mentioned. If we count the names about which there is textual uncertainty (3), the names of bodies of water (3), and the names of places that are possibly alluded to in the poem (2), we find that the poem mentions 24 separate places. Four of these places appear twice and two of them appear three times. This gives a total of 32 occurrences of

---

[49]E. Farès, *L'honneur chez les Arabes avant l'Islam* (Paris, 1932; cited in Elliott, 16).

[50]I assume that the Moabites had prophets; it seems a safe assumption given the similarity of Israelite and Moabite religion and what we know of the broad spectrum of ancient near eastern societies of the time. The story of Balak hiring an outside prophet to curse Israel does not indicate that Moab had no prophets of its own. Perhaps the hiring of Balaam is intended as a satire on the effectiveness of Moab's indigenous prophets. The humor that pervades the story—Balaam's donkey who knows the will of Yahweh better than Balaam; the repeated failure of Balaam to curse Israel; Balak's frustration and vain attempts to succeed at different locations—suggests that the author(s)/redactor(s) composed the piece in a somewhat satiric vein.

place names and possible allusions. The following chart summarizes the data.[51]

Places Clearly Named	*Places Possibly Named*	*Bodies of Water*	*Possible Allusions*
Dibon/Dimon (3x)	(Kiriath) Huzoth	Waters of Nimrim	Ar
Nebo	Admah	Wadi of Willows	Qarḥoh
Medeba	Sela	Arnon	
Heshbon (3x)			
Elealah (2x)			
Jahaz			
Zoar			
Eglath Shelishiyah			
Luhith			
Horonaim			
Eglaim			
Beer Elim			
Mount...Zion			
Kir Hares(eth) (2x)			
Sibmah (2x)			
Jazer (2x)			

Commentaries usually focus on identifying the location of these places, and this is an important pursuit. In general, however, little attention is given to *why* so many places are mentioned or *what rhetorical effect* the author achieves by this accumulation. At most, commentaries occasionally suggest that the mention of numerous specific places adds vividness to the description, and certainly this is a part of the effect. The rhetorical dynamic of the place names is, however, more complex and central to the poem's purposes than has generally been recognized.

Two other texts in the HB exhibit a similar density of place names: Mic 1:8–16, a lament over the cities of the Shephelah; and

---

[51]As we have argued in our text critical notes, Dimon is a distortion of Dibon, and for this reason it is grouped with Dibon.

Eglath Shelishiyah may be a later explanatory gloss on the name Zoar and not a distinct place.

Kir Hareseth is spelled two different ways, perhaps intentionally for the sake of paronomasia or perhaps due to the vicissitudes of textual transmission. Both spellings almost certainly refer to the same place.

The decision as to whether Kiriath Huzoth and Admah are mentioned depends on the evaluation of text critical issues. We consider the probability high for reading Kiriath Huzoth and somewhat less for reading Admah.

Sela may be read either as a proper name or as a common noun; we have argued above that it should be read as a proper name.

Isa 10:28–32, a description of the advance of an attacking army. The rhetorical effect of the names in each of these texts has received some attention. In Micah the places are listed for the sake of punning on their names and as a part of a rhetorical strategy to draw out an omen for each city from either the sound or the concept of its name: "The wordplays simultaneously focus attention on the city and the accusation against it."[52] In addition, the mention of specific cities reifies the coming destruction: "Micah connects the impending destruction so indissolubly with each individual place-name that no member of his audience could forget it."[53] There may even be "an additional note of mockery and taunting" in Micah's lament, although there is disagreement on this point.[54] The author of Isa 10:28–32 also uses place names to add vividness to description and to emphasize the threat by deriving ominous meanings from several of the names.[55] By way of contrast, Isaiah 15–16 puns only on a few names (Dibon, and perhaps Kir Hares[eth] and Qarḥoh), and the context is quite different from the two texts just mentioned, since we are dealing with an OAN and the cities are Moabite, not Israelite or Judean. The rhetorical strategy involved is, therefore, not directly comparable. Isaiah 15–16 uses place names in a manner quite distinct.

We may begin by noting the distribution of the names. In 15:2–4 we find seven city names, all of which belong to places north of the W. Mujib. The names in 15:5–8, however, designate places south of the Mujib. "Dimon" in 15:9 brings us once again back to the north. The density of place names drops dramatically in 16:1–6, quite naturally considering the nature of the content; here only Sela and Mount Zion appear. In the final section of the poem, the places mentioned are, once again, exclusively those

[52]C. Shaw, 69.

[53]H. Wolff, *Micah: A Commentary* (Minneapolis: Augsburg, 1990) 65.

[54]D. Hillers, *Micah* (Hermeneia; Philadelphia: Fortress, 1984) 28. Rejecting this suggestion is J. Mays, *Micah* (OTL; Philadelphia: Westminster, 1976) 54. The difference of opinion expressed on this point echoes that found in treatments of Isaiah 15–16.

[55]See Kaiser, *Isaiah*, 1. 246–51. This device is not at all uncommon in the HB; other examples include Jer 48:2, 31; Amos 5:5b; and Zeph 2:4. On this mode of onomastic pejorative paronomasia, see Y. Radday, "Humour in Names," *On Humour and the Comic in the Hebrew Bible*, 79–97.

north of the Mujib. J. Hayes and S. Irvine have recently pointed out that, with the exception of Kir Hareseth, all the cities mentioned in Isaiah 16:6-12 had once belonged to the Israelites.[56] The seven cities mentioned in 15:2–4 are likewise all claimed as Israelite in biblical tradition.[57] If, as we have suggested elsewhere,[58] Kir Hareseth is a taunt name for Kiriathaim or Qarḥoh, it too would belong to the group of cities formerly Israelite. Hayes and Irvine's observation provides the key to understanding the rhetorical effect of the place names in the poem. The audience would almost certainly have been aware that all the cities mentioned in the parts of the poem describing Moab's lamentation and misfortune had belonged to Israel/Judah in better times.[59] One may easily imagine that they bitterly resented the loss of these cities and the agriculturally productive fields around them. The density of place names is thus an integral part of the poem's rhetorical strategy. The "lament" deconstructs itself even as it unfolds. Underneath the lamentation of Moab we hear intoned a litany of cities once held by Israel. With each sounded name the poem calls to mind the desecration, bloodshed and sorrow entailed in the conquests by Mesha and other Moabite kings. Moab the brutal, Moab the usurper, Moab the dominant, the arrogant, the bully is evoked in the mind of the audience long before 16:6 delivers this verdict explicitly. This is the rhetorical purpose behind the place names, and the reason why we find such an unusual density of names in one place. The names are one of the markers of irony in the poem.

---

[56]*Isaiah*, 244.

[57]See Num 32:2–5, 34-38; Josh 13:8–32. Num 32:34-38 is generally considered a very old piece of tradition (E source, or at least predating J); see the summary of positions in P. Budd (*Numbers*) 337–41. Josh 21:36–39 and II Samuel 24, both sources purporting to come from David's reign, indicate that David had established his authority over the territory north of the W. Mujib (see Miller and Hayes, *History*, 172, 180–81).

[58]Jones, "In Search of Kir Hareseth," 19–21.

[59]Israel probably exercised some degree of control over Moab as late as the reign of Jeroboam II (See Miller-Hayes, 307–09). Thus the memory of Israel's claim on this territory would likely have been fresh in the latter part of the eighth century BCE.

We are left, however, to ponder why Luhith, Horonaim, Zoar, Eglaim and Beer Elim are mentioned. It seems doubtful that the route described owes only to historical fact or to geographical necessity; other cities could, no doubt, have been listed along the flight path southward. Probably these cities are mentioned for some special quality or meaning attached to them. None of these cities was ever held by the Israelites, and, apart from Zoar, none of them is mentioned in the HB outside of Isaiah 15–16 and Jeremiah 48. It is not even clear that the cities on the flight path were Moabite; we really know very little about who controlled the area south of the Mujib.[60] Perhaps specific cities are mentioned in order to continue the vividness of the poem's depiction or to maintain a consistent style in the description of Moab's lamentation. Something more may be involved, too, but we probably lack sufficient cultural and historical information to discover what this may be.

VI. The Rhetoric of the Genre

We have argued that the poem is an example of prophetic satire, specifically a mocking song in which the genre lament is ironically inverted. It now remains to say something a bit more precise about how generic elements have been combined as part of the rhetorical strategy of the poem. The structure of the poem in schematic form may be analyzed as (1) description of lament and

[60]See J. M. Miller, "Early Monarchy in Moab?" *Early Edom and Moab*, 84–88. The Mesha Inscription mentions no city south of the W. Mujib controlled by Mesha. There is, however, one possible exception. Lines 31–33a read: "And Hawronen lived in it...// And] Kemosh said to me, 'Go down, fight against Hawronen.' So I went down[// and Kemosh [retur]ned it in my days,..." (Dearman, ed., *Studies in the Mesha Inscription and Moab*, 98). Whether "Hawronen" is a city or group is not clear since בחורנן may be translated either "against Hawronen" or "against the Hawronen," and, indeed, the latter translation is indicated by line 31: "And Hawronen lived in it..." The brokenness of the text also casts doubt on the translation, "Kemosh [retur]ned it in my days." Although it is very tempting to equate Hawronen with biblical Horonaim, the brokenness and obscurity of the text suggest caution.

flight; (2) petition; (3) vow of loyalty;[61] (4) rejection of petition; (5) lament. This analysis results in part from an emphasis on certain elements not usually singled out in this way. It is intended to illuminate the similarity of the structure of the poem to that of individual and community laments in the book of Psalms.[62] Of course, in the book of Psalms one never finds an explicit rejection of the petition or a return to lamentation in response to such a rejection. The first three elements, however, are quite similar. One wonders if Isaiah 15–16 offers an example of petition to an earthly potentate of which individual and community laments are the heaven-directed counterpart.[63]

Isa 15:1–8 is, however, an unusual example of "elegy" or "lament." The passage does not lament Moab's misfortune; it describes Moab's lamentation. In vv 1–4 the Moabites are depicted in various acts of lamentation at a number of their cities. In 5b–8 they flee southward, lamenting as they travel along. The poet describes the unfavorable conditions that they encounter on this flight (v 6) but speaks not a word concerning the actual disaster over which, we must assume, they are raising a lament. Nowhere in 15:1–8 does description of the circumstances which have given rise to the lament appear. Still, the passage does bear significant marks of lament. The content, the first person expression of sympathy in 15:5a, the *qinah* meter, and the repetition of כי all suggest the lament genre.[64] It would appear that the genre has been adapted by the author in order to suit his or her rhetorical purpose. Instead of a "complaint" consisting of a description of suffering as is typical of biblical laments, Isa 15:1–8 describes the Moabites in the act of lamentation. This *mutatis mutandis* is the

---

[61]See below for a defense of this interpretation. Of course, the structure of the poem as here analyzed and compared to Psalmic laments is itself one argument in favor of this interpretation.

[62]See E. Gerstenberger, "Psalms," *Old Testament Form Criticism*, 200, for a convenient summary of the structural paradigm.

[63]This has been suggested by Petersen ("Oracles," 54) who argues that the author "addressed what was usually a plea for help to Yahweh directly to the ruling class of Jerusalem, an innovative and brilliant rhetorical tactic worthy of Isaiah's best poetry."

[64]J. Muilenburg, "The Linguistic and Rhetorical Usages of the Particle כי in the Old Testament," *HUCA* 32 (1961) 153, 157. Petersen ("Oracles," 54).

result of adapting a genre usually spoken on one's own behalf to a situation in which it is imagined in the mouth of another.

VII. Historical Situation

Before we offer our rhetorical analysis, the actual historical circumstances behind the poem need to be delineated as well as possible. The poem's heading in 15:1 introduces the lamentation of Moab; it says nothing of the destruction of cities. Nowhere in the poem do we find evidence that Moab's cities were destroyed. The poem depicts only Moab's lamentation, flight, and the destruction of its agriculture.[65]

The reason for the exodus southward is never made explicit. Are the Moabites to be imagined fleeing with the foe on their heels? Many commentaries at least imply this scenario. Several considerations make this questionable, however. First, the description of the flight in the poem never depicts the fugitives as pursued. This is not a headlong flight, but one on which the fugitives lament as they walk along. They carry a burden of supplies with them, and this suggests that they were not hotly pursued but had time to collect food stores. The poem depicts a deliberate and unharrassed exodus.

Second, at a number of points the poem indicates that some of the Moabites are still inhabiting their cities. The lamentation in the cities described in 15:1–4 makes no sense as a description of behavior following an attack that destroyed the cities, and the depiction of Moab's failure upon its own high place indicates that one of its principal cult centers (Dibon?) is intact. Some of the Moabites have fled, but apparently not all. Those in the cities seem to have remained behind. Perhaps the exodus included only some of those in the coutryside and in the small open villages.

---

[65]See A. Jenkins, "The Development of the Isaiah Tradition in Is 13–23," *The Book of Isaiah: Le Livre D'Isaïe* (ed. J. Vermeylen; Leuven: Leuven University, 1989) 241–42. Jenkins cites Isa 15:6b and 16:8a as evidence that the poem deals with Moab's loss of fertility rather than with a major invasion. He notes that 15:2–4 and 16:12 focus on Moab's worship and suggests that the reason for this focus is that "worship was intended to ensure fertility." In this regard, he suggests that 16:12 is thematically similar to Isa 1:12–17.

And what of the delegation sent to Judah, what did it hope to secure? The petition of the embassy (16:3–4) suggests that the Moabites were seeking asylum, a safe harbor in which to ride out the storm. Why was this necessary, however, if the cities were intact? To answer this we must consider why the lament sections of the poem do not describe the destruction of cities or the death of warriors or inhabitants but focus on Moab's loss of its agriculture. This is true not only of 16:7–11, where the case is obvious, but also of 15:5–9. The depiction of the Moabites carrying their "surplus" with them through the desolate Ghor is designed to call to mind their problem: the only food they have left is that which was kept in their storehouses. This is their real plight. At the height of the summer drought an invader has destroyed all their crops, and they are left with no product to sell and little food to eat. They flee from their decimated land where the enemy still harasses the populace. Their appeal to Judah is couched in stereotypical language, but the real point is that they need food and temporary shelter.

The attack seems to have been aimed not at conquering Moab, but at weakening it. The enemy slipped in by night and destroyed Moab's croplands, leaving its cities untouched. Perhaps the enemy inflicted as much damage as quickly as it could in a single night, and then conducted a series of harassing raids to keep the Moabites pinned down in their cities with no chance to replant their fields. The effect of this would have been devastating for a country such as Moab with its economic base set squarely on agriculture. The description of the coalition attack on Moab in 2 Kings 3 suggests that a similar strategy was used in that case: "on every good piece of land everyone threw a stone, until it was covered; every spring of water they stopped up, and every good tree they felled" (2 Kgs 3:25). The difficulty involved in overthrowing Moab's fortified cities might explain why an attacking foe would choose to destroy fields and vineyards as a means of weakening Moab.[66]

---

[66]Jeremiah refers to Kiriathaim as Moab's "lofty stronghold" (48:1), and throughout his adaptation of Isaiah's poem he adds references to the destruction (or hoped-for destruction) of Moab's cities (48:8, 9, 15, 21–24, 28, 41).

The statement in Jer 48:11 substantiates this picture: "Moab has been at ease from his youth, settled like wine on its dregs; he has not been emptied from vessel to vessel, nor has he gone into exile; therefore his flavor has remained and his aroma is unspoiled." Surely if Moab's cities had been destroyed in the late eighth century the writer would not have said that the country was "at ease" and "settled," never having "gone into exile." Moab's cities are still intact in Zephaniah's and later in Ezekiel's time (Zeph 2:8–10; Ezek 25:8–11). Over a long period of time Israel and Judah hoped for and expected the destruction of Moab, but apparently this hope was disappointed again and again. Moab kept hanging on.

VIII. A Sequential Reading of Isaiah 15–16

Having examined the rhetoric of the poem synoptically, we may now complete our analysis with a sequential reading. For the sake of convenience we shall repeat our translation here.

15

1 Massah concerning Moab
Indeed, in the night of the destroyer the cities of Moab lament.
Indeed, in the night of the destroyer the cities of Moab lament.
2 Dibon has gone up to the temple, to the high places to weep.
On Nebo and on Medeba Moab wails.
On every head is baldness, and every beard is shorn.
3 In Huzoth they put on sackcloth.
On its rooftops and in its plazas
everyone wails, sinking in tears.
4 Heshbon and Elealah cried out;
unto Jahaz their voice was heard.
Therefore the loins of Moab cry out; his whole being quivers.
5 My heart cries out for Moab.
His fugitives [flee] as far as Zoar (Eglath Shelishiyah).

Ezekiel refers to Beth-jeshimoth, Baal-meon and Kiriathaim as "the flank of Moab...the glory of the land" (25:8, 10). These references demonstrate that Moab was well known for its fortified cities.

For the ascent of Luhith they ascend with tears.
For on the road of Horonaim they raise a shattering cry.
6 For the waters of Nimrim are a desolation.
For the grass is withered, the young grass is finished,
nothing green remains.
7 Therefore the surplus it acquired and their stockpile
they carry over the Wadi of the Willows.
8 For the cry has encompassed the territory of Moab.
Unto Eglaim its wailing; unto Beer Elim its wailing.
9 Because the waters of Dimon are full of blood,
indeed, I will place upon Dimon additional [woes].
For the fugitives of Moab a lion,
as well as for the remnant of Admah.

16

1 Send a lamb to the ruler of the land,
from Sela toward the wilderness
to the mount of maiden Zion.
2 And it will come to pass:
Like fleeing birds, like scattered nestlings
shall be the daughters of Moab beyond the Arnon.
3 Give counsel! Assume responsibility!
Cast your shadow as the night at high noon!
Hide the displaced! Do not betray the fugitive!
4 Let Moab's displaced sojourn among you.
Be a shelter to him from the destroyer.
When the violent one has ceased, destruction has ended,
the trampler has vanished from the land,
5 Then a throne will be established in faithfulness,
and one will sit on it in truth,
in the tent of David a judge and a seeker of justice
and an expert in righteousness.
6 We have heard about the majesty of Moab,
the exceedingly proud one,
about its hauteur and its haughtiness and its arrogance
—his boasting is not right.
7 Therefore let Moab howl.
As for all Moab, let it howl.

On behalf of the raisin-cakes of Kir Hareseth
you will groan, utterly stricken.
8 For the fields of Heshbon languish.
As for the vine of Sibmah, the lords of the nations
its choicest vines have smitten.
They extended to Jazer; they wandered [to] the wilderness.
Its shoots spread out; they crossed the sea.
9 Therefore I weep with the weeping of Jazer
[for] the vine of Sibmah.
I drench with my tears Heshbon and Elealah.
For on your fruit harvest and on your grain harvest
fell the victory shout.
10 Joy and rejoicing have been taken away from the garden land,
and in the vineyards no cry rings out and no one cheers.
No treader treads wine in the vats.
I have brought an end to the victory shout.
11 Therefore, my bowels growl like a lyre for Moab
and my innards for Kir Hares.
12 And it will come about that although he presents himself,
although Moab exhausts himself upon the high place
and enters his sanctuary to pray,
he will not succeed.

Our reading is based on the following structural analysis:

I. Description of Moab's lamentation and flight (15:1b–9)
  A. Description of Moab's lamentation
    1. Thematic heading: the nocturnal lamentation in Moab's cities (1b)
    2. Description of lamentation in Dibon (2a)
    3. Description of lamentation in Nebo and Medeba (2b)
    4. Description of lamentation in Huzoth (3)
    5. Description of lamentation in Heshbon and Elealah, reaching to Jahaz (4a)
    6. Summary: Moab's great distress (4b)
  B. Description of Moab's flight (5–8)
    1. Thematic heading: Expression of sympathy; Summary of the Moabites' flight as a journey to Zoar (5a)

2. Description of flight by way of Luhith and Horonaim (5b)
3. Description of dry conditions at the waters of Nimrim (6)
4. Description of Moab carrying provisions due to dry conditions (7)
5. Summary: the all-encompassing lamentation (8)
6. Threat of additional punishment (9)

II. Petition of the Moabites for sanctuary (16:1–5)
  A. Call to send a present to Jerusalem (1)
  B. Caricature of Moabite appeal (2-5)
    1. Description of emissaries as frightened birds (2)
    2. Appeal for aid (3–4a)
  C. Promise to be loyal to the Judean king (4b–5)
    1. Condition (4b)
    2. Promise (5)

III. Response to petition (6–12)
  A. Rejection of petition (6)
  B. Ironic lament (7–11)
    1. Call to lamentation (7a)
    2. Description of lamentation over loss of Kir Hareseth's raisin cakes (7b)
    3. Description of loss of crops (8–10)
      a. the fields of Heshbon (8aα)
      b. ironic eulogy to the vine of Sibmah (8aβ–b)
    4. Declaration of "grief" (9a)
      a. for the vine of Sibmah (9aα)
      b. for Heshbon and Elealeh (9aβ)
    5. Description of silent, joyless harvest time at Heshbon and Elealeh (9b–10)
    6. Declaration of "grief" for Kir Hares[eth] (11)
  C. Prediction of Moab's failure to find help from its god (12)

Indeed, in the night of the destroyer,
the cities [ער] of Moab lament.
Indeed, in the night of the destroyer,
the cities [קיר] of Moab lament.

These lines introduce the theme of the poem. Moab has been visited by the destroyer, and its cities now lament their misfortune. The nearly precise repetition of the lines draws the audience's attention to the single element that is changed, the word "cities." In the first line the word is spoken in Hebrew; in the second line the poet speaks the word in Moabite. Highlighted is that which divides two peoples; what is Judean and what is Moabite are brought into sharp contrast. The subject of this contrast is cities. The expression, "the night of the destroyer" is unusual. Does it merely indicate the bare fact that the attack was nocturnal, or is there something more implied? The expression בליל seems to introduce onomopoetically the lamentation (יליל) repeatedly mentioned in the chapters (15:2, 3, 8, 8; 16:7, 7).[67] Night-time and weeping are thereby poetically linked, as they are also in the Psalms (e.g., 6:7; 22:3; 77:3; etc.). Perhaps the expression derives from what may have been a common proverbial saying, a saying found in its full form in Obad 5.[68] The proverb employs the image of gleanings left by grape gatherers and the fact that nocturnal thieves seldom steal everything, to express the idea that there are natural limits to an invader's destruction. The "destroyer of the night" (שדד לילה) leaves "a gleaning" behind. Later we will learn that Moab was left with a gleaning of their former abundance (15:7); it was not completely destroyed.

The theme of the poem is explicated in 15:2–4a. Moab's lamentation in six cities is depicted: Dibon, Nebo, Medeba, (Kiriath) Huzoth, Heshbon and Elealah. Jahaz is also mentioned, but it is unclear whether it participates in the lamentation; it represents the far point to which the cries of Heshbon and Elealah reach. The listing of specific cities renders the description vivid and suggests the comprehensiveness of the disaster. From Dibon, the capital, in

[67]I owe this insight to F. Landy, "Prophetic Burdens in Isaiah 13–23," a paper presented at the national meeting of the Society of Biblical Literature, Chicago, November 21, 1994.

[68]See text and translation notes.

the south, to the central plains of Medeba, to the important northern cities of Heshbon and Elealah, the whole land is convulsed with sorrow. The totality of the mourning is emphasized also by a spatial symmetry. The Moabites ascend (עלה) the *bamah* at Dibon (2a) and they descend, or "sink" (ירד), in tears at Huzoth (3c). The whole depiction is one of vivid action—they ascend the high place, they shave head and beard, they put on sackcloth in the city square and on the rooftops, they wail out their grief and sink in tears. Perhaps the final action described by ירד alludes to the fate Moab has suffered; the one who went up (in fortunes and pride) has now been forced to come down. The poet drives home the comprehensiveness of the disaster with a summarizing synecdoche: "Therefore the loins of Moab cry out; his whole being quivers" (4b).

The usual force of such description is to set the audience's sympathetic faculties in motion. The audience is, however, confused. Moab is an old enemy, frequently the target of low humor and satiric jibes. In addition, the poet has subtly contrasted Moabite cities and Israelite cities and has named as sites of Moabite lamentation cities formerly claimed by Israel. This has stirred long-standing resentments and hostility that are incompatible with the attitude of lament. Dimly, the audience is aware that something is amiss.

The על־כן in 15:4b marks the conclusion to part one of the first movement. Thus far the poet has described Moab's lamentation. In 15:5 a description of their flight southward begins. The first-person expression of sympathy in 15:5a (לבי למואב יזעק) comes in response to the outcry of Moab in 15:4 (תזעק) and thus serves as a transitional element. It is the expected response, but the audience has reason to doubt its appropriateness, if not its sincerity. The poet tells us that Moab's fugitives are "as far as Zoar."[69] Zoar represents the farthest point to which the fugitives have fled, and perhaps it is their goal. It was the goal of their putative ancestor,

---

[69]As we have noted in our text and translation notes, it is possible that 15:5a should be read, "My heart cries out for Moab, from Riḥa to Zoar..." In this case, the line would be an ellipsis designating the territory through which the fugitives must travel in search of safety and succor.

Lot, when he fled from Sodom. Its mention here reminds the audience of this old story and of Moab's rather tainted beginnings.[70] Zoar, we are told (Gen 19:20–22), means "small, insignificant." As did their father, the Moabites set their sights on an insignificant destination when they are in trouble.

A brief description of their route follows in 15:5b–7. As in the previous section, the poet plays with the idea of ascending and descending. The fugitives are first depicted climbing the ascent of Luhith and then shown on "the road of Horonaim," apparently a route leading down to the Ghor.[71] Where they might have expected to find water and a pleasant camp, they discover the wadis dried up and the surrounding pasturage burned by the scorching sun until "nothing green remains."[72] The description of the desolate conditions serves to emphasize Moab's plight. They have been forced to flee to the Ghor, apparently during the time of the annual drought.[73] The water supply at Nimrim is dried up, all the

---

[70]So H. Cowles, *Isaiah* (New York: D. Appleton & Co., 1869) 126; Alexander, 316. The suggestion dates back at least to Vitringa.

[71]Jer 48:5 makes this movement more explicit by changing Isa 15:5's "the road of Horonaim" to "the descent [ירד] of Horonaim." This descent may have been a road following the Wadi Kerak or a route just south of this. See Jones, "In Search of Kir Hareseth," 15–21, and J. A. Dearman, "The Moabite Sites of Horonaim and Luhith," *PEQ* 122 (1990) 41–46.

[72]The precise location of the waters of Nimrim is disputed, but it is generally agreed that they are to be identified with one of the wadis descending from the plateau to the Ghor between Kerak and the Wadi el-Heṣa.

[73]The annual drought in the southern Ghor is a regular feature of the region. S. Mittmann has argued that 15:5–8 describes the Moabites' flight *northward,* away from the Ghor in order to escape a drought there ("The Ascent of Luhith," *Studies in the History and Archaeology of Jordan I* [ed. A. Hadidi; Amman: Department of Antiquities, 1982] 177). His argument is based on the assumption that ascending at Luhith necessarily indicates an ascent from the Ghor. Isaiah 15, however, indicates that one climbed the ascent of Luhith on a southward journey. 15:5 specifies Zoar as the destination of the Moabite fugitives; the following verses most likely describe the journey toward this city lying at the southern end of the Dead Sea. Moreover, Mittmann's argument asserts that two separate accounts of misfortune have been combined, the account of an attack in the north and the account of a drought in the Ghor. Why two accounts of very different kinds of disasters would have been combined is not explained. The idea that the poem describes only one misfortune provides a simpler and more straightforward explanation. The account of the drought in the Ghor serves to intensify the plight of the Moabites by showing the difficulties they encounter as they flee

vegetation in the Ghor has been scorched brown, and through this desolation the once-proud Moabites carry "the surplus it acquired and their stockpile," eventually across the wadi of the willows (probably the Wadi el-Heṣa). The burden on their shoulders is the substance of their former pride. This hoarded wealth they haul with them, perhaps as provision and perhaps as a gift to those who might help them.[74] The lamb soon to be mentioned in 16:1 is perhaps a part of this surplus and a token of the larger gift to be offered. The surplus borne by the Moabites reminds the Judean audience, in any case, of former times when Moab sent some of its produce regularly as an act of subservience to the Israelite king (2 Kgs 3:4). It also plays upon that theme common in prophetic satire, "how the mighty have fallen."[75] Implicit in "the surplus it acquired and their stockpile" is a reminder of Moab's former state in which they had extra to save. Now this excess is all that remains.

In verse 8 the poet summarizes Moab's cry of distress; the whole territory of Moab is caught up in the lamentation. The sound of this weeping reaches as far as the sites of Eglaim and

---

the destruction north of the Arnon. Mittmann's thesis also requires that the Moabites had been staying down in the Ghor and were forced to leave when a drought came. The idea that the Moabites would have been living in the Ghor is unlikely given that, as far as we know, they never controlled this territory. Finally, the Ghor suffers a yearly drought, and this fact would have been well-known by the local inhabitants. The necessary shifting of camp to a more hospitable clime would hardly have surprised anyone or constituted the grounds for a lament.

[74]The עַל־כֵּן at the beginning of v 7 suggests that at least part of the motivation for carrying along the surplus was the dry conditions along the way. But specific words chosen suggest that more than simple provision is involved. The author emphasizes that the cargo was Moab's surplus, its stockpile against hard times. This would probably have consisted of more than would have been needed for the short journey to Zoar, or Judah for that matter. The idea that they carry their surplus as a gift is suggested by comparision to the מַשָּׂא in Isa 30:6–7, a text bearing several similarities to Isaiah 15–16: "Through a land of trouble and distress, of lioness and roaring lion, of viper and flying serpent, they carry their riches on the backs of donkeys, and their treasures on the humps of camels to a people [Egypt] that cannot profit them" (cf. 30:1–5).

[75]See D. Fishelov, "The Prophet as Satirist," 198.

Beer Elim.[76] This summary is functionally parallel to the summary in 4a and serves as an inclusion at the end of the first section.

Verse 9 concludes the first movement with a threat. It contains a pair of כי clauses that function syntactically rather than paratactically: "Because the waters of Dimon are (pf.) full of blood, indeed I will give (impf.) to Dimon additional [woes]...."[77] Here again there is a shift from perfect to imperfect. It is *because* the waters of Dimon were full of blood that "I [YHWH] will give to Dimon additional woes." Verse 9aα does not, however, describe Moab's plight, as if many Moabites had been slain near a body of water. It gives a reason for the additional punishment for Moab. How does the fact that the waters of Dibon are full of blood warrant further punishment? According to the Mesha Inscription, Mesha used Israelite captives in the building of Qarḥoh, which was probably his royal residence and a suburb of Dibon.[78] This building project included the construction of an extensive water system. It may be that "the waters of Dimon" refers to this water system.[79] Thus it is possible that the poet is alluding to Israelite

---

[76]The locations of Eglaim and Beer Elim are not known. It is possible that paronomasia is behind the choice of these two names. Eglaim (אגלים) may mean something such as "collection, stores, reserve-supply" (BDB, 8) in which case it would correspond to the "surplus" mentioned in the previous verse. Beer Elim clearly means "the well of the gods." Perhaps there is an intentional irony in the juxtaposition of this name with the description of the dry waste through which the Moabites flee. Perhaps the author intends to communicate that the well of Moab's god has run dry (cf. 16:12). Ewald (145) pointed out paronomasia in the sound play between the two names and the thematic word ילל.

[77]These two כיs are set apart in function from those in the preceding verses by their position (following the general summary), proximity, and the syntax of the line: כי + perfect, כי + imperfect (first person). It is unlikely that the first kî is to be taken with v 8 since v 8 is a general summary. It makes little sense to move from such a summary back toward the particular, and v 9a would be strangely isolated between a summary and a divine word. Following the scribes who added the *sillûq*, we should take v 9aα with 9aβ. The first כי should be construed as causal. The second כי is a typical usage to mark divine speech (Jer 1:8, Isa 43:3, cf. Amos 5:3–4, Isa 18:4, 21:16). See Muilenburg, "Usages," 144–45.

[78]MI, lines 21–26. See Dearman, "Historical Reconstruction," 171–74.

[79]Scholars are divided on the question of the identity of "the waters of Dimon [=Dibon]." The Arnon is commonly suggested as the most likely candidate. Others note that the Arnon lies several miles south of Dibon, and

blood spilled during the building of the water works associated with Qarḥoh: "because the waters of Dimon are filled with [Israelite] blood, I will place upon Dimon additional [woes]."

A further pun underlining the poetic justice of Moab's fate may be contained in the unusual word "additions" (נוספות). If the bloody waters of Dibon are associated with the water-related building projects of Mesha, "additions" may allude to Mesha's additions to his royal center or, more broadly, to his general program of expansion. Twice in the MI the root יסף is used to refer to Mesha's annexation of towns (יספתי in line 29, לספח in line 21)—most notably of the King of Israel's stronghold at Jahaz which Mesha captured "to annex (it) [לספח] to Dibon" (ln 21). The poet declares the word of Yahweh: just as Moab has made "additions" to Dibon, so now Yahweh will put "additions" on Dibon. In the case of the fugitives, the additional punishment involves a lion in some way. It is not clear whether the lion is a literal lion, in which case one might imagine the fugitives suffering attack during their flight, or a symbol for some other danger, in which case the poet might be alluding to another nation.

The ballast variant at the end of 15:9 refers to the "remnant of Admah." The poet uses "Admah" as a byword for Moab. Admah is associated in tradition with Sodom, Gomorrah and Zeboiim, cities reputedly lying at the south end of the Dead Sea, near Zoar. These cities are symbols of divine punishment in biblical tradition. The area in which they were supposedly built is largely desolate and uninhabitable; it served as a moral object lesson in conjunction with the stories of the great destruction once meted out there. "Admah" (a sound pair with "Dimon") is thus an epithet connect-

---

far below the plateau. Since the Mesha Inscription (lines 23–25) reveals that at Qarḥoh Mesha built extensive water works, some have thought of these as the referent of "the waters of Dimon." The phrase "waters of X" appears to designate a water source nearby "X" and probably used by the inhabitants of "X" for drinking and sanitation (BDB, 565; see Josh 15:7, 9; 18:15). This is the most obvious reason for naming a water source as if it belonged to "X." The idea that a large water system such as the Arnon should be referred to as the property of one city is difficult, and it seems preferable to understand this reference as designating a small water system quite close to Dibon, one that the local inhabitants would have used for their daily needs.

ing Moab both with the sin of these proverbial cities and with the just punishment that they suffered.[80] Possibly, this comparison was (or became) a topos in the case of Moab. In Zeph. 2:9 we read, "Moab shall become like Sodom and the Ammonites like Gomorrah, a land possessed by nettles and salt pits, and a waste forever...this shall be their lot in return for their pride." The arid conditions through which the Moabites had just come would not have improved much when they arrived at Zoar. They have fled into a desolation. Those who once enjoyed "the waters of Dimon" and Moab's successful agriculture are now reduced to "the remnant of Admah." This first section of the poem thus concludes with a threat and a taunt. The audience now sees Moab's lamentation and flight from the poet's perspective. Divine justice has overtaken Moab. The cities it took from Israel are now filled with lamentation and those who have fled to seek help struggle through a desolate wasteland. Moab's practice of *adding* to its territory has won for it *additions* from the divine judge.

With the divine threat still in their ears, the audience hears the poet summon the Moabites to "send a lamb." Here the poet dramatically quotes an anonymous voice calling for Moab to send tribute to the "ruler of the land."[81] The reason for the unusual title is unclear. Perhaps a certain grandiloquence is intended, and we should understand the phrase as "ruler of the earth" or something similar. In this case, the summons would be imagined to be spoken by a Moabite and the honorific title would constitute flattery of the Judean king similar to that present in 16:5. Alterna-

---

[80]See text critical note on 15:9. Texts in which Admah appears include Gen 10:19, 14:2, 8; Deut 29:22; Hos 11:8. Lowth (*Isaiah*, 229) notes that "Michaelis thinks, that the Moabites might be called the remnant of Admah, as sprung from Lot and his daughters escaped from the destruction of that and the other cities; or metaphorically, as the Jews are called the princes of Sodom and people of Gomorrah, chap. i.10." Similarly, see Alexander, 320.

[81]The problem of identifying voices and transitions between voices in prophetic rhetoric is a challenging one. The task is fairly straightforward in cases such as Isa 14:4–21, but becomes more difficult in texts such as Isa 21:2–10. The summons in Isa 21:5b is analogous to the present case; it too appears suddenly in the poem and is spoken by an anonymous voice. See Y. Gitay, "Rhetorical Criticism and the Prophetic Discourse," *Persuasive Artistry: Studies in New Testament Rhetoric in Honor of George A. Kennedy*, 15.

tively, the voice addresses the king of Moab with the vocative "O ruler of the land." The vocative might be a sarcastic hyperbole. Or perhaps it is a subtle term of derision based on a double entendre: מֹשֵׁל, "ruler," is very close to מָשָׁל, "taunt, proverb."[82] If indeed it is the voice of the poet that speaks in 16:1, the summons is spoken ironically and is akin to the sarcastic imperative found typically in satiric OAN texts. Luther catches the nuance of this verse: "...it is prophetic irony, namely: 'Send a lamb to Jerusalem now. Up until now you have despised us. Do you now crawl to the cross? Do you now wish to bring a sacrifice to Jerusalem? But it is too late. So you come at long last?'"[83]

Moab's lowly position compared to Judah is emphasized by the implicit comparison in the latter part of verse one between "Sela [rock] toward the wilderness" and the "mount of maiden Zion."[84] Moab no longer enjoys the produce of its fertile tableland; it must send for help from a wilderness berg to the glorious mount of maiden Zion.[85] The petition section of the poem thus begins on a derisive note.

16:2 sets the scene for the depiction of Moab's petition in 16:3–5.[86] The initial verb is a converted perfect (והיה) and indicates that the poet is describing something that will happen in the future, not something that has already happened.[87] The emissaries from Moab are depicted as women and startled birds (cf. Isa 10:14). The bird simile conveys an impression of panic and helplessness. This impression is strengthened when the poet refers to the emissaries

---

[82]Cf. the paronomasia based on these two usages in Isa 14:4–5. For the pejorative use of מָשָׁל as "taunt, proverb," see Deut 28:37; Ps 69:12; Num 23:7; Hab 2:6.

[83]Luther, 149.

[84]Isa 25:10 shows a similar focus of comparison: "For the hand of the LORD will rest on this mountain [Zion], but Moab shall be trampled under his feet..." (NEB).

[85]On the highly positive connotations of "maiden Zion," see E. Follis, "The Holy City As Daughter," 176–178.

[86]Cf. 13:2–4 for an example of a similar movement from imperative summons to description of future event.

[87]Gray (*Isaiah*, 288) refers to it as "predictive." The force of the imperfect aspect here is, however, not so much predictive as hypothetical and imaginative. The poet is satirizing not a petition that has actually been made, but one which will probably (or is about to) be made.

as "daughters of Moab," that is, as fearful and weak women. This strategy appears also in Isa 19:16: "In that day the Egyptians will become like women, and they will tremble and be in dread..."[88] The poet in this way undercuts the dignity of the emissaries and reduces their request to the twittering of birds and the hysterical pleas of terrified women. The distress and hysteria of the "daughters of Moab" is apparent in the breathless imperatives delivered in rapid succession: "Give counsel! Assume responsibility! Cast your shadow as the night at high noon! Hide the displaced! Do not betray the fugitive!" (16:3). This is not the formal language of diplomacy; this is the language of panic. The first two imperatives are masculine, and the last three are feminine, although there is sufficient textual evidence to warrant reading the first two as feminine also. The grammatical confusion might be designed to emphasize the confused panic into which the Moabites have been thrown. If we emend the text, the feminine forms would indicate that the petition is addressed to "maiden Zion." In either case, the picture is the same. The poet presents a caricature of the Moabite embassy as thrown into a mindless dither, unable to restrain itself and wholly ridiculous.

The tone of the petition changes subtly in 16:4. This is indicated by the more relaxed pace of the syntax, by the shift to the jussive mood, and by the fact that the outcasts are referred to as a third party. This new voice speaks more calmly and seeks to negotiate a deal with Judah. It requests that Moab's displaced persons should be given *gēr* status in Judah, that is, given a special class of citizenship and protection.[89] In exchange for this protection, the emissary vows that Moab will become loyal to the Judean

---

[88]The use of women as a symbol of weakness, prone to fear and panic, and emotionally overwrought is common in prophetic literature; see Isa 3:12; 13:7, 8; 19:16; 48:41; 49:22; Jer 49:23–24; 50:37, 43; 51:30; Nah 2:7; 3:5, 13. See also Smith, "Destruction," 165–68. For a treatment of women as the objects of satire, see Hodgart, *Satire*, 79–107. We need not approve of this attitude toward women to acknowledge the fact that it was common in the ancient world, and, to be honest, in our own. It helps in the present case to realize that the implicit contrast between the "daughters of Moab" and "maiden Zion" indicates that the author can also use a feminine symbol positively.

[89]On this point, see Wildberger, 621.

king (4bα) as soon as the enemy has departed the land.[90] The vow is made in highly stereotyped language, the language of diplomacy. It is stated obliquely, and its actual intention becomes apparent only when one recognizes that the vocabulary is all drawn from the semantic domain of treaty making and enthronement ritual.[91] The promise to "establish a throne" is an indirect offer of loyalty. According to the ideology of kingship expressed in the HB, one of the chief duties of a king is the protection of those in need or trouble.[92] The petitions in 16:3 are clearly aimed at obtaining protection,[93] and the wording of the vow may have been chosen to emphasize the Judean king's obligations to provide help. Although the vow is spoken by a Moabite

---

[90]The enemy is apparently still present, and this vow depends in some way on its departure. Perhaps the condition on the vow indicates only that subservience to Judah cannot effectively begin until a reasonable amount of order is restored in Moab. 16:4 implies that Moab expects this enemy to depart its land without establishing any significant hegemony over it. If the enemy had established some kind of suzerainty over Moab, the vow to serve Judah in exchange for protection would be quite empty.

[91]Gottwald has observed that 16:5 sounds like "a quotation from an enthronement hymn" (*Kingdoms*, 204–205). The language points to the context of enthronement, but also to that of the covenant that is formed between a king and his subjects as a part of the enthronement (cf. 2 Sam 5:3). On "establishing a throne," see 2 Sam 3:10; 7:13, 16. "Faithfulness" and "truth" are language typical in contexts dealing with kingship and covenant (e.g., Psalm 89; Isa 11:5). The interpretation of Gesenius (153; cf. Rudolph, 140), that 16:5 is a "benediction...an inducement to hearken to their petition," moves in the right direction, but the syntax of 16:4b–5, the structure which suggests that a vow should be found at this point, and the treaty language all indicate that this "benediction" implies something more.

[92]See Isa 32:1–2. This idea is frequently found in contexts dealing with the kingship of YHWH (e.g., Isa 25:3–4; Ps 9:8–11 [7–10]; 72:12–14), and it is probably safe to assume that it is based on an analogy to a similar idea concerning the obligations of human kings. B. Ollenburger (*Zion, the City of the Great King: A Theological Symbol of the Jerusalem Cult* [JSOTS 41; Sheffield: JSOT, 1987] 70–71) has pointed out that the security and refuge provided by Zion is based on YHWH's kingship and the establishing of YHWH's throne there. In this regard, Isa 14:32 is quite significant for the present discussion since it raises the issue of refuge in Zion in the immediate context of the poem.

[93]Compare 16:3, "Give counsel [הביאו עצה]... Cast your shadow [צל] as the night at high noon," with Isa 30:1–2, "who carry out a plan [לעשות עצה], but not mine; who make an alliance...to take refuge in the protection of Pharaoh, and to seek shelter in the shadow [צל] of Egypt."

emissary, we must not forget that it is put in the emissary's mouth by the poet. By having the Moabite spokesperson emphasize the "faithfulness" (חסד) and "truth" (אמת) of the proposed arrangement, the poet may evoke memories of Moab's earlier faithlessness with regard to its treaty obligations to the Davidic and Omride dynasties. The "establishing" of the throne with one from "the tent of David" to sit on it may hint at a return to a time when Israel/Judah controlled most, if not all, the land of Moab.

The poet has depicted the Moabite petition in carefully selected images. The ambassadors sent to Judah flap about like startled birds, they blurt out their petition in hysteria. When a calmer voice promises Moab's subservience to the Judean throne, the words of flattery sound calculating and inauthentic. The audience has already been reminded that Moab inhabits land once controlled by Israel. They have heard the divine decree of further punishment for the refugees. Now they see the Moabite petition delivered in a manner both ridiculous and, given their history, suspiciously ingratiating.

The response given in 16:6 is the turning point in the rhetoric of the poem. Prior to this verse the decision about the Moabite plea is, at least ostensibly, under consideration; following it, the plea is officially rejected. The response makes explicit what has been implicit throughout the first two sections of the speech: Moab is suffering the just punishment for its arrogance.

We have heard about the majesty of Moab, the exceedingly proud one. About its hauteur and its haughtiness and its arrogance—his boasting is not right.	שָׁמַעְנוּ גְאוֹן־מוֹאָב גֵּא מְאֹד גַּאֲוָתוֹ וּגְאוֹנוֹ וְעֶבְרָתוֹ לֹא־כֵן בַּדָּיו׃

The first person plural form of address unites the Judean audience as one voice. As we have seen, it is probable that most members of the audience agreed that Moab was exceedingly arrogant. The "we" language of the verdict, however, gives public expression to this opinion and thereby collects and focuses it.[94] The four-fold

[94] Aristotle comments on a similar technique: "To a certain extent an audience will be impressed by a device which speech-writers use to nauseous excess: 'who does not know...?' 'we all know...' The hearer, ashamed to be ignorant, agrees to the fact, so as to have his part in common knowledge"

use of forms based on גאו drives home the point. Such repetition is the language of taunt and sarcasm. The communal acknowledgment of Moab's overweening pride leads naturally to the communal verdict: "his boasting is not right." The clear implication in the context is that Judah will not (should not, from the audience's temporal perspective) provide the requested help. Moab's suffering is the just reward for its attitude and actions.[95] Yahweh has brought low the haughty nation, and its petitions fail to arouse the sympathy of rulers both human (16:6) and divine (16:12). The Judeans will offer no aid, for to do so would contradict the divine will.

The third section of the speech confirms and celebrates this decision. The speaker's attitude toward Moab has been made clear. This lament for Moab, far from being sympathetic, is patently ironic. The lament form, turned on its head, has become a song of rejoicing. The introduction to section three is formally a summons to lamentation (16:7).[96] The speaker's ironic tone, however, marks this summons as an example of the "sarcastic imperative" common in prophetic speeches against foreign na-

---

(*Rhetoric* §3.7). See also E. Conrad, *Reading Isaiah* (Minneapolis: Fortress, 1991) 84–88.

[95]The expression לא־כן often denotes impropriety or taboo behavior that merits punishment; cf. Deut 18:14; 2 Kgs 7:9; Jer 23:10. Even if this explicit verdict were removed, the repetitive harping on Moab's pride would be sufficient answer to the petition. As we have seen, hubris is an exceedingly common—even the prototypical—reason for divine judgment in the HB, and Moab's pride is frequently cited as grounds for judgment. The explicit statement of Moab's pride is in itself, therefore, a sufficient answer to the Moabite petition.

[96]We have noted in our chapter on text and translation the semantic ambiguity in 16:7a. Following the suggestion of Berlin (*Dynamics*, 70), we have translated "Therefore let Moab howl; As for all Moab, let it howl." It is also possible to translate "Therefore let Moab howl; for Moab let everyone howl." The term ילל, "to lament, howl," can denote either a cry of grief or a howl of mocking (cf. Isa 52:5; G. Knight, *Deutero-Isaiah* [New York and Nashville: Abingdon, 1965] 222–24)—somewhat as the English word "howl" denotes expressions both of pain and of hilarity. The summons for everyone to howl for haughty Moab can thus be a summons ironically equivocal, at first calling Moab to lamentation, but then, in 16:7aβ, inviting everyone to mock Moab.

tions.[97] Such imperatives (here a jussive) amount to: "Go ahead and howl; your just punishment has finally come. How richly you deserve it! Howl on, now it is your turn."

The third section of the poem consists primarily of the "description of suffering" traditional in individual and communal laments, intermingled with expressions of sympathy. The formal similarity of the first and third sections of the poem has often been noted. There are, however, clear differences between the two sections. Unlike the first section, the third section does in fact describe the problem, and not just the lamentation itself. Also, the expressions of sympathy are both more frequent and more extreme.

Additionally, in 16:7b the poet introduces a new theme: the destruction of Moab's crops.[98] The speaker addresses the stricken nation directly and predicts that the Moabites will "groan, utterly stricken" over the lost raisin cakes of Kir Hareseth. The nature of these raisin cakes is unclear; they had some connection with the cultic sphere, but they also served as a profane delicacy.[99] In the latter case, the groaning over these delicacies once provided by Kir Hareseth might serve to emphasize Moab's former elitism. If they are associated with the Moabite cultus, the loss of the raisin cakes might adumbrate the cultic failure predicted in 16:12.[100] The symbolic value of these cakes in the poem is difficult to determine, but an allusion to Moab's cultus suits the poem and may bear witness to that anxiety over Moab's cultic prowess which is implicit elsewhere in the HB.

As we have argued elsewhere, Kir Hareseth is not to be identified with modern-day Kerak but with some city north of the

---

[97]Cf. Isa 23:1, 6, 14; Jer 25:34. For a fuller discussion, see chapter four.

[98]The closest HB parallel to this description of ruined crops is Joel 1:4–20. In Joel the destruction of the crops is the work of locusts and not of an army. The response urged by the prophet to this disaster (vv 13–14; 2:12–17) is quite similar to the response of the Moabites in Isa 15:2 and 16:12. Note also that ridicule from surrounding nations is mentioned repeatedly as one of the unpleasant results of the agricultural devastation (2:17b, 19b, 26b, 27b).

[99]On their sacral use see Hos 3:1; 2 Sam 6:19. For the profane use see Cant 2:5.

[100]The verb הגה, "groan, moan," may have been used as a technical term in the vocabulary of magical incantation (cf. Isa 8:19; BDB, 211).

Wadi Mujib. Furthermore, we have noted that the name may be a taunt-name (either "city of potsherds" or "city of silence").[101] If we are correct on the second point, the poet has used a taunt-name as an inclusion device to mark the beginning and end of the satiric lament in 16:7b–11. Verses 7–11 contain five Moabite place names in the following sequence: Kir Hareseth, Heshbon, Sibmah, Jazer, Jazer, Sibmah, Heshbon, Elealeh, Kir Hareseth. This chiasm consists of four easily identifiable members repeated in a section of text sufficiently short that the chiasm is easily perceived.[102] The rhetorical effect of this device derives from its artistry. The pleasingly balanced structure demonstrates the speaker's artistic ability, and artistic merit is easily confused with credibility in the mind of an audience. Additionally, the delight that an audience experiences in discovering such structures is its own form of persuasion.

Beginning with Heshbon and Sibmah, in 16:8 the speaker describes the conditions in Moab. "The fields of Heshbon languish." Initially, it is not clear what has happened to the fields. The description of the fate of Sibmah's vines clarifies the situation: "As for the vine of Sibmah, the lords of the nations its choicest vines have smitten." This verse is intentionally ambiguous (see chapter five). A "janus parallelism" enables the poet to point out both the former glory of the vine of Sibmah and its present state of ruin. The fine wine produced by its vineyards once smote with drunkenness the nations; now the lords of the nations have smitten the vineyards.

The second half of v 8 appears to recount the international success of Sibmah's fine viniculture which had "reached [נגע] to Jazer...wandered to the wilderness[103]... its shoots [שלחותיה] spread out [נטש]... crossed the sea." The subject is not clear, however. Either the vines or the lords of the nations may be the subject of

---

[101]Jones, "In Search of Kir Hareseth," 14–21.

[102]The inclusion of Elealeh disrupts the symmetry of the chiasm slightly. The context would suggest, however, that Elealeh should be considered together with Heshbon as a single entity (cf. Isa 15:4).

[103]See Isa 19:13–14; 28:7 where "strayed" [תעה] denotes drunken behavior. Perhaps the image here is of vines spreading uncontrollably and erratically as if intoxicated.

the verbs.[104] In fact, the verbs appear to have been chosen in order to prolong the double entendre begun in 8a. The semantic fields of נגע and נטש overlap at one point; both may denote warfare and the actions of soldiers.[105] The word שלחותיה, "its shoots," is a *hapax legomenon* and is usually understood as referring to the tendrils of Sibmah's vines.[106] But like נגע and נטש, שלחותיה is used in military contexts; it may refer to missiles and weapons or to those who wield them.[107] If we make the lords of the nations the subject, 16:8b recounts how an invading army roamed that land. It struck as far as Jazer and wandered to the wilderness; "its shooters" spread out like an encamped army and reached the sea. In a subtle and brilliant manner, the poet's double entendre turns a description of the success of Sibmah's viniculture into a recital of its destruction; the celebrated characteristics of its former weal provide the pattern for its present woe.[108] Perhaps the poet has borrowed and parodied an existing poem in praise of Sibmah's vineyards.

The speaker's description in 16:9a of his weeping over Sibmah's destroyed vineyards drips with sarcasm. By overstating the expression of sorrow, the poet ridicules Moab's loss and grief. These "crocodile tears" are mock sympathy and plain sarcasm.[109]

---

[104]While it is true that the 3fs suffix attached to "shoots" can only refer to the vine of Sibmah, one should not for this reason rule out a possible secondary reference to the "lords." The poet's double entendre is limited somewhat by the necessity of grammatical agreement. The use of the perfect 3 cpl avoids the agreement problem in the case of the verbs.

[105]On נגע see Jer 4:6, Mic 1:9, 1 Sam 6:9, etc.; on נטש see Judg 15:9, 2 Sam 5:18, 22.

[106]See the verb of similar meaning based on this stem in Jer 17:8, Ps 80:12, Ezek 31:5, and the related noun משלוח in Isa 11:14.

[107]See the use of the noun שלח in this sense and related verbal usages in 1 Sam 20:20: "to shoot (arrow)"; and 2 Kgs 24:2 "to send (invaders)."

[108]Fishelov (198) notes that prophetic satire frequently contrasts "the sinners' speech or thoughts about their 'success' with the humiliating fall awaiting them. The prophet may 'quote' various boastings of the target of the satire in the form of either speech or hidden thoughts." A similar technique appears to be at work in the present case.

[109]On the use of overstatement see D. C. Muecke, "Irony Marker," 368–73. Muecke uses the term "over-dissimulation" for this ironic technique; see esp. paragraph 3.4.2, p. 327. Ironic overstatement signals its intent by expressing

The phrase "with the weeping of Jazer" (בבכי יעזר) is difficult to interpret, and it is possible that the text is slightly corrupt.[110] Given the context, some satiric barb is probably intended. The following line, "I drench with my tears Heshbon and Elealah," paints a ridiculous picture. The verb רוה, "drench, saturate," (cf. Isa 55:10) depicts the quantity of the prophet's tears. רוה is used nowhere else in the HB to describe weeping; its usual meaning suggests complete saturation or satiation of persons (with food, sexual delight, things/money), of land (with water, blood), and of the sword (with blood). The speaker uses the verb to describe weeping as irrigation, an idea which in the context is not a little ridiculous.[111]

---

praise or sorrow in excess of what the audience would normally expect from the speaker in the context.

[110]The meaning of this phrase is unclear, but it is possible that the text should be emended to read מבכי, a word found in Ugaritic meaning "fountain, spring," although there is no manuscript evidence for this reading. Given the context of the phrase, it is tempting to read כמבכי and translate 16:9aα, "I will weep like the fountain of Jazer [for] the vine of Sibmah." Cf. Job 38:16 and text critical notes above, s.v.

[111]This profuse weeping reminds one of the Walrus in Lewis Carroll's poem "The Walrus and the Carpenter." Carroll's unlikely pair sit eating a group of young oysters whom they have enticed into "a pleasant walk, a pleasant talk,/ Along the briny beach."

> "I weep for you," the Walrus said,
> "I deeply sympathize."
> With sobs and tears he sorted out
> Those of largest size,
> Holding his pocket handkerchief
> Before his streaming eyes."

(*Alice's Adventures in Wonderland and Through the Looking Glass* [no place given: Harper & Row, 1949] 111). This poem demonstrates nicely how irony is marked. The context and intra-text give us the needed clues to realize the ironic intention. Expressions of grief over one's dinner will almost always arouse a reader's suspicions, and the activity of "sorting out those [oysters] of largest size" indicates a level of calculation (and appetite!) incongruent with genuine grief. Should we be tempted to think the Walrus's tears genuine, the narrative following the poem would disabuse us of this notion. Alice says that she likes the Walrus best, "because you see, he was a *little* sorry for the poor oysters." To which Tweedledee replies, "He ate more than the Carpenter, though... You see, he held his handkerchief in front, so that the Carpenter couldn't count how many he took."

16:9b–10 describes Heshbon and Elealah's loss of agricultural productivity with an image striking both for its vividness and for its stillness. The scene is harvest season, a happy, busy, and noisy time of the year. But Moab's fields are not filled with workers; no joyful shouts fill the air. The picture is still. The emotional impact resembles the effect in cinema when the camera pans slowly across a blasted battlefield with only the sound of the wind as background.

The three lines of 9b–10 contain three alliterative word pairs: קיצך/קצירך (v 9b), הכרמל/בכרמים (v 10a), ידרך/הדרך (v 10b). The first pair encompasses all of the fruit and grain harvest. This harvest has been destroyed; instead of the reaper's cry of joy, the victorious battle cry of the enemy has fallen upon it. No fruit and grain are gathered from the garden land; instead, "joy and rejoicing have been taken away (harvested)."[112] No cries ring out in the vineyard (בכרמים); no treader (הדרך) treads out (ידרך) the vintage. The final line of v 10 spells out the reason for the silence in the fields: "I have made an end of the victory shout."

The silence described in this final section of the poem contrasts with the noisy lamentation depicted in the first section. The poet uses impersonal syntactic constructions and passive verbs in 16:9b–10 to emphasize the stillness at harvest time. The fields lie empty and silent when they should be full of the shouts of the reapers, and the cities are loud with lamentation over the loss when they should be empty and quiet while everyone is out enjoying the harvest time. YHWH has turned Moab's noisy boasting into noisy lamentation.

The prophet concludes the "lament" by saying, "My bowels growl like a lyre for Moab" (מעי למואב ככנור יהמו). It is not unusual to find mention of bowels or belly in lament (cf. Isa 63:15; Jer 4:19; 31:20; Lam 1:20, 2:11; Ps 22:15), and mourning or distress is often expressed with the verb המה (Isa 49:11; Ezek 7:16; Ps 42:6, 12; 43:5; Jer 31:20; 4:19). But nowhere else is such digestive distress com-

---

[112]אסף is used frequently of harvesting crops. The choice of verb is an ironic stroke.

pared to the sound of a lyre.[113] How should we interpret this unusual expression? Hayes and Irvine have suggested that the prophet here indulges in humor bordering on the scatological and that the growling of the bowels like a lyre refers to flatulence.[114] Scatological humor appears elsewhere in Isaiah. Isa 25:10–12 depicts Moab swimming in the water of a manure pile, and B. Halpern has argued that Isa 28:10 satirizes the priests of Judah by portraying them playing with ordure.[115] This interpretation entails a shockingly crude form of satire, and perhaps some will object that this speaker would not sink so low. Another interpretation is possible. The lyre is an instrument not of mourning, but of praise and rejoicing (e.g., Isa 5:12; 24:8; Ezek 26:13). The speaker's bowels and innards growl for Moab, but the musical sound to which this growling is compared is songs of joy. Thus the growling of sympathy is in fact the happy sound of rejoicing; over the misfortune of Moab and Kir Hares(eth) the poet's bowels play a happy tune. With the second reference to Kir Hares(eth) we come to the end of the lament.

As a conclusion to the speech, the poet predicts that just as Moab will fail to obtain help from Judah, so too it will fail in its petitions at its own high place. The Moabites' failure at their own high place proves their guilt. The final לא יוכל, "He will not succeed," indicates Moab's inability to elicit Chemosh's sympathy, and it confirms the justice of the Judean rejection of Moab's petition (16:6 לא־כן בדיו). Inasmuch as 16:12 is a prediction of the divine rejection of Moab, it is thematically parallel to the threat of "additions" in 15:9. The structure of movements one and three is similar in this respect since both conclude with predictions of divine judgment. 16:12 is also thematically linked to the beginning of the poem. The depiction of Moab at its sanctuary recalls the description in 15:2 of Dibon ascending the high place to weep. In this way, all of Moab's lamentation described in the first part of the poem is retrospectively brought under the judgment of לא יוכל.

---

[113]Jer 48:36 changes the instrument to "flutes" (כחללים), an equally unexpected word choice.

[114]Hayes and Irvine, *Isaiah*, 245.

[115]Halpern, "The Excremental Vision," 109–21, esp. 114–16.

This is the final word, the final judgment on Moab. The once arrogant nation has been brought to its knees, and the great clamor of its lamentation will have no effect.

Summary

When the evidence of irony provided by the contextual clues discussed in chapter four is considered together with the indications of irony pointed out in the present chapter, the case for an ironic interpretation becomes quite compelling. A summary of the evidence brings this into focus. The foremost evidence is the apparent contradiction between the unrelievedly negative attitude toward Moab displayed in the HB and the expressions of sympathy in the poem. To this we may add the preponderance in the HB of prophetic satire directed at the foreign nations and the lack of expressions of sympathy that are truly comparable to what we find in Isaiah 15–16. Finally, there is the inter-textual evidence: the implicit comparison of Hebrew cities (ער) and Moabite cities (קיר) in 15:1; the naming almost exclusively of cities formerly held by Israel; the threat of "additions" and the reference to Moab as the "remnant of Admah" in 15:9; the derisive manner in which the petitioning Moabites are portrayed in 16:2–4; the straightforward condemnation of Moab's arrogance and rejection of its petition in 16:6; the subtle artistry of 16:8 which emphasizes the poetic justice of Moab's troubles; the ironic hyperbole and unusual semantics in the expressions of sympathy in 16:9 and 11; and the straightforward note of judgment in 16:12 which makes it clear that Moab's lamentation has aroused sympathy neither in heaven nor on earth. The accumulation of these signals of an ironic intention strongly suggests that Isaiah 15–16 contain not a sympathetic elegy, but a satiric lament celebrating the troubles of Moab, Israel and Judah's old enemy.

WORKS CITED

ABD. ed. David Noel Freedman. New York: Doubleday, 1992. S. v. "Oracle."

Abel, F. M. *Géographie de la Palestine*. 2 vols. Paris: Gabalda, 1967[3].

Abrams, Meyer Howard. *A Glossary of Literary Terms*. Fifth ed. New York: Holt, Rinehart and Winston, 1988.

Ackerman, James S. "Satire and Symbolism in the Song of Jonah." *Traditions in Transformation: Turning Points in Biblical Faith*, ed. Baruch Halpern and Jon Levenson, 213–46. Winona Lake: Indiana University, 1981.

Aharoni, Yohanon. *The Land of the Bible: A Historical Geography*. Philadelphia: Westminster, 1967.

Albright, William F. "The Archaeological Results of an Expedition to Moab and the Dead Sea." *BASOR* 14 (1924) 1–12.

_____. *Yahweh and the Gods of Canaan*. London: University of London, Athlone, 1968.

Alexander, Joseph Addison. *Commentary on the Prophecies of Isaiah*. 2 vols. abridged in 1. Grand Rapids: Zondervan, 1970.

Alter, Robert. *The Art of Biblical Narrative*. New York: Basic Books, 1981.

_____. *The Art of Biblical Poetry*. New York: Basic Books, 1985.

Andersen, Francis I., and David Noel Freedman. *Amos*. AB. New York: Doubleday, 1989.

Anderson, A. A. *The Book of Psalms*. Vol. 1. NCBC. Grand Rapids: Eerdmans, 1972.

Aristotle. *The Rhetoric of Aristotle*. Englewood Cliffs, NJ: Prentice-Hall, 1932.

Auvray, Paul. *Isaïe 1–39*. Paris: Gabalda, 1972.

Baltzer, K. "Considerations Regarding the Office and Calling of the Prophet." *HTR* 61 (1968) 567–81.

Baly, Denis. *The Geography of the Bible.* Rev. ed. New York: Harper & Row, 1974.

Bardtke, H. "Jeremia der Fremdvölkerprophet." *ZAW* 54 (1936) 240–62.

Barnes, Albert. *Notes: Critical, Explanatory, and Practical on the Book of the Prophet Isaiah.* 2 vols. Boston: Crocker & Brewster, 1840.

Barrick, W. Boyd. "The Bamoth of Moab." *Maarav* 7 (1991) 67–89.

Barstad, Hans M. "No Prophets? Recent Developments in Biblical Prophetic Research and Ancient Near Eastern Prophecy." *JSOT* 57 (1993) 39–60.

Bartlett, John R. "The Conquest of Sihon's Kingdom: A Literary Re-examination." *JBL* 97 (1978) 347–51.

_____. *Edom and the Edomites.* JSOTS 77. Sheffield: JSOT, 1989.

_____. "The Historical Reference of Numbers 21:27–30." *PEQ* 101 (1969) 94–100.

_____. "The Moabites and Edomites." *Peoples of Old Testament Times,* ed. D. Wiseman, 229–44. Oxford: Clarendon, 1973.

_____. "The 'United' Campaign against Moab in 2 Kings 3.4-27." *Midian, Moab and Edom: The History and Archaeology of Late Bronze and Iron Age Jordan and North West Arabia,* ed. J. G. A. Sawyer and D. J. A. Clines, 135–46. JSOTS 24. Sheffield: JSOT, 1983.

Barton, John. "Form Criticism: Old Testament." *ABD* 2. 838–41.

_____. "History and Rhetoric in the Prophets." *The Bible as Rhetoric,* ed. M. Warner, 51–64. London: Routledge, 1990.

_____. *Reading the Old Testament.* Philadelphia: Westminster, 1984.

Beentjes, P. C. "Notitie: Oracles Against the Nations: A Central Issue in the 'Latter Prophets.'" *Tijdschrift voor Filosofie en Theologie* 50 (1989) 203–09.

Berlin, Adele. *The Dynamics of Biblical Parallelism.* Bloomington: Indiana University Press, 1985.

_____. "On the Meaning of *pll* in the Bible." *RB* 96 (1989) 345–51.

Bienkowski, Piotr, ed. *Early Edom and Moab: The Beginning of the Iron Age in Southern Jordan.* Sheffield Archaeological Monographs 7. Sheffield: J. R. Collis/National Museums and Galleries on Merseyside, 1992.

Bitzer, Lloyd. "Functional Communication: A Situational Perspective." In *Rhetoric in Transition: Studies in the Nature and Uses of Rhetoric*, ed. E. White, 21–38. University Park: Pennsylvania State University, 1980.

_____. "The Rhetorical Situation." *Philosophy and Rhetoric* 1 (1968) 1–14. Reprinted in *Rhetoric: A Tradition in Transition*, ed. W. R. Fisher, 247–60. Ann Arbor: University of Michigan, 1974.

Black, C. Clifton. "Keeping up with Recent Studies. XVI. Rhetorical Criticism and Biblical Interpretation." *ET* 100 (1988–89) 252–58.

Black, Edwin. *Rhetorical Criticism: A Study in Method*. New York: Macmillan, 1965.

Blenkinsopp, Joseph. *A History of Prophecy in Israel*. Philadelphia: Westminster, 1983.

_____. *Prophecy and Canon: A Contribution to the Study of Jewish Origins*. Notre Dame: University of Notre Dame, 1977.

Boadt, Lawrence. "Ezekiel, Book of." *ABD* 2. 711–22.

Boer, P. A. H. de. "An Inquiry into the Meaning of the Term משא." *OTS* 5 (1948) 197–214.

Booth, Wayne. *A Rhetoric of Irony*. Chicago: University of Chicago, 1961.

Borée, Wilhelm. *Die alten Ortsnamen Palästinas*. Leipzig: Pfeiffer, 1930.

Brangenberg, John H. "A Reexamination of the Date, Authorship, Unity and Function of Isaiah 13–23." Ph.D. dissertation, Golden Gate Baptist Seminary, 1989.

Brenner, Athalya. "On the Semantic Field of Humour, Laughter and the Comic in the Old Testament." *On Humour and the Comic in the Hebrew Bible*, ed. A. Brenner and Y. Radday, 39–58. JSOTS 92. Sheffield: Almond, 1990.

Brenner, Athalya, and Yehuda T. Radday. *On Humour and the Comic in the Hebrew Bible*. JSOTS 92. Sheffield: Almond, 1990.

Bright, John. *Jeremiah*. AB. Garden City: Doubleday, 1984^{2}.

Budd, Philip J. *Numbers*. WBC. Waco: Word, 1984.

Buhl, Franz. *Geographie des alten Palästina*. Freiburg and Leipzig: Mohr, 1896.

Burckhardt, Ludwig. *Travels in Syria and the Holy Land*. Ed. William Martin Leake, for the Association for Promoting the

Discovery of the Interior Parts of Africa. London: Murray, 1822.

Burrows, Millar. *The Dead Sea Scrolls of St. Mark's Monastery*. Vol. 1. New Haven: American Schools of Oriental Research, 1950.

Buss, Martin J. *The Prophetic Word of Hosea*. Berlin: Töpelmann, 1969.

Calvin, John. *Commentary on the Book of the Prophet Isaiah*. Vol. 1. Tr. William Pringle. Grand Rapids: Eerdmans, 1948.

Carroll, Lewis. *Alice's Adventures in Wonderland and Through the Looking Glass*. N. p.: Harper & Row, 1949.

Carroll, Robert P. "The Elijah-Elisha Sagas: Some Remarks on Prophetic Succession in Ancient Israel." *VT* 19 (1969) 400–415.

_____. "Is Humour Among the Prophets?" *On Humour and the Comic in the Hebrew Bible*, ed. A. Brenner and Y. Radday, 169–89. JSOTS 92. Sheffield: Almond, 1990.

_____. *Jeremiah*. OTL. Philadelphia: Westminster, 1986.

_____. "Poets Not Prophets: A Response to 'Prophets Through the Looking Glass.'" *JSOT* 27 (1983) 25–31.

_____. "Rebellion and Dissent in Ancient Israelite Society." *ZAW* 89 (1977) 176–204.

Casanowicz, I. M. *Paronomasia in the Old Testament*. Boston: Norwood, 1894. Reprint ed. Jerusalem: Makor, 1970.

Ceresko, Anthony R. "Janus Parallelism in Amos's 'Oracles Against the Nations.'" *JBL* 113 (1994) 485–90.

Cheyne, Thomas K. *The Book of Isaiah, Chronologically Arranged*. London: MacMillan, 1870.

_____. "Kir-Heres." *Encyclopædia Biblica*. New York: Macmillan, 1901.

_____. *The Prophecies of Isaiah*. Vol. 1. 5th ed. New York: Thomas Whittaker, 1892.

Childs, Brevard S. *Introduction to the Old Testament As Scripture*. Philadelphia: Fortress, 1979.

Chilton, Bruce D. *The Isaiah Targum*. Wilmington, DE: Michael Glazier, 1987.

Chotzner, Joseph. *Hebrew Humour and Other Essays*. London: Luzac, 1905.

_____. *Hebrew Satire*. London: Paul, Trench, Trubner, 1911.

Christensen, Duane. *Transformations of the War Oracle in Old Testament Prophecy*. HDR 3. Missoula: Scholars, 1975.

Churgin, P. *Targum Jonathan to the Prophets*. Yale Oriental Series—Researches XIV. New Haven: Yale University, 1927; New York: Ktav, 1983.

Clarke, E. G. et al., eds. *Targum Pseudo-Jonathan of the Pentateuch: Text and Concordance*. Hoboken, NJ: Ktav, 1984.

Clements, Ronald E. *Isaiah 1–39*. NCBC. Grand Rapids: Eerdmans; London: Marshall, Morgan & Scott, 1980.

_____. *Prophecy and Tradition*. Atlanta: John Knox, 1975.

Coats, George W. "Genres: Why Should They Be Important for Exegesis?" *Saga, Legend, Tale, Novella, Fable: Narrative Forms in Old Testament Literature*, ed. G. W. Coats, 7–15. JSOTS 35. Sheffield: JSOT, 1985.

Colenso, John William. *Lectures on the Pentateuch and the Moabite Stone*. London: Longmans, Green, 1873.

The Compact Edition of the Oxford English Dictionary. Vol. 1. Oxford: University Press, 1971.

Conley, Thomas. "The Linnaean Blues: Thoughts on the Genre Approach." *Form, Genre and the Study of Political Discourse*, ed. Herbert W. Simons and Aram A. Aghazarian, 59–78. Columbia: University of South Carolina, 1986.

Consigny, Scott. "Rhetoric and Its Situations." *Philosophy and Rhetoric* 7 (1974) 175–86.

Cooper, Allan. "Imagining Prophecy." *Poetry and Prophecy: The Beginnings of a Literary Tradition*, ed. J. L. Kugel, 26–44. Ithaca, NY and London: Cornell University, 1990.

Cowles, Henry. *Isaiah*. New York: Appleton, 1869.

Craigie, Peter C. *The Book of Deuteronomy*. NICOT. Grand Rapids: Eerdmans, 1976.

Cross, Frank M. "The Priestly Tabernacle in the Light of Recent Research." *Temples and High Places in Biblical Times*, ed. A. Biran, 169–80. Jerusalem: Keter, 1981.

Culler, Jonathan L. *Structuralist Poetics*. Ithaca, NY: Cornell University, 1975.

Dahood, Mitchell. "The Moabite Stone and Northwest Semitic Philology." *The Archaeology of Jordan and Other Studies*, ed. L.

Geraty and L. Herr, 429–41. Berrien Springs: Andrews University, 1986.

_____. "A New Metrical Pattern in Biblical Poetry." *CBQ* 29 (1967) 574–79.

_____. "Textual Problems in Isaiah." *CBQ* 22 (1960) 400–409.

Davis, Ellen. *Swallowing the Scroll: Textuality and the Dynamics of Discourse in Ezekiel's Prophecy*. Sheffield: Almond, 1989.

De Vries, Simon. *Prophet Against Prophet*. Grand Rapids: Eerdmans, 1978.

Dearman, J. Andrew. "Historical Reconstruction and the Mesha Inscription." *Studies in the Mesha Inscription and Moab*, ed. J. A. Dearman, 155–210. Atlanta: Scholars, 1989.

_____. "The Moabite Sites of Horonaim and Luhith." *PEQ* 122 (1990) 41–46.

Delitzsch, Franz. *Biblical Commentary on the Prophecies of Isaiah.* Grand Rapids: Eerdmans, 1960.

Dicou, Bert. *Edom, Israel's Brother and Antagonist: The Role of Edom in Biblical Prophecy and Story*. JSOTS 169. Sheffield: JSOT, 1994.

Dietrich, W. *Jesaja und die Politik*. BEvT 74. Munich: Kaiser, 1976.

Dimant, Devorah. "Targum Jonathan to Isa. XVI. 6 and Jer. XLVIII. 29f." *JSS* 18 (1973) 55–58.

Donner, H., and W. Röllig. *Kanaanäische und Aramäische Inschriften.* 3 Vols. Wiesbaden: Harrassowitz, 1962–4.

Dozeman, Thomas. "OT Rhetorical Criticism." *ABD*. 5. 712–15.

Driver, Samuel Rolles. "Isaiah I–XXXIX: Textual and Linguistic Problems." *JSS* 13 (1968) 36–57.

_____. "Linguistic and Textual Problems: Isaiah I–XXXIX." *JThSt* 38 (1937) 36–50.

Duhm, Bernard. *Das Buch Jesaia.* 2d ed. HKAT. Göttingen: Vandenhoek and Ruprecht, 1902.

Duke, Paul D. *Irony in the Fourth Gospel*. Atlanta: John Knox, 1985.

Duke, Rodney K. *The Persuasive Appeal of the Chronicler*. Sheffield: Almond, 1990.

Easterly, Ellis. "Is Mesha's qrḥh Mentioned in Isaiah XV 2?" *VT* 41 (1991) 215–19.

Eichhorn, J. G. *Die hebräischen Propheten*. Göttingen: Vandenhoeck and Ruprecht, 1816.

Eichrodt, Walther. *Der Herr der Geschichte: Jesaja 13–23 und 28–39*. BKAT. Stuttgart: Calwer, 1967.

Eissfeldt, Otto. *The Old Testament: An Introduction*. New York: Harper & Row, 1965.

Elliott, Robert C. *The Power of Satire: Magic, Ritual, Art*. Princeton: Princeton University, 1960.

Erlandsson, Seth. *The Burden of Babylon: A Study of Isaiah 13:2–14:23*. ConBOT 4. Lund: Gleerup, 1970.

Ewald, Heinrich George August. *Commentary on the Prophets of the Old Testament*. Vol. 2. Translated by J. F. Smith. London and Edinburgh: Williams and Norgate, 1876.

_____. *Die Propheten des alten Bundes*. Vol. 2, *Jesaja mit den übrigen älteren Propheten*. Göttingen: Vandenhoeck & Ruprecht, 1867.

Exum, Cheryl. "Of Broken Pots, Fluttering Birds and Visions in the Night: Extended Simile and Poetic Technique in Isaiah." *CBQ* 43 (1981) 347–50.

Fanwar, W. "Sela." *ABD* 5. 1073–74.

Feinberg, L. *Introduction to Satire*. Ames, Iowa: Iowa State University Press, 1967.

Fewell, Danna Nolan, and David M. Gunn. *Compromising Redemption: Relating Characters in the Book of Ruth*. Louisville: Westminster/John Knox, 1990.

Fiore, B. "NT Rhetoric and Rhetorical Criticism." *ABD* 5. 715–19.

Fishbane, Michael A. *Biblical Interpretation in Ancient Israel*. Oxford: Clarendon, 1985.

Fishelov, David. "The Prophet as Satirist." *Prooftexts* 9 (1989) 195–211.

Floyd, Michael. "The Chimerical Acrostic of Nahum 2:1–10." *JBL* 113 (1994) 421–37.

_____. "Oral Tradition As a Problematic Factor in the Historical Interpretation of Poems in the Law and the Prophets." Ph.D. dissertation, Claremont Graduate School, 1980.

Fohrer, Georg. *Das Buch Jesaja*. Vol. 1 (chapters 1–23). Zürich/Stuttgart: Zwingli, 1960.

_____. *Introduction to the Old Testament*. Tr. D. Green. Nashville: Abingdon, 1965.

Follis, Elaine R. "The Holy City As Daughter." *Directions in Biblical Hebrew Poetry*, ed. E. Follis, 173–84. JSOTS 40. Sheffield: JSOT, 1987.

Forbes, A. Dean. "Statistical Research on the Bible." *ABD* 6. 185–206.

Fox, Michael V. *Character and Ideology in the Book of Esther*. Columbia, SC: University of South Carolina, 1991.

_____. "The Rhetoric of Ezekiel's Vision of the Valley of the Bones." *HUCA* 51 (1980) 1–15.

Freedman, David Noel. "A Second Mesha Inscription." *BASOR* 175 (1964) 50–51.

Frye, Northrup. *Anatomy of Criticism: Four Essays*. New York: Atheneum, 1968.

Gehman, Henry S. "The 'Burden' of the Prophets." *JQR* 31 (1940–41) 107–21.

Gerstenberger, E. "Psalms." *Old Testament Form Criticism*, ed. John H. Hayes, 179–224. San Antonio: Trinity University, 1974.

Gesenius, Wilhelm. *Philologisch-kritischer und historischer Commentar über den Jesaia*. Leipzig: Vogel, 1821. Treatment of chs 15–16 translated by W. Tyler in "Exegesis of Isaiah XV. XVI." *Biblical Repository and Quarterly Observer* 7 (1836) 107–61.

Ginsberg, H. Louis. "Some Emendations in Isaiah." *JBL* 69 (1950) 51–60.

Gitay, Yehoshua. "Isaiah and His Audience." *Prooftexts* 3 (1983) 223–30.

_____. *Prophecy and Persuasion*. Forum Theologicae Linguisticae 14. Bonn: Linguistica Biblica, 1981.

_____. "Reflections on the Study of Prophetic Discourse." *VT* 33 (1983) 207–221.

_____. "Rhetorical Criticism and the Prophetic Discourse." *Persuasive Artistry: Studies in New Testament Rhetoric in Honor of George A. Kennedy*, ed. D. Watson, 13–24. JSNTS 50. Sheffield: JSOT, 1991.

_____. "Rhetorical Criticism." *To Each its Own Meaning*, ed. S. McKenzie and S. Haynes, 135–49. Louisville: Westminster/John Knox, 1993.

Goldstein, J. A. *II Maccabees*. New York: Doubleday, 1983.

Good, Edwin M. *Irony in the Old Testament*. Sheffield: Almond, 1981[2]; Philadelphia: Westminster, 1965[1].

Goshen-Gottstein, Moshe H., ed. *The Book of Isaiah*. Vol. 1. Jerusalem: Magness, 1975.

Gottwald, Norman K. *All the Kingdoms of the Earth*. New York: Harper, 1964.

Gray, George B. *A Critical and Exegetical Commentary on the Book of Isaiah*. Vol. 1. ICC. Edinburgh: T. & T. Clark, 1912.

Gray, John. *I–II Kings*. 2d ed. OTL. Philadelphia: Westminster, 1970.

Greenberg, Moshe. *Ezekiel, 1–20*. AB. Garden City: Doubleday, 1983.

Greenstein, Edward L. *Essays on Biblical Method and Translation*. Brown Judaic Studies 92. Atlanta: Scholars, 1989.

Greenwood, David. "Rhetorical Criticism and Formgeschichte: Some Methodological Considerations." *JBL* 89 (1970) 418–26.

Grohman, Edward D. "A History of Moab." Ph.D. dissertation, Johns Hopkins, 1958.

Grossfeld, Bernard. *The Targum Onqelos to Leviticus and The Targum Onqelos to Numbers: Translated, with Apparatus, and Notes*. Aramaic Bible 8. Wilmington, DE: Michael Glazier, 1988.

Guilhamet, Leon. *Satire and the Transformation of Genre*. University of Pennsylvania, 1987.

Gutwein, K. C. *Third Palestine: A Regional Study in Byzantine Urbanization*. Washington, DC: University Press of America, 1981.

Halpern, Baruch. "'The Excremental Vision': The Doomed Priests of Doom in Isaiah 28." *HAR* 10 (1986) 109–21.

Hamborg, Graham. "Reasons for Judgment in the Oracles Against the Nations of the Prophet Isaiah." *VT* 31 (1981) 145–59.

Handy, Lowell K. "Uneasy Laughter: Ehud and Eglon as Ethnic Humor." *SJOT* 6 (1992) 233–46.

Haran, Menahem (Diman-). "An Archaic Remnant in the Prophetic Call to War." *Bulletin of the Israel Exploration Society* 13 (1946–47) 7–15.

Harrington, Daniel J., and Anthony J. Saldarini. *Targum Jonathan of the Former Prophets: Introduction, Translation and Notes.* Wilmington, DE: Michael Glazier, 1987.

Hatch, Edwin and Henry A. Redpath. *A Concordance to the Septuagint and the Other Greek Versions of the Old Testament.* 3 vols. Oxford: Clarendon, 1897; reprint edn. Grand Rapids: Baker, 1983.

Hayes, John H. *Amos: the Eighth-Century Prophet: His Times and His Preaching.* Nashville: Abingdon, 1988.

_____. "The History of the Form-Critical Study of Prophecy." *Society of Biblical Literature 1973 Seminar Papers,* 1. 60–99. Missoula: Scholars, 1973.

_____. "The Usage of Oracles Against Foreign Nations in Ancient Israel." *JBL* 87 (1968) 81–92.

Hayes, John H., and Stuart Irvine. *Isaiah, the Eighth-Century Prophet: His Times and His Preaching.* Nashville: Abingdon Press, 1987.

Hendewerk, C. L. *Des Propheten Jesaja Weissagungen.* Königsberg: Gebrüder Bornträger, 1838.

Hertzberg, Hans Wilhelm. *Der erste Jesaja.* Kassel: Oncken, 1952.

Hill, Gray. *With the Beduins.* London: T. Fisher Unwin, 1891.

Hillers, Delbert R. *Micah.* Hermeneia. Philadelphia: Fortress, 1984.

Hitzig, F. *Der Prophet Jesaja.* Heidelberg: Winter, 1833.

_____. *Des Propheten Jonas Orakel über Moab, kritisch vindicirt und durch Übersetzung nebst Anmerkungen erläutert.* Heidelberg: Mohr, 1831.

Hodgart, Matthew. *Satire.* New York: McGraw-Hill, 1969.

Holbert, J. "Deliverance Belongs to Yahweh: Satire in the Book of Jonah." *JSOT* 21 (1981) 59–81.

Holladay, John S., Jr. "Assyrian Statecraft and the Prophets of Israel." *HTR* 63 (1970) 29–51.

Jastrow, M. *A Dictionary of the Targumim: The Talmud Babli and Yerushalmi, and the Midrashic Literature.* 2 vols. New York: Putnam, 1903.

Jemielity, Thomas. *Satire and the Hebrew Prophets.* Louisville, KY: Westminster/John Knox, 1992.

Jones, Brian C. "In Search of Kir Hareseth: A Case Study in Site Identification." *JSOT* 52 (1991) 3–24.

_____. "Isaiah 8.11 and Isaiah's Vision of Yahweh." *History and Interpretation: Essays in Honour of John H. Hayes*, ed. M. P. Graham, W. Brown and J. Kuan, 145–59. JSOTS 173. Sheffield: JSOT, 1993.

Kaiser, Otto. *Isaiah 13–39: A Commentary*. OTL. Philadelphia: Westminster, 1974.

Kaufmann, Yehezkel. *The Religion of Israel*. Chicago: University of Chicago, 1960; New York: Schocken Books, 1972.

Keil, K. F. *Commentary on the Books of Kings*. 2 vols. Edinburgh: T. & T. Clark, 1857.

Kennedy, George A. *New Testament Interpretation through Rhetorical Criticism*. Chapel Hill and London: University of North Carolina, 1984.

Kinneavy, James L. "Contemporary Rhetoric." *The Present State of Scholarship in Historical and Contemporary Rhetoric*, ed. W. Horner, 186–246. Rev. ed. Columbia and London: University of Missouri, 1990.

Kissane, E. J. *The Book of Isaiah*. 2 vols. Rev. ed. Dublin: Browne and Nolan, 1960.

Klein, Lillian R. *The Triumph of Irony in the Book of Judges*. JSOTS 68. Sheffield: Almond, 1988.

Knauf, Ernst Axel. "Jeremia XLIX 1–5: Ein Zweites Moab-Orakel im Jeremia-Buch." *VT* 42 (1992) 124–28.

_____. "Toponymy of the Kerak Plateau." *Archaeological Survey of the Kerak Plateau*, ed. J. M. Miller, 281–90. ASOR Archaeological Reports 01. Atlanta: Scholars, 1991.

Knierim, Rolf. "Criticism of Literary Features, Form, Tradition and Redaction." *The Hebrew Bible and Its Modern Interpreters*, ed. G. Tucker and D. Knight, 123–66. Chico: Scholars, 1985.

Knight, Douglas A. "The Understanding of 'Sitz im Leben' in Form Criticism." *SBL 1974 Seminar Papers*, 1. 105–25. Scholars: Missoula, 1974.

Knight, George A. F. *Deutero-Isaiah*. New York and Nashville: Abingdon, 1965.

Knobel, August W. *Der Prophet Jesaia*. KHAT 5. Leipzig: Weidmann'sche, 1843.

Knös, Gustavo. *Scholia Selecta in Esai XIII-XXXIX*. Uppsala: Regiæ Academiæ Typographi, 1826-27.

König, Eduard. *Das Buch Jesaja*. Gütersloh: Bertelsmann, 1926.

Koppe, Johann Benjamin von. *D. Robert Lowth's Lord Bischofs zu London und der Londner und Göttingschen Societäten der Wissenschaften Mitglieds; Jesaias: neu ubersetzt nebst einer Einleitung und kritischen philologischen und erlauternden Anmerkungen; aus dem Englischen; mit Zusatzen und Anmerkungen*. Vol. 2. Leipzig: Weidmanns Erben und Reich, 1780.

Kugel, James L. *The Idea of Biblical Poetry; Parallelism and Its History*. New Haven: Yale University, 1981.

_____. "Poets and Prophets: An Overview." *Poetry and Prophecy: The Beginnings of a Literary Tradition*, ed. J. L. Kugel, 1–25. Ithaca, NY and London: Cornell University, 1990.

_____, ed. *Poetry and Prophecy: The Beginnings of a Literary Tradition*. Ithaca, NY and London: Cornell University, 1990.

Kuschke, A. "Jer. 48,1–8: Zugleich ein Beitrag zur historischen Topographie Moabs." *Verbannung und Heimkehr: Beiträge zur Geschichte und Theologie Israels im 6. und 5. Jahrh. v. Chr.: Festschrift für W. Rudolph*, ed. A. Kuschke, 181–96. Tübingen: Mohr, 1961.

Landes, George. "The Fountain at Jazer." *BASOR* 144 (1956) 30–37.

Landy, Francis. "Prophetic Burdens in Isaiah 13–23." A paper presented at the national meeting of the Society of Biblical Literature, Chicago, November, 21, 1994.

Lang, Bernhard. *Kein Aufstand in Jerusalem: Die Politik des Propheten Ezekiel*. Stuttgart: Katholisches Bibelwerk, 1978.

Leon, Judah Messer. *The Book of the Honeycomb's Flow*. [*Sēpher Nōpheth Ṣūphīm*]. Translated and edited by I. Rabinowitz. Ithaca and London: Cornell University, 1983.

Leupold, H. C. *Exposition of Isaiah*. 2 vols. Grand Rapids: Baker, 1963–1971.

Levenson, Jon. "Is There a Counterpart in the Hebrew Bible to New Testament Antisemitism?" *Journal of Ecumenical Studies* 22 (1985) 242–60.

Liver, J. "The Wars of Mesha, King of Moab." *PEQ* 99 (1967) 14–31.

Long, Burke O. "Recent Field Studies in Oral Literature and the Question of Sitz im Leben." *Oral Tradition and Old Testament*

Studies, ed. R. Culley, 35–49. *Semeia* 5. Missoula: Scholars, 1976.

Lowth, Robert. *Isaiah: A New Translation with a Preliminary Dissertation and Notes*. Boston: William Hilliard, 1778; Cambridge: James Munroe and Company, 1834.

_____. *Lectures on the Sacred Poetry of the Hebrews*. Tr. G. Gregory. London: S. Chadwick & Co., 1847.

Luther, Martin. *Lectures on Isaiah: Chapters 1–39*. Vol. 16, *Luther's Works*, ed. J. Pelikan, et al. Saint Louis: Concordia, 1969.

Malamat, Abraham. "New Light from Mari (ARM XXVI) on Biblical Prophecy (III–IV)." *Storia e tradizioni di Israele: Scritti in onore di J. Alberto Soggin*, ed. D. Garrone and F. Israel, 186–90. Brescia: Paideia, 1991.

March, W. Eugene. "Prophecy." *Old Testament Form Criticism*, ed. J. H. Hayes, 141–78. San Antonio: Trinity University, 1974.

Margulis, Barry. "Studies in the Oracles Against the Nations." Ph.D. dissertation, Brandeis, 1967.

Marti, Karl. *Das Buch Jesaja*. KHAT 10. Tübingen: Mohr, 1900.

May, Herbert G., ed. *Oxford Bible Atlas*. New York: Oxford University, 1984[3].

Mays, James Luther. *Micah*. OTL. Philadelphia: Westminster, 1976.

Melamed, E. Z. "Break-Up of Stereotype Phrases as an Artistic Device in Biblical Hebrew." *Scripta Hierosolymitana* 8 (1961) 115–153.

Melugin, Roy F. "Muilenburg, Form Criticism, and Theological Exegesis." *Encounter with the Text*, ed. M. Buss, 91–100. Philadelphia: Fortress; Missoula, MT: Scholars, 1979.

Migne, J. P. *Patrologia Cursus Completus, Series Latina*. Vol. 24 of 221. Paris: Venit Apud Editorem, 1844–1864.

Miller, J. Maxwell, ed. *Archaeological Survey of the Kerak Plateau*. ASOR Archaeological Reports 01. Atlanta: Scholars, 1991.

_____. "Early Monarchy in Moab?" *Early Edom and Moab: The Beginning of the Iron Age in Southern Jordan*, ed. Piotr Bienkowski, 77–92. Sheffield Archaeological Monographs 7. Sheffield: J. R. Collis/National Museums and Galleries on Merseyside, 1992.

_____. "The Israelite Journey Through (Around) Moab and Moabite Toponymy." *JBL* 108 (1989) 590–92.

_____. "Moab and the Moabites." *Studies in the Mesha Inscription and Moab*, ed. J. A. Dearman, 1–40. Atlanta: Scholars, 1989.

_____. "Site Identification: A Problem Area in Contemporary Biblical Scholarship." *ZDPV* 99 (1983) 119–29.

Miller, J. Maxwell, and John H. Hayes. *A History of Ancient Israel and Judah*. Philadelphia: Westminster, 1986.

Mittmann, Siegfried. "The Ascent of Luhith." *Studies in the History and Archaeology of Jordan I*, ed. A. Hadidi, 175–80. Amman: Department of Antiquities, 1982.

Montgomery, J. A. *A Critical Commentary on the Books of Kings*. ICC. Edinburgh: T. & T. Clark, 1951.

Mowinckel, Sigmund. *Prophecy and Tradition: The Prophetic Books in the Light of the Study of the Growth and History of the Tradition*. Oslo: Jacob Dybwad, 1946.

Muecke, D. C. "Irony Marker." *Poetics* 7 (1978) 363–75.

Muilenburg, James. "Form Criticism and Beyond." *JBL* 88 (1969) 1–18.

_____. "The Linguistic and Rhetorical Usages of the Particle כי in the Old Testament." *HUCA* 32 (1961) 135–60.

Musil, Alois. *Arabia Petraea: I Moab*. Kaiserliche Akademie der Wissenschaften. Wien: Alfred Hölder, 1907.

Myers, Jacob M. *II Chronicles*. AB. Garden City, NY: Doubleday, 1965.

Neusner, Jacob. *The Mother of the Messiah in Judaism: The Book of Ruth*. The Bible of Judaism Library. Valley Forge, PA: Trinity International, 1993.

Newsom, Carol. "A Maker of Metaphors: Ezekiel's Oracles Against Tyre." *Interpreting the Prophets*, ed. J. Mays and P. Achtemeier, 188–199. Philadelphia: Fortress, 1987.

Nissinen, M. "Prophecy and Power Struggle in the Neo-Assyrian Empire." A paper presented at the 1994 annual meeting of the Society of Biblical Literature, Chicago.

O'Connor, Michael P. *Hebrew Verse Structure*. Winona Lake, IN: Eisenbrauns, 1980.

O'Day, Gail R. "Irony and the Johannine Theology of Revelation: An Investigation of John 4." Ph.D. dissertation, Emory University, 1983.

Olivier, Hannes. "Archaeological Evidence Pertaining to a Possible Identification of Ar-Moab and er-Rabbah." *NedTTs* 30 (1989) 179–89.

Ollenburger, Ben C. *Zion, the City of the Great King: A Theological Symbol of the Jerusalem Cult*. JSOTS 41. Sheffield: JSOT, 1987.

Orelli, C. von. *The Prophecies of Isaiah*. Edinburgh: T & T Clark, 1889.

Orlinsky, Harry M. "Studies in the St. Mark's Scroll–V." *IEJ* 4 (1954) 5–8.

Osborn, Michael. "Rhetorical Depiction." *Form, Genre and the Study of Political Discourse*, ed. Herbert W. Simons and Aram A. Aghazarian, 79–107. Columbia: University of South Carolina, 1986.

Oswalt, John. *The Book of Isaiah: Chapters 1–39*. NICOT. Grand Rapids, MI: Eerdmans, 1986.

Palmer, E. H. *The Desert of the Exodus. Journeys on Foot in the Wilderness of the Forty Years Wanderings*. Cambridge: Deighton, Bell and Co., 1871.

Parpola, Simo. *The State Archives of Assyria IX*. (forthcoming).

Patton, John. "Causation and Creativity in Rhetorical Situations." *Quarterly Journal of Speech* 65 (1979) 36–55.

Paul, Shalom M. *Amos*. Hermeneia. Minneapolis: Fortress, 1991.

Perelman, Chaim, and L. Olbrechts-Tyteca. *The New Rhetoric: A Treatise on Argumentation*. Notre Dame: University of Notre Dame, 1969.

Perry, Menakhem. "Literary Dynamics." *Poetics Today* 1 (1979) 35–64.

Petersen, David L. "The Oracles Against the Nations: A Form Critical Analysis." *Society of Biblical Literature Abstracts and Seminar Papers*. 1. 39–61. Missoula: Scholars, 1975.

_____, ed. *Prophecy in Israel: Search for an Identity*. Philadelphia: Fortress, 1987.

Pfeiffer, Robert H. *Introduction to the Old Testament*. NY: Harper, 1941.

Pomeroy, Ralph. "Fitness of Response in Bitzer's Concept of Rhetorical Discourse." *Georgia Speech Communication Journal* 4 (1972) 42–71.

Pope, Marvin H. "'Pleonastic' Waw before Nouns in Ugaritic and Hebrew." *JAOS* 73 (1953) 95–98.

Power, E. "The Prophecy of Isaias against Moab (Is. 15, 1–16, 5)." *Biblica* 13 (1932) 435–51.

Procksch, Otto. *Geschichtsbetrachtung und geschichtliche Überlieferung bei den vorexilischen Propheten*. Leipzig: Hinrichs, 1902.

_____. *Jesaia*. Vol. 1. KAT. Leipzig: Deichertsche, 1930.

Propp, W. H. *Water in the Wilderness: The Mythological Background of a Biblical Motif*. HDR. Ann Arbor: University Microfilms, 1985.

Rabin, Chaim. "Hebrew *Baddim* 'Power.'" *JSS* 18 (1973) 57–58.

Rad, Gerhard von. *Genesis: A Commentary*. Tr. J. H. Marks. London: SCM, 1963[2].

Radday, Yehuda T. "Humour in Names." *On Humour and the Comic in the Hebrew Bible*, ed. Y. T. Radday and A. Brenner, 59–98. JSOTS 92. Sheffield: Almond, 1990.

Randall, C. "Satire in the Bible." Ph.D. dissertation, Hebrew Union College, 1969.

Rauber, D. F. "Jonah—The Prophet as Shlemiel." *BToday* 49 (1970) 29–37.

Reed, William L., and Fred V. Winnett. "A Fragment of an Early Moabite Inscription from Kerak." *BASOR* 172 (1963) 1–9.

Reider, Joseph. "Contributions to the Scriptural Text." *HUCA* 24 (1952/3) 85–106.

Rendtorff, Rolf. *The Old Testament: An Introduction*. Philadelphia: Fortress, 1986.

Robertson, David A. *Linguistic Evidence in Dating Early Hebrew Poetry*. SBLDS 3. Missoula: Scholars, 1972.

Robinson, Edward. *Biblical Researches in Palestine: A Journal of Travels in the Year 1838*. 11th ed. Boston: Crocker and Brewster, 1874.

Rofé, Alexander. "The Classification of Prophetical Stories." *JBL* 89 (1970) 427–40.

Rosenheim, Edward W., Jr. *Swift and the Satirist's Art*. Chicago: University of Chicago, 1963.

Rowlands, Elwyn R. "Mistranscriptions in the Isaiah Scroll." *VT* (1951) 226–29.

Rudolph, Wilhelm. *Jeremia*. HAT. Tübingen: Mohr, 1968[3].

_____. "Jesaja XV–XVI." *Hebrew and Semitic Studies Presented to Godfrey Rolles Driver*, ed. D. Thomas and W. McHardy, 130–43. Oxford: Clarendon, 1963.

Saebø, Magne. *Sacharja 9–14*. WMANT 34. Neukirchen-Vluyn: Neukirchener, 1969.

Saulcy, Félicien de. *Narrative of a Journey round the Dead Sea and in the Bible Lands in 1850 and 1851. Including an Account of the Discovery of the Sites of Sodom and Gomorrah*. Philadelphia: Parry and McMillan, 1854.

Schottroff, Willy. "Horonaim, Nimrim, Luhith und der Westrand des 'Landes Ataroth.'" *ZDPV* 82 (1966) 184.

Schweizer, Harald. *Elischa in den Kriegen. Literaturwissenschaftliche Untersuchung von 2 Kön. 3; 6,8–23; 6,24–7,20*. SANT 37. Munich: Kösel, 1974.

Scott, R. B. Y. "The Meaning of maśśā' as an Oracle Title." A paper read at the 83rd meeting of the Society of Biblical Literature and Exegesis, New York, NY, 29 and 30 December 1947. Summarized in *JBL* 67 (1948) v-vi.

Seeligman, I. L. "On the History and Nature of Prophecy in Israel." *EI* 3 (1954) 125–32.

Seetzen, Ulrich. *A Brief Account of the Counties Adjoining the Lake Tiberias, the Jordan and the Dead Sea*. 2 vols. London: Palestine Association of London, 1810.

Seitz, Christopher. *Isaiah 1–39*. Interpretation. Louisville: John Knox, 1993.

Shafer, Byron E. "*rwxbm/rxbm* = 'Fortress.'" *CBQ* 33 (1971) 389–96.

Shaw, Charles. "The Speeches of Micah: A Rhetorical-Historical Analysis." Ph.D. dissertation, Emory University, 1990.

Simons, J. *The Geographical and Topographical Texts of the Old Testament*. Leiden: Brill, 1959.

Sloane, Thomas O. "Rhetoric: Rhetoric in Literature." *The New Encyclopaedia Britannica*. 15th ed.

Smelik, Klaus. *Converting the Past: Studies in Ancient Israelite and Moabite Historiography*. Leiden: Brill, 1992.

Smith, J. *A Compendious Syriac Dictionary*. Oxford: Clarendon, 1903.

Smith, J. E. "The Destruction of Foreign Nations in Hebrew Prophetic Literature." Ph.D. dissertation, Hebrew Union College-Jewish Institute of Religion, 1969.

Smyth, Herbert Weir. *Greek Grammar*. Rev. ed. Cambridge, MA: Harvard University, 1956.

Soden, Wolfram von. "Ist im Alten Testament schon von Schwimmen die Rede?" *ZAH* 4 (1991) 165–70.

Sperber, Alexander, ed. *The Bible in Aramaic*. Leiden: Brill, 1959.

Stenning, J. F. *The Targum of Isaiah*. Oxford: Clarendon, 1949.

Stinespring, William F. "Irony and Satire." *IDB* 2. 727–28.

_____. "No Daughter of Zion." *Encounter* 26 (1965) 133–41.

Stolz, F. "נשׂא nśʾ aufheben, tragen." *Theologisches Handwörterbuch zum Alten Testament*, ed. K. Jenni and C. Westermann, 2. 109–17. Munich: Kaiser, 1976.

Sumner, W. "Israel's Encounters with Edom, Moab, Ammon, Sihon and Og according to the Deuteronomist." *VT* 18 (1968) 216–28.

Sweeney, Marvin. *Isaiah 1–4 and the Post-Exilic Understanding of the Isaianic Tradition*. Berlin: de Gruyter, 1988.

Thiselton, Anthony. *The Two Horizons: New Testament Hermeneutics and Philosophical Description*. Grand Rapids: Eerdmans, 1980.

Timm, Stefan. *Die Dynastie Omri*. Göttingen: Vandenhoeck & Ruprecht, 1982.

Trible, Phyllis. *Rhetorical Criticism*. Minneapolis: Augsburg Fortress, 1994.

Tristram, H. B. *The Land of Moab: Travels and Discoveries on the East Side of the Dead Sea and the Jordan*. New York: Harper, 1873; London: John Murray, 2d ed., 1874.

Tucker, Gene M. *Form Criticism of the Old Testament*. Philadelphia: Fortress, 1971.

_____. "Prophecy and Prophetic Literature." *The Hebrew Bible and Its Modern Interpreters*, ed. G. Tucker and D. Knight, 325–68. Chico: Scholars, 1985.

_____. "Prophetic Superscriptions and the Growth of a Canon." *Canon and Authority*, ed. G. W. Coats and B. O. Long, 56–70. Philadelphia: Fortress, 1977.

_____. Review of *The Burden of Babylon*, by Seth Erlandsson. *JBL* 90 (1971) 486–88.

Tyler, W. S. "Exegesis of Isaiah XV. XVI." *Biblical Repository and Quarterly Observer* 7 (1836) 107–61.

Ullendorff, Edward. "The Contribution of South Semitics to Hebrew Lexicography." *VT* 6 (1956) 190–98.

Van Seters, John. "The Conquest of Sihon's Kingdom: A Literary Examination." *JBL* 91 (1972) 182–97.

_____. "Once Again—the Conquest of Sihon's Kingdom." *JBL* 99 (1980) 117–19.

Vatz, Richard E. "The Myth of the Rhetorical Situation." *Philosophy and Rhetoric* 6 (1973) 154–61.

Vaux, Roland de. *Les Livres des Roi.* La Bible de Jérusalem. Paris: Cerf, 1949.

Vitringa, Campegius. *Commentarius in Librum Prophetiarum Jesaiae.* 2 vols. N. p.: Johan. Nicolai Andreae, 1715-1722. First pub. Leuwarden, 1714.

Waard, Jan de. "The Interim and Final HOTTP Reports and the Translator: a Preliminary Investigation." *Tradition of the Text: Studies Offered to Dominique Barthélemy in Celebration of his 70th Birthday,* ed. G. Norton and S. Pisano, 277–84. OBO 109. Freiburg, Switzerland: Universitätsverlag; Göttingen: Vandenhoeck and Ruprecht, 1991.

Walker, Williston. *A History of the Christian Church.* New York: Charles Scribner's Sons, 1970[3].

Waltke, Bruce K., and Michael P. O'Connor. *An Introduction to Biblical Hebrew Syntax.* Winona Lake: Eisenbrauns, 1990.

Watts, John D. W. *Isaiah 1–33.* WBC. Waco: Word, 1985.

Weis, Richard D. "A Definition of the Genre Maśśāʾ in the Hebrew Bible." Ph.D. dissertation, Claremont, 1986.

Weiser, Artur. *The Psalms: A Commentary.* London: SCM, 1962.

Wernberg-Møller, Preben. "'Pleonastic' Waw in Classical Hebrew." *JSS* 3 (1958) 321–26.

Wildberger, Hans. *Jesaja.* BKAT 10/2. Neukirchen-Vluyn: Neukirchener, 1978.

_____. "Die Völkerwallfahrt zum Zion: Jes. II 1–5." *VT* 7 (1957) 62–81.

Wilkerson, K. E. "On Evaluating Theories of Rhetoric." *Philosophy and Rhetoric* 3 (1970) 82–96.

Williams, James G. "Irony and Lament: Clues to Prophetic Consciousness," *Semeia* 8 (1977) 51–74.

Wilson, Robert R. *Prophecy and Society in Ancient Israel*. Philadelphia: Fortress, 1980.

Wolff, Hans Walter. *Amos the Prophet*. Philadelphia: Fortress, 1973.

_____. *Micah: A Commentary*. Minneapolis: Augsburg, 1990.

Worschech, Udo. *Die Beziehungen Moabs zu Israel und Ägypten in der Eisenzeit. Siedlungsarchäologische und siedlungshistorische Untersuchungen im Kernland Moabs (Ard el-Kerak)*. Ägypten und Altes Testament. Studien zu Geschichte, Kultur und Religion Ägyptens und des Alten Testaments 18. Wiesbaden: Otto Harrassowitz, 1990.

Worschech, Udo, and Ernst Axel Knauf. "Alte Strassen in der nordwestlichen Arḍ al-Kerak: Ein Vorbericht." *ZDPV* 101 (1985) 128-33.

_____. "Dimon und Horonaim." *BN* 31 (1986) 70–75.

Wuellner, Wilhelm. "The Rhetorical Genre of Jesus' Sermon in Luke 12.1–13.9." *Persuasive Artistry: Studies in New Testament Rhetoric in Honor of George A. Kennedy*, ed. D. F. Watson, 93–118. JSNTS 50. Sheffield: JSOT, 1991.

_____. "Where is Rhetorical Criticism Taking Us?" *CBQ* 49 (1987) 448–63.

Wyatt, N. "A New Look at Ugaritic *šdmt*." *JSS* 37 (1992) 149–53.

Young, Edward J. *The Book of Isaiah*. 3 vols. NICOT. Grand Rapids: Eerdmans, 1965–72.

Ziegler, Joseph, ed. *Isaias*. Septuaginta: Vetus Testamentum Graecum. Vol. 14. Göttingen: Vandenhoeck & Ruprecht, 1983.

Zyl, A. H. van. *The Moabites*. Leiden: Brill, 1960.